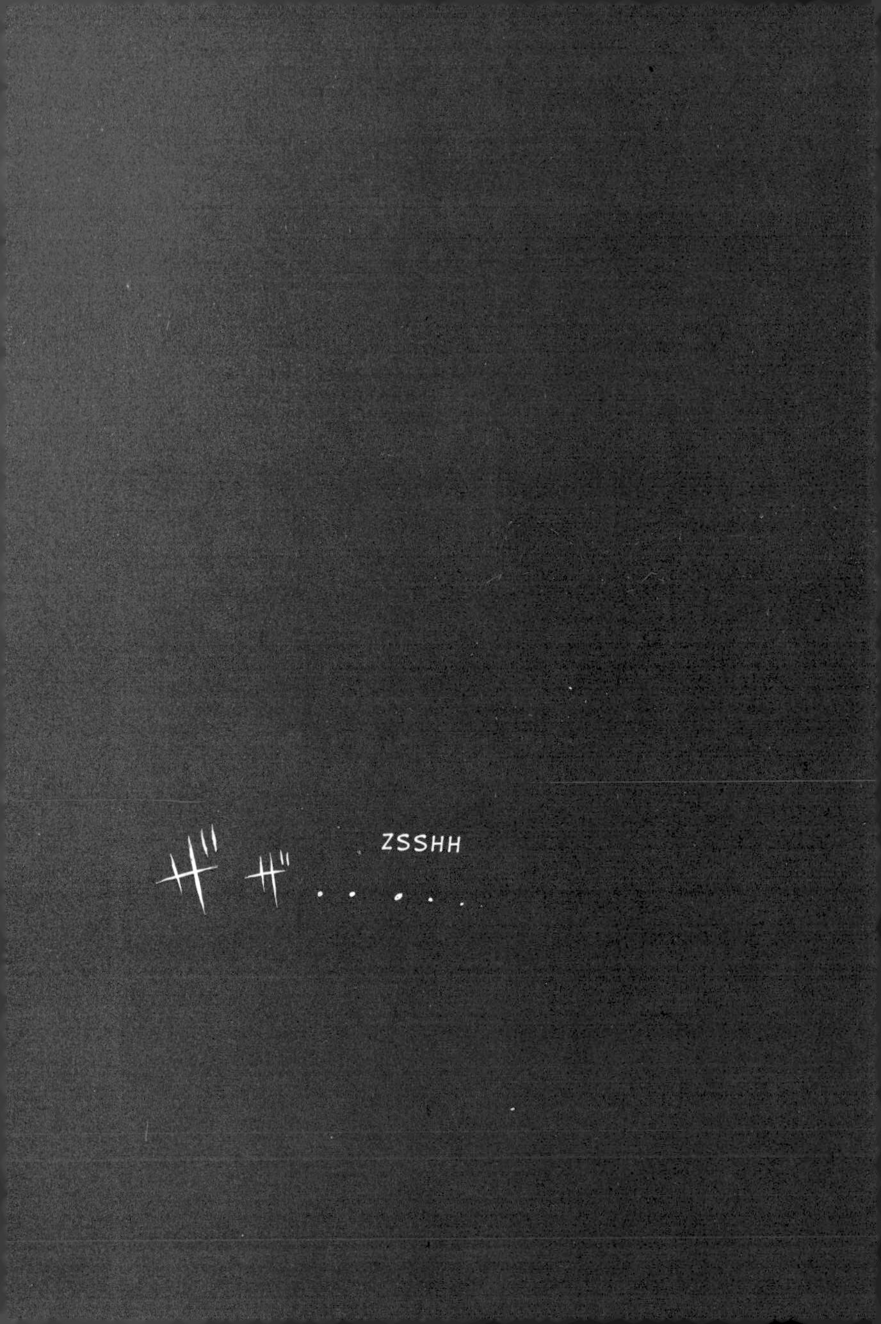
ZSSHH

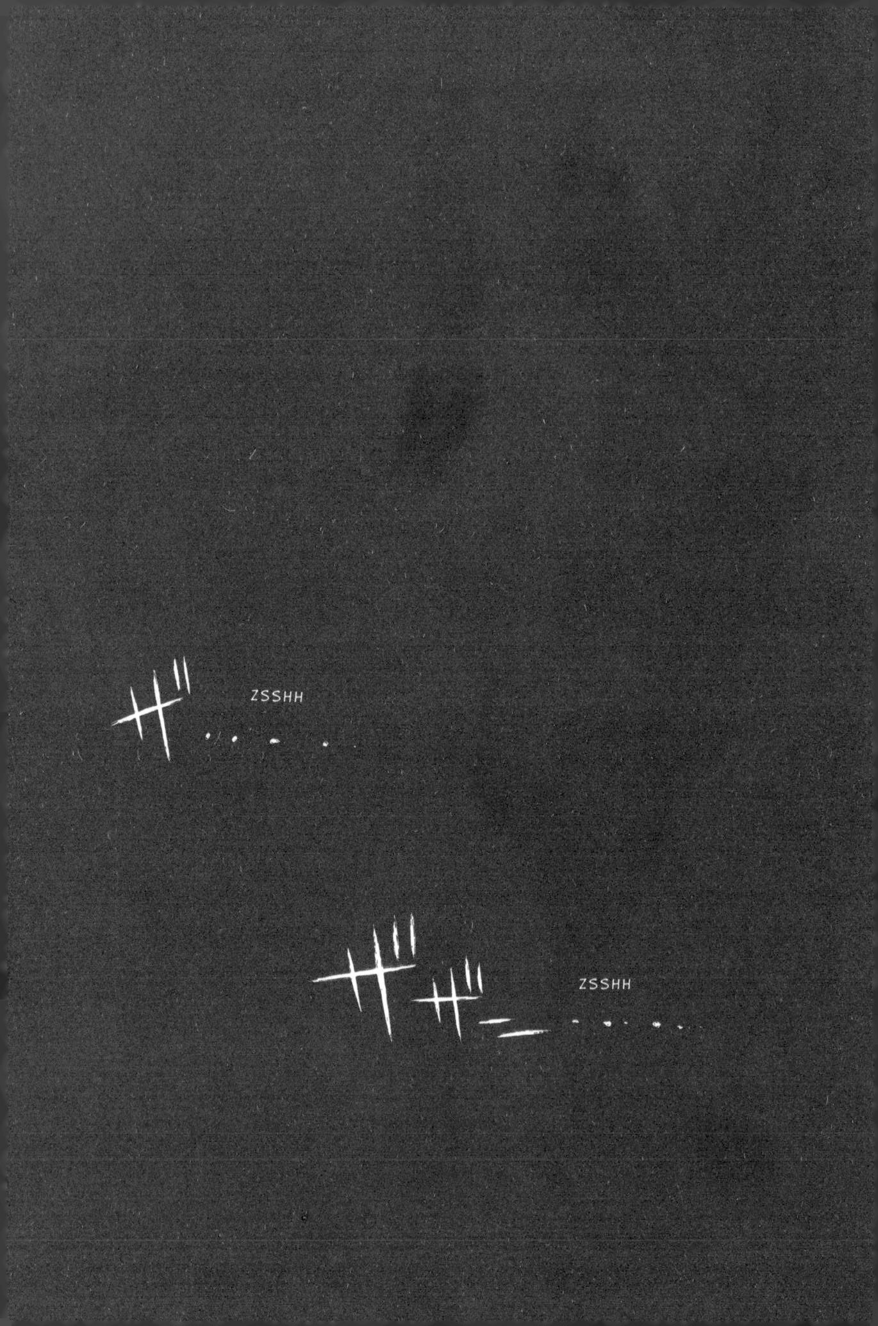
ZSSHH
ZSSHH

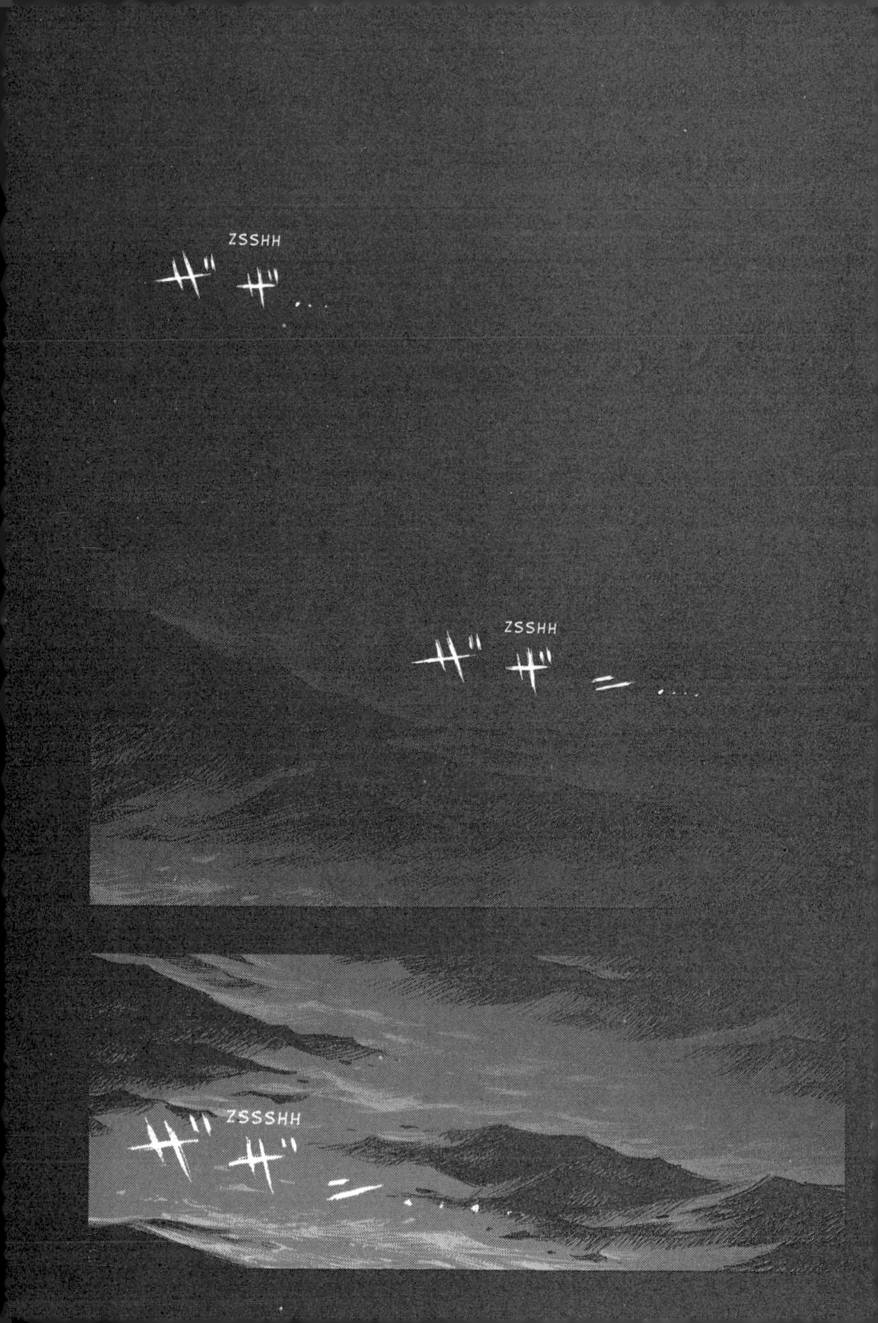
ZSSHH
ZSSHH
ZSSSHH

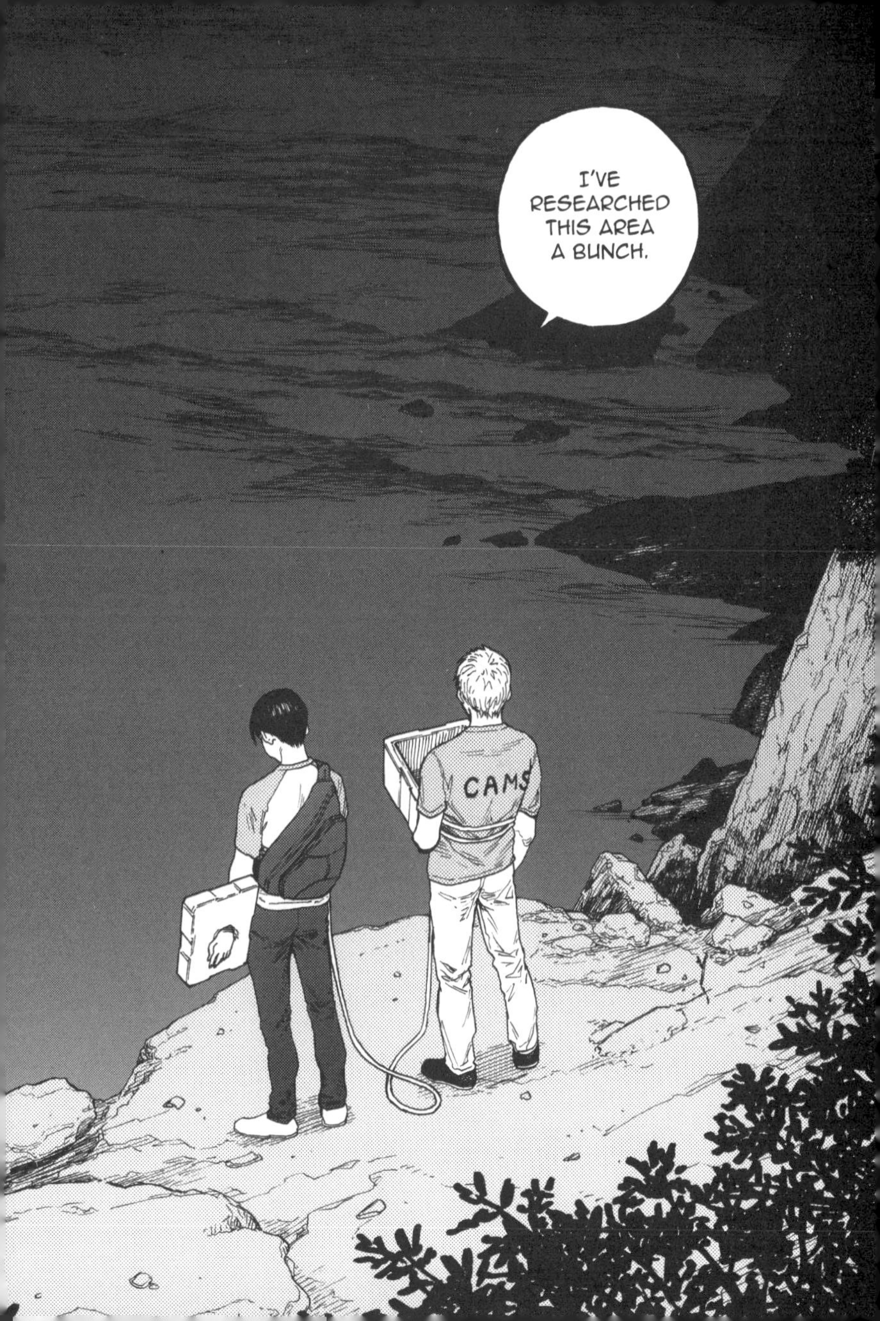
I'VE RESEARCHED THIS AREA A BUNCH.
CAMS

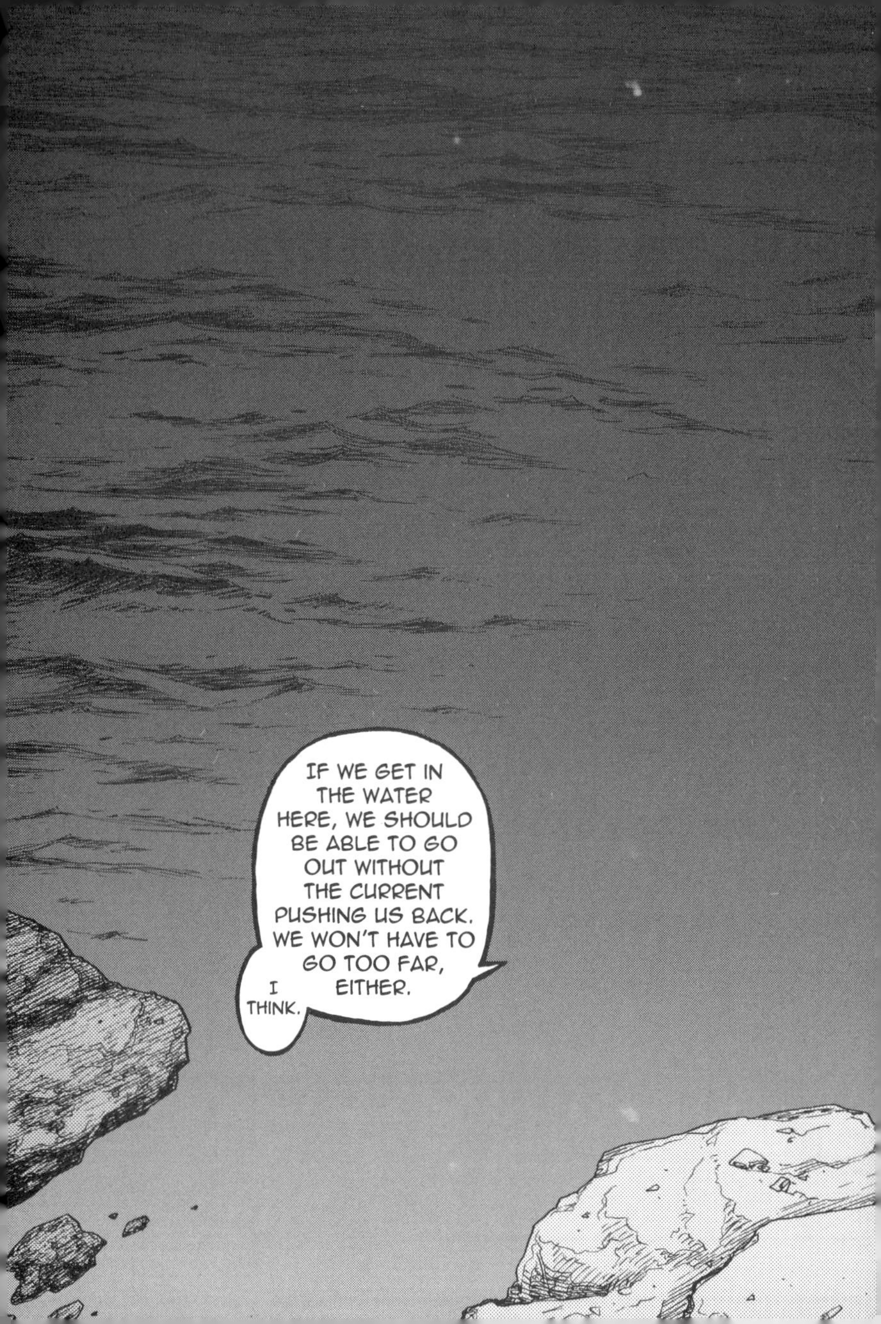
IF WE GET IN THE WATER HERE, WE SHOULD BE ABLE TO GO OUT WITHOUT THE CURRENT PUSHING US BACK. WE WON'T HAVE TO GO TOO FAR, EITHER.
I THINK.

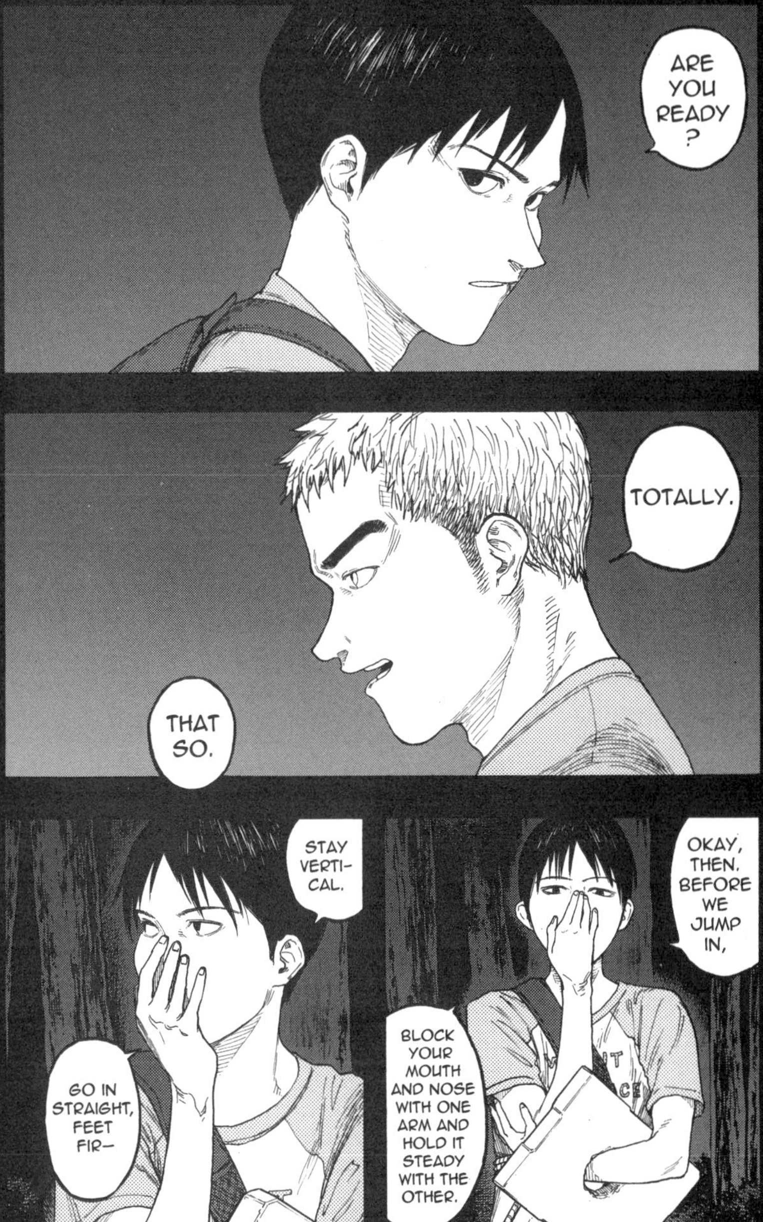
ARE YOU READY?
TOTALLY.
THAT SO.
OKAY, THEN. BEFORE WE JUMP IN,
BLOCK YOUR MOUTH AND NOSE WITH ONE ARM AND HOLD IT STEADY WITH THE OTHER.
STAY VERTI-CAL.
GO IN STRAIGHT, FEET FIR—

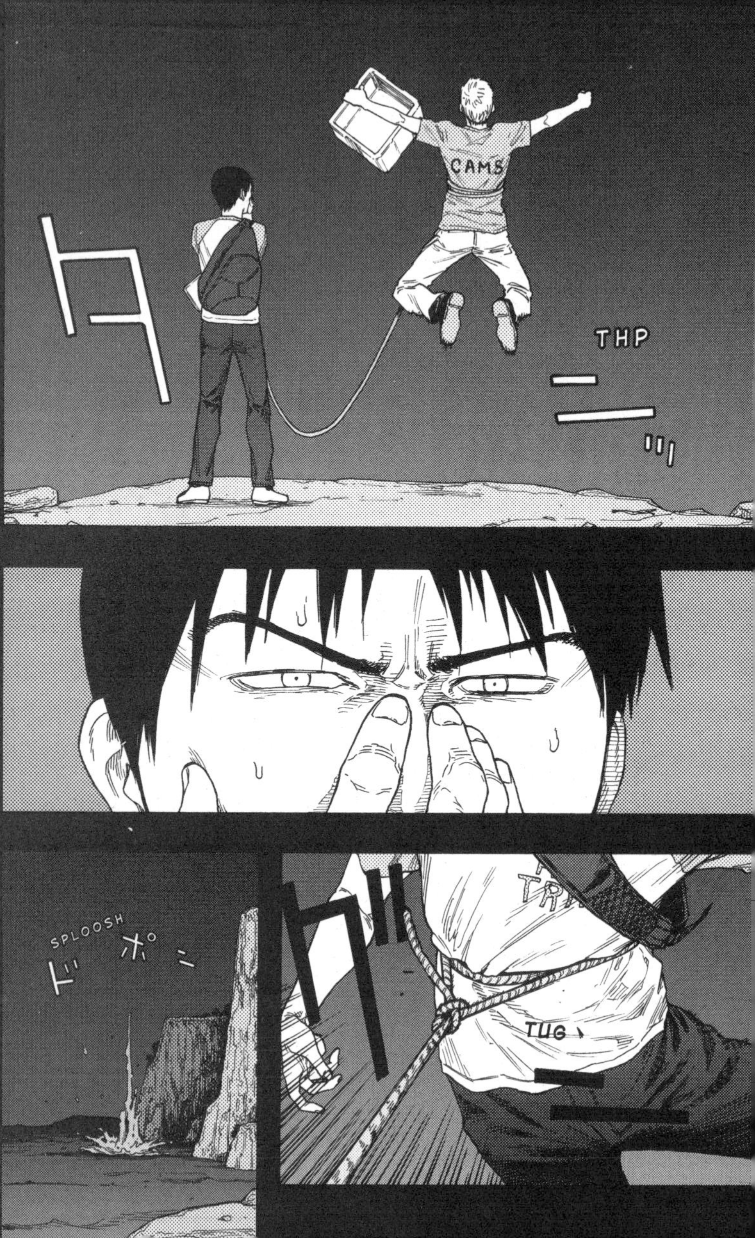
CAMS
THP
TUG
SPLOOSH

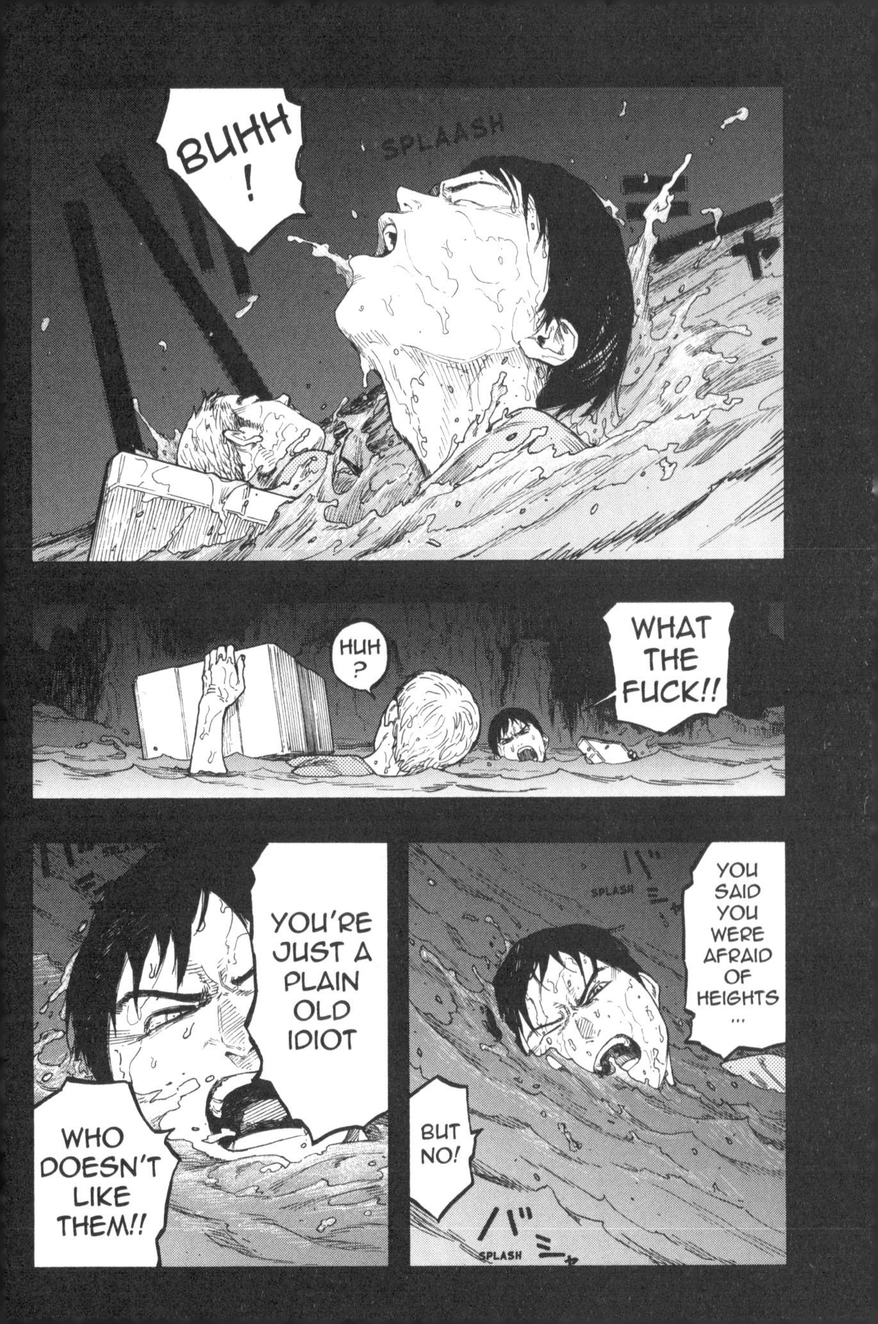
SPLAASH
BUHH!
WHAT THE FUCK!!
HUH?
SPLASH
YOU SAID YOU WERE AFRAID OF HEIGHTS...
BUT NO!
SPLASH
SPLASH
YOU'RE JUST A PLAIN OLD IDIOT
WHO DOESN'T LIKE THEM!!

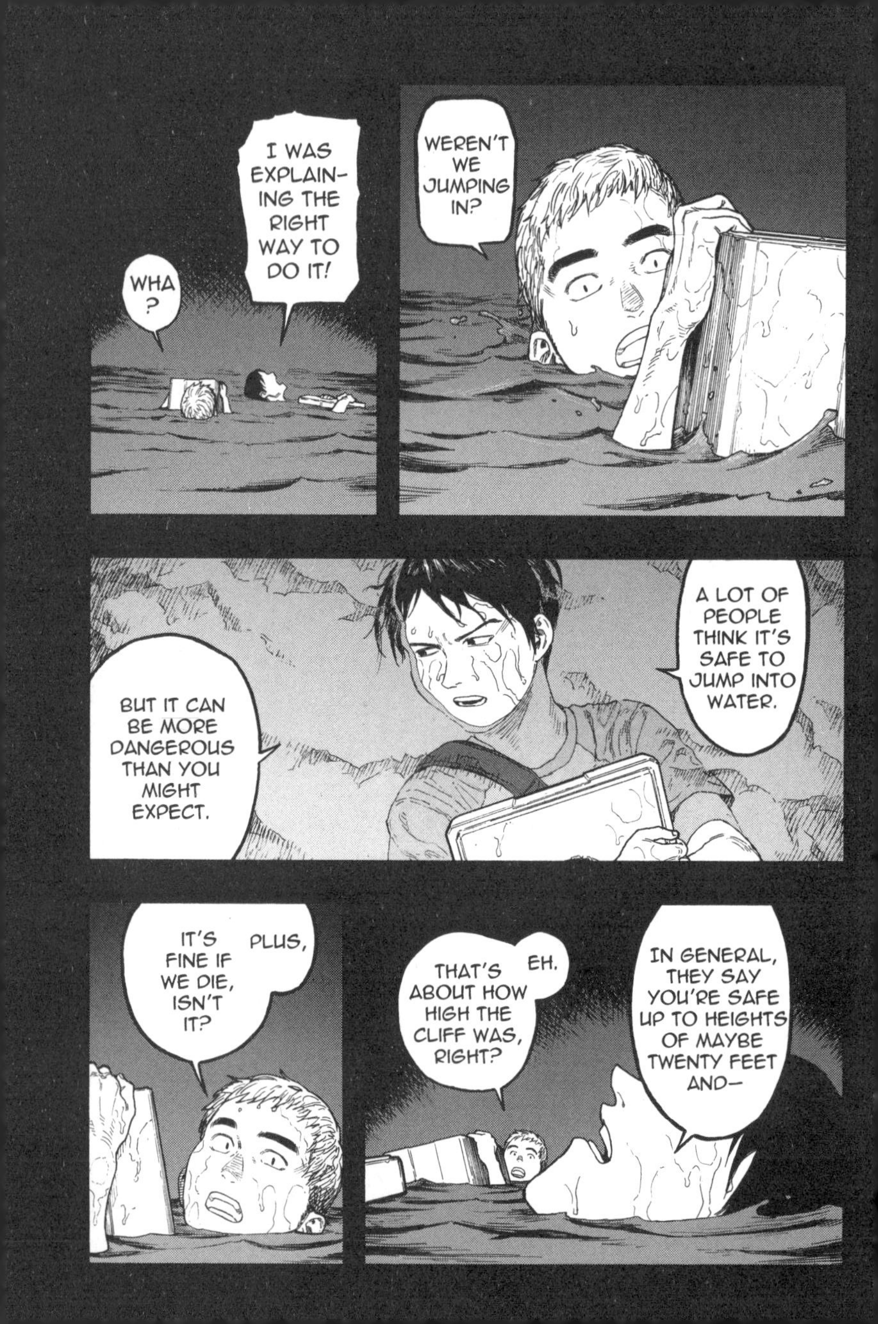
WEREN'T WE JUMPING IN?
I WAS EXPLAIN-ING THE RIGHT WAY TO DO IT!
WHA ?
A LOT OF PEOPLE THINK IT'S SAFE TO JUMP INTO WATER.
BUT IT CAN BE MORE DANGEROUS THAN YOU MIGHT EXPECT.
IN GENERAL, THEY SAY YOU'RE SAFE UP TO HEIGHTS OF MAYBE TWENTY FEET AND—
EH.
THAT'S ABOUT HOW HIGH THE CLIFF WAS, RIGHT?
PLUS,
IT'S FINE IF WE DIE, ISN'T IT?

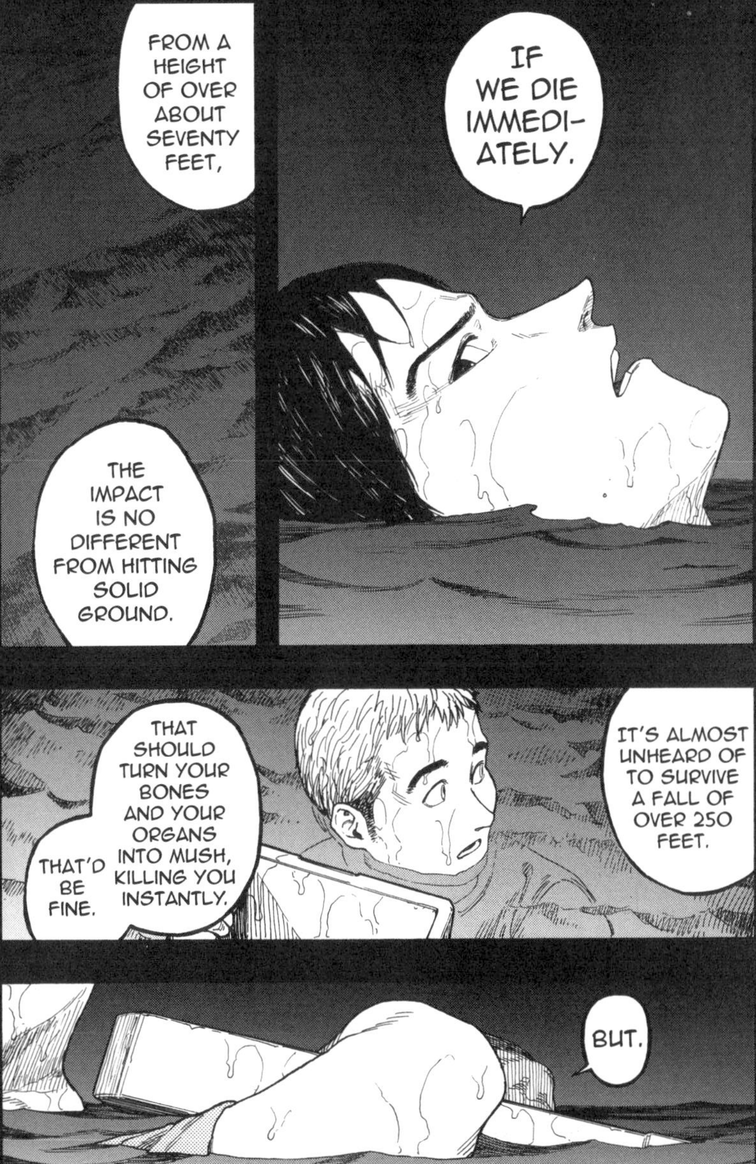
IF WE DIE IMMEDIATELY.
FROM A HEIGHT OF OVER ABOUT SEVENTY FEET,
THE IMPACT IS NO DIFFERENT FROM HITTING SOLID GROUND.
IT'S ALMOST UNHEARD OF TO SURVIVE A FALL OF OVER 250 FEET.
THAT SHOULD TURN YOUR BONES AND YOUR ORGANS INTO MUSH, KILLING YOU INSTANTLY.
THAT'D BE FINE.
BUT.

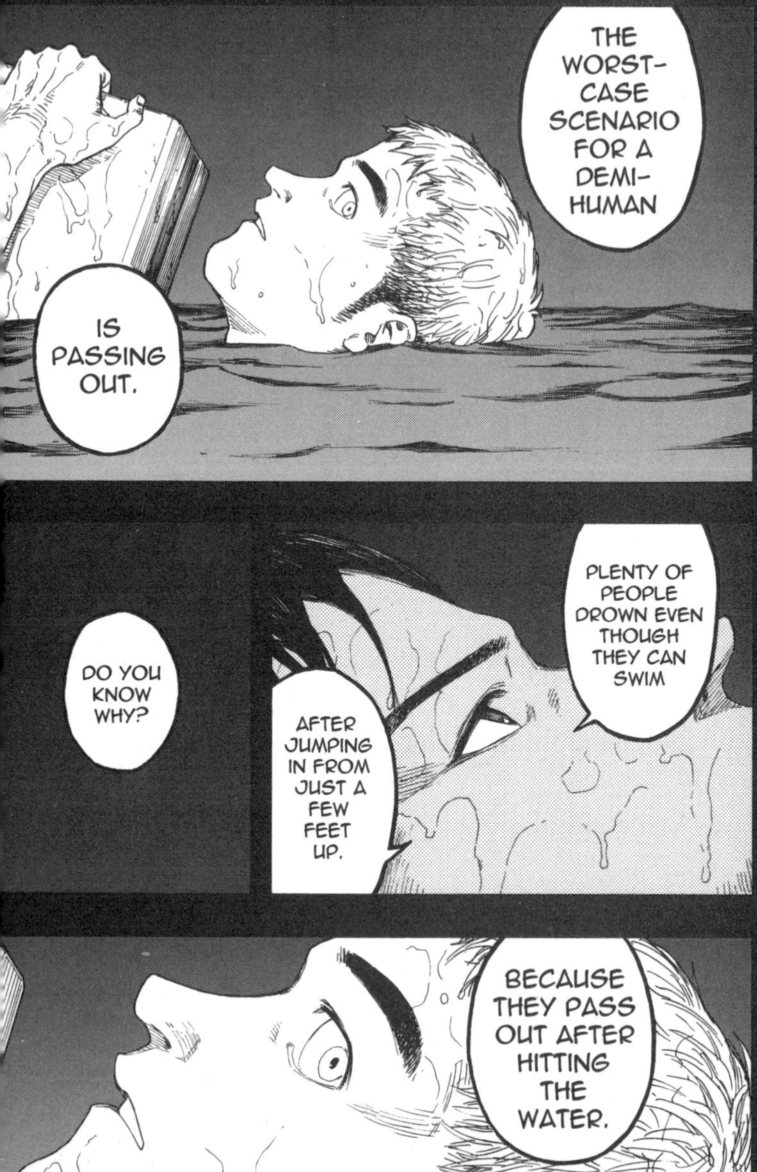
THE WORST-CASE SCENARIO FOR A DEMI-HUMAN
IS PASSING OUT.
PLENTY OF PEOPLE DROWN EVEN THOUGH THEY CAN SWIM
AFTER JUMPING IN FROM JUST A FEW FEET UP.
DO YOU KNOW WHY?
BECAUSE THEY PASS OUT AFTER HITTING THE WATER.

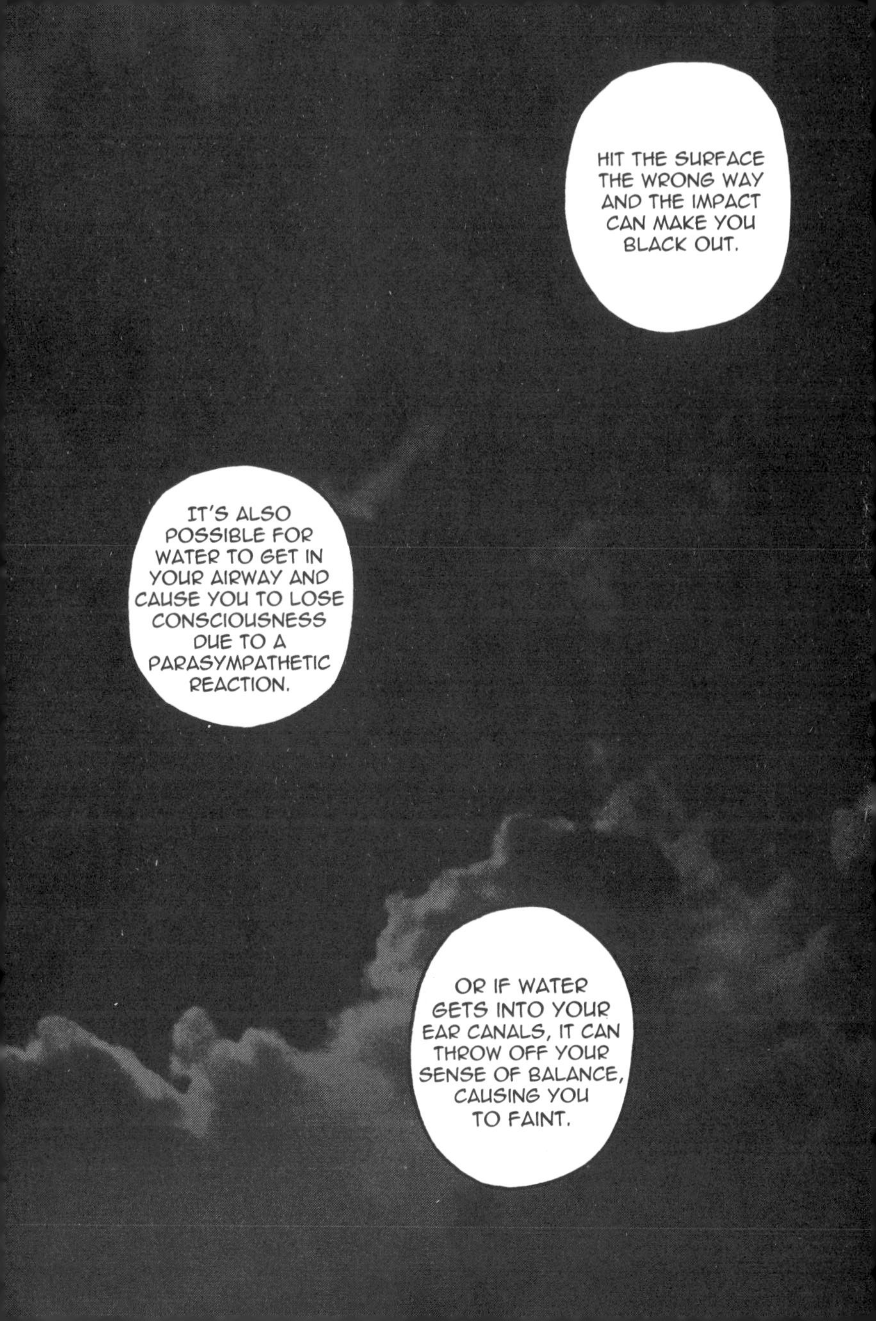
HIT THE SURFACE THE WRONG WAY AND THE IMPACT CAN MAKE YOU BLACK OUT.
IT'S ALSO POSSIBLE FOR WATER TO GET IN YOUR AIRWAY AND CAUSE YOU TO LOSE CONSCIOUSNESS DUE TO A PARASYMPATHETIC REACTION.
OR IF WATER GETS INTO YOUR EAR CANALS, IT CAN THROW OFF YOUR SENSE OF BALANCE, CAUSING YOU TO FAINT.

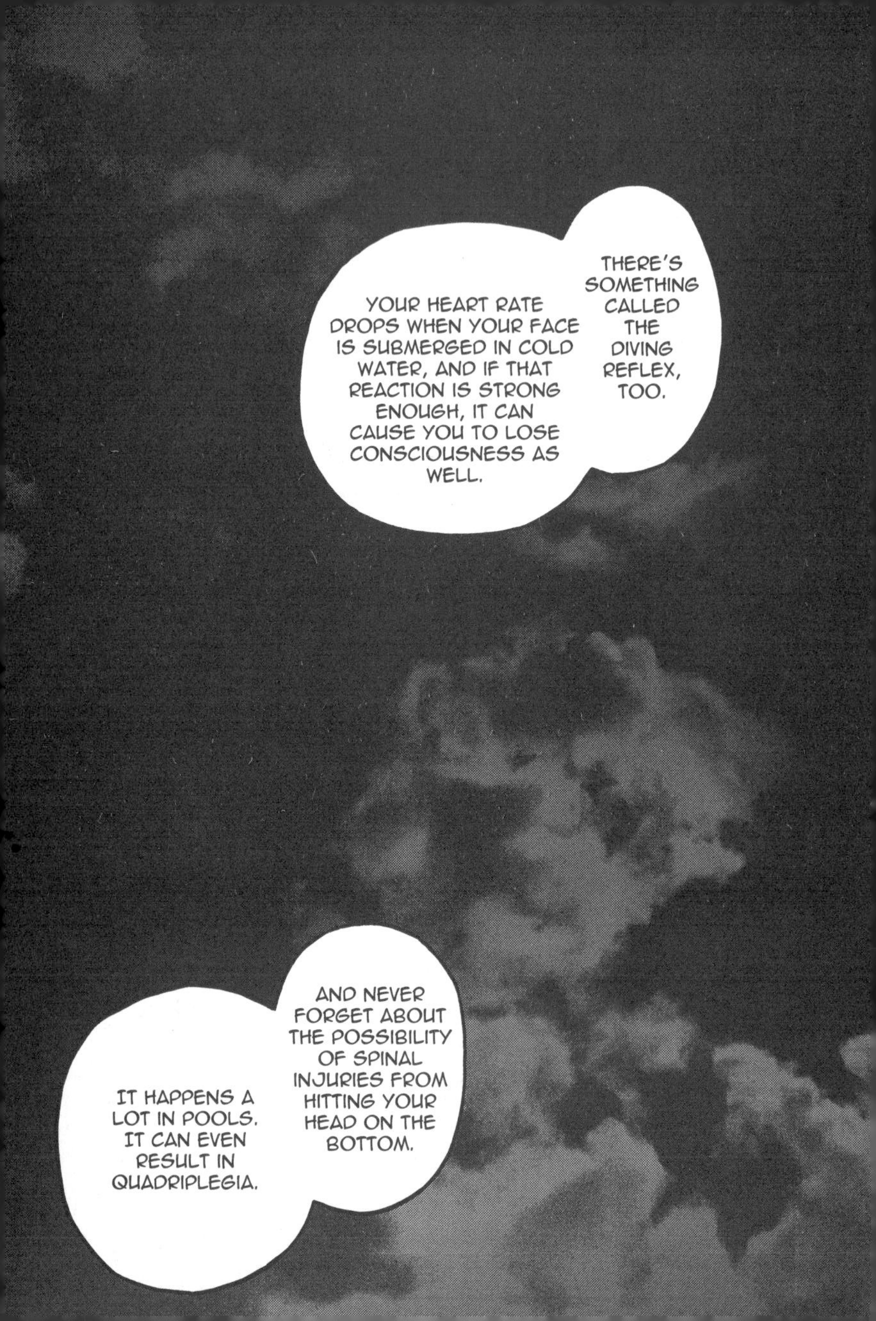
THERE'S SOMETHING CALLED THE DIVING REFLEX, TOO.
YOUR HEART RATE DROPS WHEN YOUR FACE IS SUBMERGED IN COLD WATER, AND IF THAT REACTION IS STRONG ENOUGH, IT CAN CAUSE YOU TO LOSE CONSCIOUSNESS AS WELL.
AND NEVER FORGET ABOUT THE POSSIBILITY OF SPINAL INJURIES FROM HITTING YOUR HEAD ON THE BOTTOM.
IT HAPPENS A LOT IN POOLS. IT CAN EVEN RESULT IN QUADRIPLEGIA.

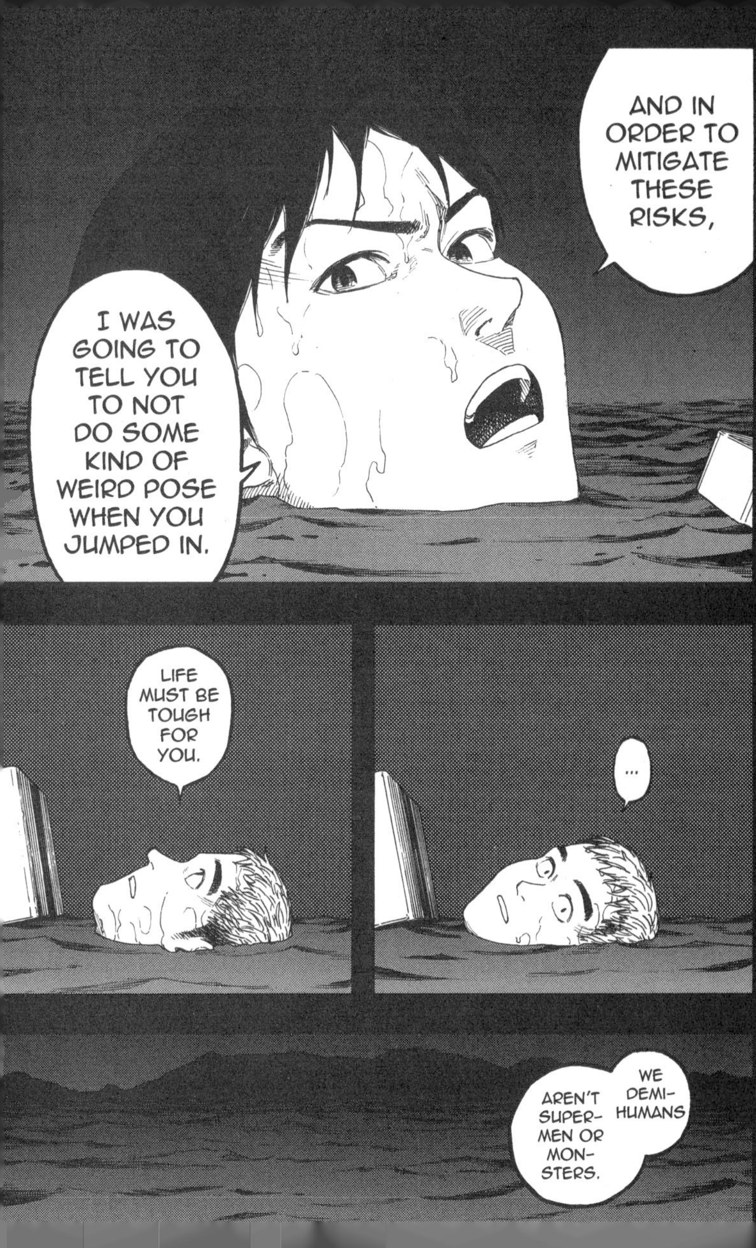
AND IN ORDER TO MITIGATE THESE RISKS,
I WAS GOING TO TELL YOU TO NOT DO SOME KIND OF WEIRD POSE WHEN YOU JUMPED IN.
...
LIFE MUST BE TOUGH FOR YOU.
WE DEMI-HUMANS
AREN'T SUPER-MEN OR MON-STERS.

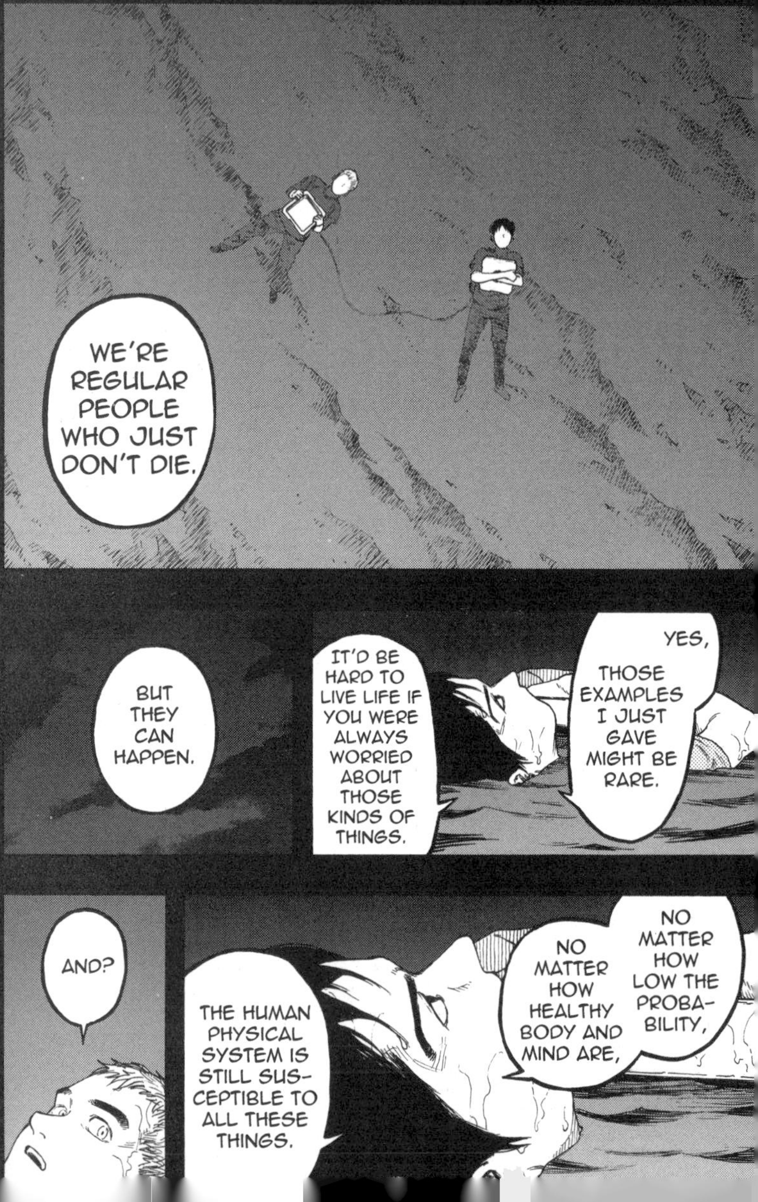
WE'RE REGULAR PEOPLE WHO JUST DON'T DIE.
YES, THOSE EXAMPLES I JUST GAVE MIGHT BE RARE.
IT'D BE HARD TO LIVE LIFE IF YOU WERE ALWAYS WORRIED ABOUT THOSE KINDS OF THINGS.
BUT THEY CAN HAPPEN.
NO MATTER HOW LOW THE PROBA-BILITY,
NO MATTER HOW HEALTHY BODY AND MIND ARE,
THE HUMAN PHYSICAL SYSTEM IS STILL SUS-CEPTIBLE TO ALL THESE THINGS.
AND?

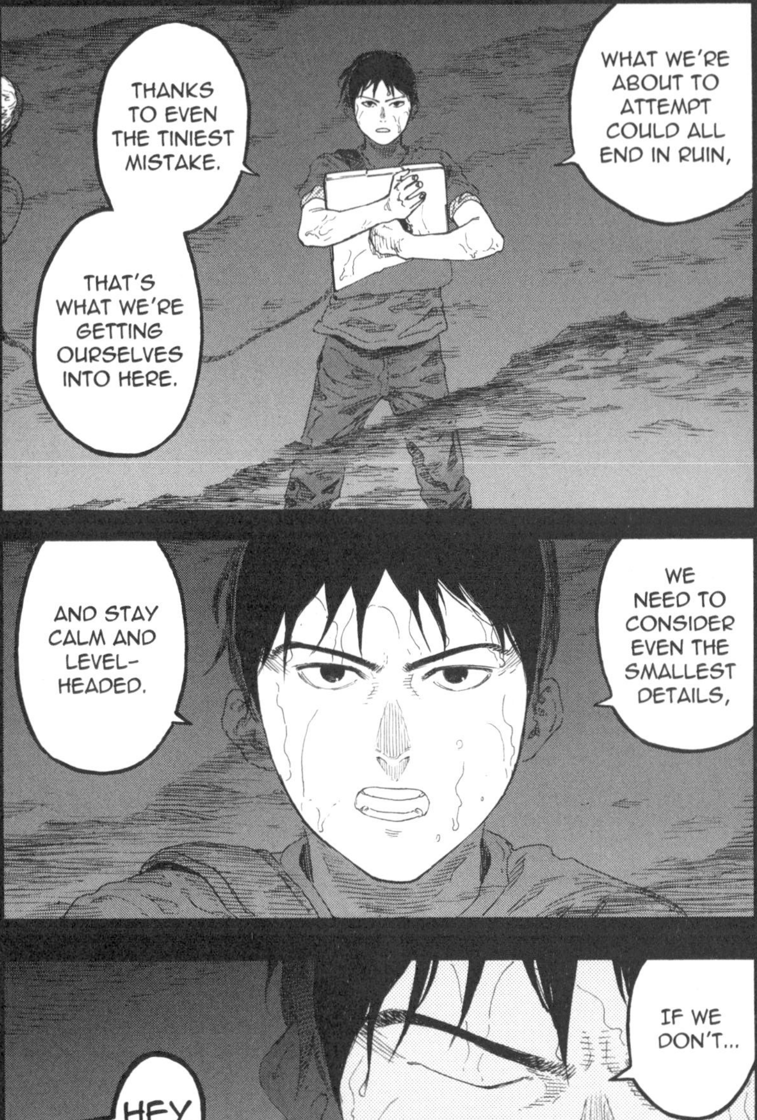
WHAT WE'RE ABOUT TO ATTEMPT COULD ALL END IN RUIN,
THANKS TO EVEN THE TINIEST MISTAKE.
THAT'S WHAT WE'RE GETTING OURSELVES INTO HERE.
WE NEED TO CONSIDER EVEN THE SMALLEST DETAILS,
AND STAY CALM AND LEVEL-HEADED.
IF WE DON'T...
HEY.

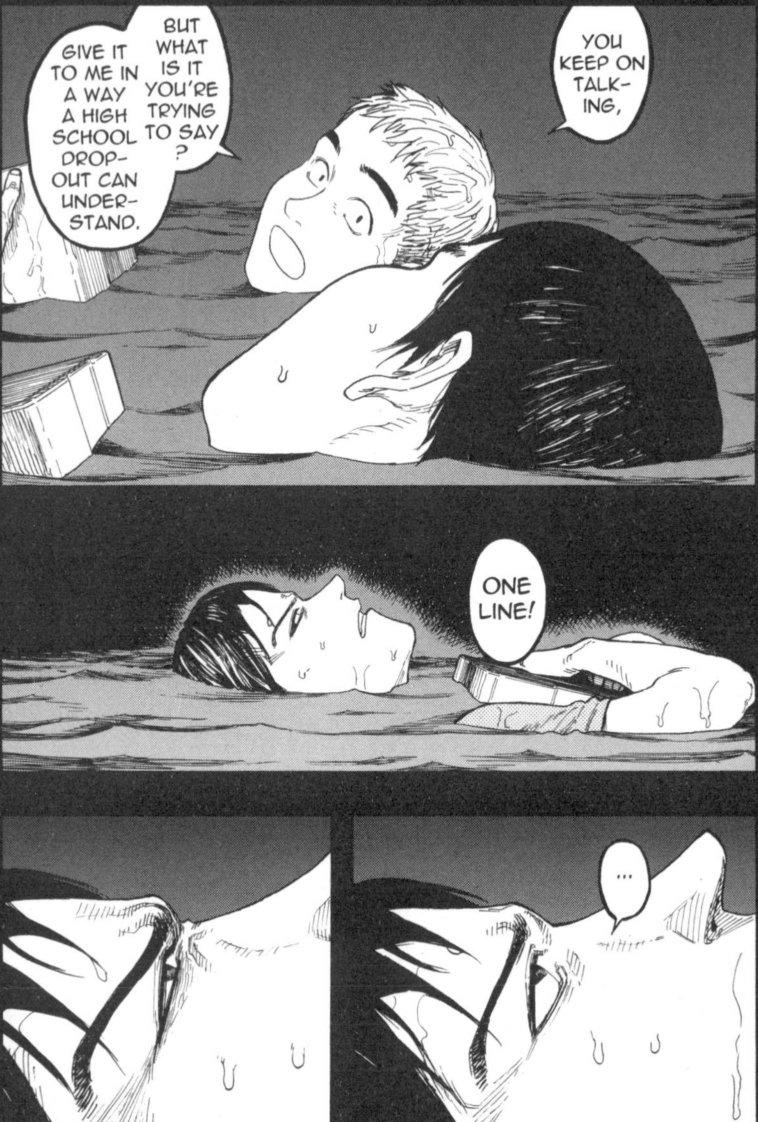
YOU KEEP ON TALKING,
BUT WHAT IS IT YOU'RE TRYING TO SAY?
GIVE IT TO ME IN A WAY A HIGH SCHOOL DROPOUT CAN UNDERSTAND.
ONE LINE!
...

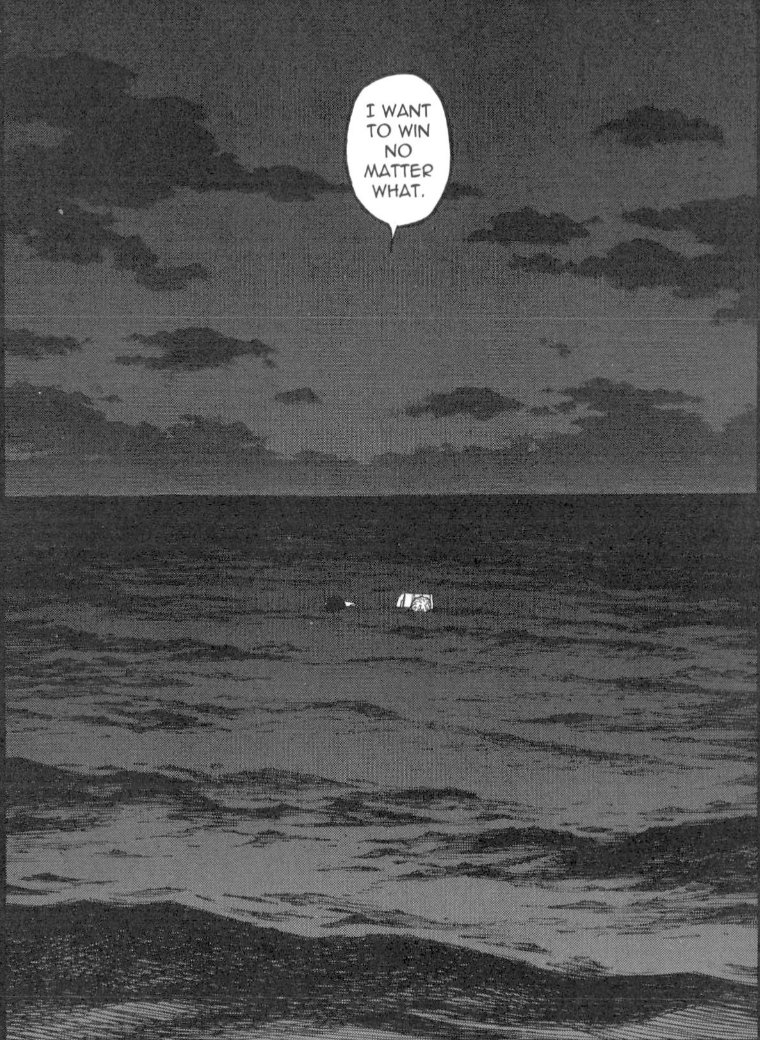
I WANT TO WIN NO MATTER WHAT.

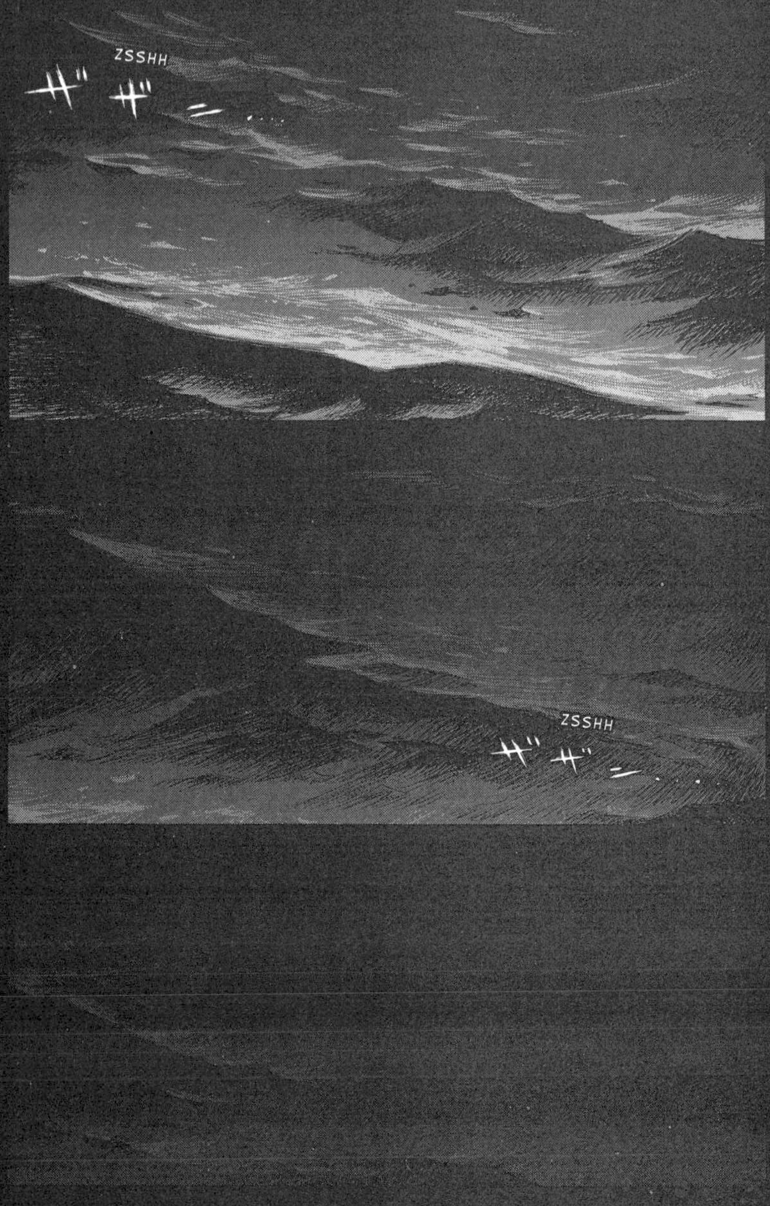
ZSSHH
ZSSHH

FINAL VOLUME

AJIN
DEMI-HUMAN

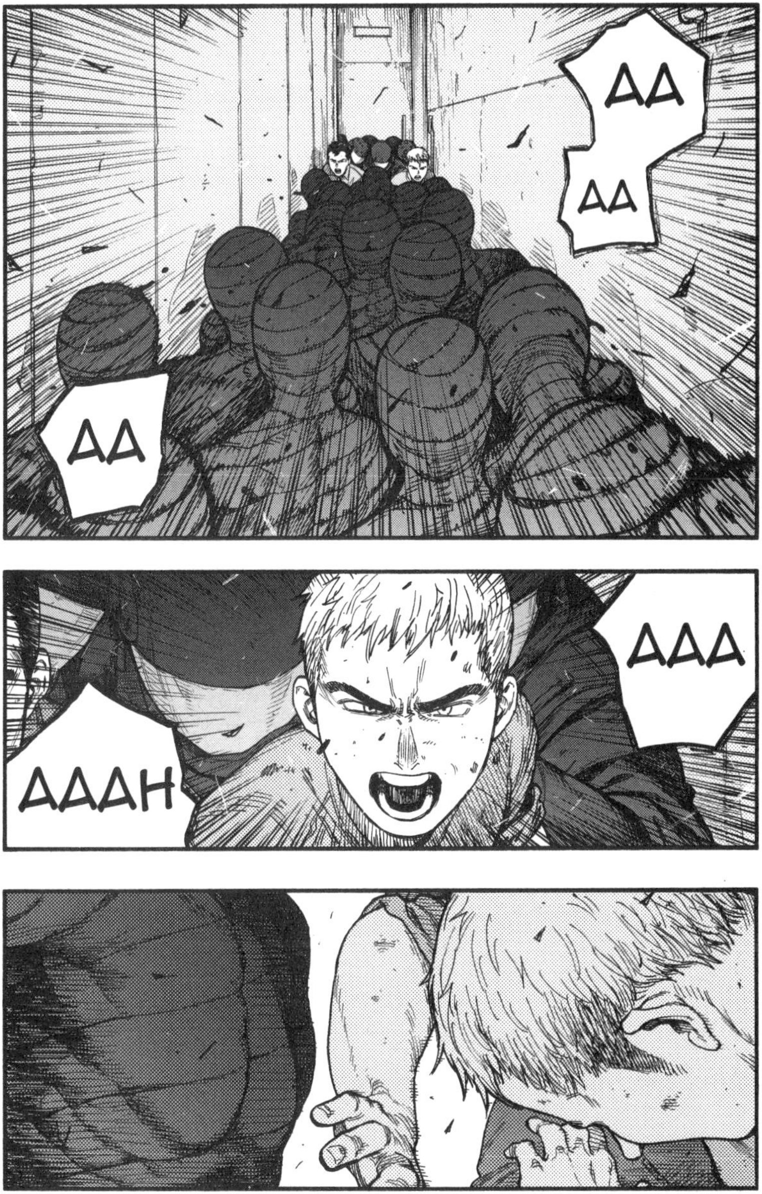
AA
AA
AA
AAA
AAAH

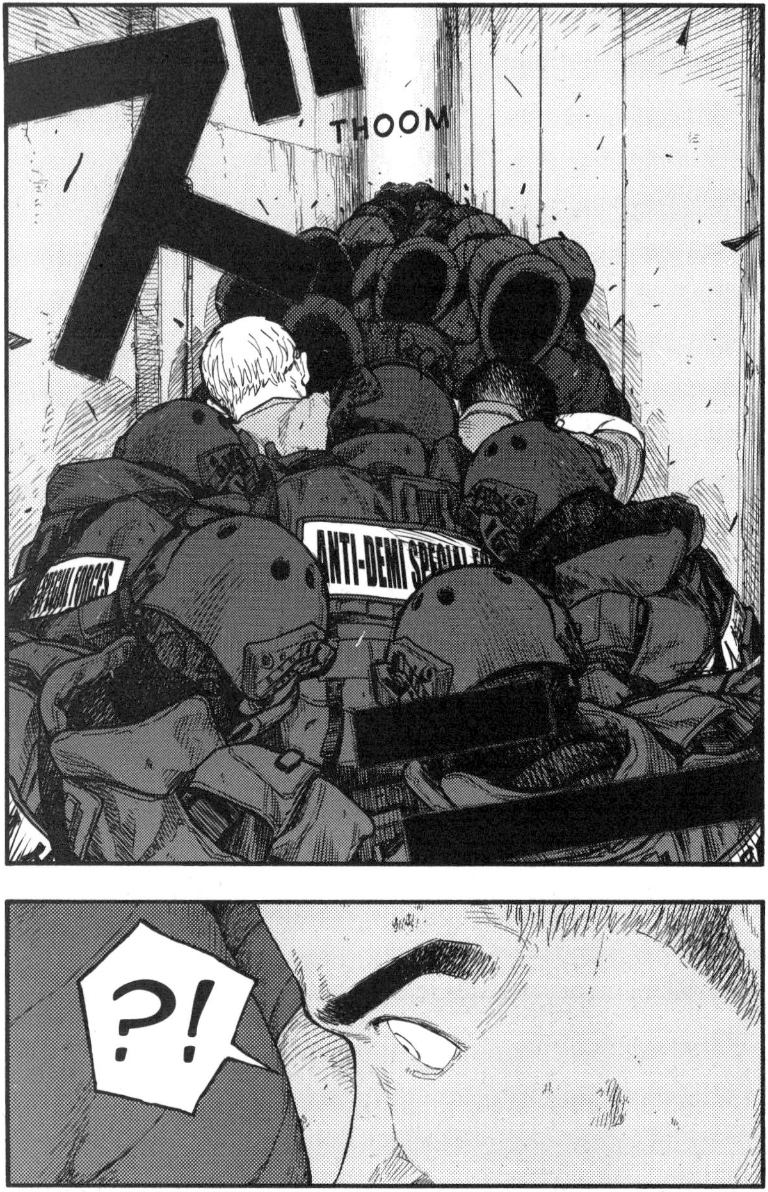
THOOM
ANTI-DEMI SPECIAL
SPECIAL FORCES
?!

CRUMBLE
ボロ
ボロ
CRUMBLE

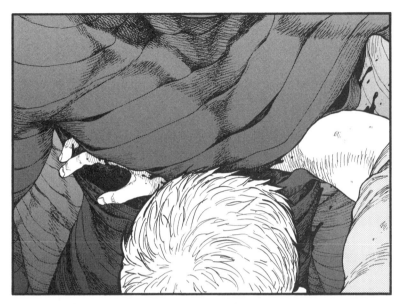

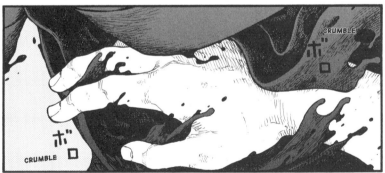

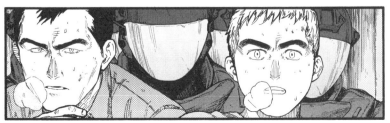

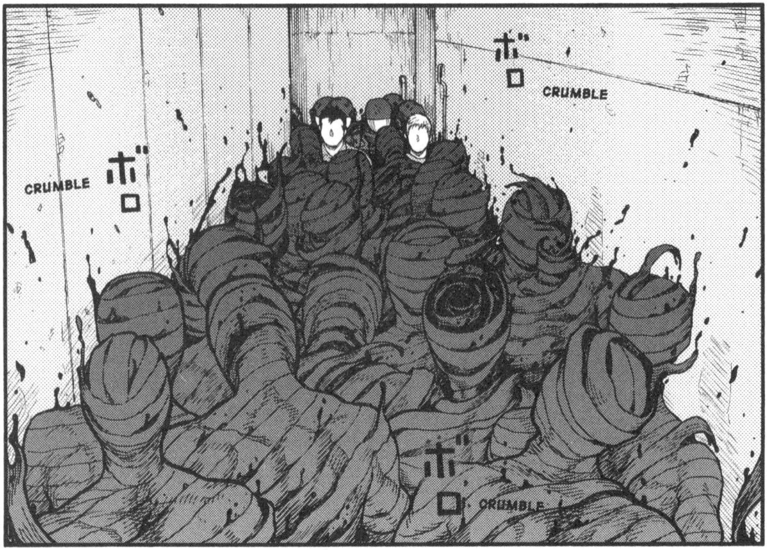
ボロ
CRUMBLE
ボロ
CRUMBLE
ボロ
CRUMBLE

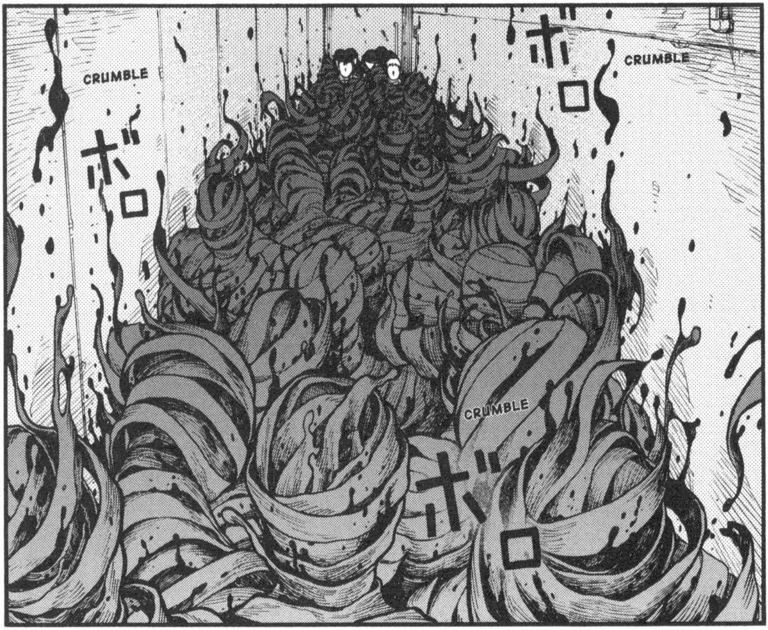
ボロ
CRUMBLE
CRUMBLE
ボロ
CRUMBLE
ボロ

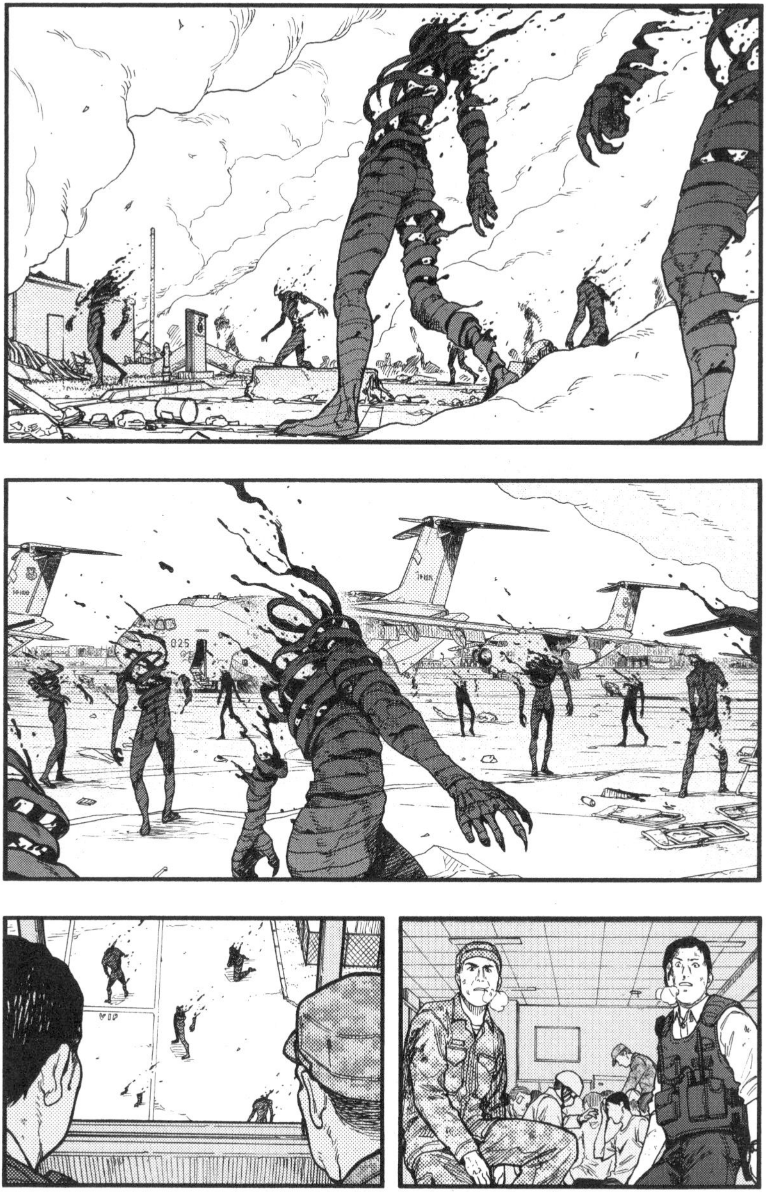
025
VIP

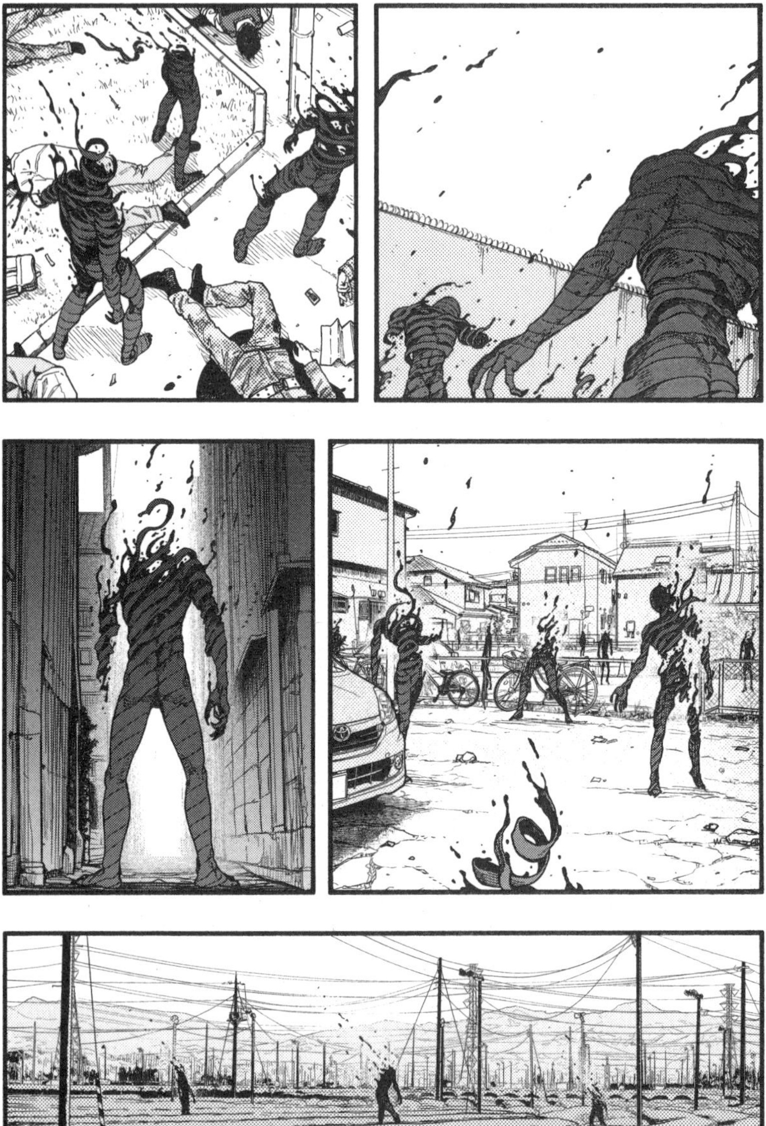

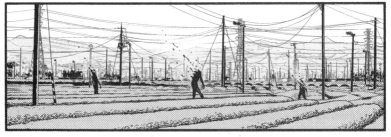

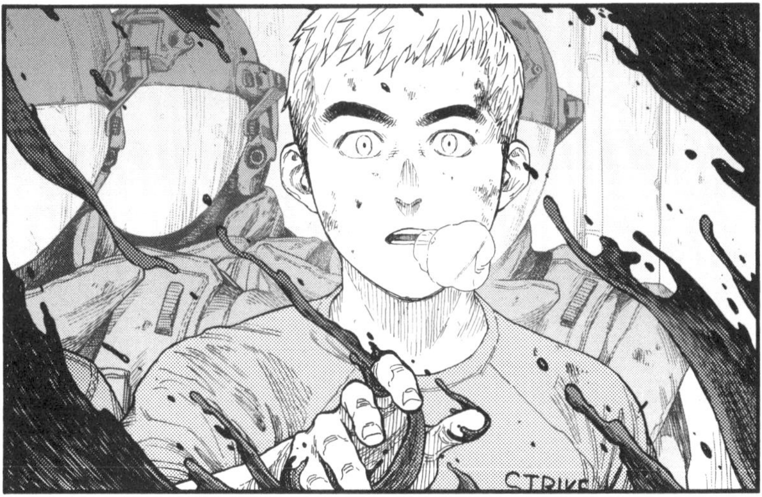
STRIKE

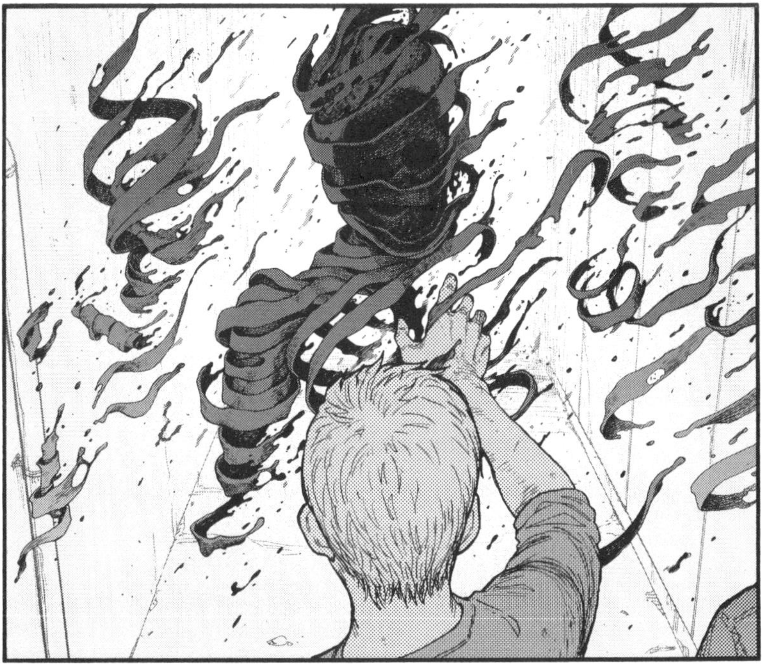

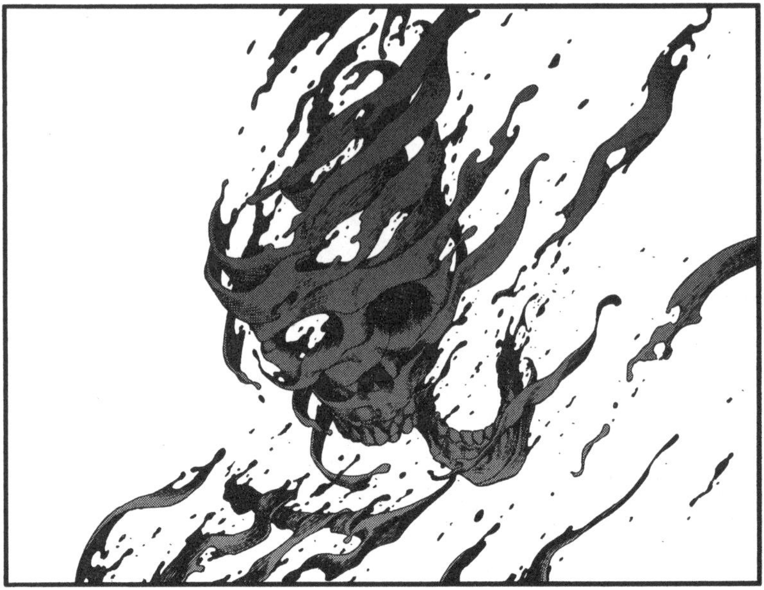
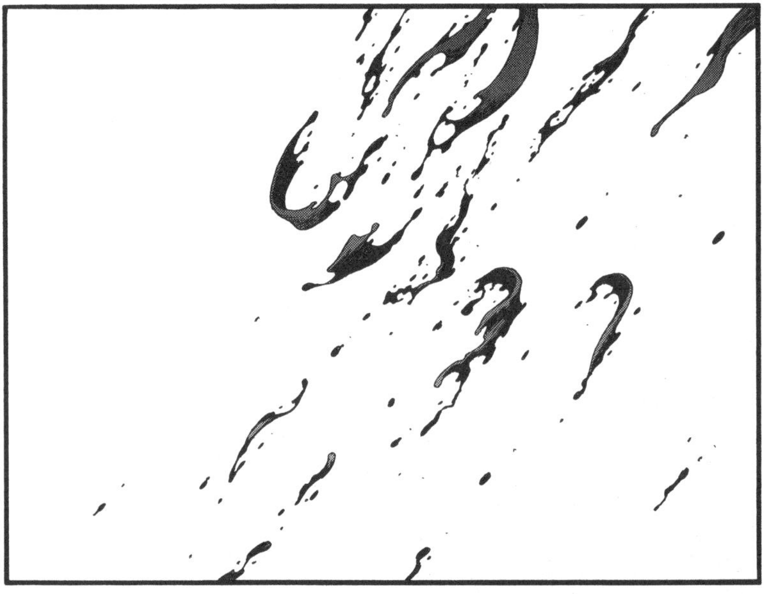

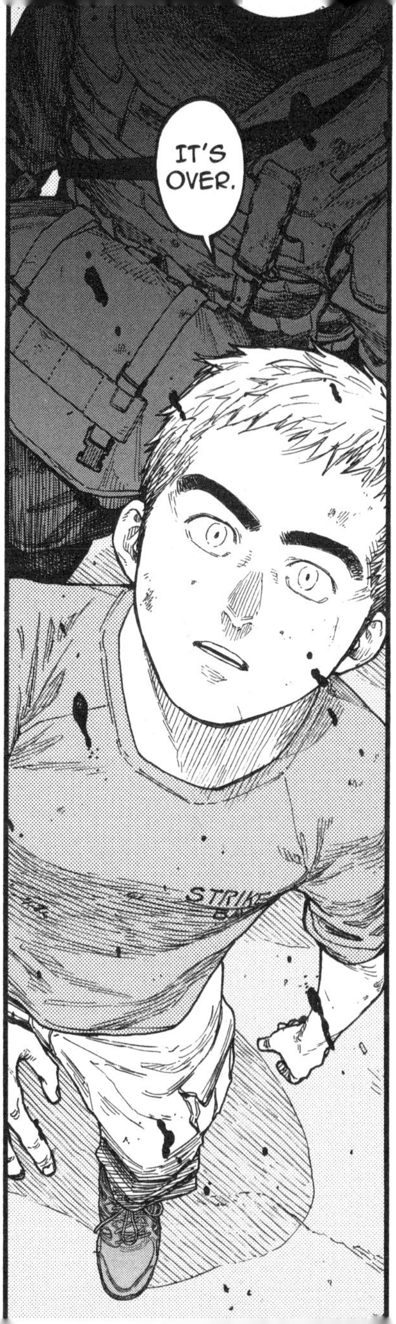
IT'S OVER.
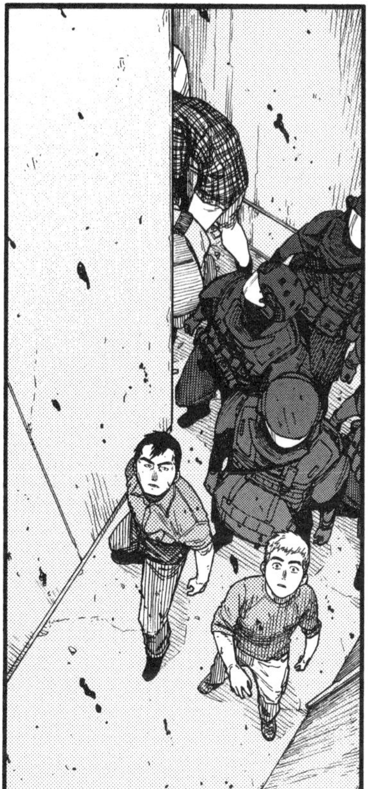

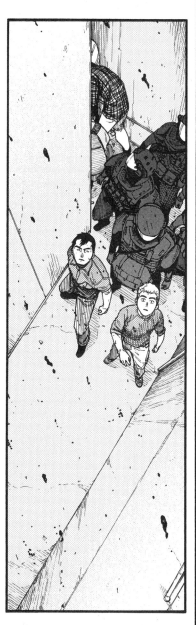

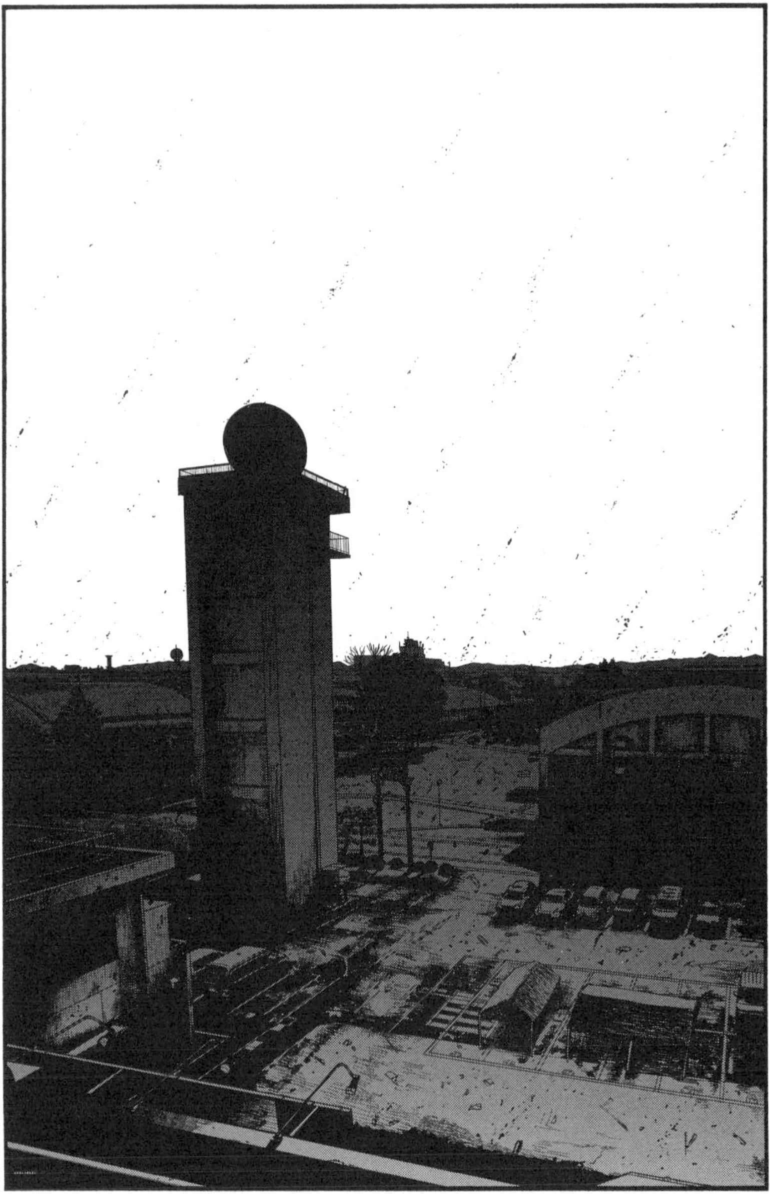

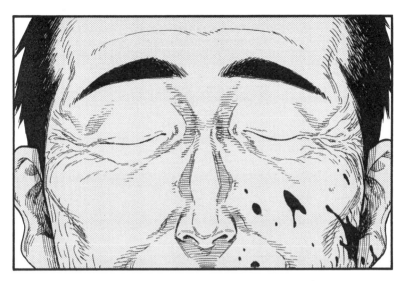

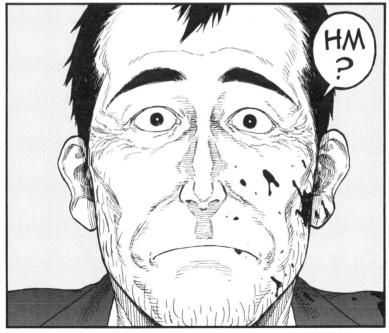

HM
?

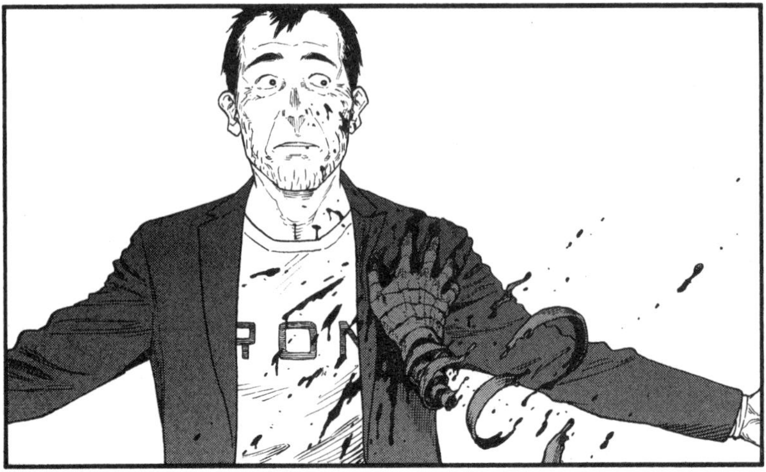
RON

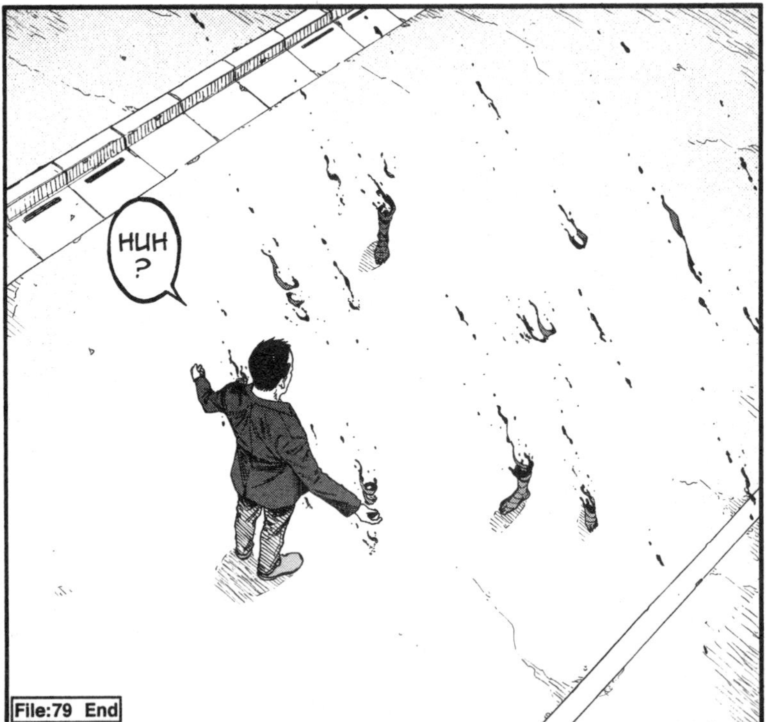
HUH ?
File:79 End

File: 80

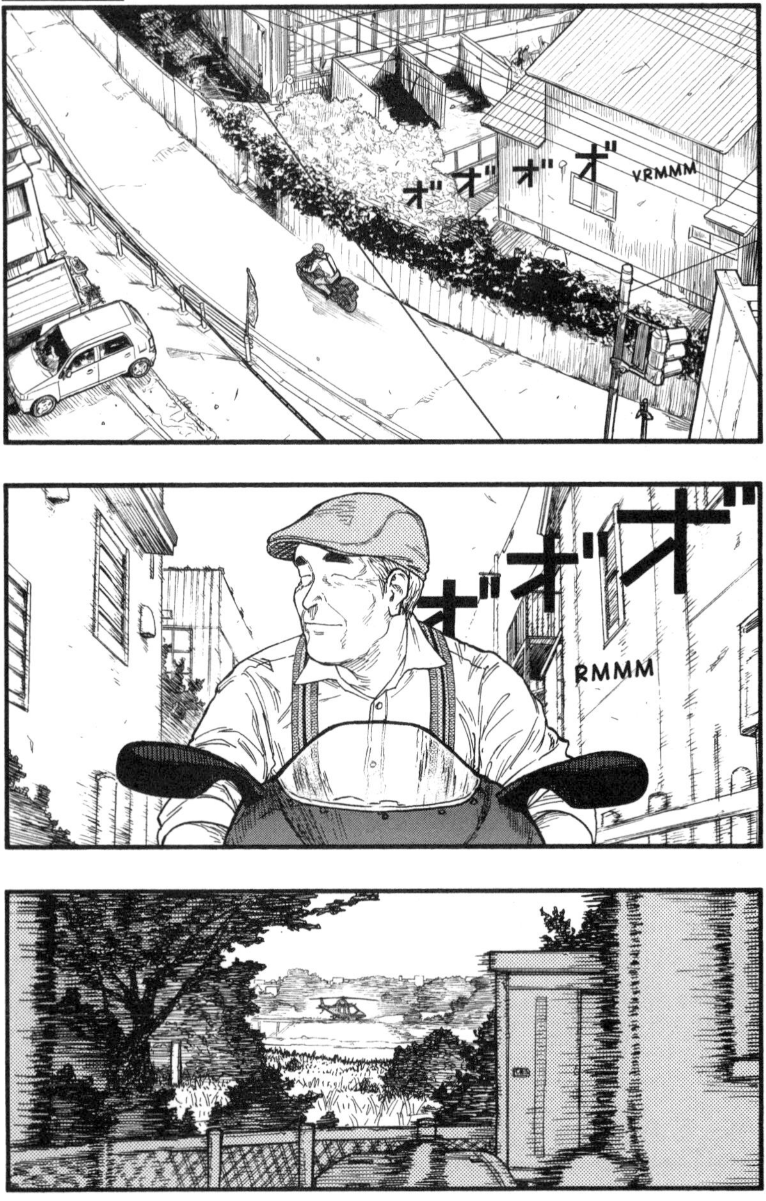

オ゛オ゛オ゛オ゛
VRMMM
オ゛オ゛オ゛
RMMM

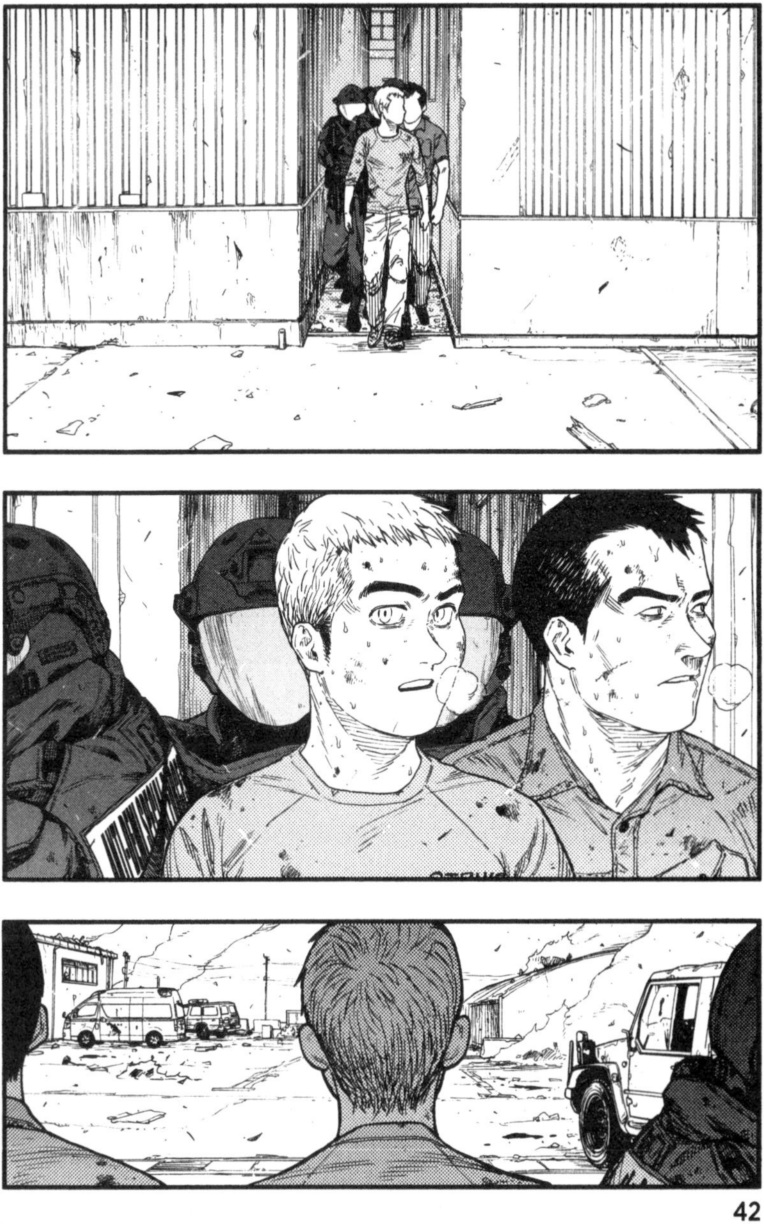

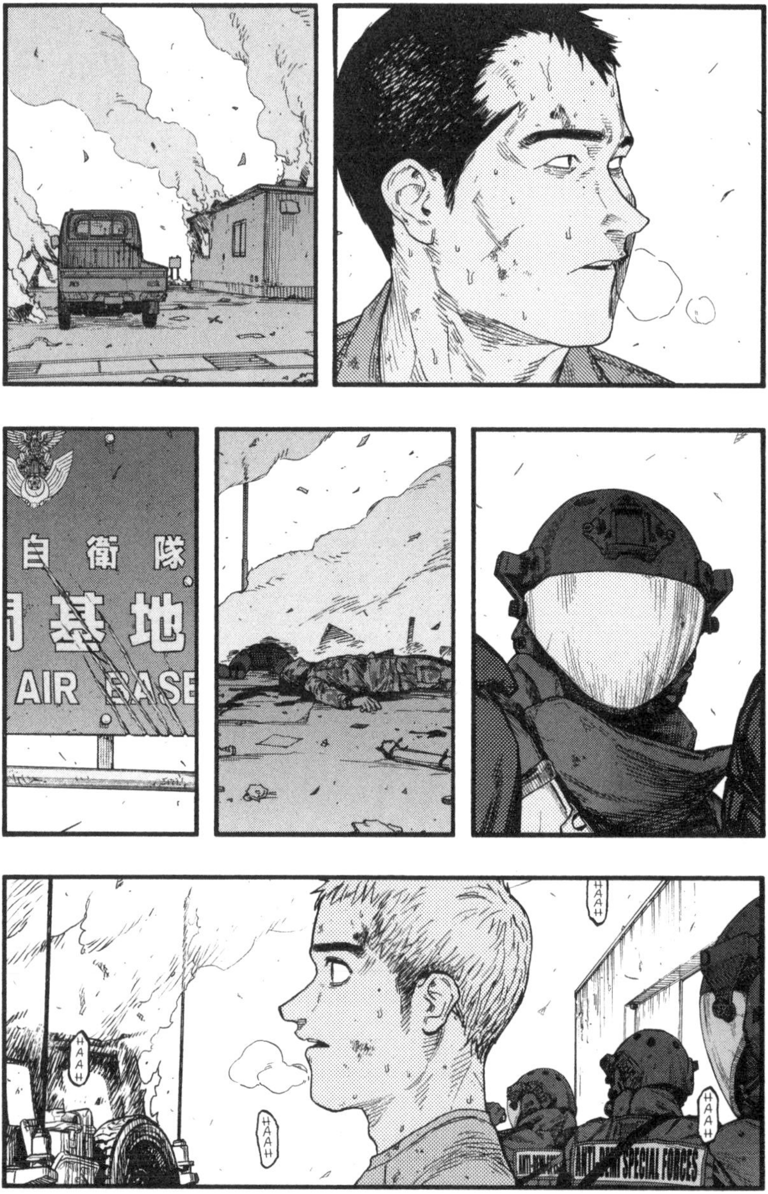
自衛隊
基地
AIR BASE
HAAH
SPECIAL FORCES
HAAH
HAAH
HAAH

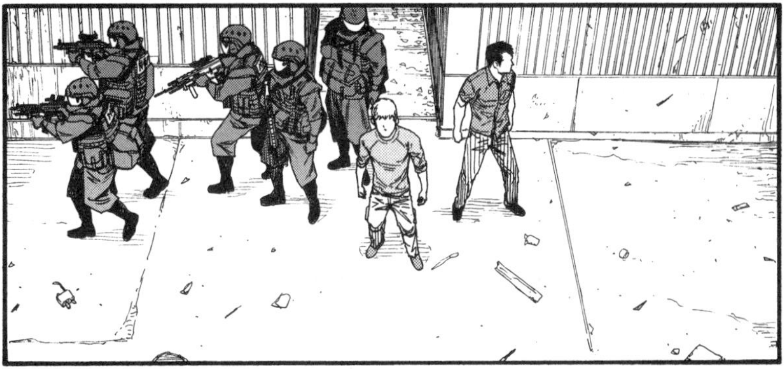

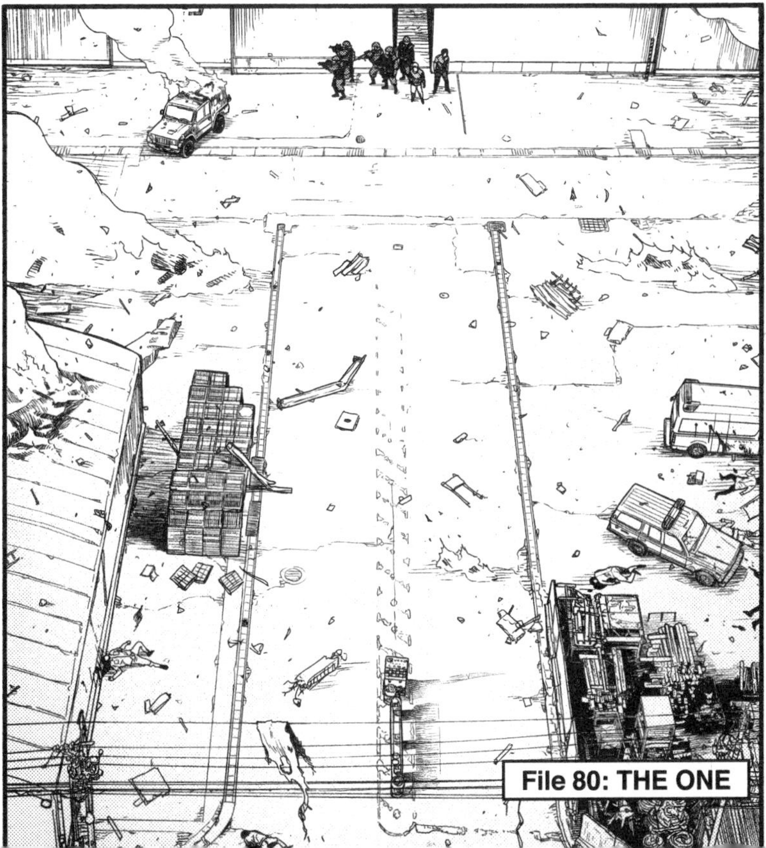
File 80: THE ONE

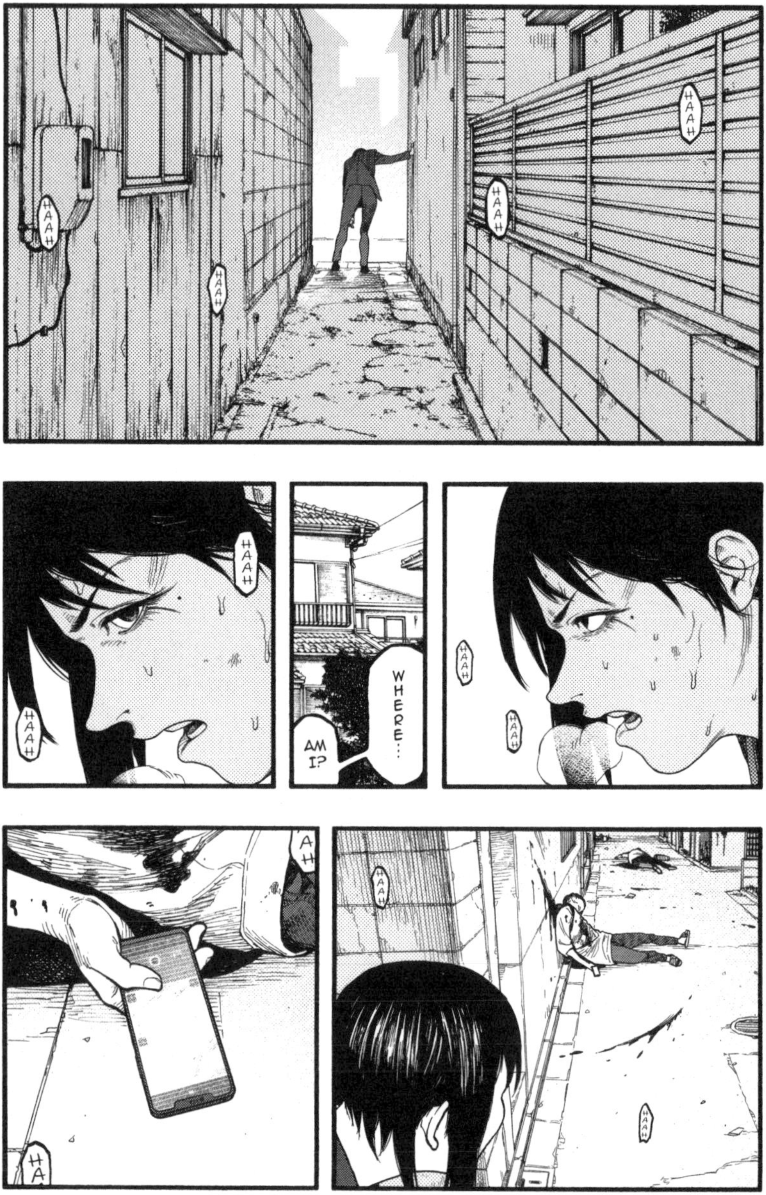
HAAH
HAAH
HAAH
HAAH
HAAH
HAAH
WHERE...
AM I?
HAAH
HAAH
HAAH
HAAH
AH
HA
A

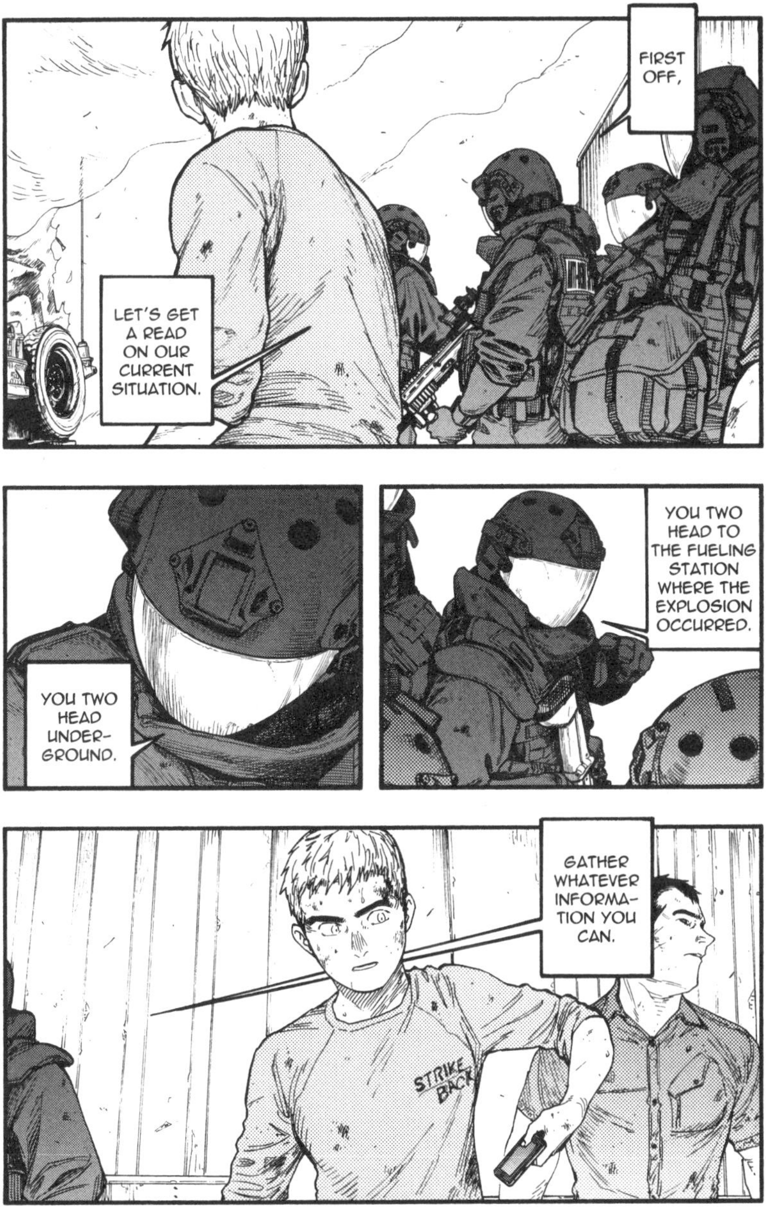
FIRST OFF,
LET'S GET A READ ON OUR CURRENT SITUATION.
YOU TWO HEAD TO THE FUELING STATION WHERE THE EXPLOSION OCCURRED.
YOU TWO HEAD UNDER-GROUND.
GATHER WHATEVER INFORMA-TION YOU CAN.
STRIKE BACK

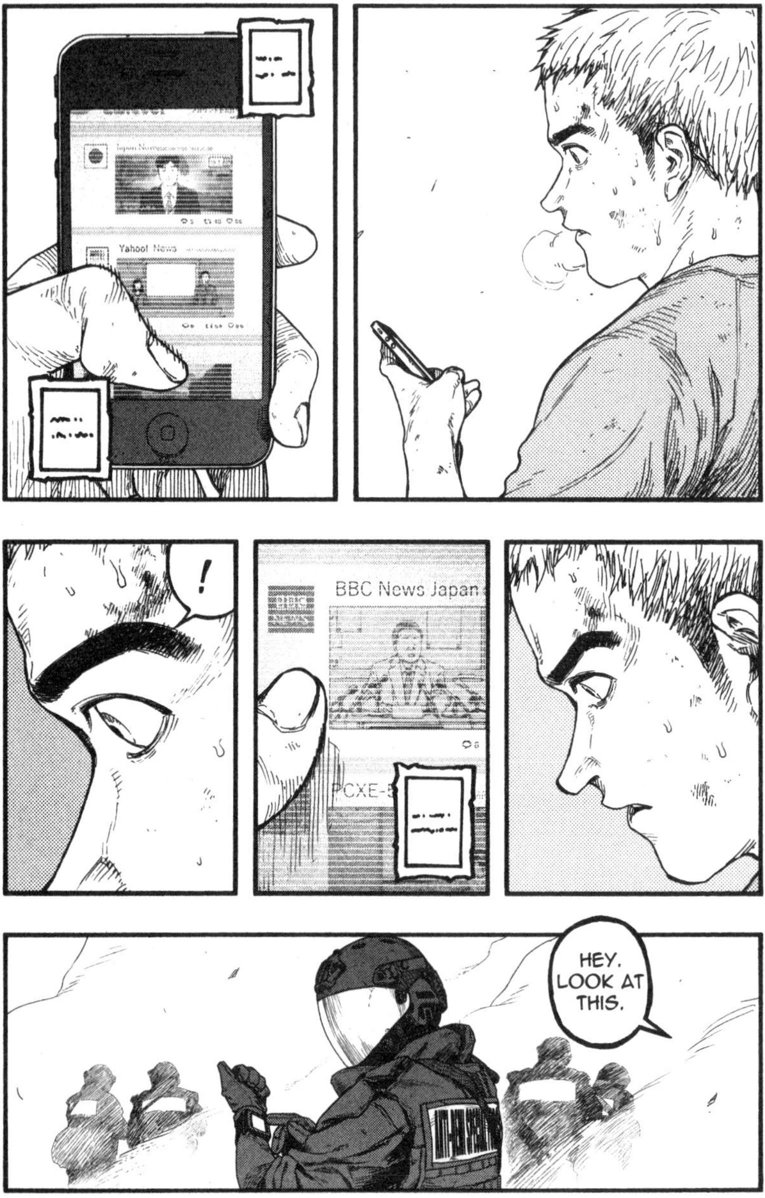
Yahoo! News
BBC News Japan
!
HEY. LOOK AT THIS.

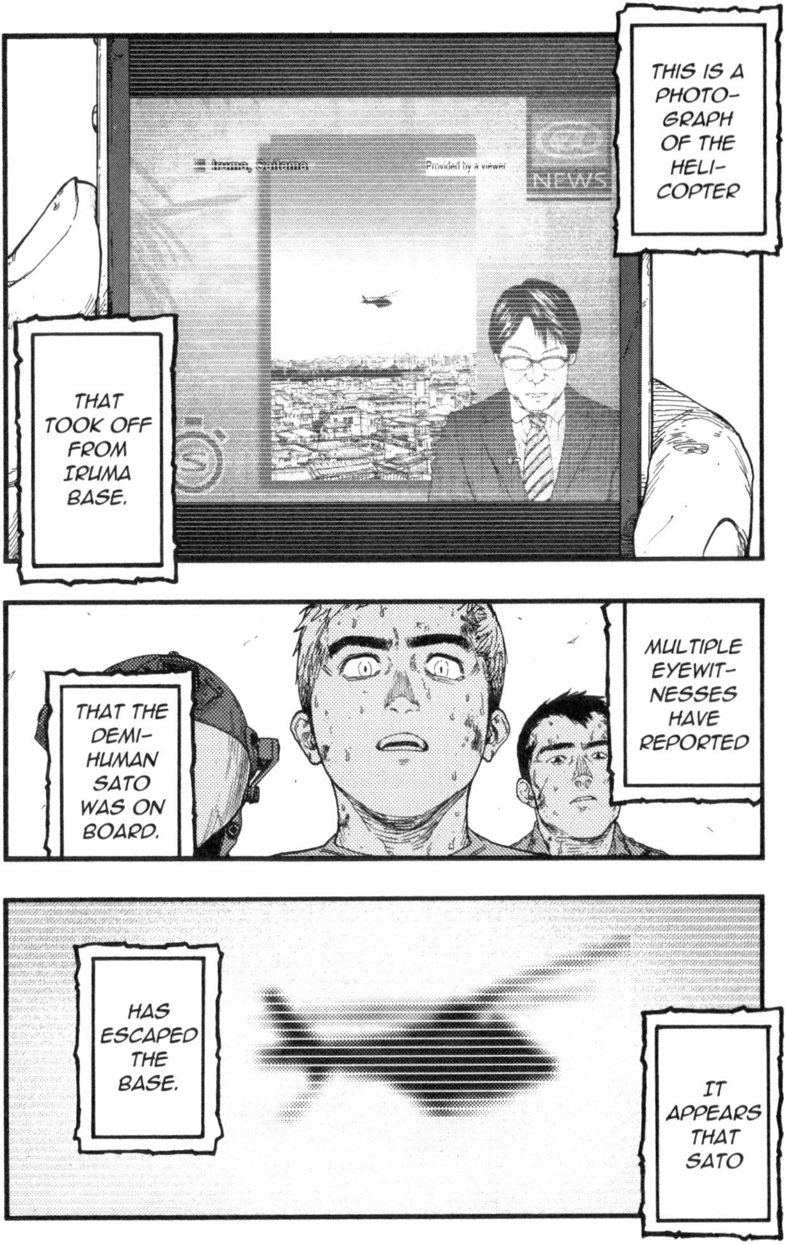
THIS IS A PHOTOGRAPH OF THE HELICOPTER
Iruma, Saitama
Provided by a viewer
NEWS
THAT TOOK OFF FROM IRUMA BASE.
MULTIPLE EYEWITNESSES HAVE REPORTED
THAT THE DEMI-HUMAN SATO WAS ON BOARD.
IT APPEARS THAT SATO
HAS ESCAPED THE BASE.

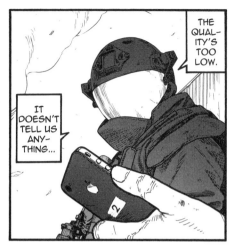

THE QUAL- ITY'S TOO LOW.

IT DOESN'T TELL US ANY- THING...

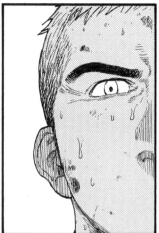

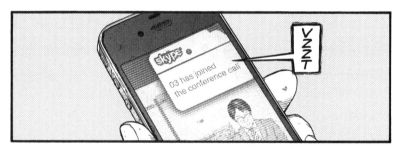

skype

03 has joined the conference call

VZZT

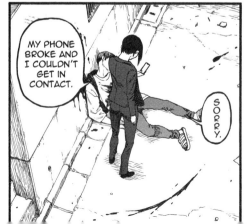

MY PHONE BROKE AND I COULDN'T GET IN CONTACT.

SORRY.

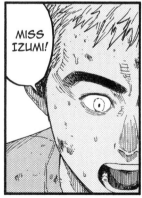

MISS IZUMI!

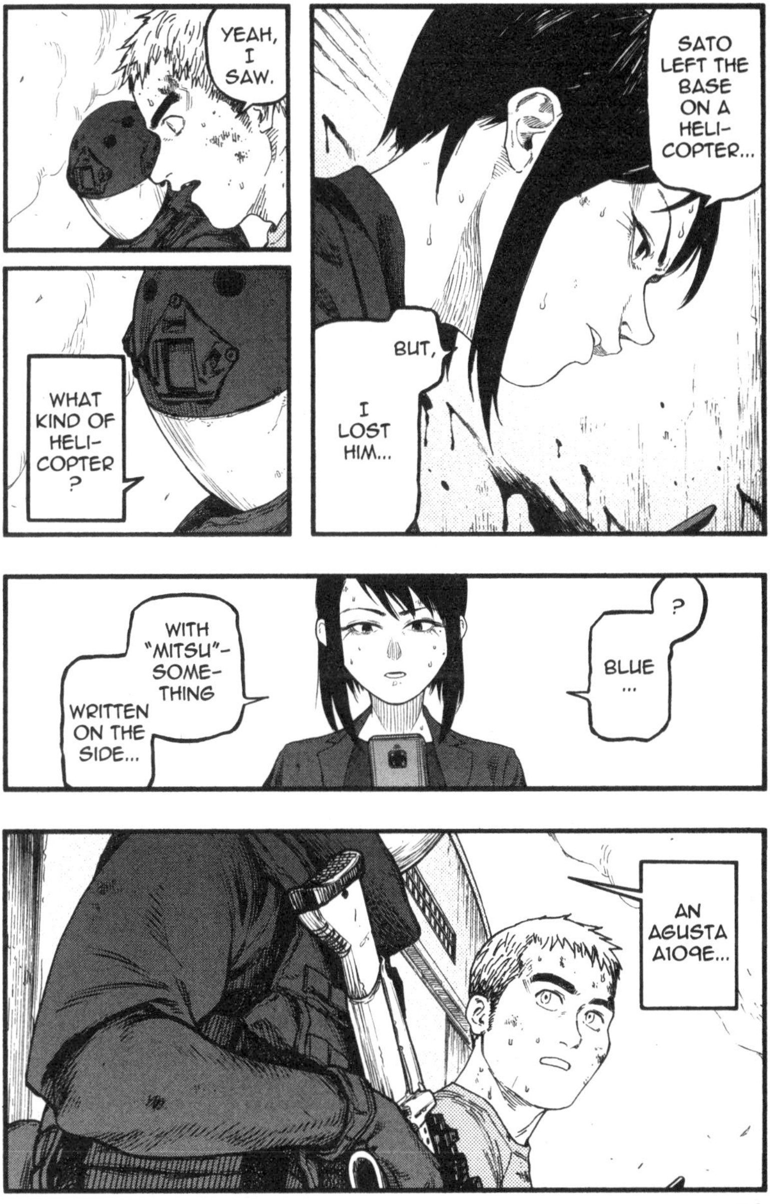
SATO LEFT THE BASE ON A HELI-COPTER...
BUT,
I LOST HIM...
YEAH, I SAW.
WHAT KIND OF HELI-COPTER ?
?
BLUE ...
WITH "MITSU"-SOMETHING
WRITTEN ON THE SIDE...
AN AGUSTA A109E...

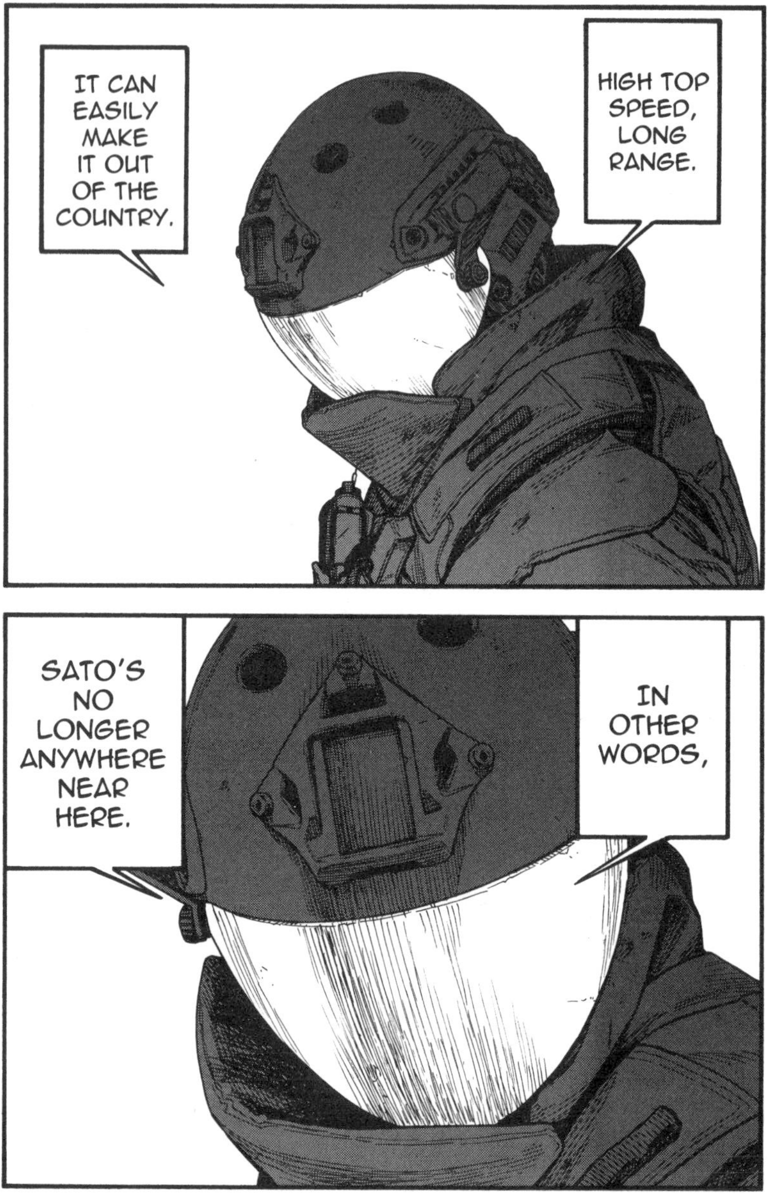
HIGH TOP SPEED, LONG RANGE.
IT CAN EASILY MAKE IT OUT OF THE COUNTRY.
IN OTHER WORDS,
SATO'S NO LONGER ANYWHERE NEAR HERE.

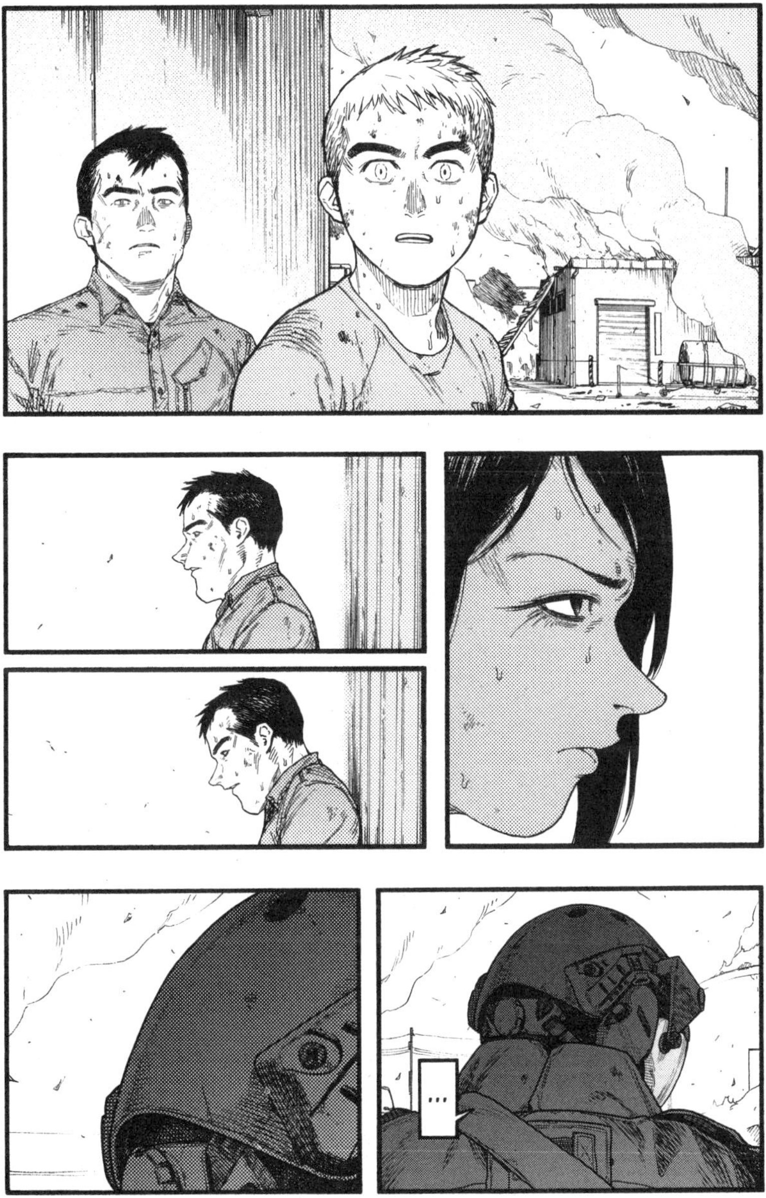
...

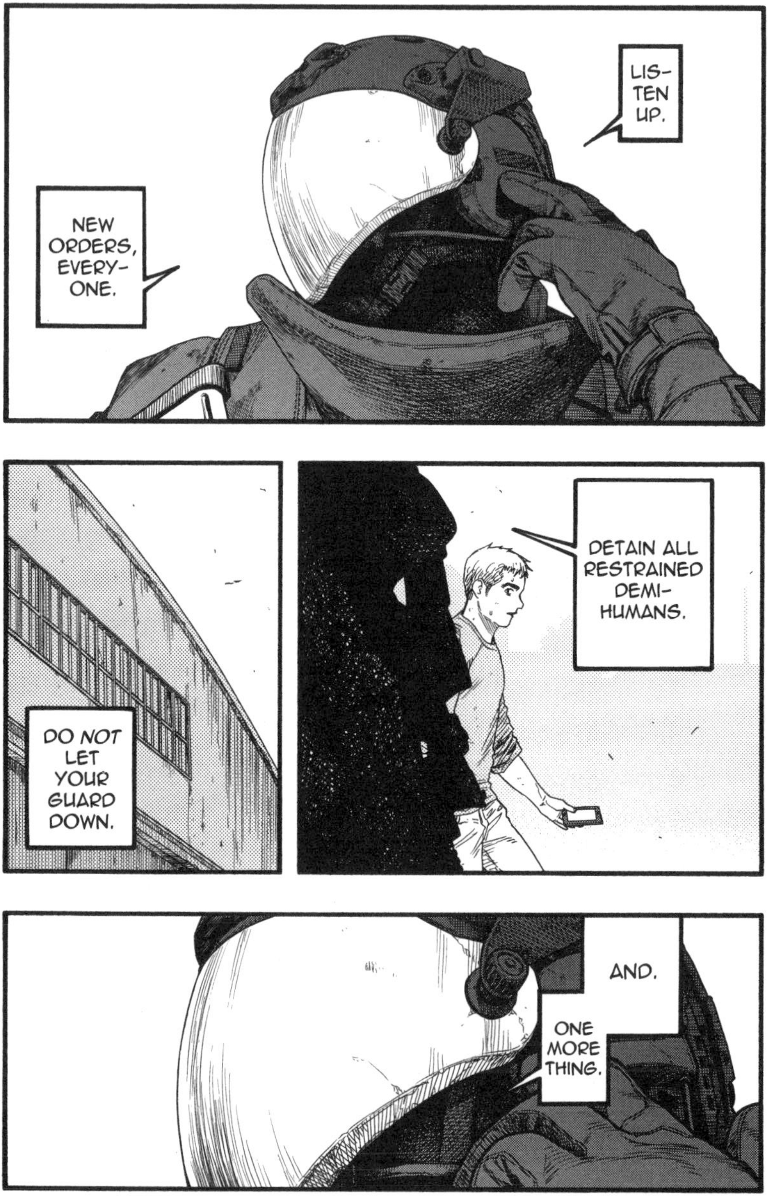
LIS-TEN UP.
NEW ORDERS, EVERY-ONE.
DETAIN ALL RESTRAINED DEMI-HUMANS.
DO *NOT* LET YOUR GUARD DOWN.
AND.
ONE MORE THING.

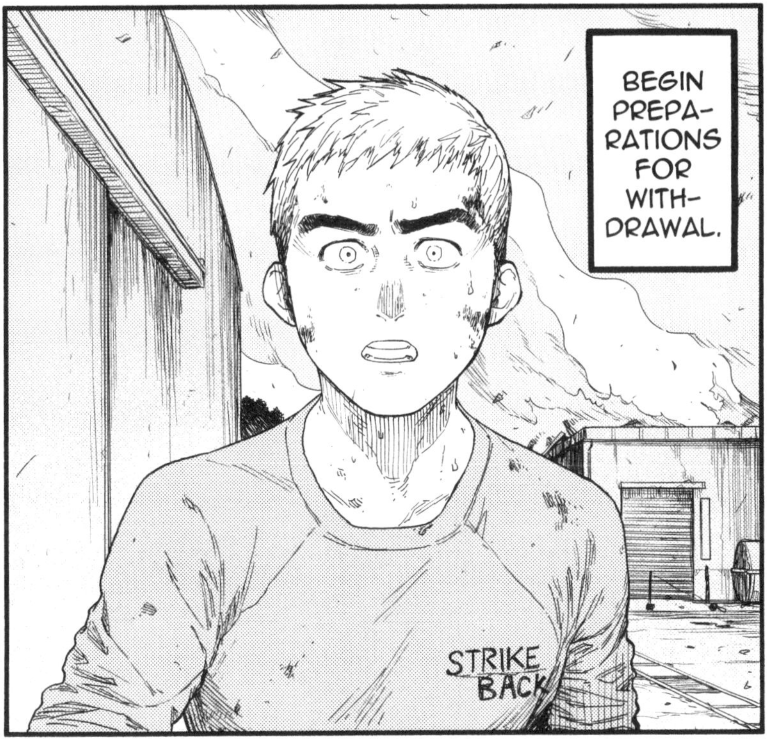
BEGIN PREPARATIONS FOR WITHDRAWAL.
STRIKE BACK
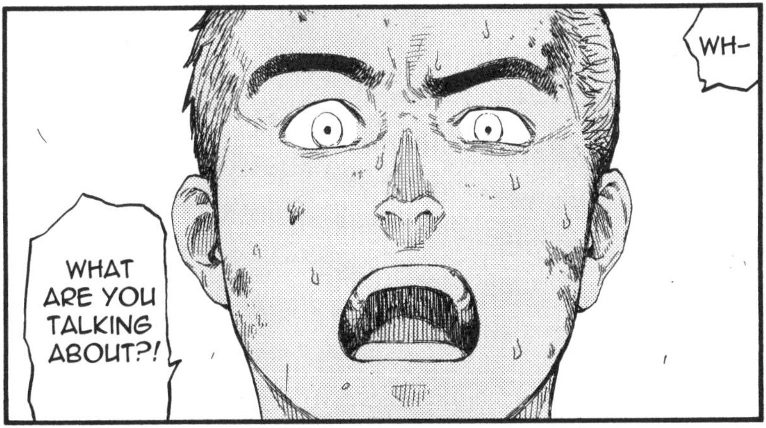
WH-
WHAT ARE YOU TALKING ABOUT?!

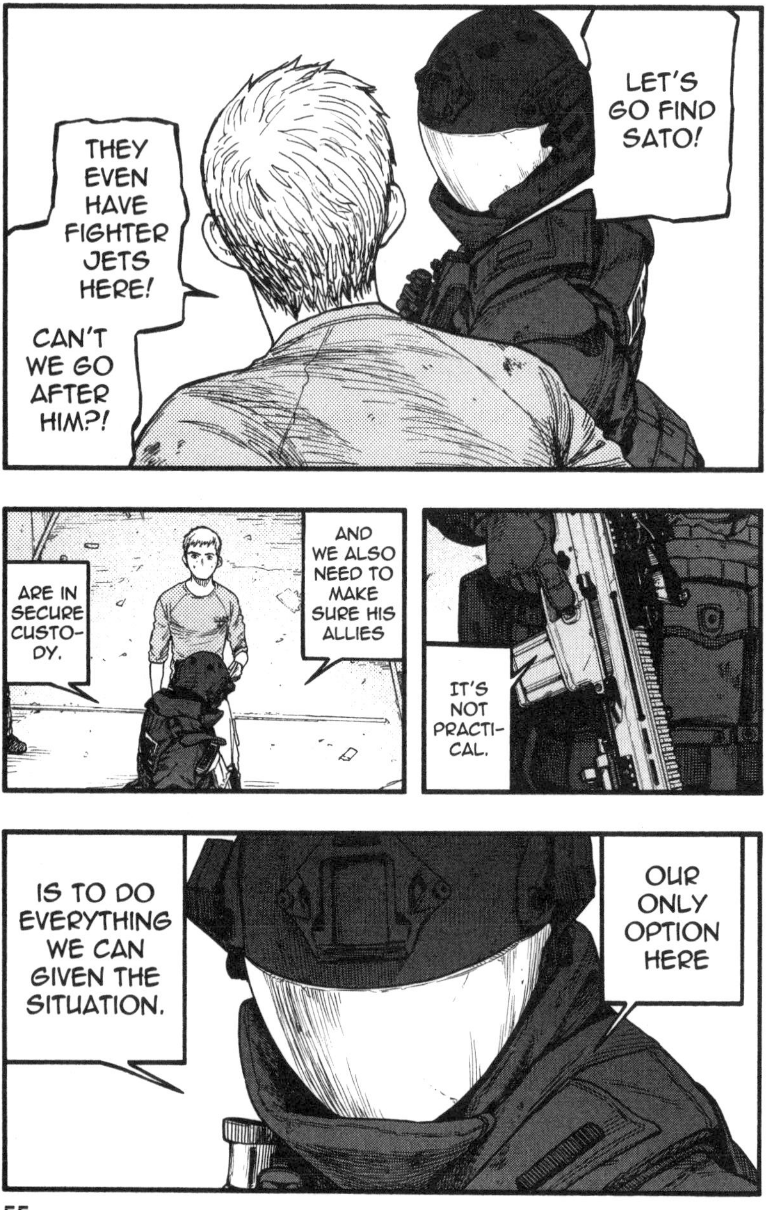
LET'S GO FIND SATO!
THEY EVEN HAVE FIGHTER JETS HERE!
CAN'T WE GO AFTER HIM?!
IT'S NOT PRACTICAL.
AND WE ALSO NEED TO MAKE SURE HIS ALLIES
ARE IN SECURE CUSTODY.
OUR ONLY OPTION HERE
IS TO DO EVERYTHING WE CAN GIVEN THE SITUATION.

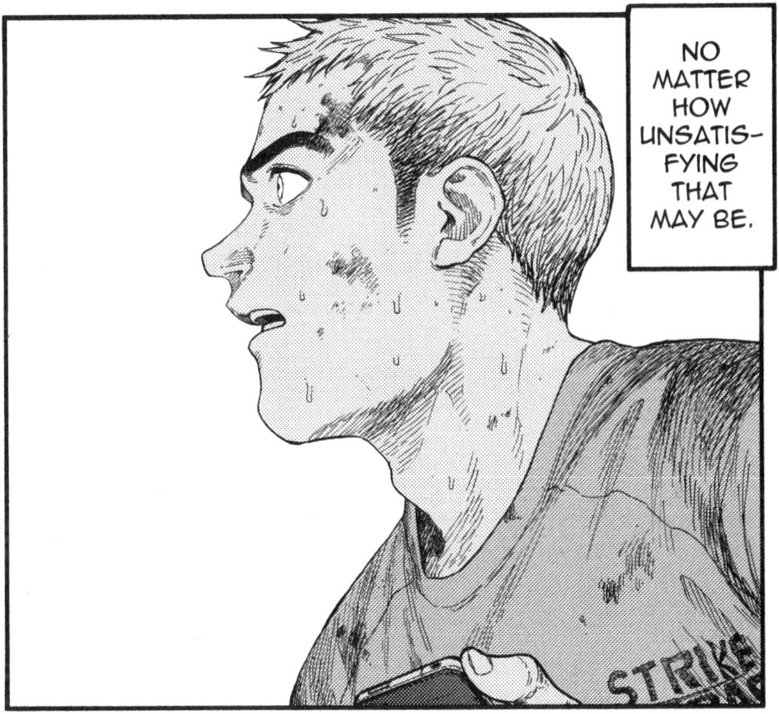
NO MATTER HOW UNSATIS- FYING THAT MAY BE.

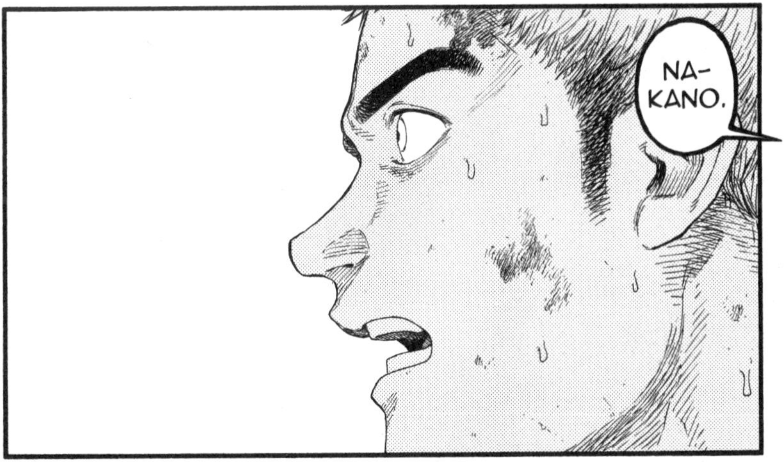
NA- KANO.

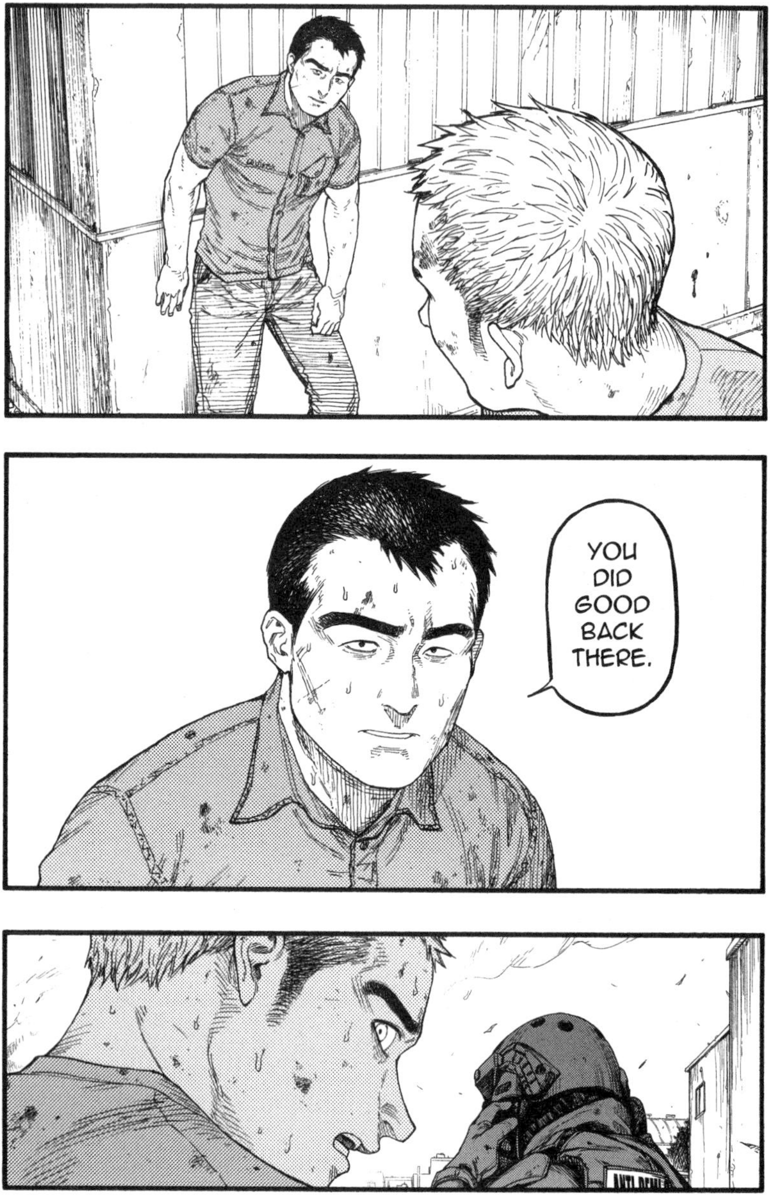
YOU DID GOOD BACK THERE.

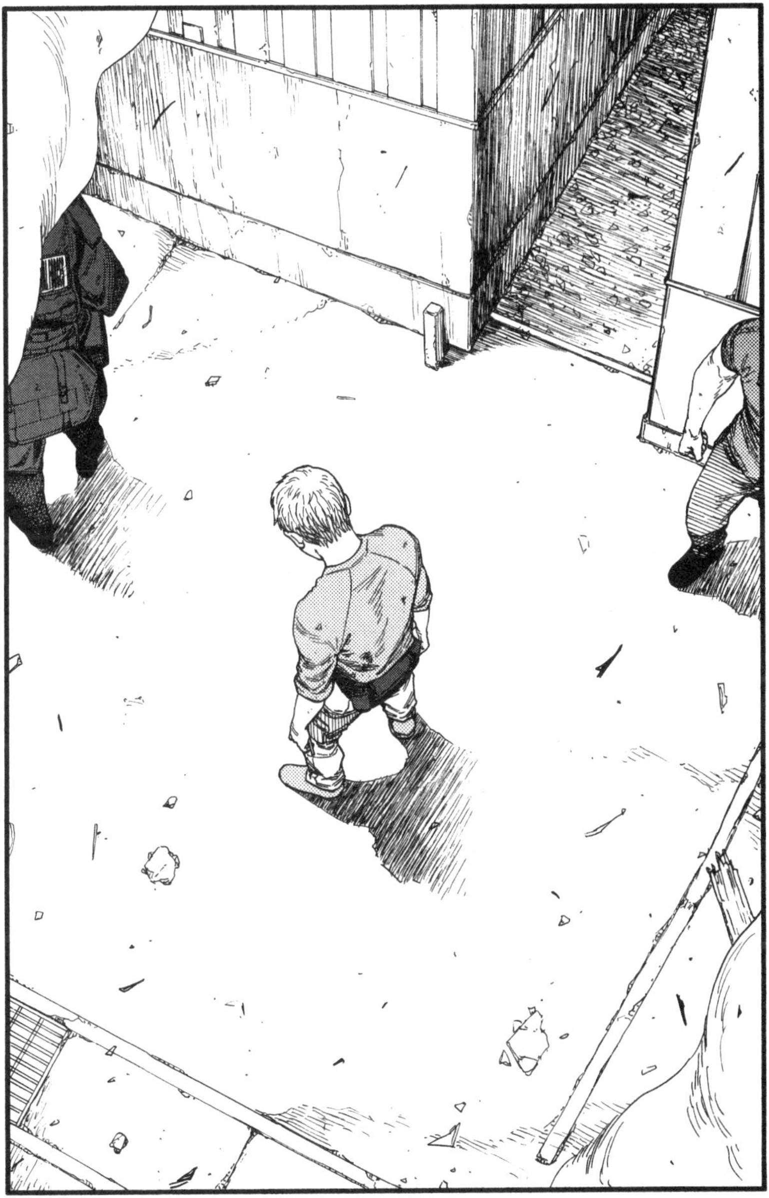

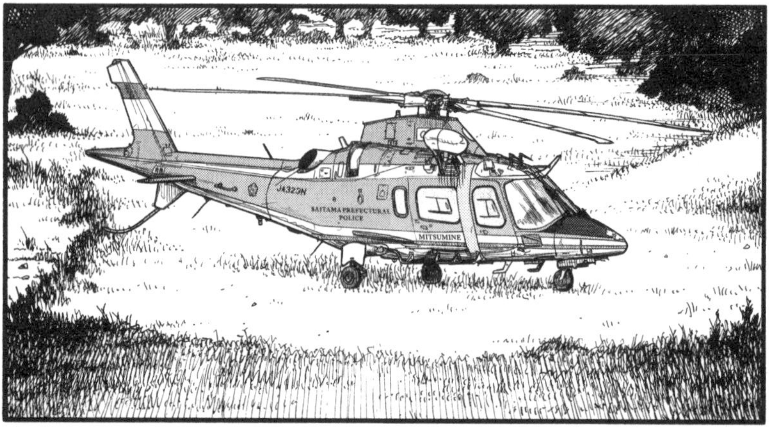
JA323N
SAITAMA PREFECTURAL POLICE
MITSUMINE

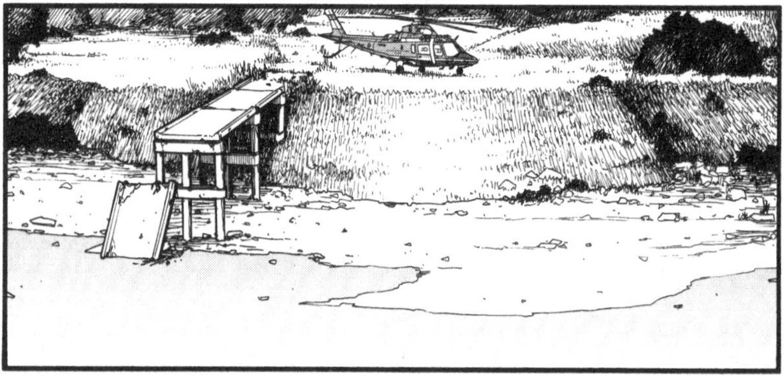

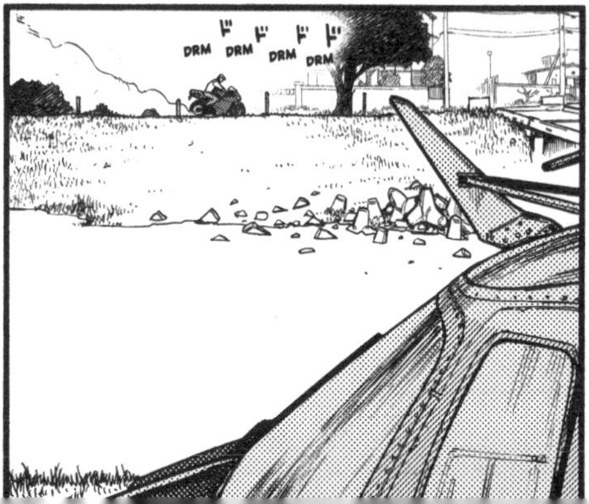
ド DRM
ド DRM
ド DRM
ド DRM

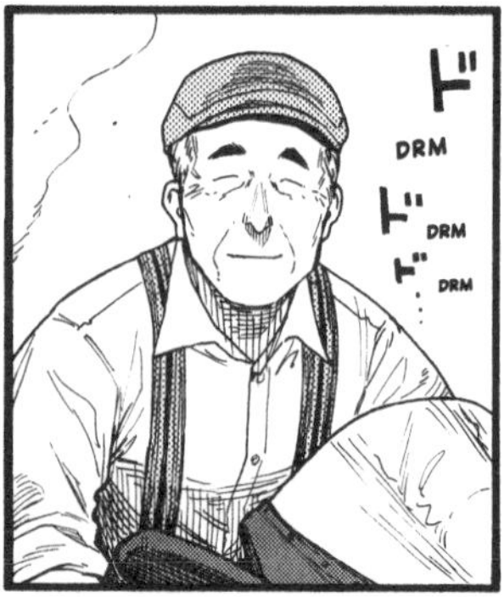
ド DRM
ド DRM
ド DRM

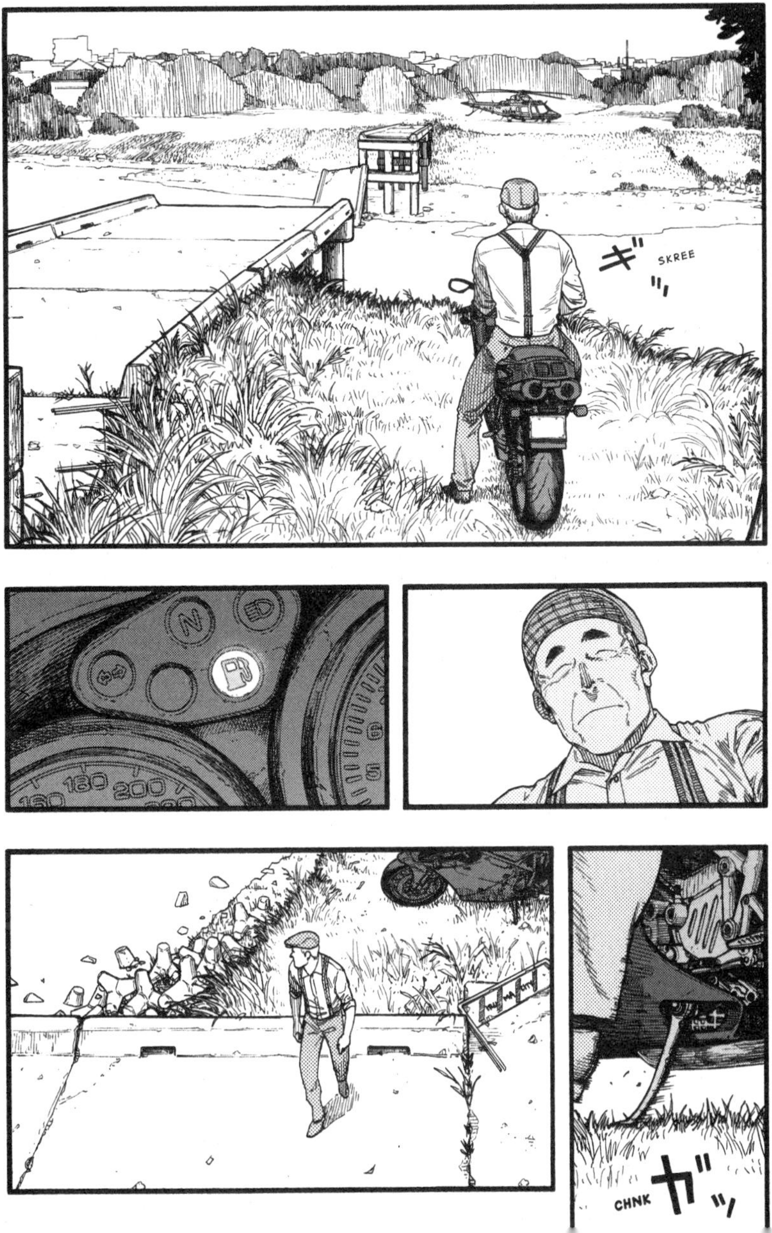
ギッ
SKREE
ガッ
CHNK

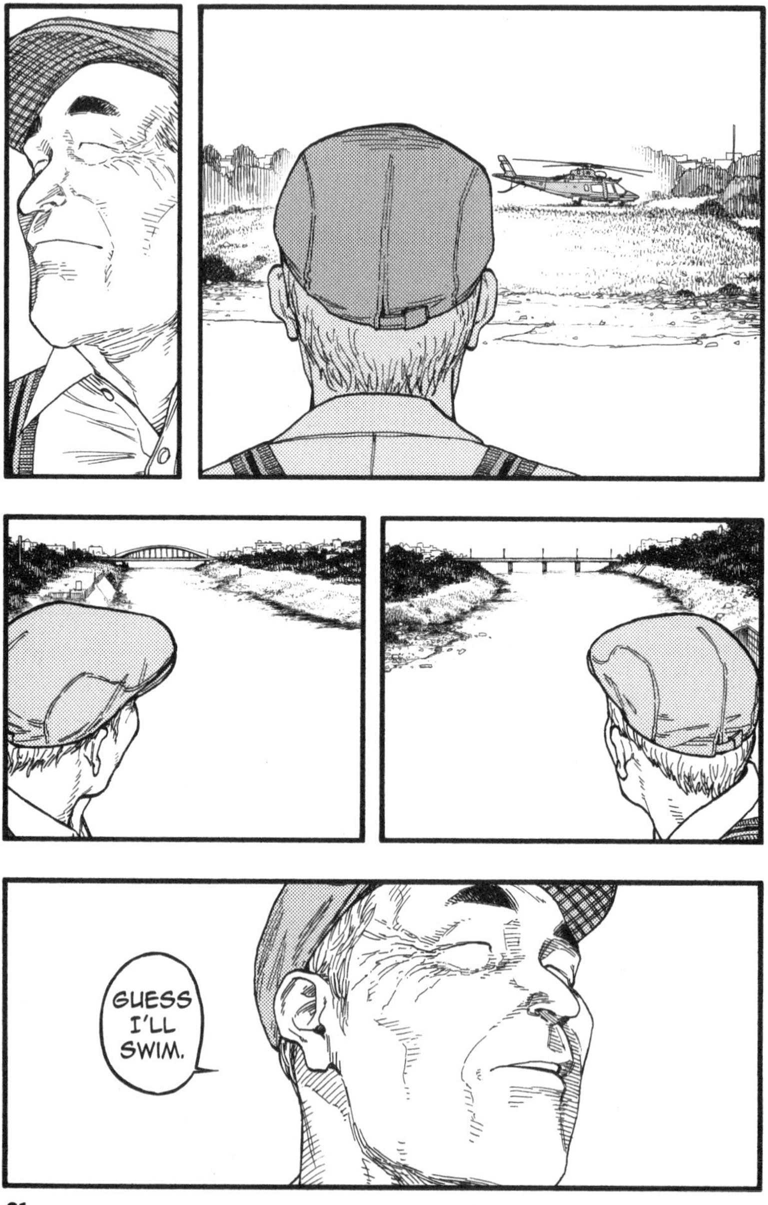
GUESS I'LL SWIM.

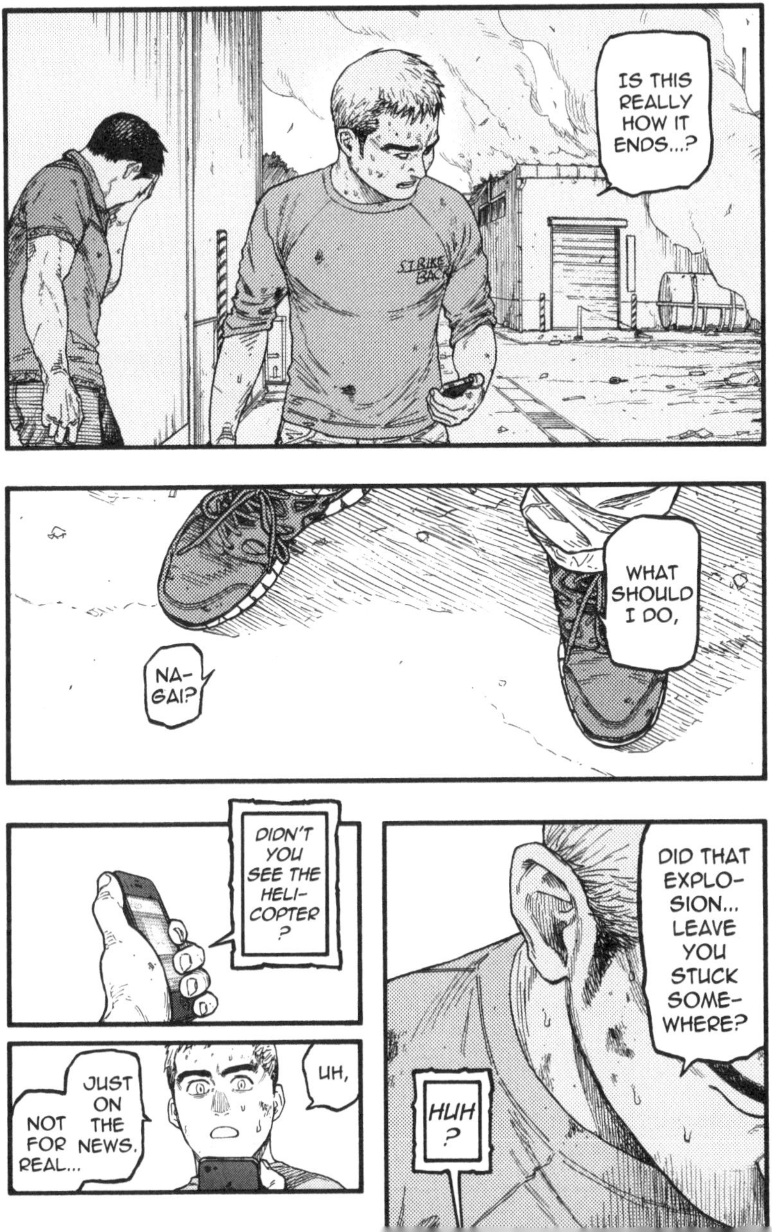
IS THIS REALLY HOW IT ENDS...?
WHAT SHOULD I DO,
NA-GAI?
DID THAT EXPLO-SION... LEAVE YOU STUCK SOME-WHERE?
HUH?
DIDN'T YOU SEE THE HELI-COPTER?
UH,
JUST ON THE NEWS.
NOT FOR REAL...

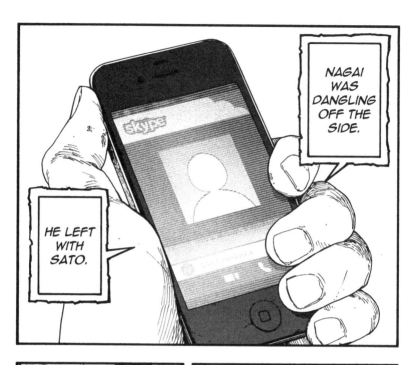

NAGAI WAS DANGLING OFF THE SIDE.

HE LEFT WITH SATO.

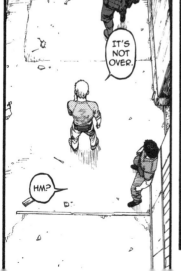

IT'S NOT OVER.

HM?

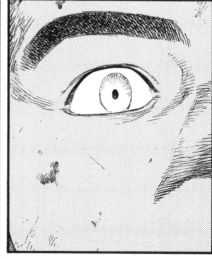

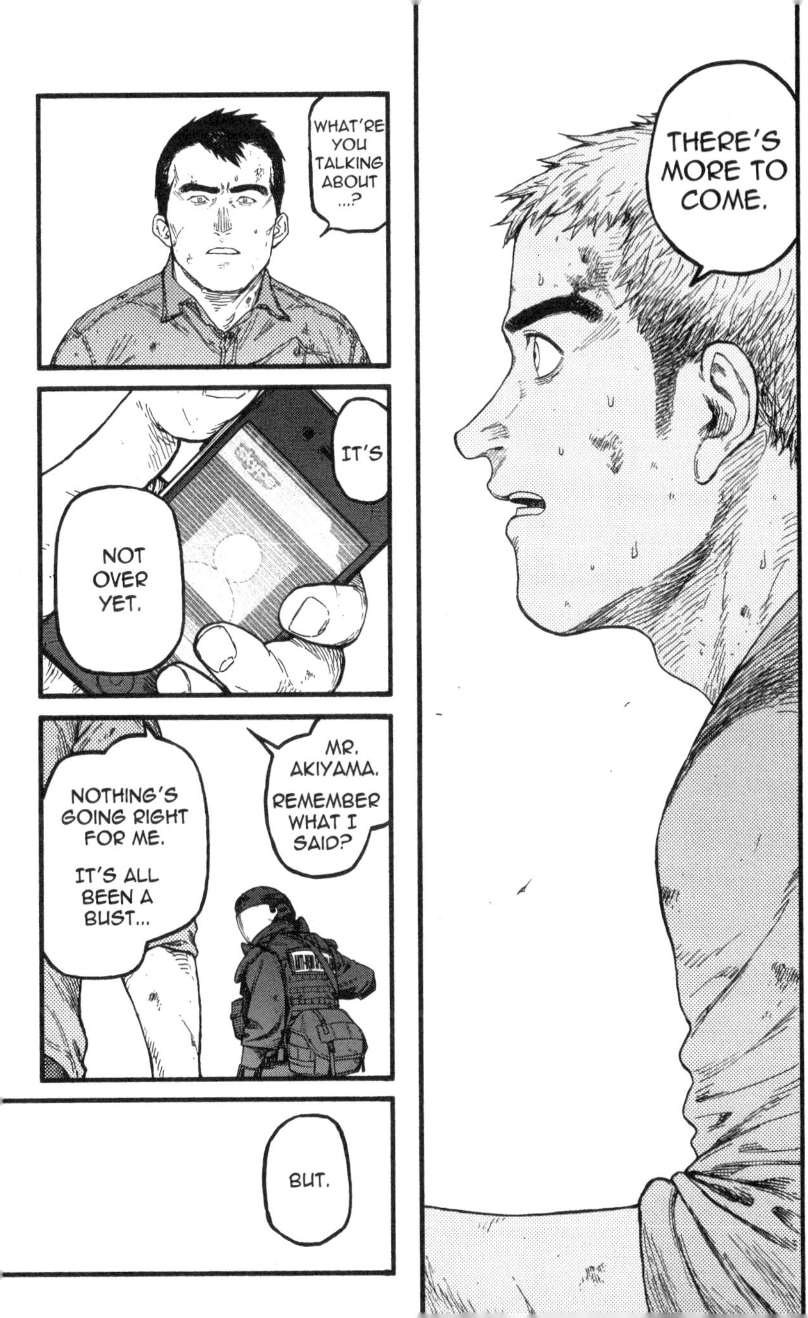
THERE'S MORE TO COME.
WHAT'RE YOU TALKING ABOUT ...?
IT'S
NOT OVER YET.
MR. AKIYAMA.
REMEMBER WHAT I SAID?
NOTHING'S GOING RIGHT FOR ME.
IT'S ALL BEEN A BUST...
BUT.

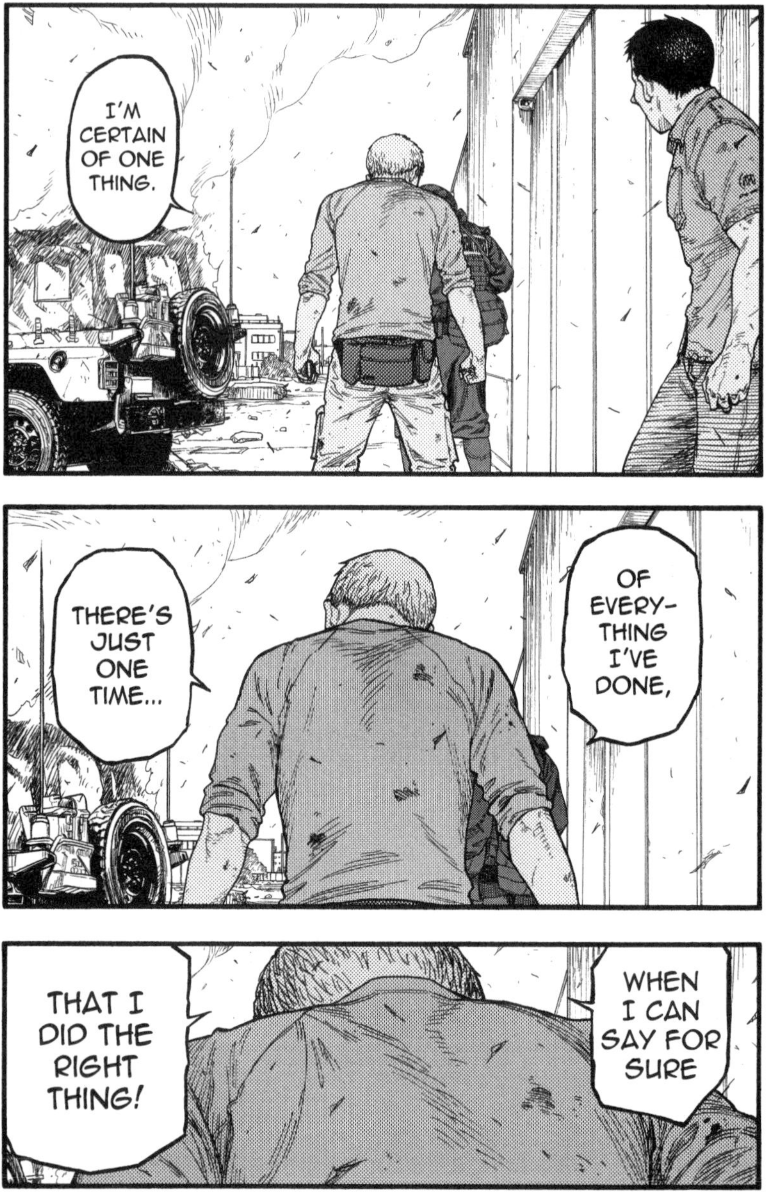
I'M CERTAIN OF ONE THING.
OF EVERY-THING I'VE DONE,
THERE'S JUST ONE TIME...
WHEN I CAN SAY FOR SURE
THAT I DID THE RIGHT THING!

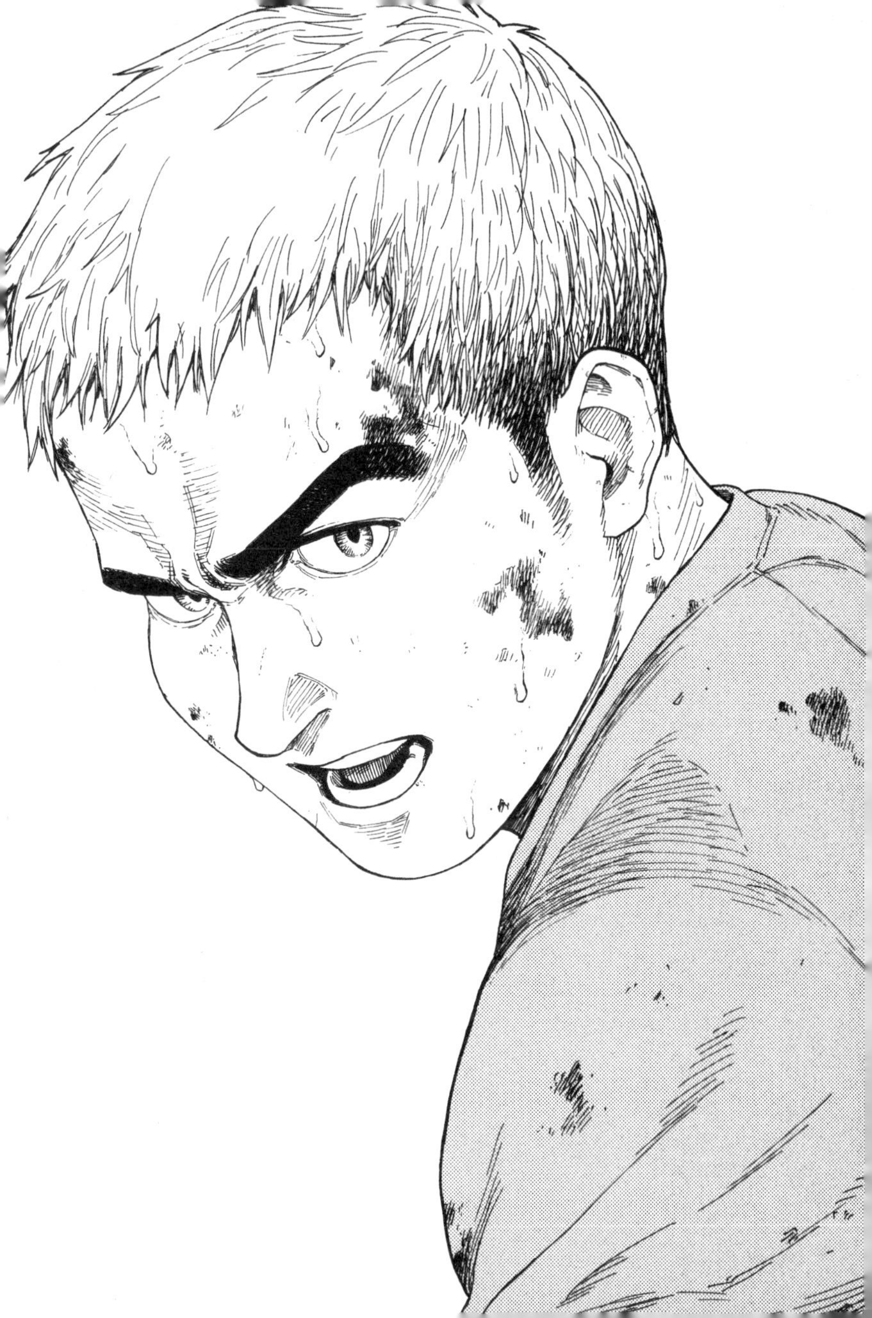

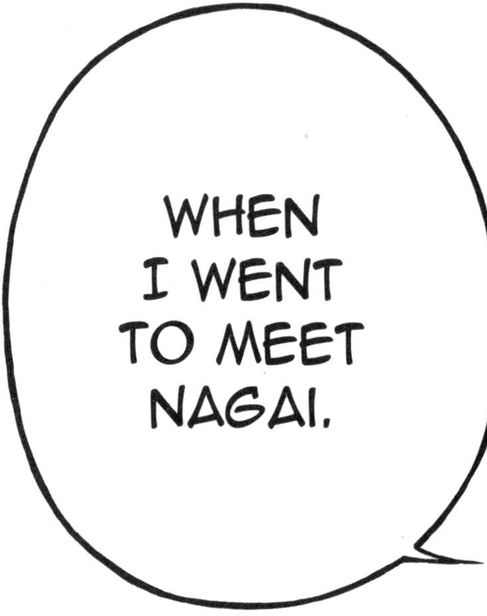
WHEN I WENT TO MEET NAGAI.

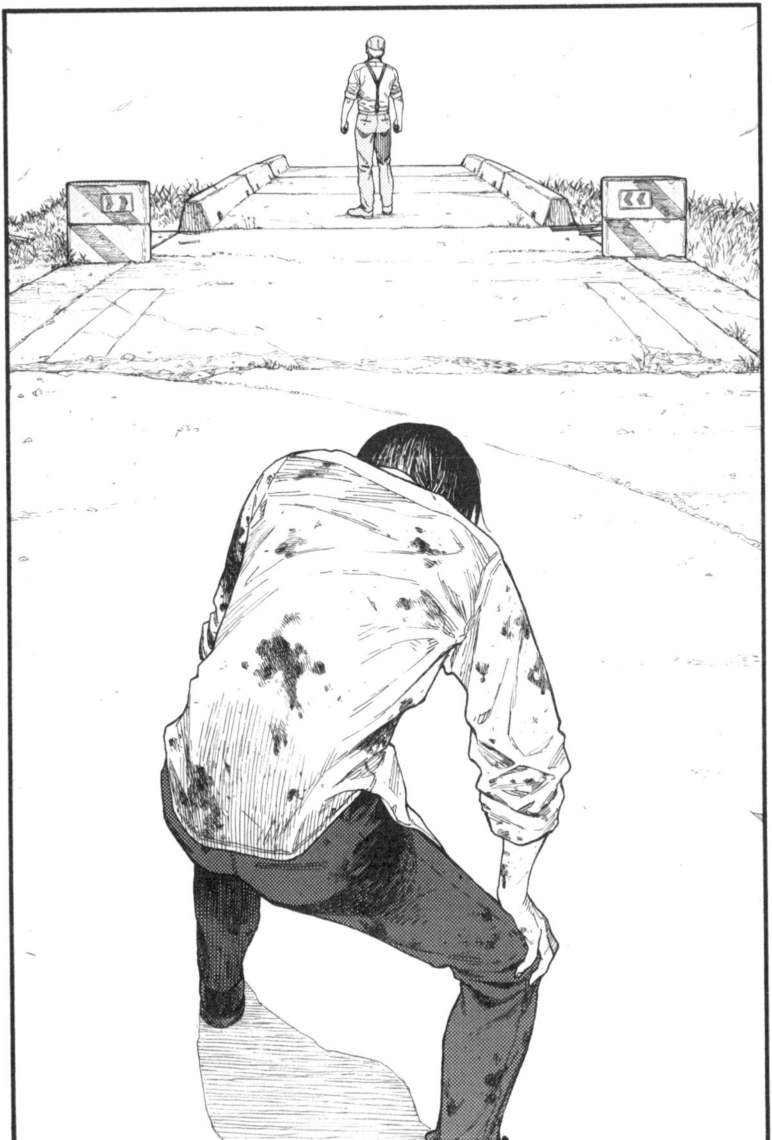

File:80 End

File: 81

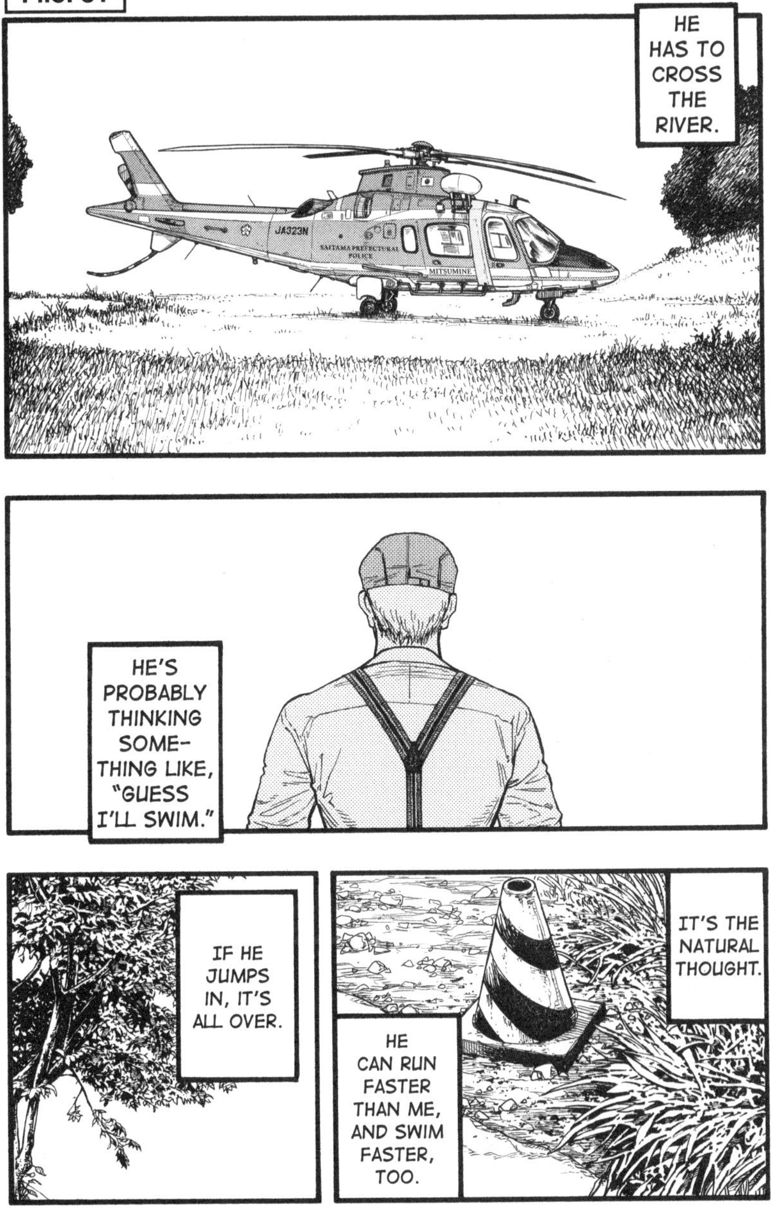
HE HAS TO CROSS THE RIVER.
JA323N
MITSUMINE
HE'S PROBABLY THINKING SOME-THING LIKE, "GUESS I'LL SWIM."
IT'S THE NATURAL THOUGHT.
HE CAN RUN FASTER THAN ME, AND SWIM FASTER, TOO.
IF HE JUMPS IN, IT'S ALL OVER.

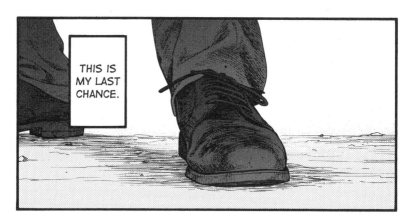

THIS IS
MY LAST
CHANCE.

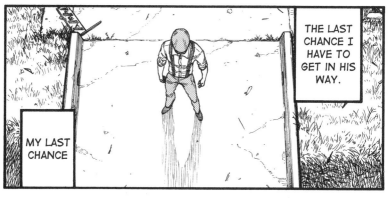

THE LAST
CHANCE I
HAVE TO
GET IN HIS
WAY.

MY LAST
CHANCE

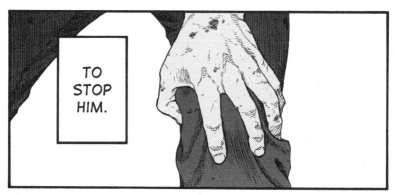

TO
STOP
HIM.

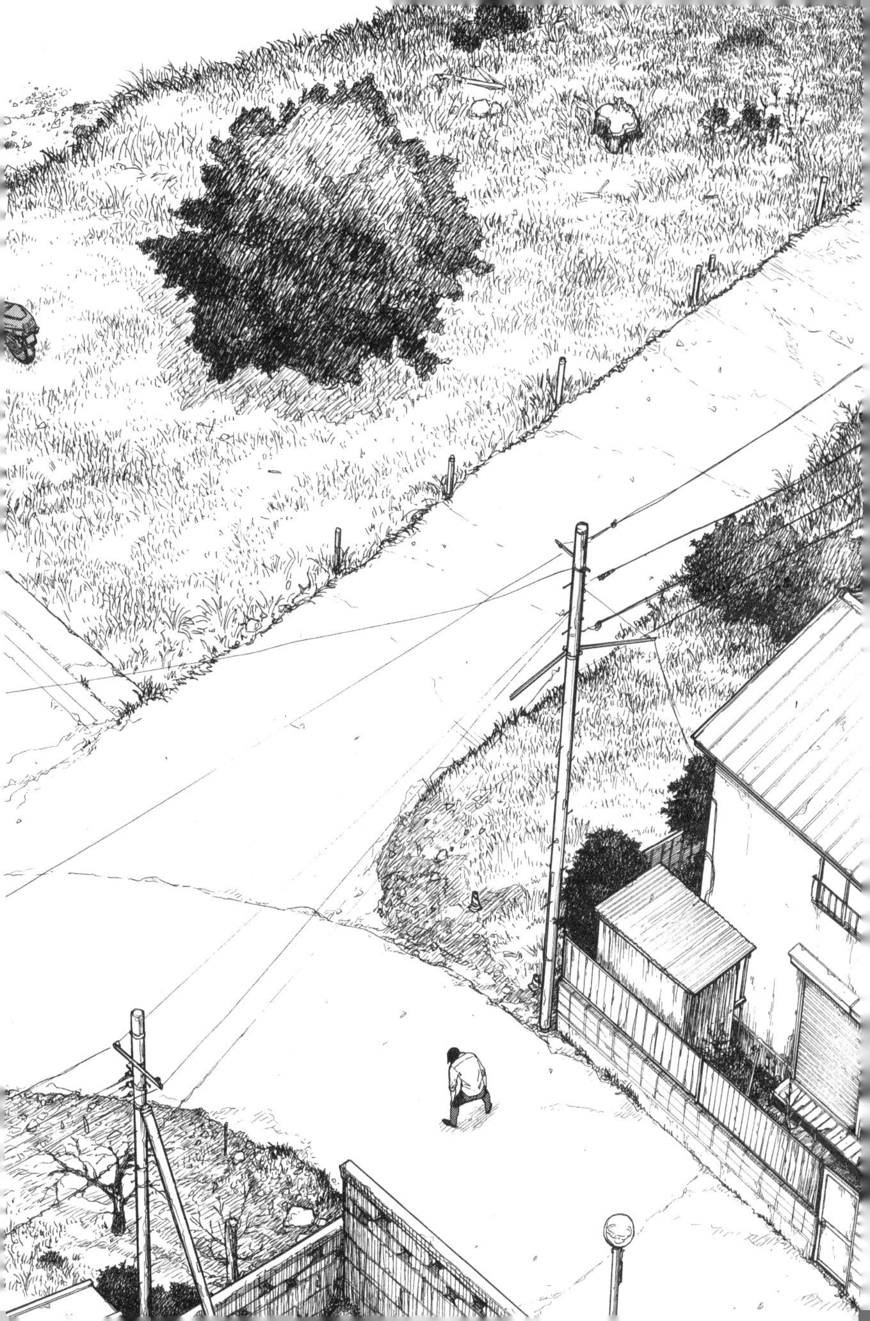

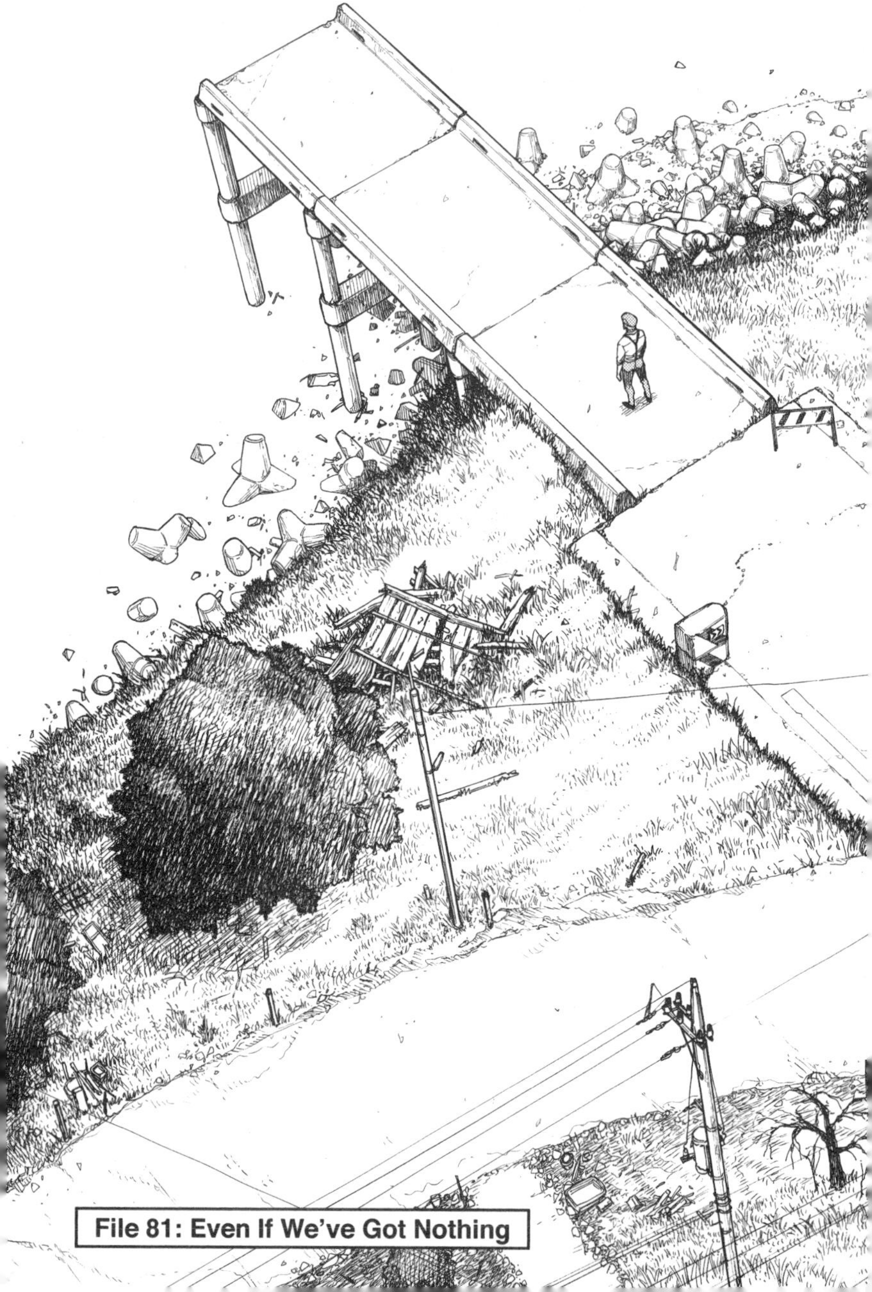

File 81: Even If We've Got Nothing

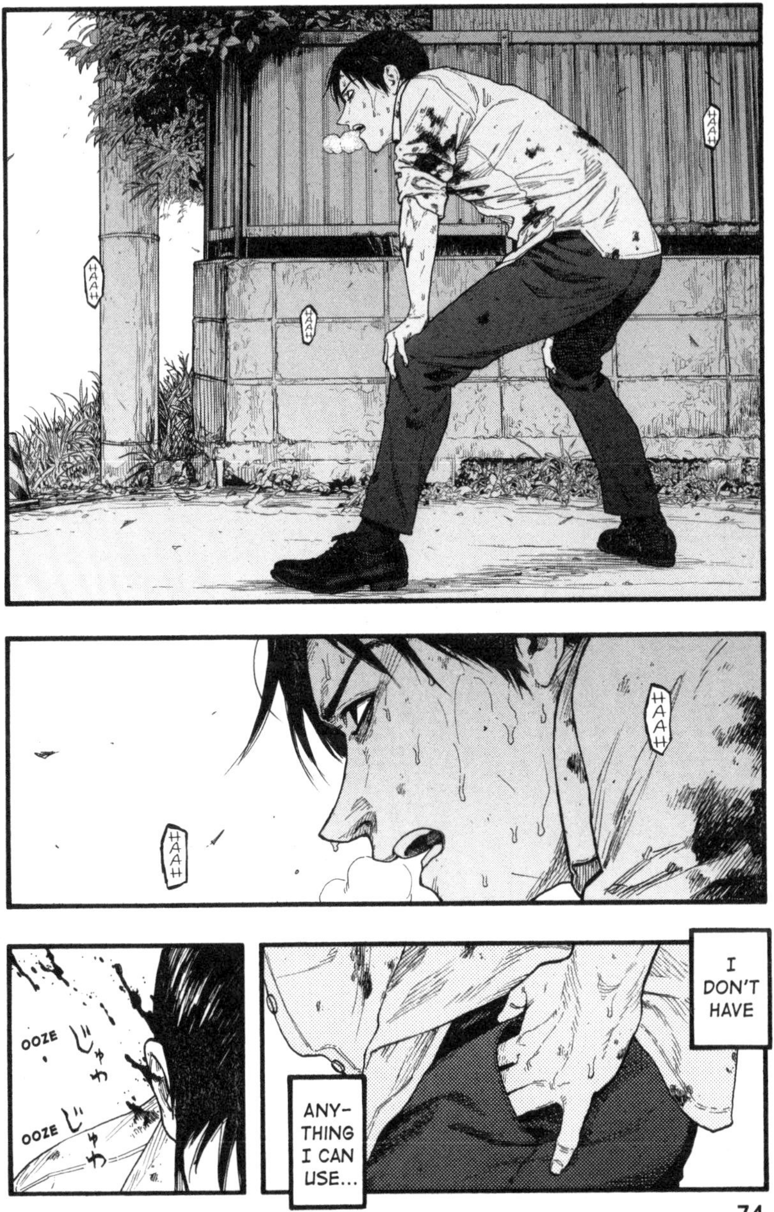
HAAH
HAAH
HAAH
HAAH
HAAH
I DON'T HAVE
ANY-THING I CAN USE...
OOZE
じゅわ
OOZE
じゅわ

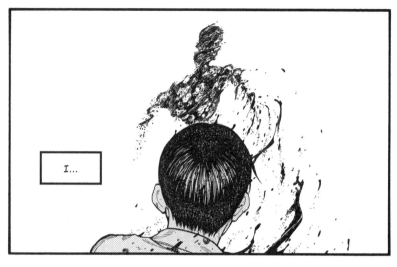

I...
CAN'T FORM MY IBM.
PROBABLY BECAUSE THERE WAS JUST A FLOOD...
FSSSS
FSSSS
WHAT CAN I DO?

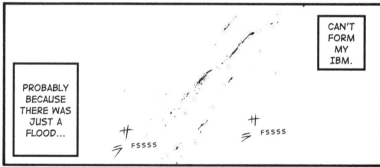

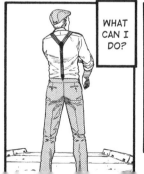

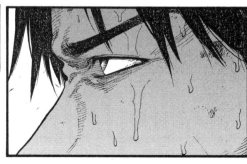

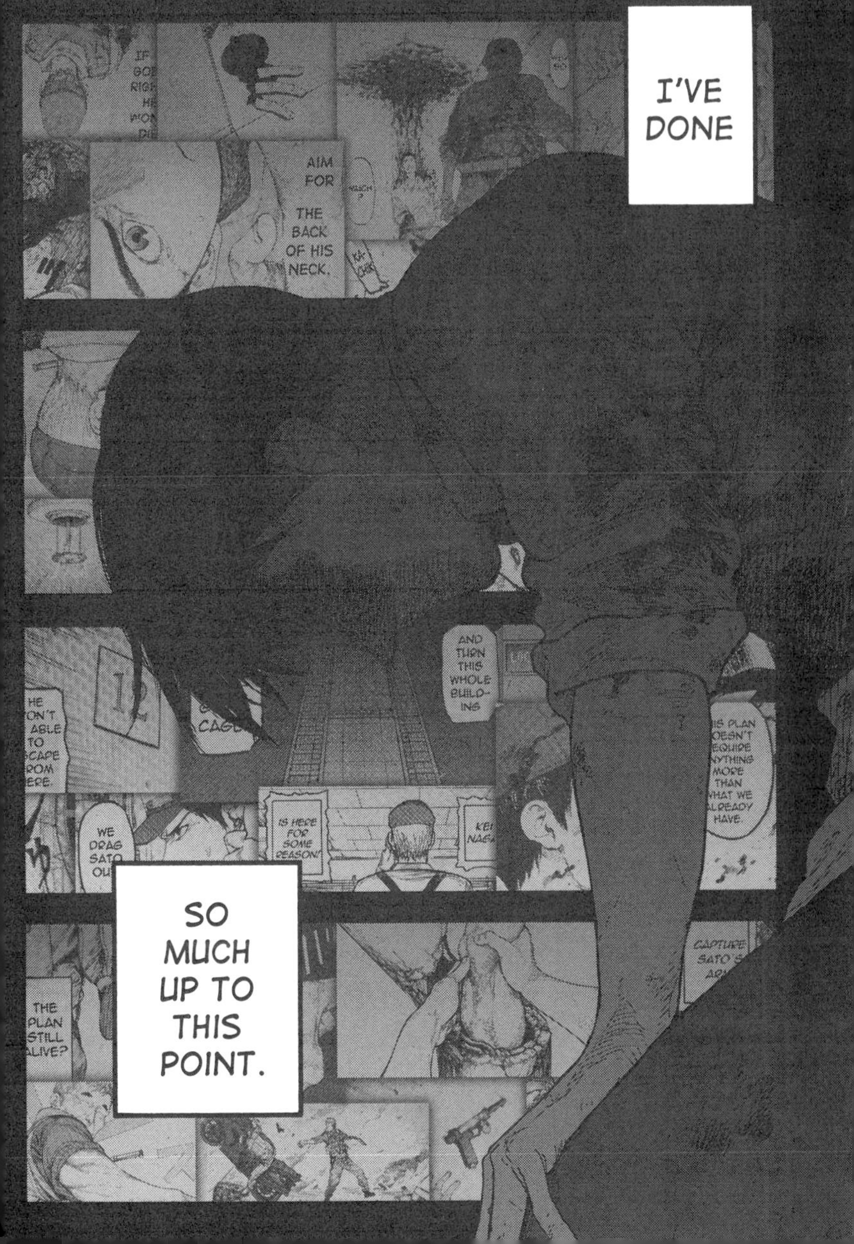

I'VE DONE
AIM FOR THE BACK OF HIS NECK.
AND TURN THIS WHOLE BUILD-ING
IS HERE FOR SOME REASON!
SO MUCH UP TO THIS POINT.
THE PLAN STILL ALIVE?

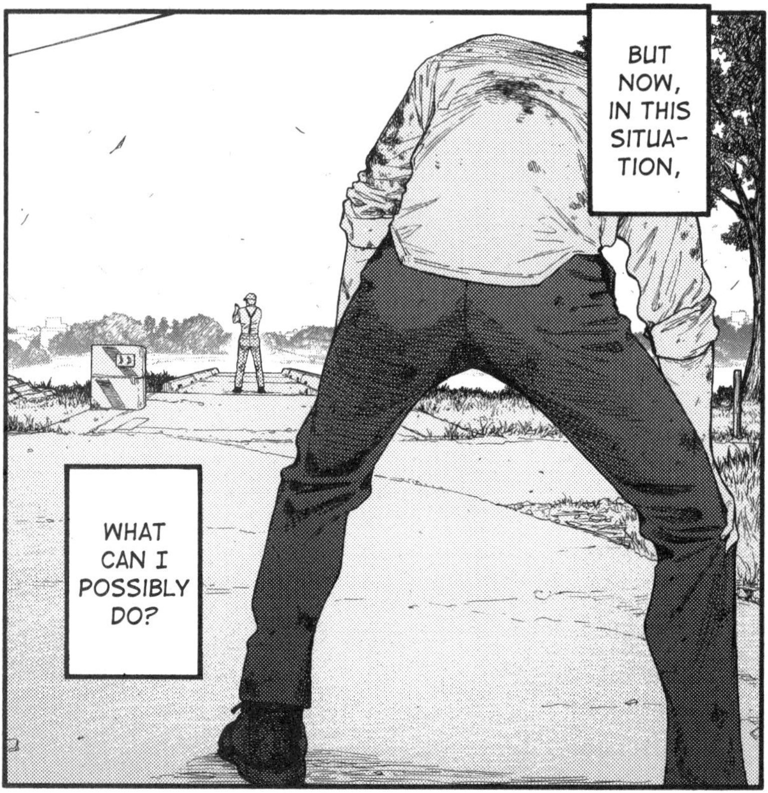
BUT NOW, IN THIS SITUATION,
WHAT CAN I POSSIBLY DO?

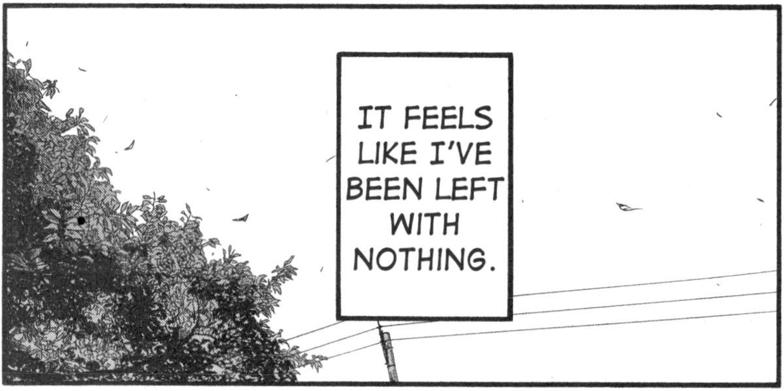
IT FEELS LIKE I'VE BEEN LEFT WITH NOTHING.

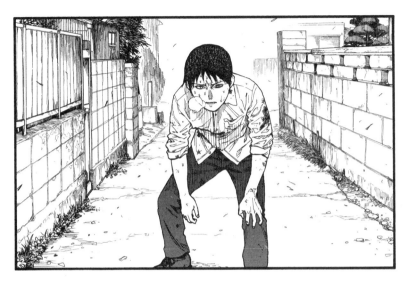

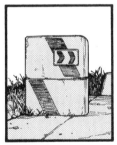
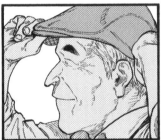
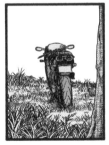

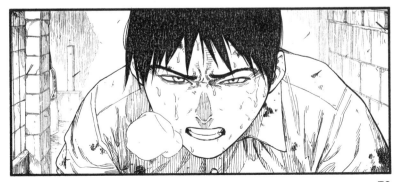

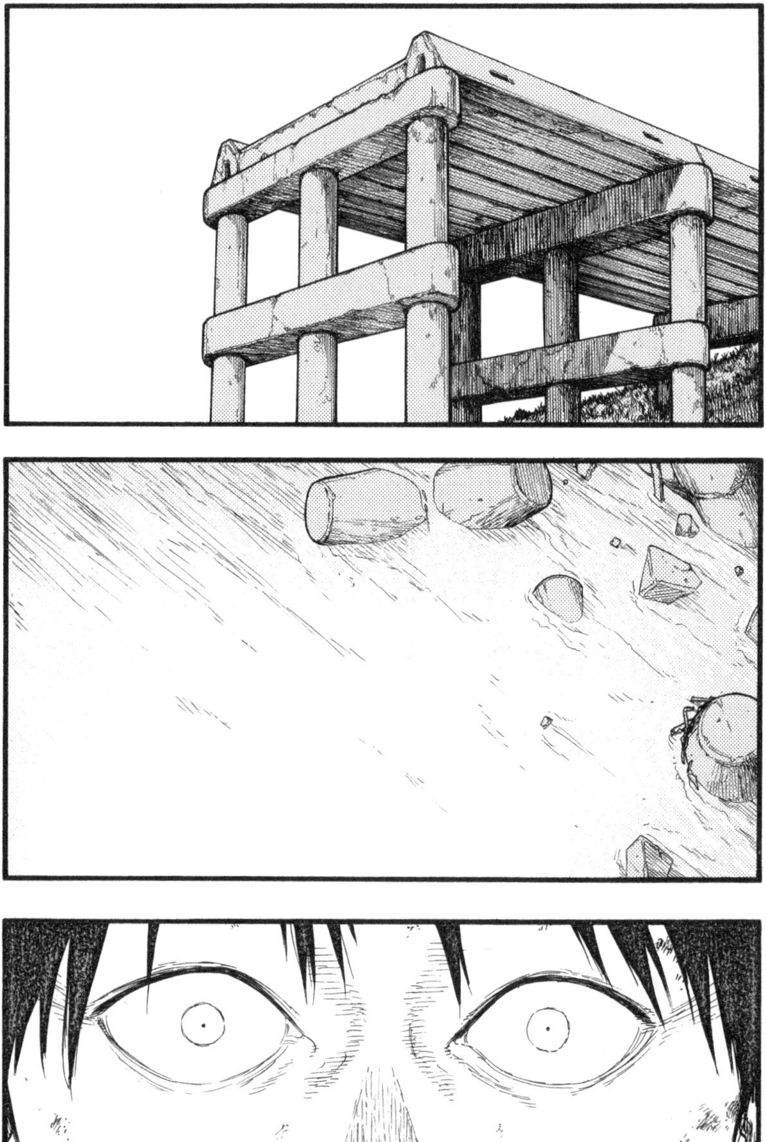

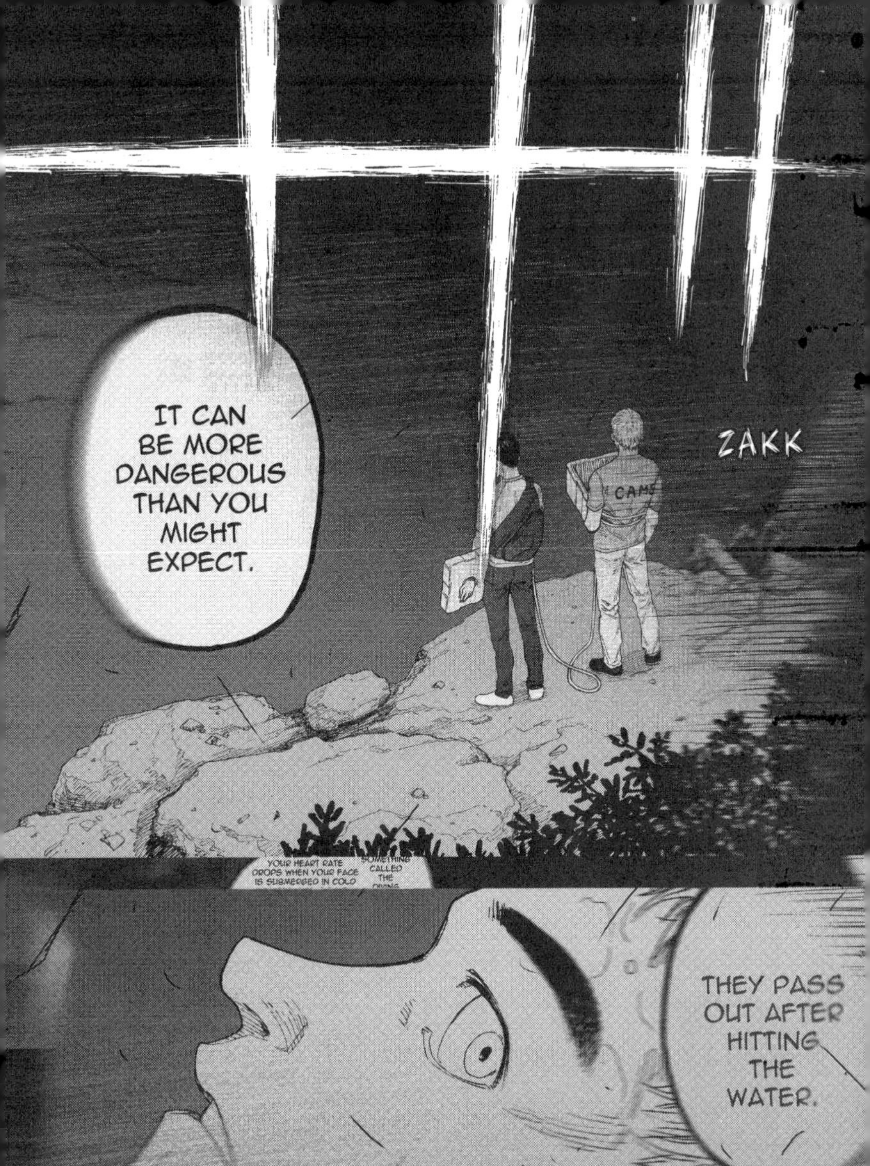
IT CAN BE MORE DANGEROUS THAN YOU MIGHT EXPECT.
ZAKK
SOMETHING CALLED THE
YOUR HEART RATE DROPS WHEN YOUR FACE IS SUBMERGED IN COLD
THEY PASS OUT AFTER HITTING THE WATER.

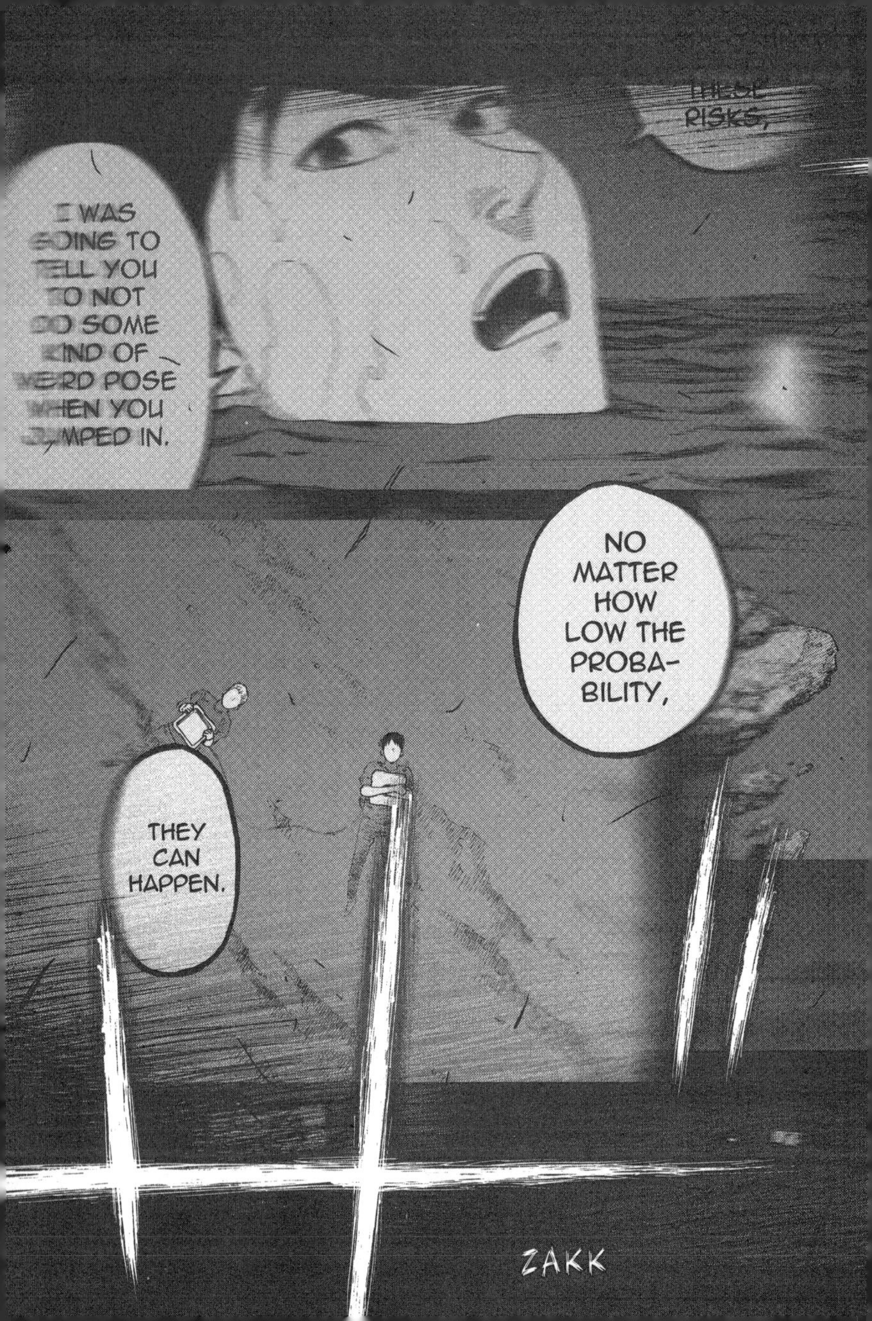
THESE RISKS,
I WAS GOING TO TELL YOU TO NOT DO SOME KIND OF WEIRD POSE WHEN YOU JUMPED IN.
NO MATTER HOW LOW THE PROBA-BILITY,
THEY CAN HAPPEN.
ZAKK

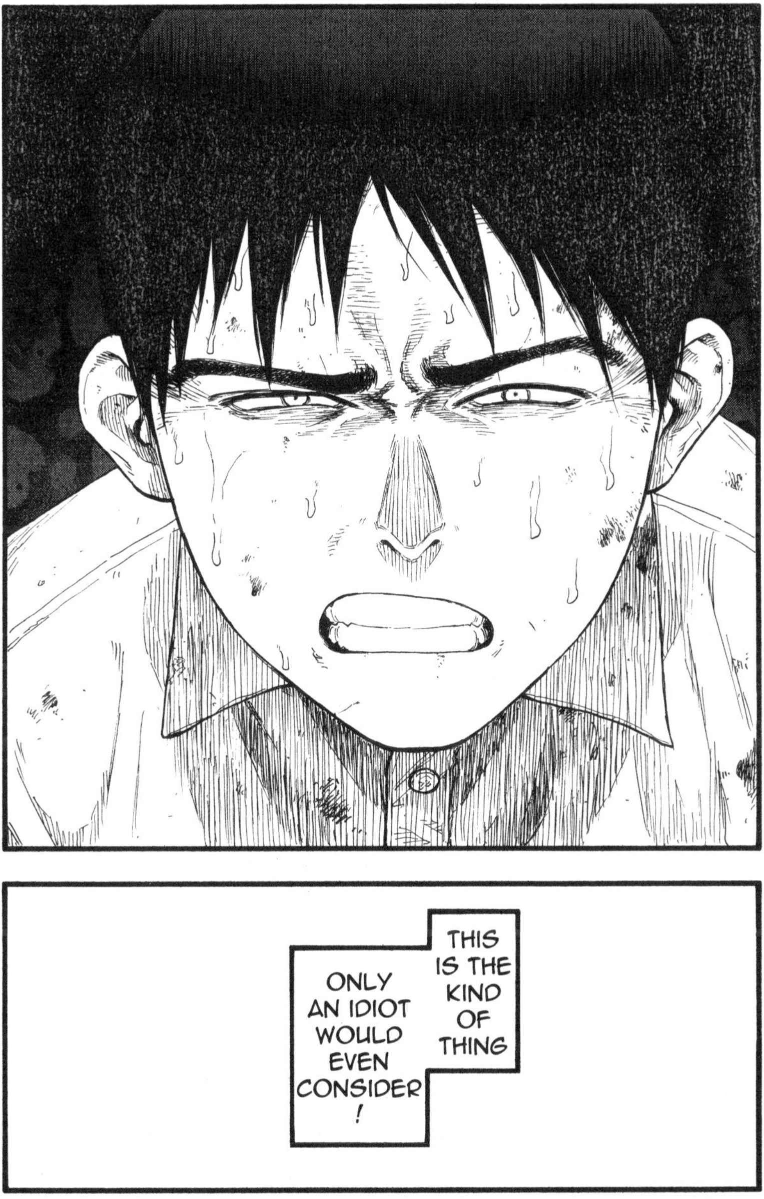
THIS IS THE KIND OF THING
ONLY AN IDIOT WOULD EVEN CONSIDER!

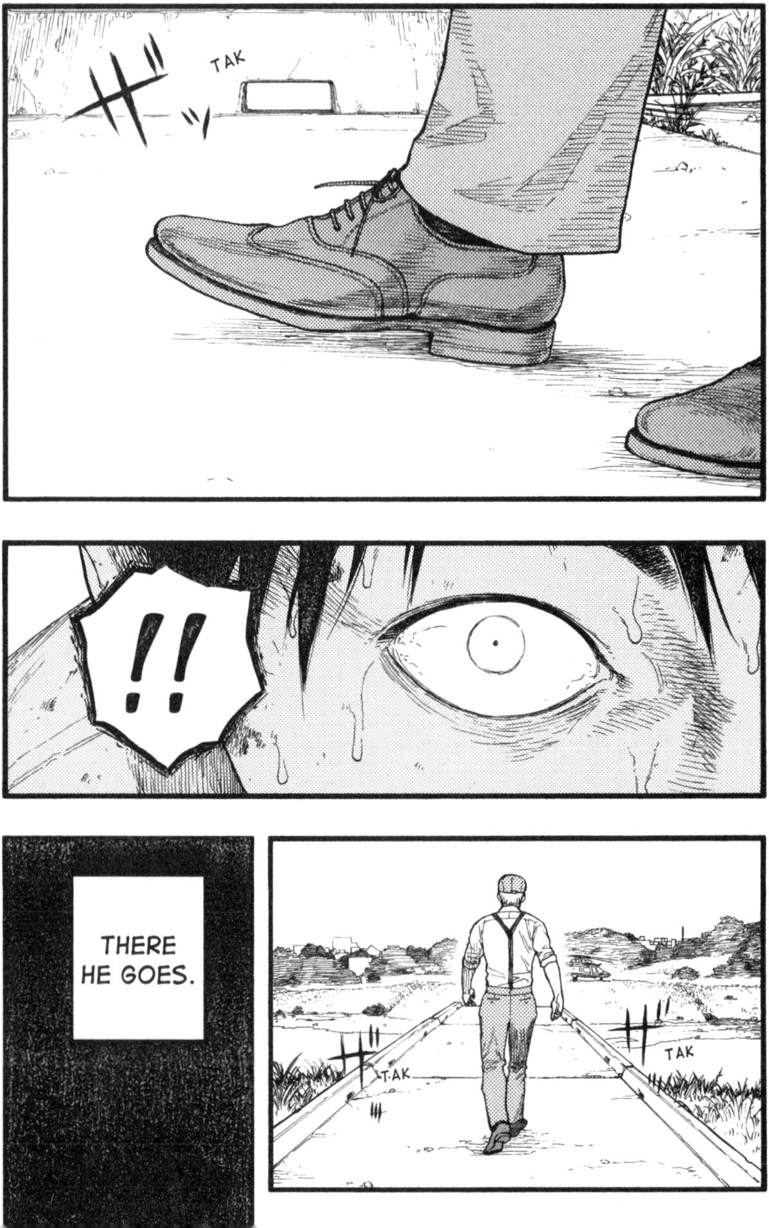
TAK
!!
TAK
TAK
THERE HE GOES.

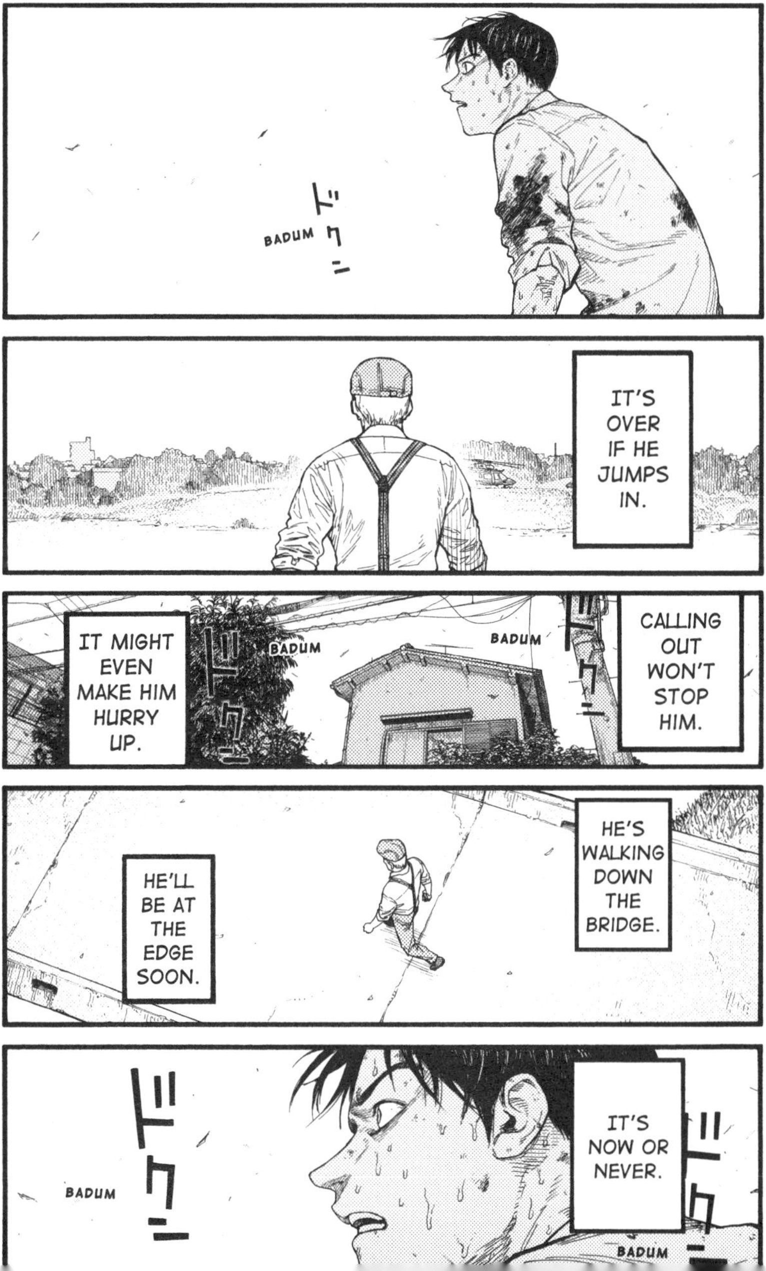

ドクン
BADUM
IT'S OVER IF HE JUMPS IN.
CALLING OUT WON'T STOP HIM.
ドクン
BADUM
ドクン
BADUM
IT MIGHT EVEN MAKE HIM HURRY UP.
HE'S WALKING DOWN THE BRIDGE.
HE'LL BE AT THE EDGE SOON.
ドクン
BADUM
IT'S NOW OR NEVER.
ドクン
BADUM

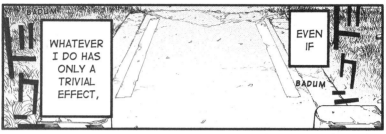

EVEN IF
BADUM
WHATEVER I DO HAS ONLY A TRIVIAL EFFECT,
BADUM
BADUM
IF I DON'T START RUNNING THIS VERY MOMENT,
BADUM
I'LL LOSE
BADUM
EVEN THAT.
BADUM
BADUM
I'LL NEVER AGAIN HAVE EVEN THE SMALLEST CHANCE TO MEDDLE IN HIS FATE.

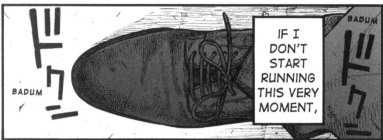

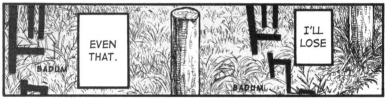

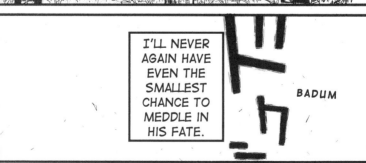

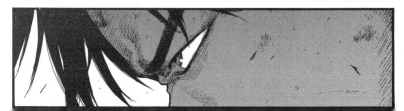

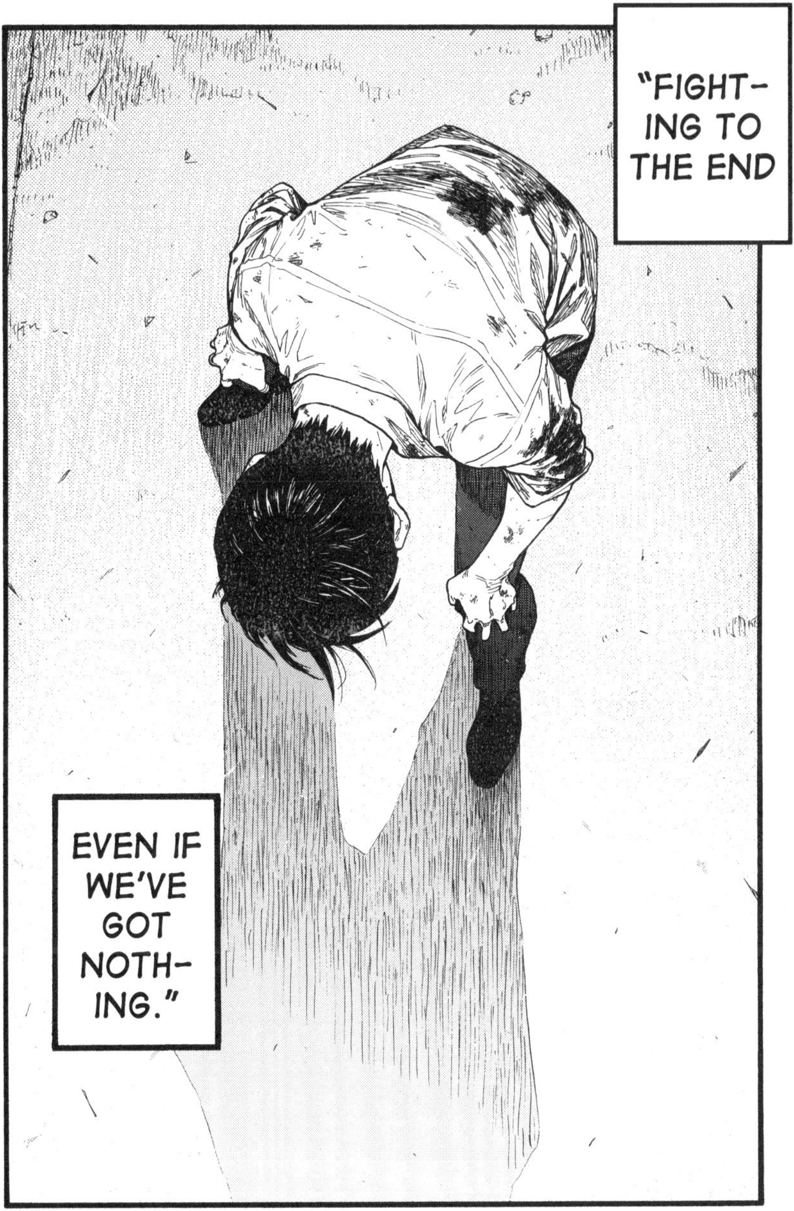
"FIGHTING TO THE END
EVEN IF WE'VE GOT NOTHING."

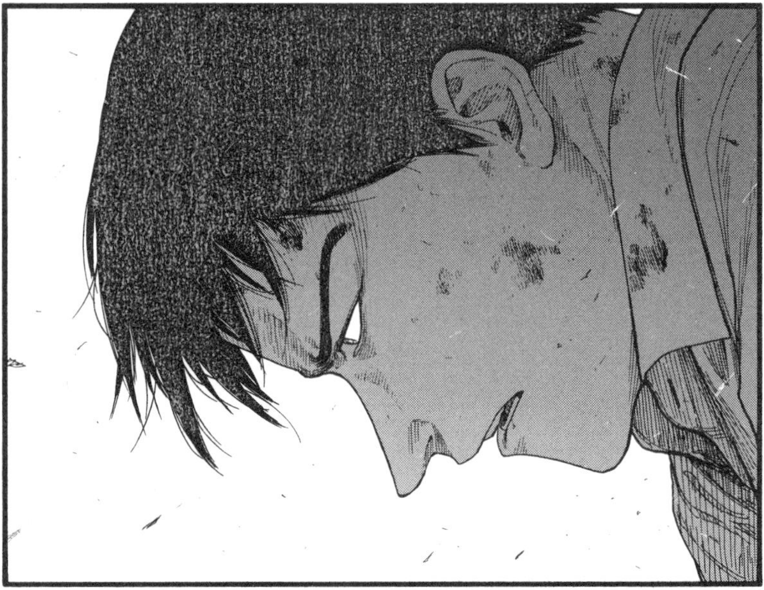
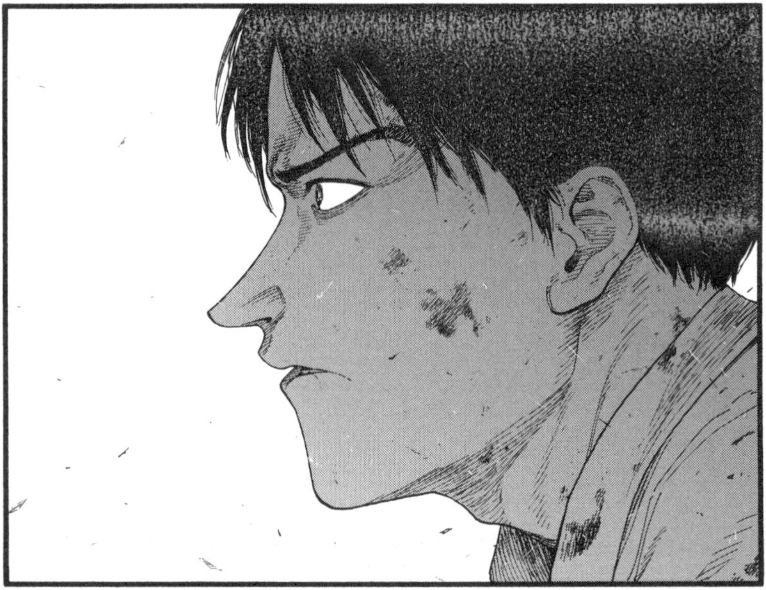

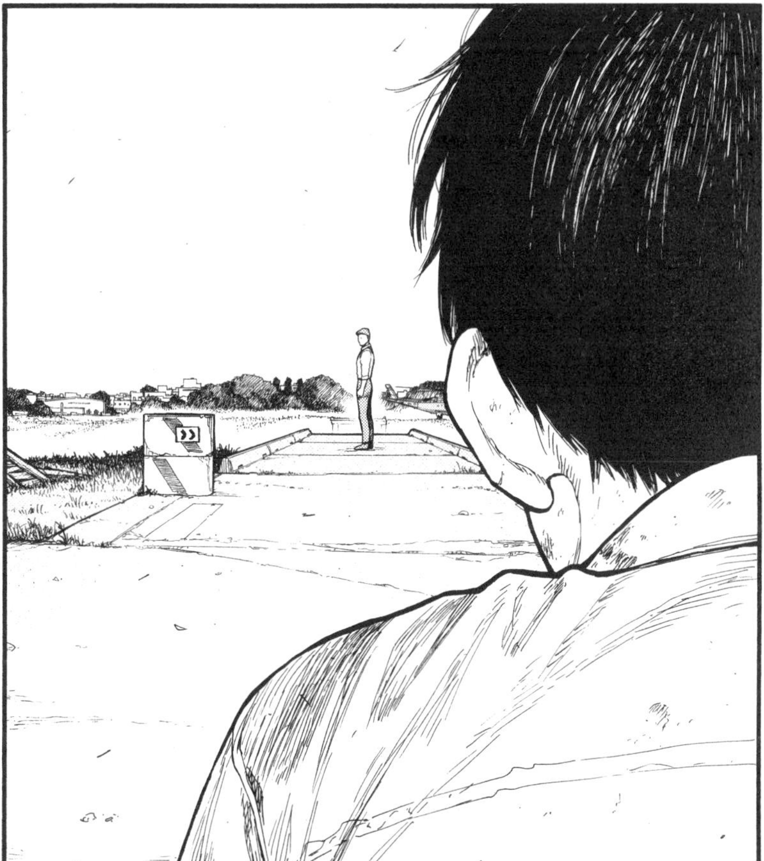

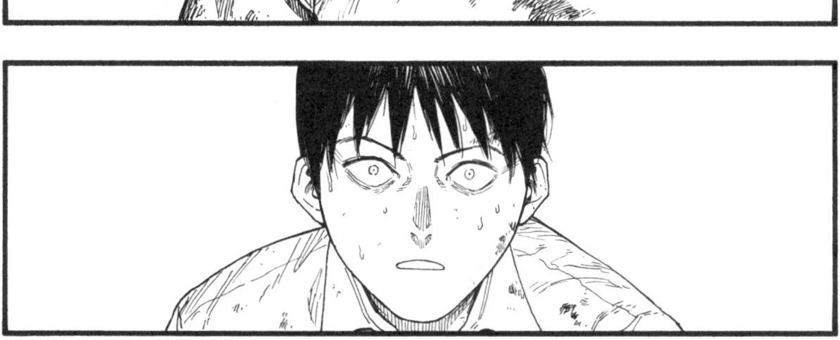

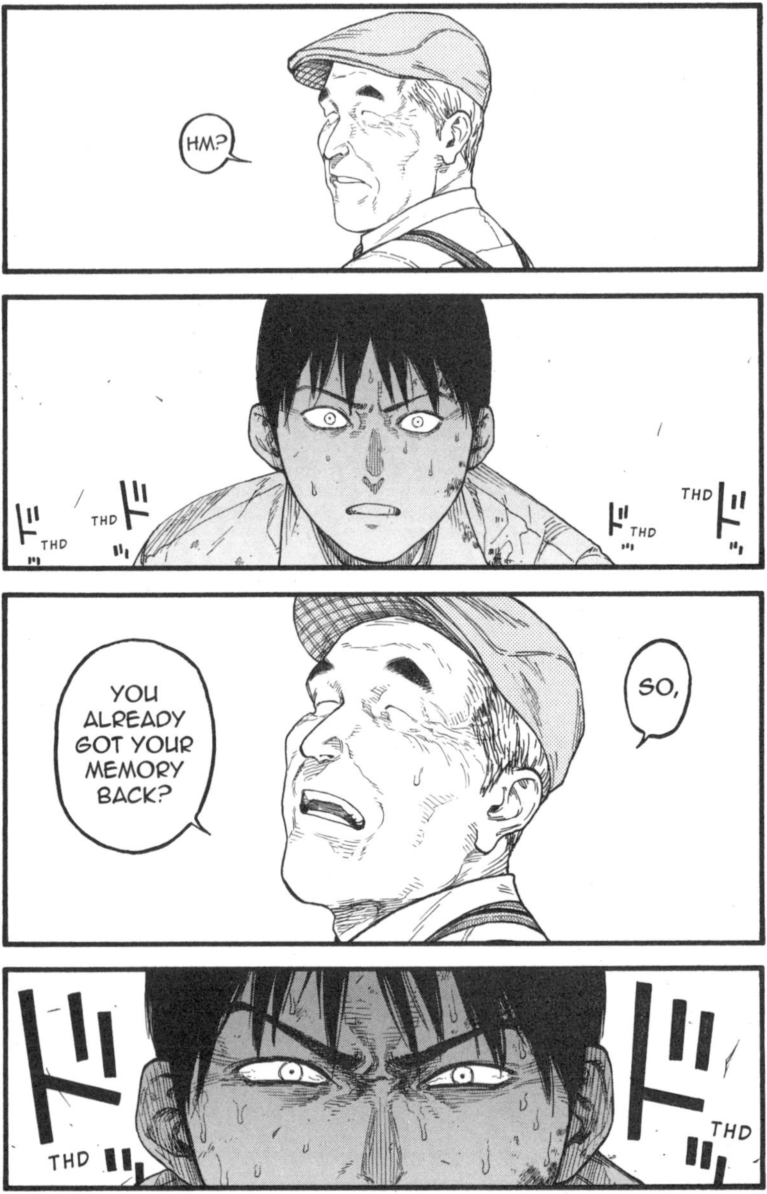
HM?
THD
THD
THD
THD
SO,
YOU ALREADY GOT YOUR MEMORY BACK?
THD
THD

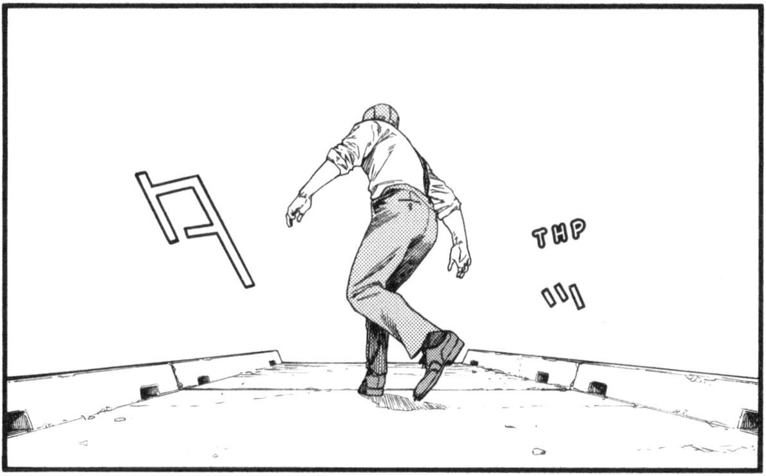
THP
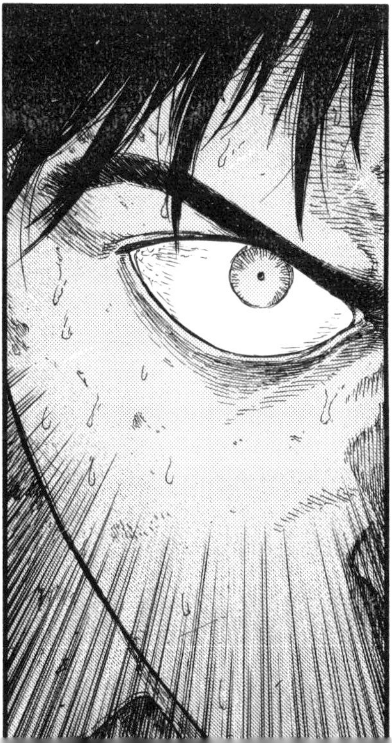
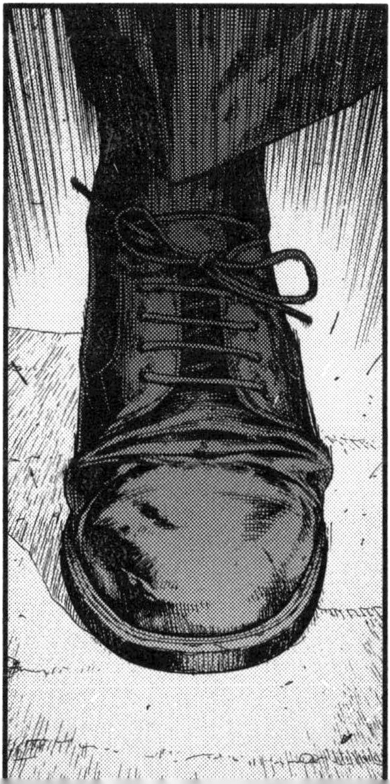

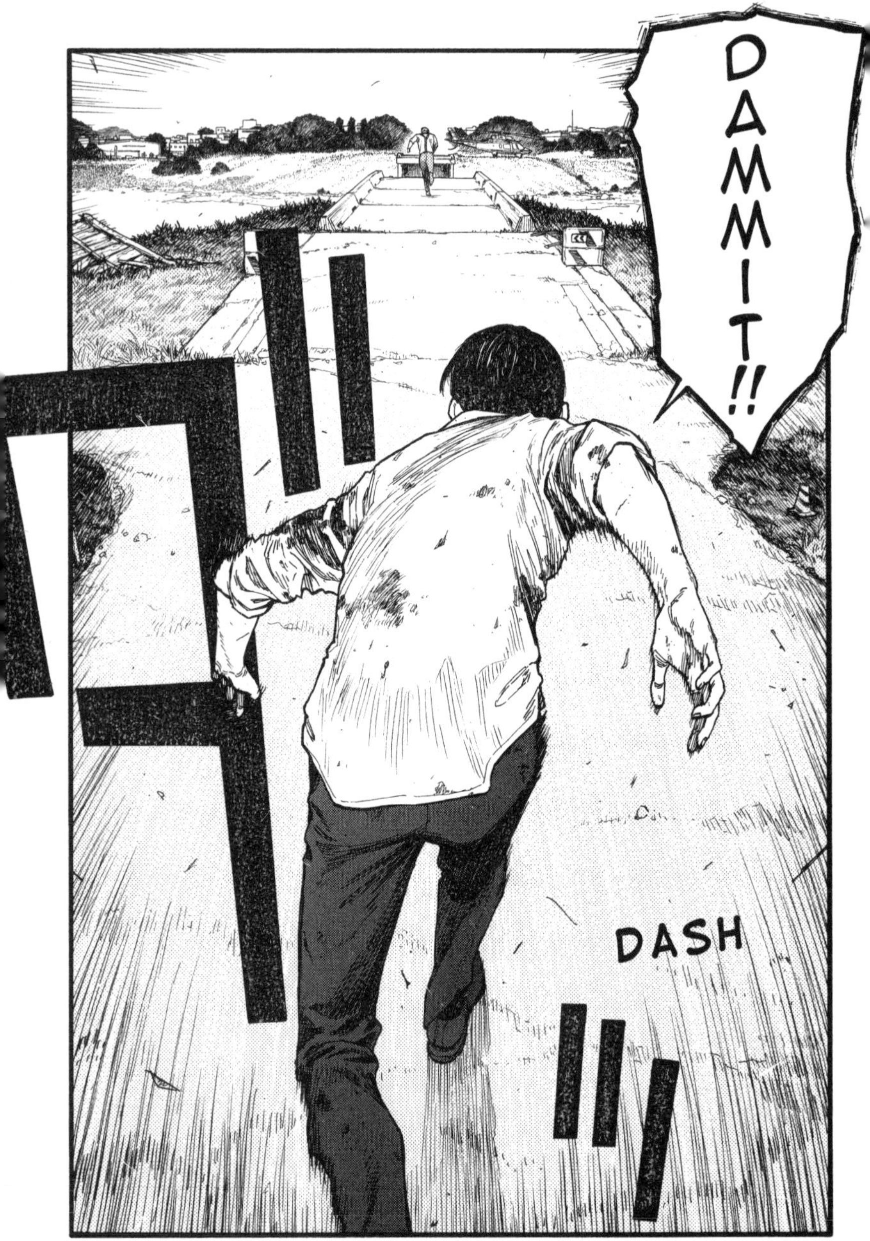
DAMMIT!!
DASH

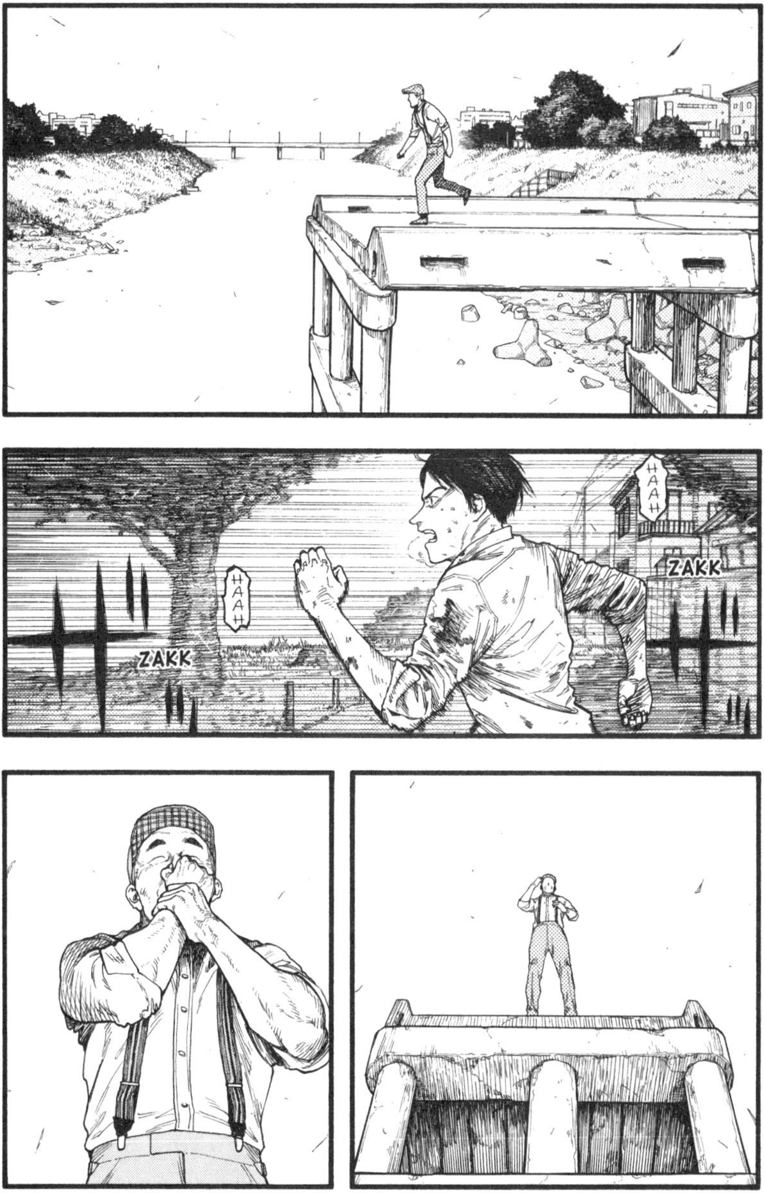
HAAH
ZAKK
HAAH
ZAKK

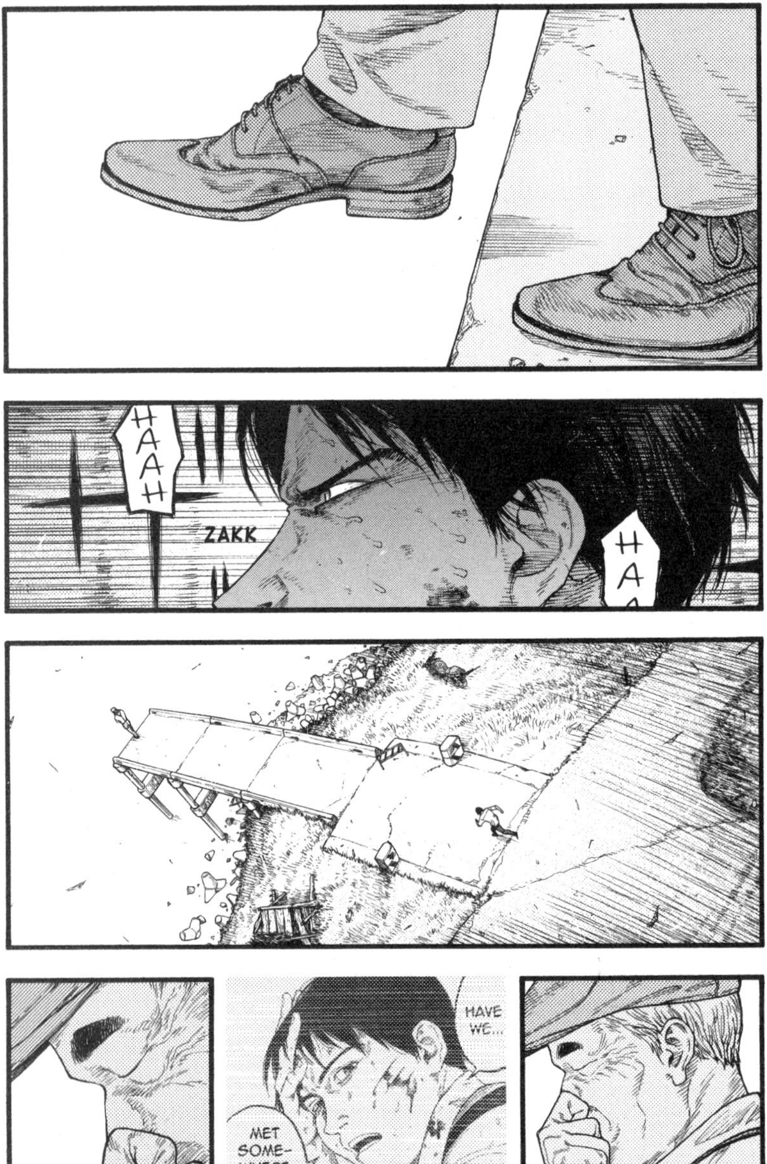
HA
ZAKK
HAAH
HAVE WE...
MET SOME-WHERE BEFORE?

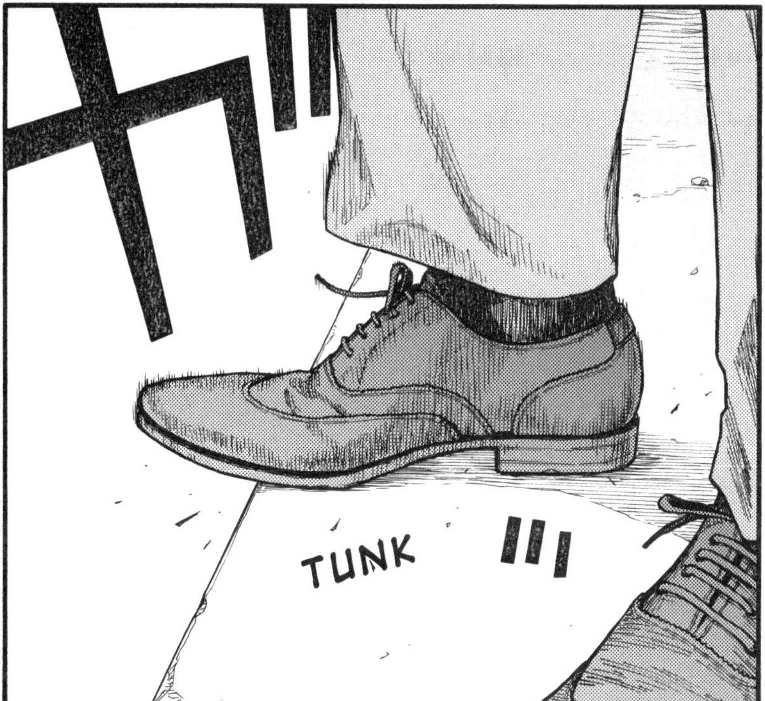
ガ
TUNK

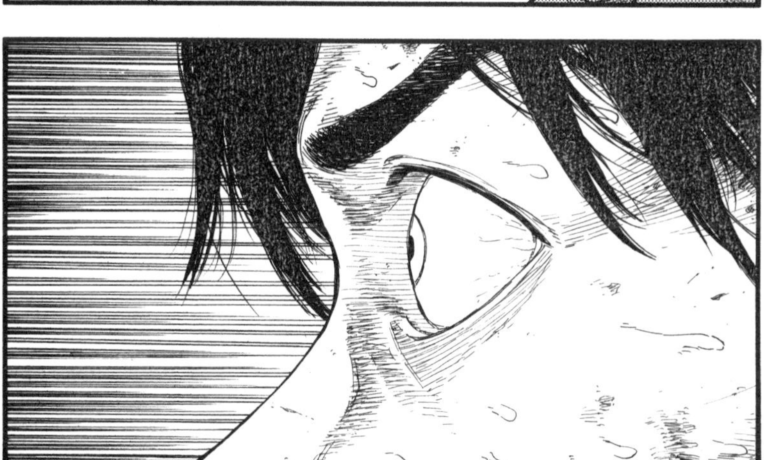

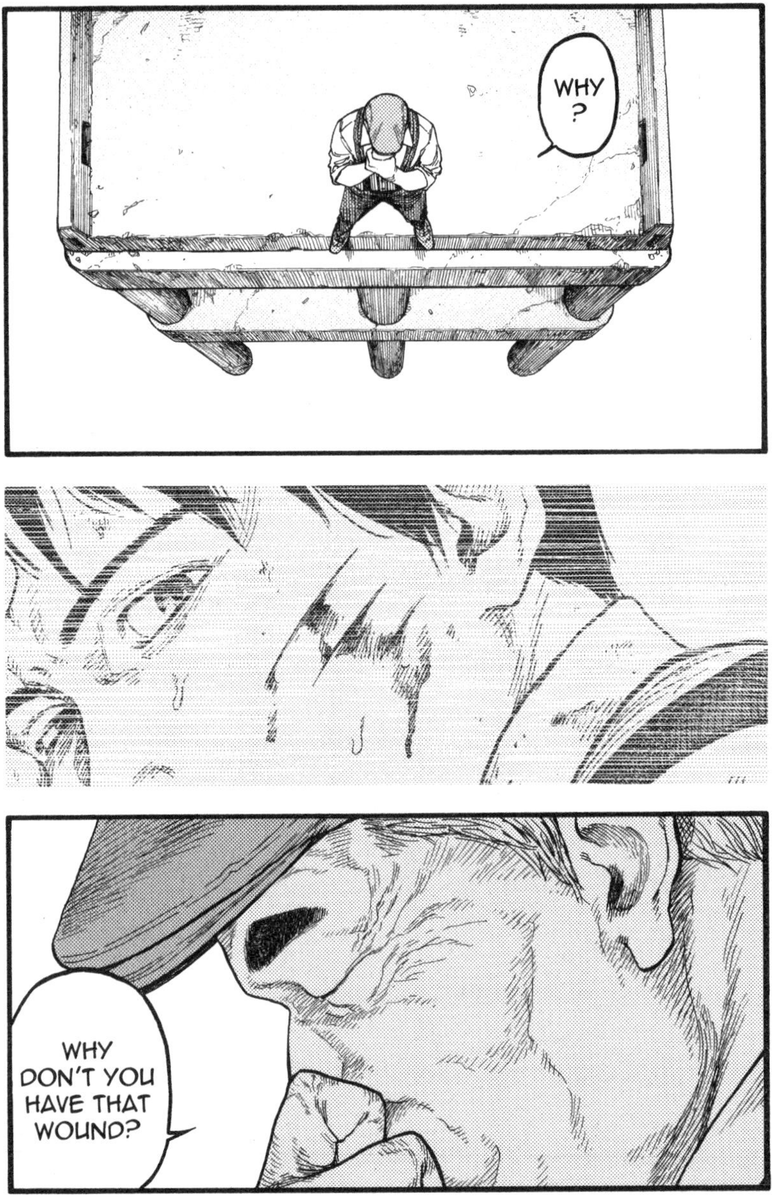
WHY?
WHY DON'T YOU HAVE THAT WOUND?

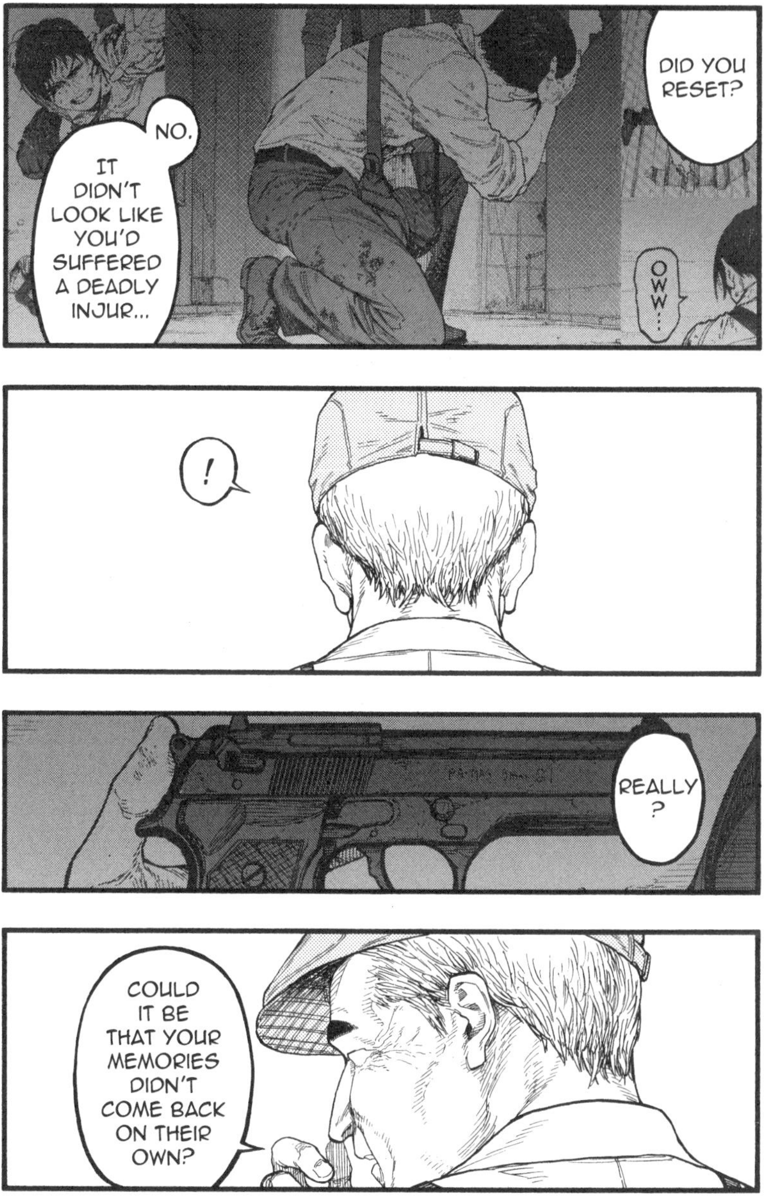
DID YOU RESET?
OWW...
NO.
IT DIDN'T LOOK LIKE YOU'D SUFFERED A DEADLY INJUR...
!
REALLY?
COULD IT BE THAT YOUR MEMORIES DIDN'T COME BACK ON THEIR OWN?

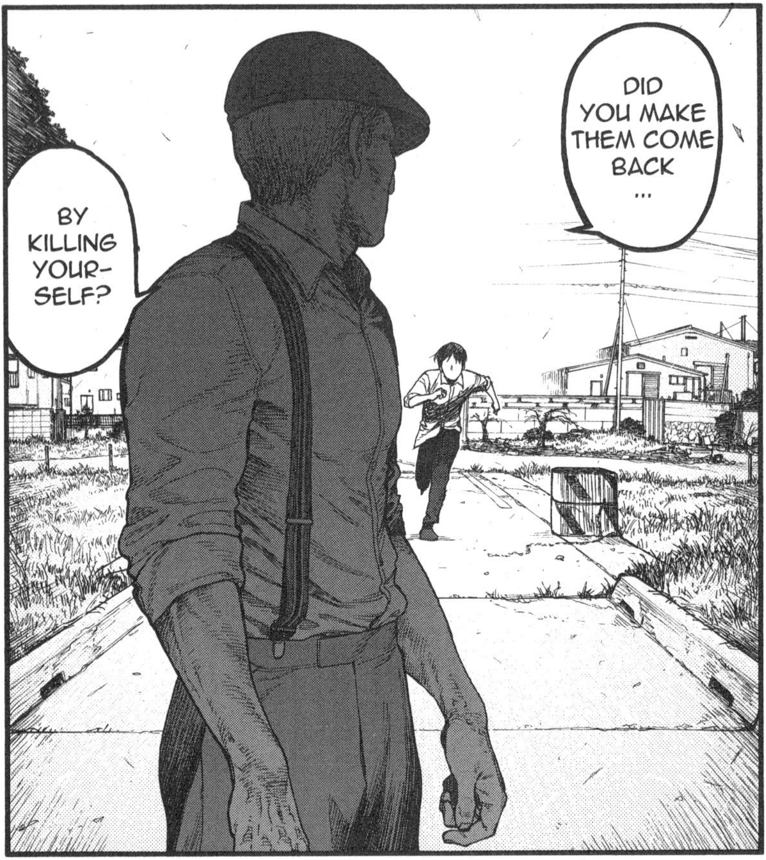
DID YOU MAKE THEM COME BACK ...
BY KILLING YOURSELF?

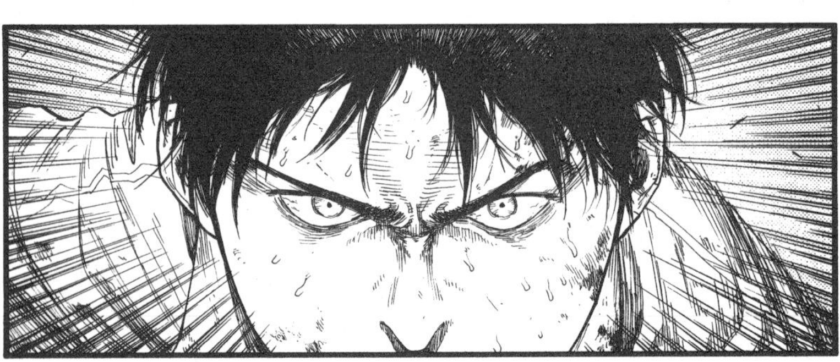

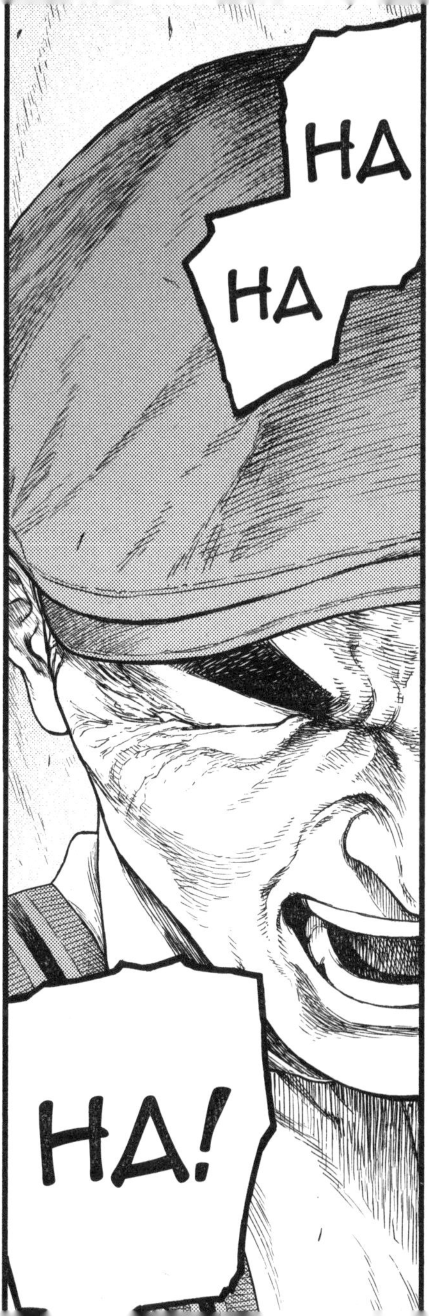
HA
HA
HA!
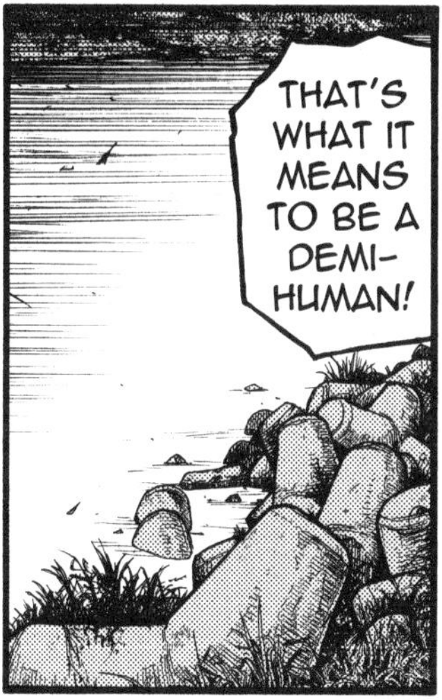
THAT'S WHAT IT MEANS TO BE A DEMI-HUMAN!
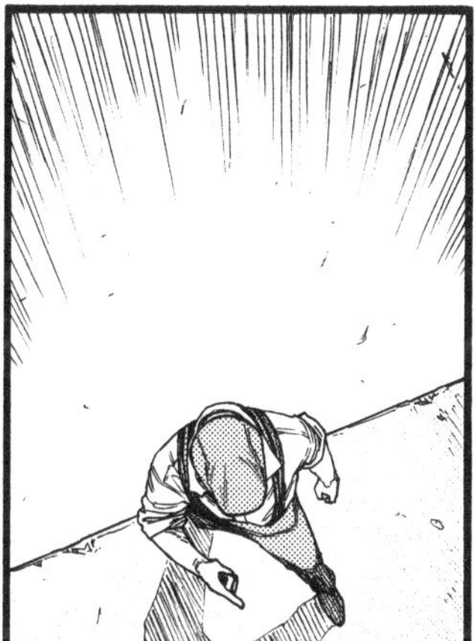
LOOK HOW FAR YOU'VE COME! WELL DONE!!

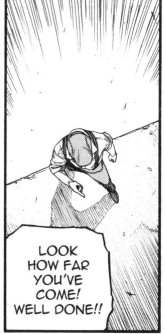

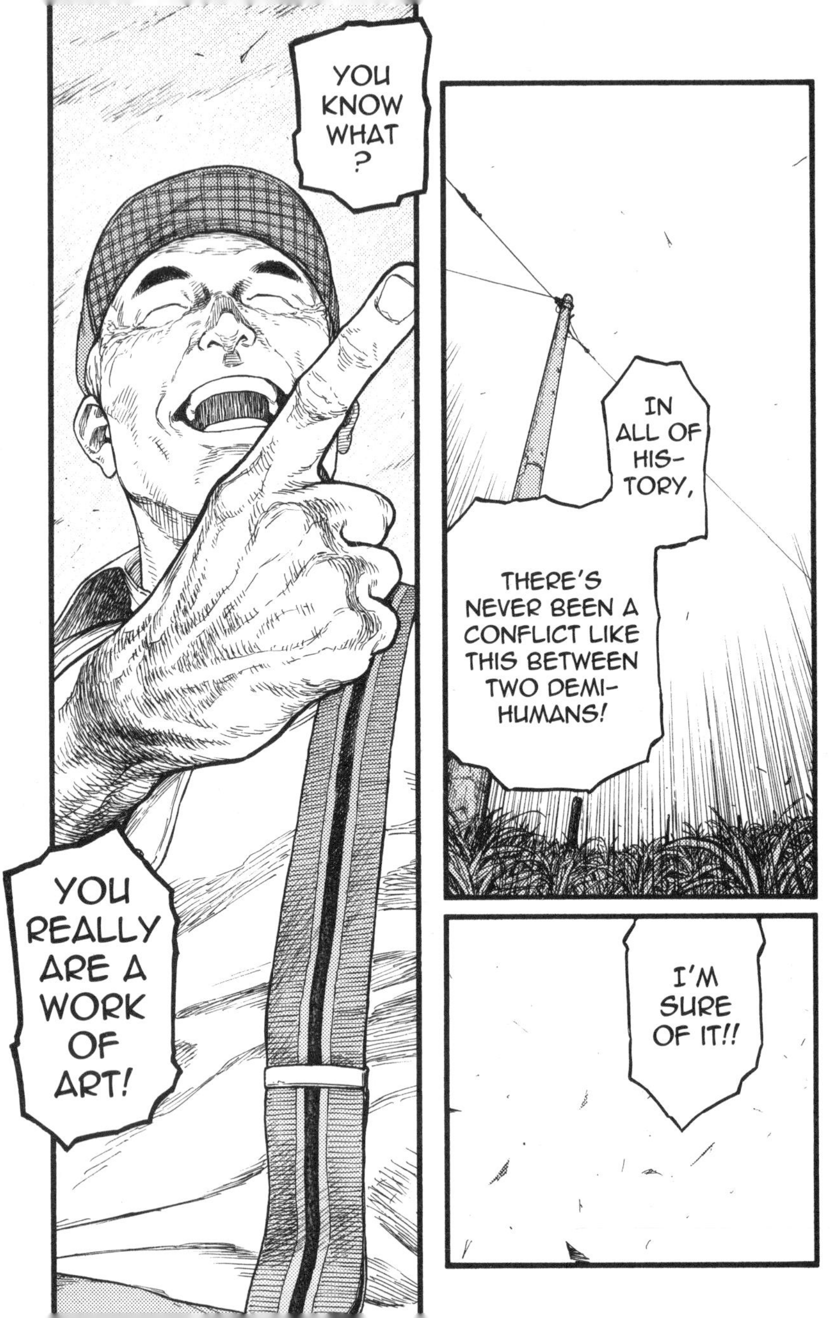
IN ALL OF HIS-TORY,
THERE'S NEVER BEEN A CONFLICT LIKE THIS BETWEEN TWO DEMI-HUMANS!
I'M SURE OF IT!!
YOU KNOW WHAT?
YOU REALLY ARE A WORK OF ART!

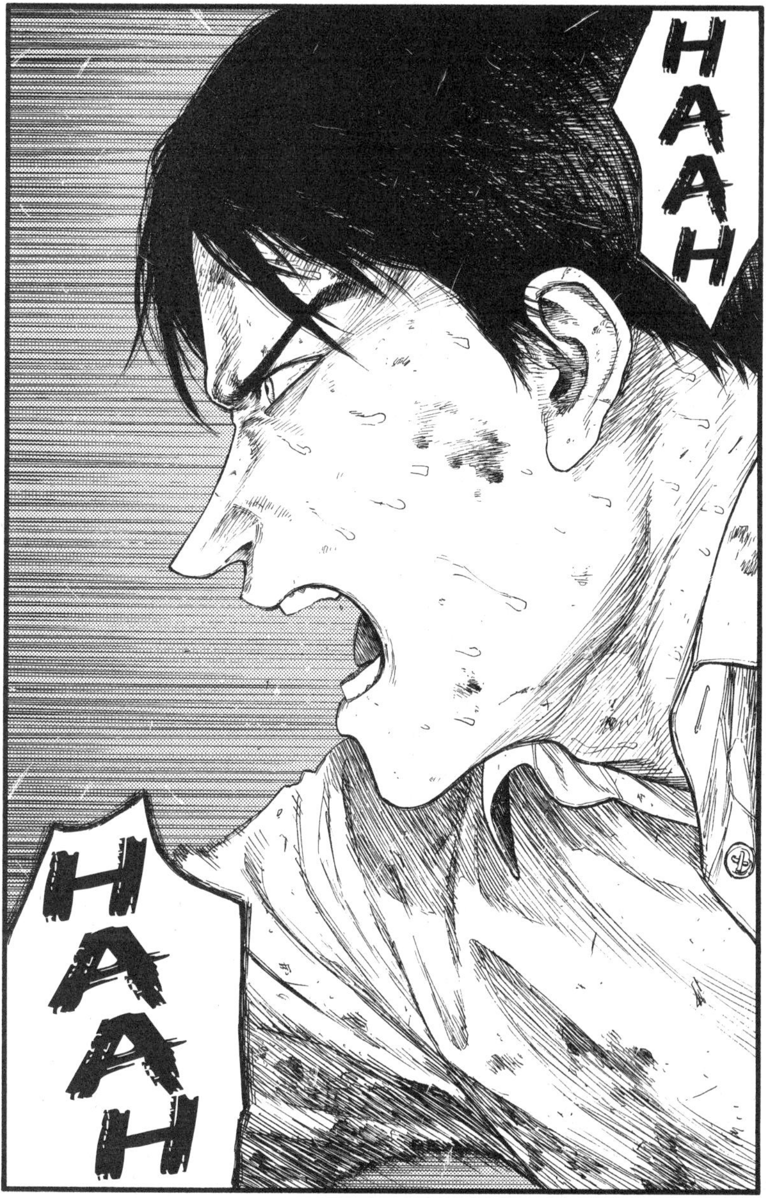
HAAH
HAAH

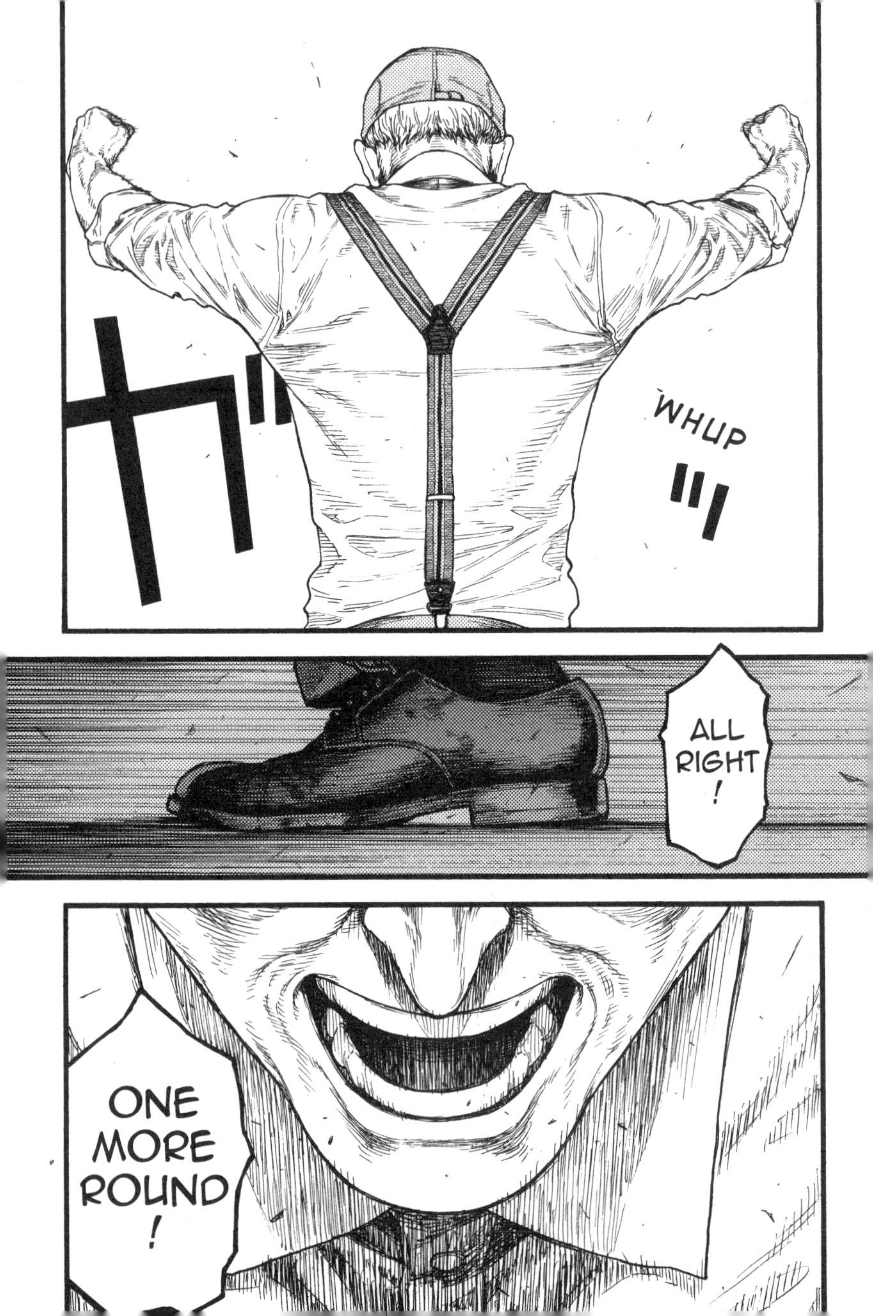
ガ
WHUP
ッ
ALL RIGHT!
ONE MORE ROUND!

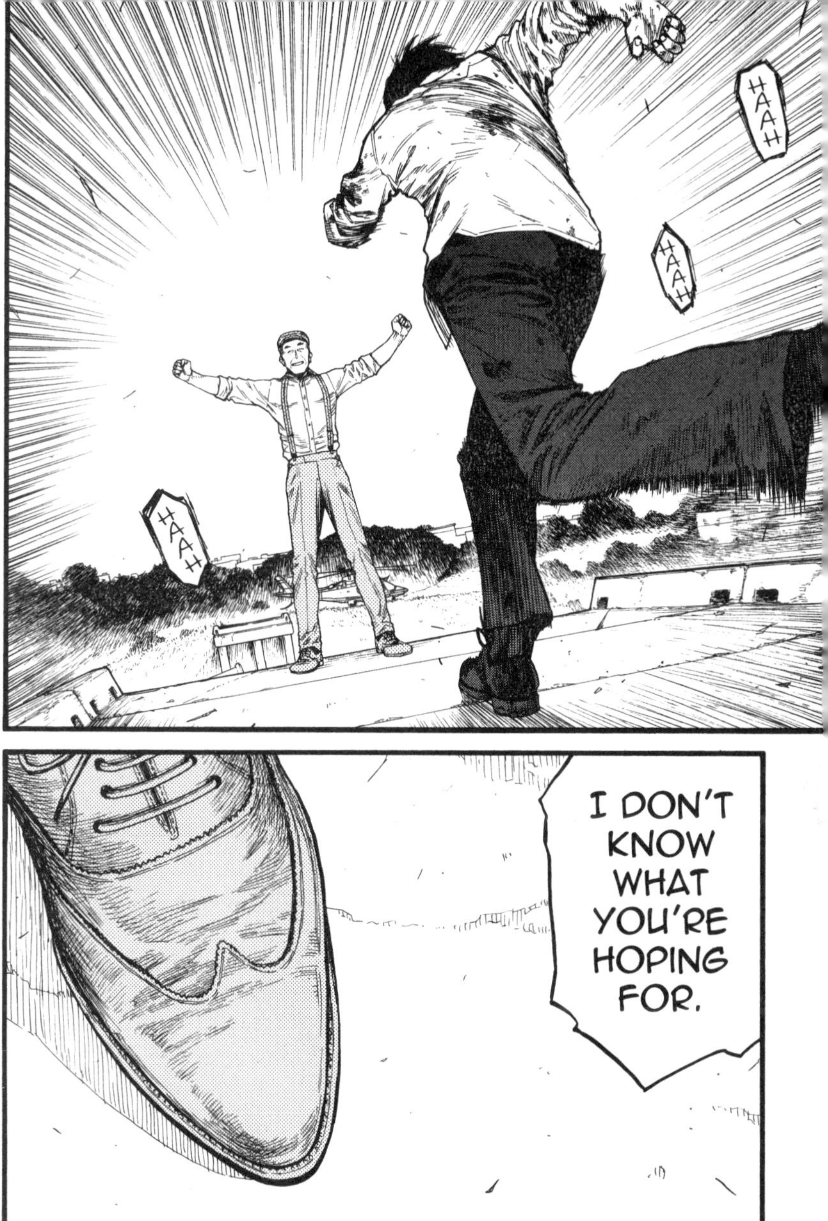
HAAH
HAAH
HAAH
I DON'T KNOW WHAT YOU'RE HOPING FOR.

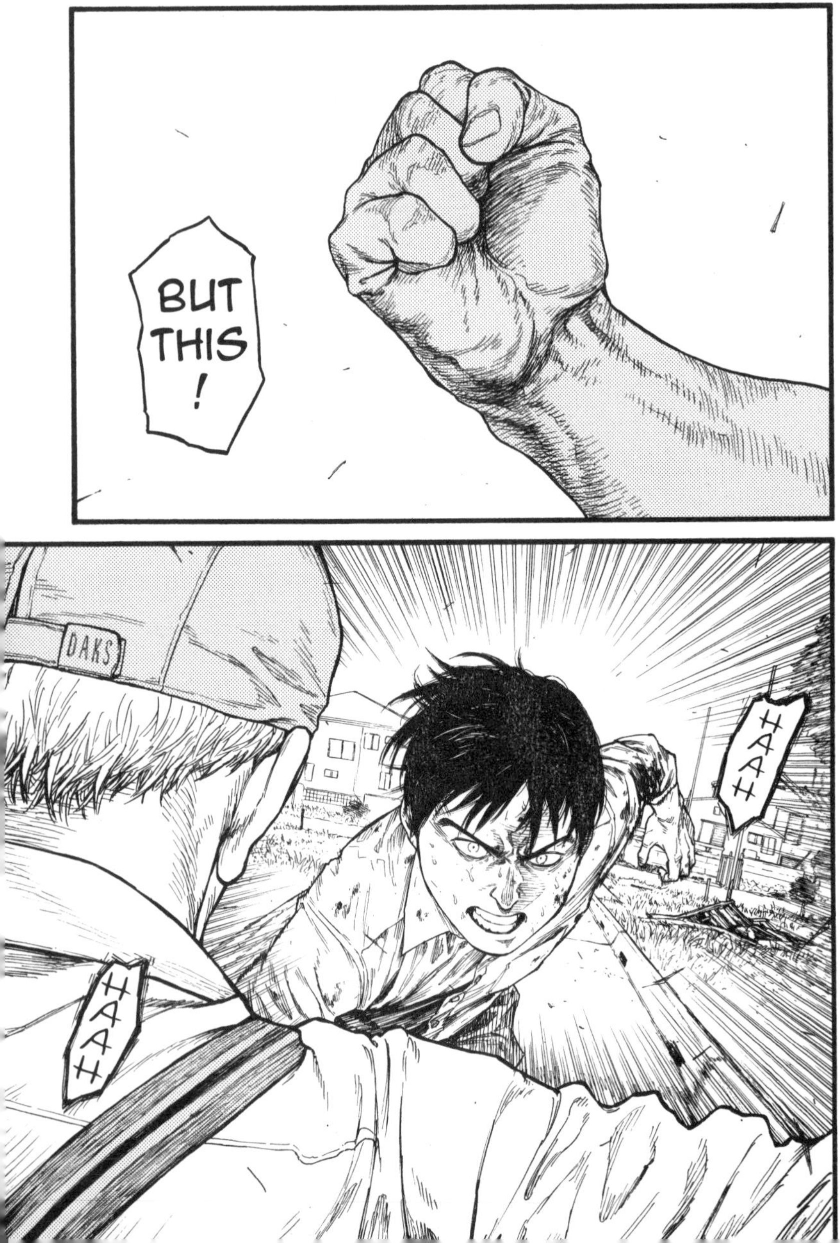
BUT THIS !
DAKS
HAAH
HAAH

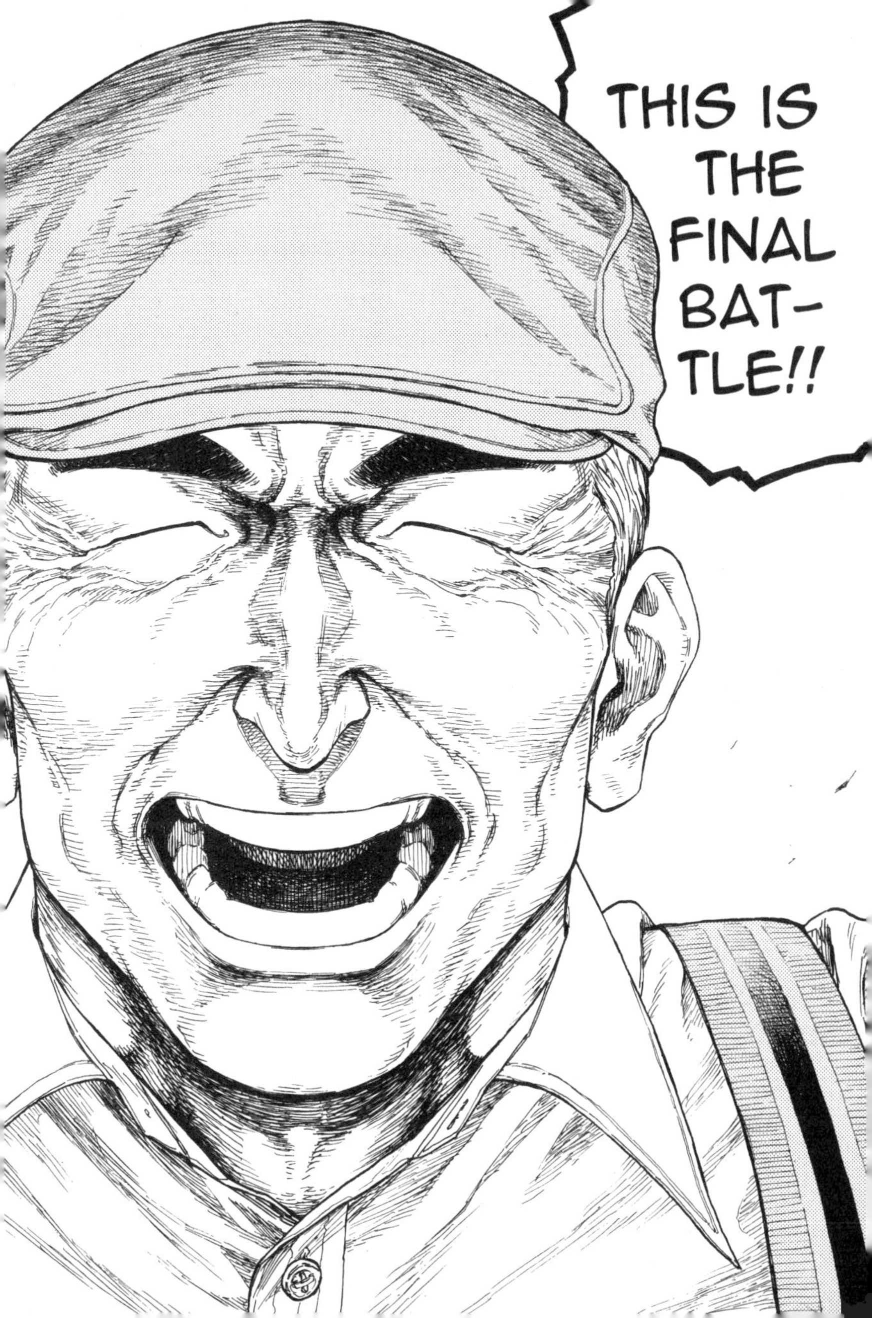
THIS IS THE FINAL BAT-TLE!!

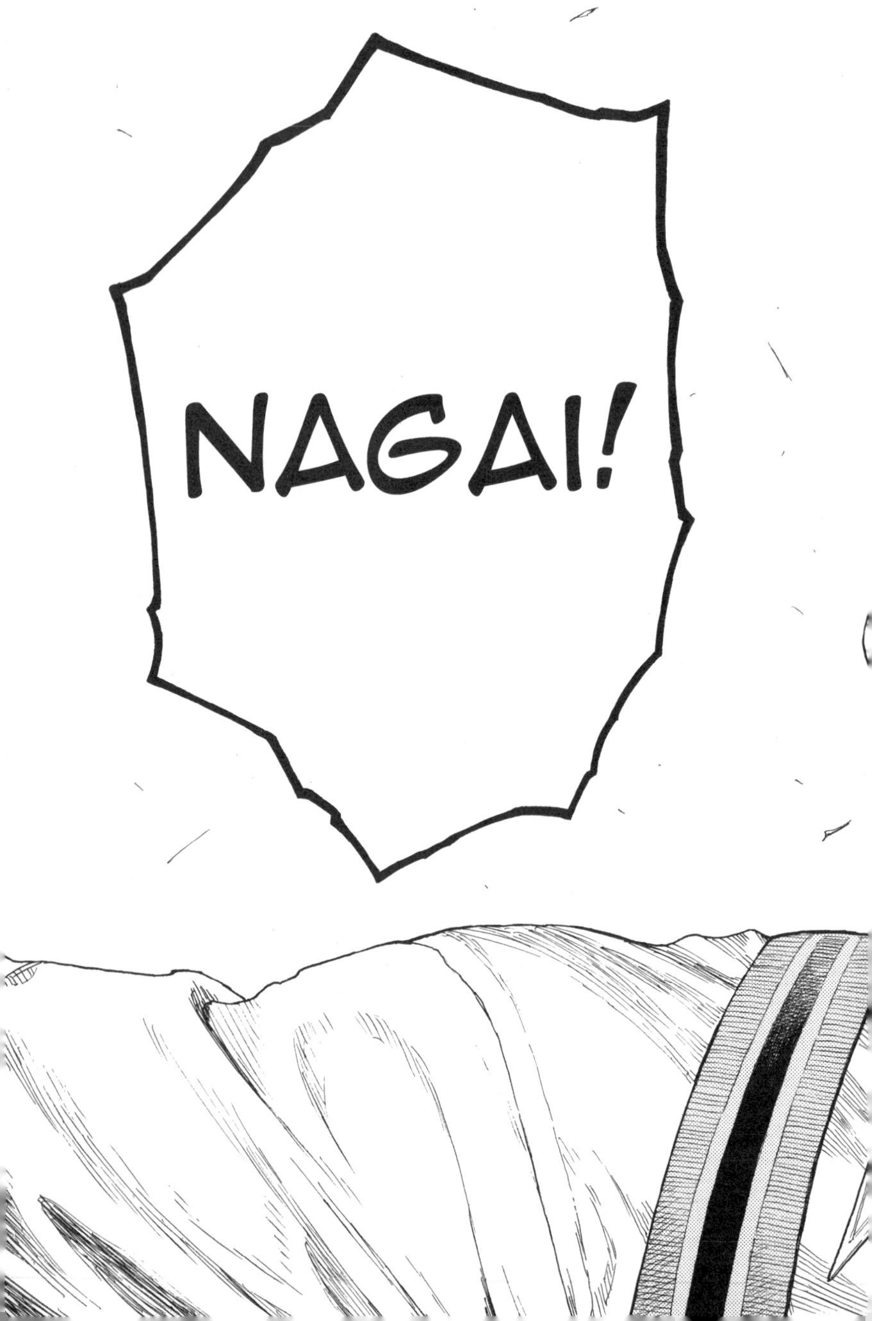
NAGAI!

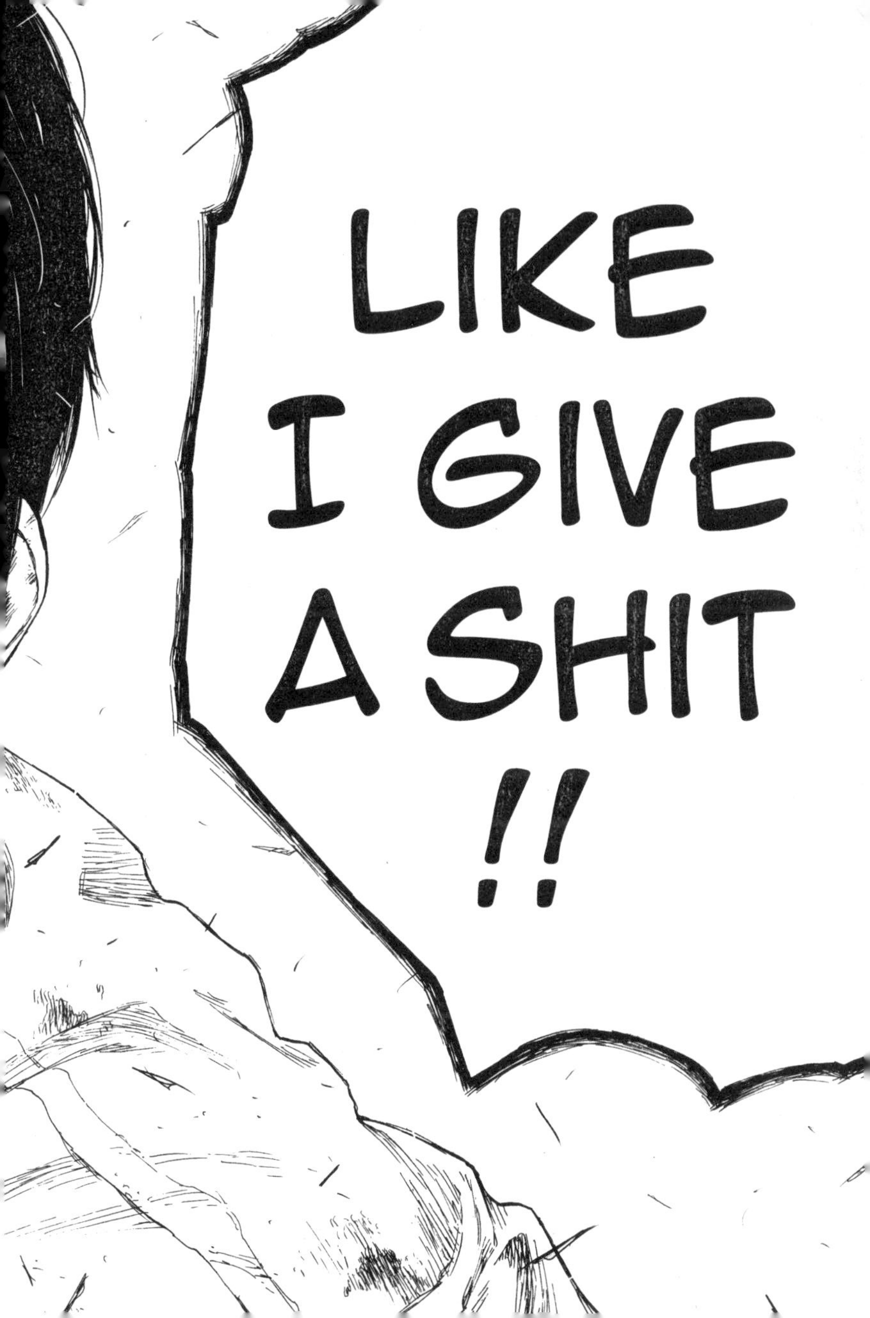
LIKE I GIVE A SHIT!!

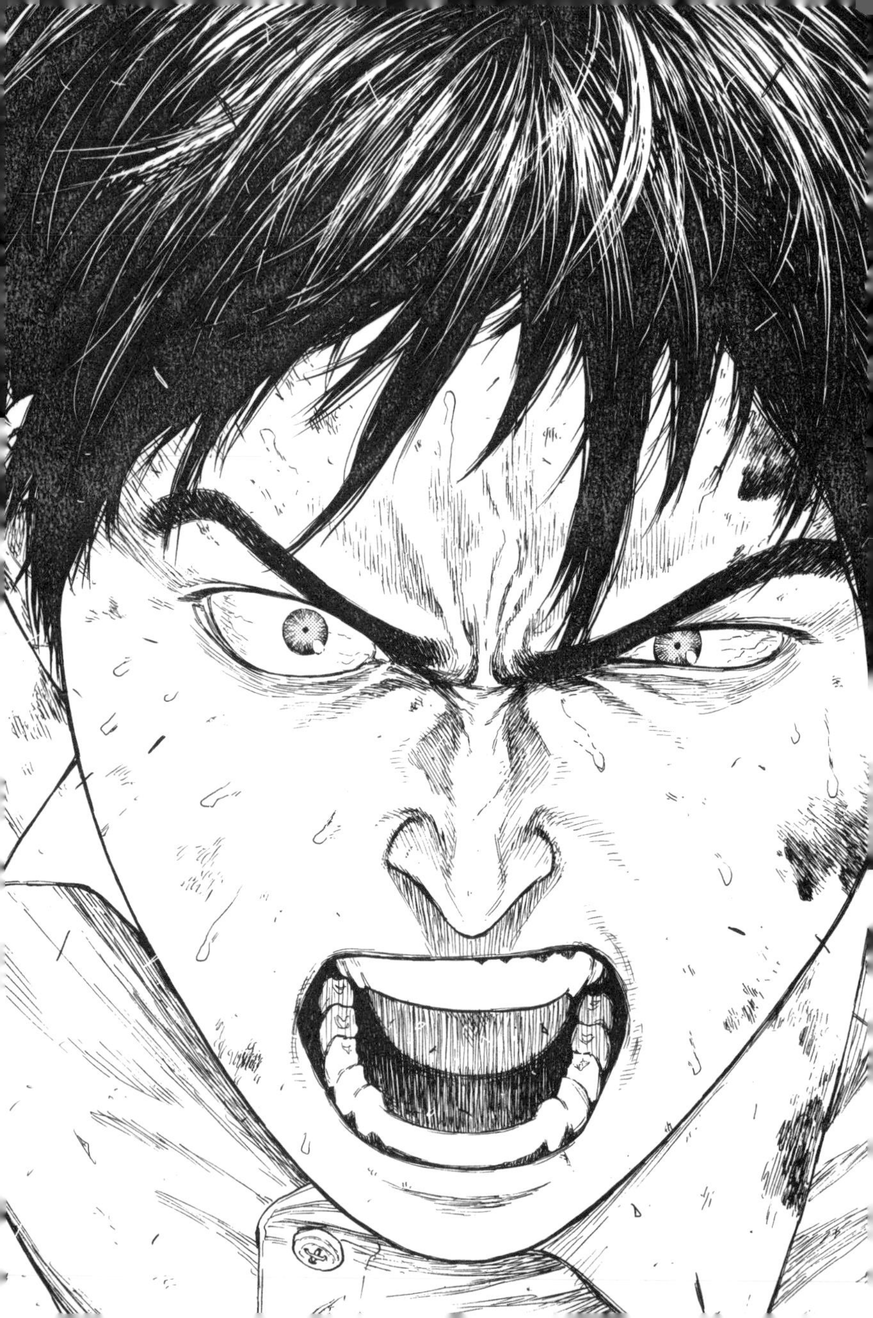

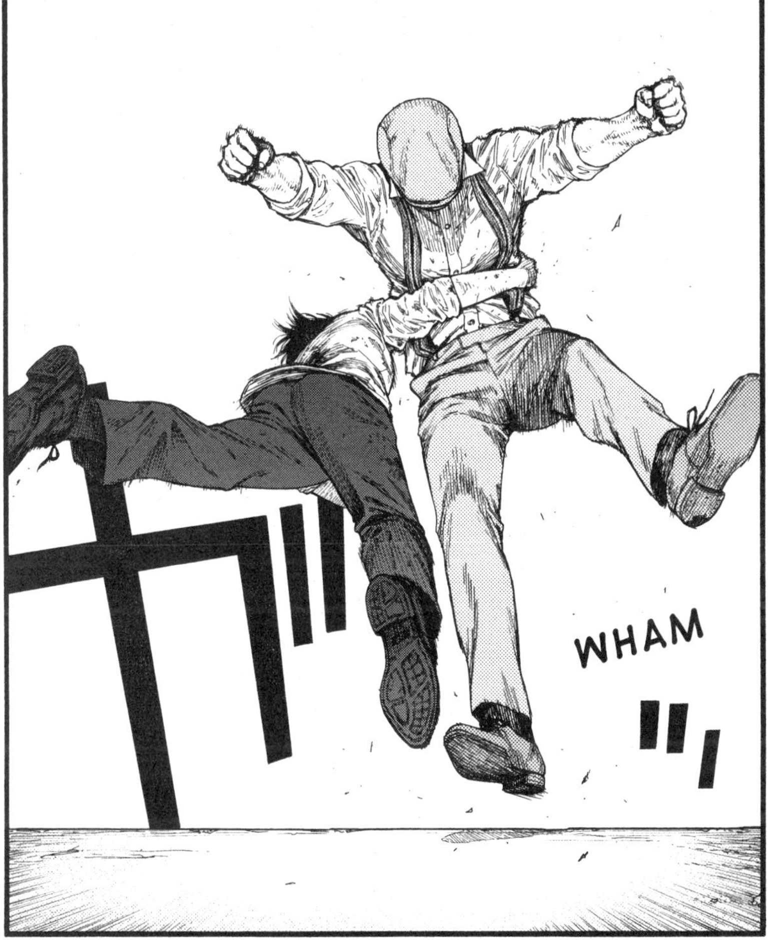
WHAM
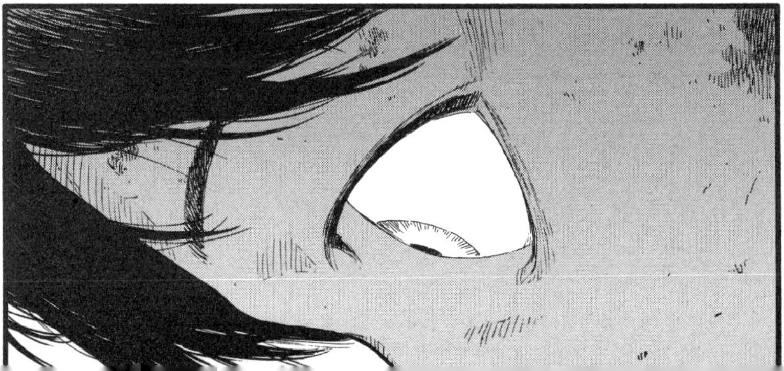

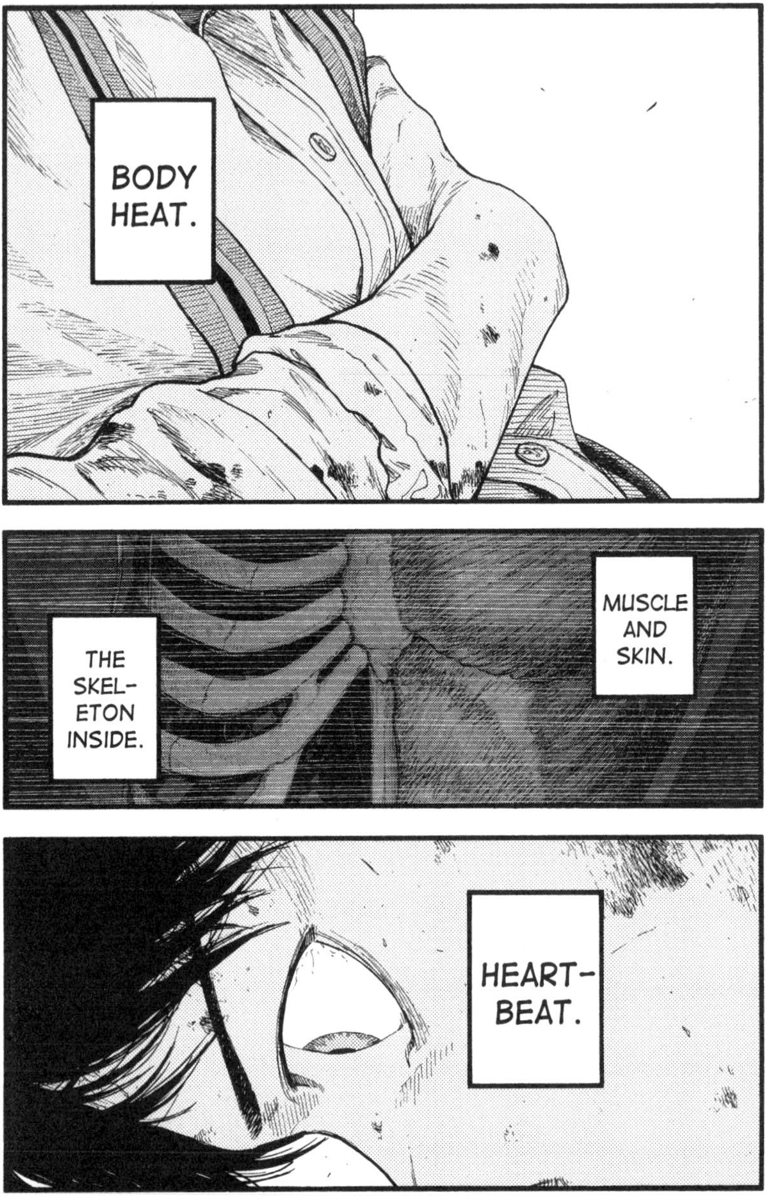
BODY HEAT.
MUSCLE AND SKIN.
THE SKEL- ETON INSIDE.
HEART- BEAT.

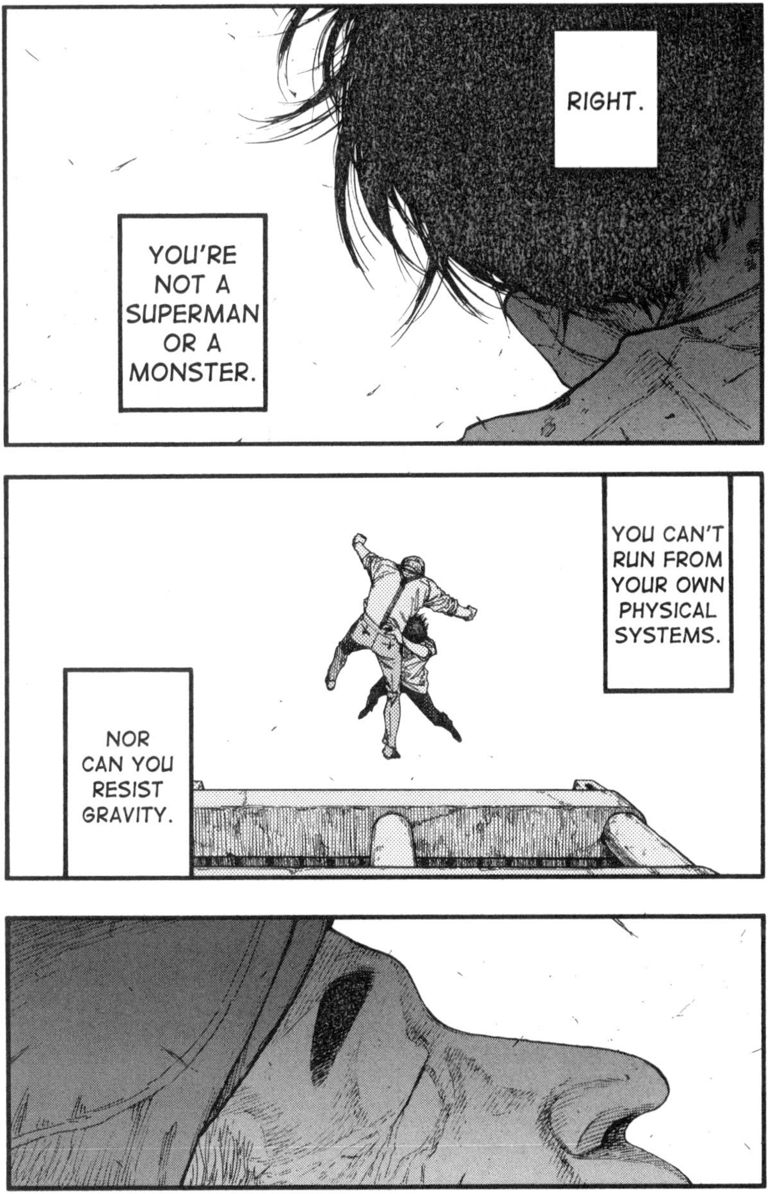
RIGHT.
YOU'RE NOT A SUPERMAN OR A MONSTER.
YOU CAN'T RUN FROM YOUR OWN PHYSICAL SYSTEMS.
NOR CAN YOU RESIST GRAVITY.

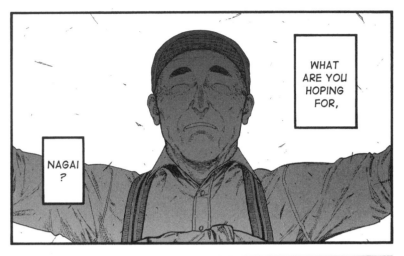

WHAT ARE YOU HOPING FOR,

NAGAI?

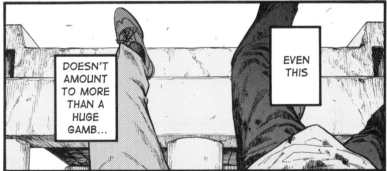

DOESN'T AMOUNT TO MORE THAN A HUGE GAMB...

EVEN THIS

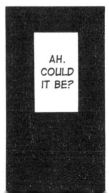

AH. COULD IT BE?

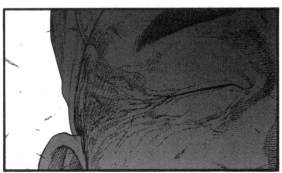

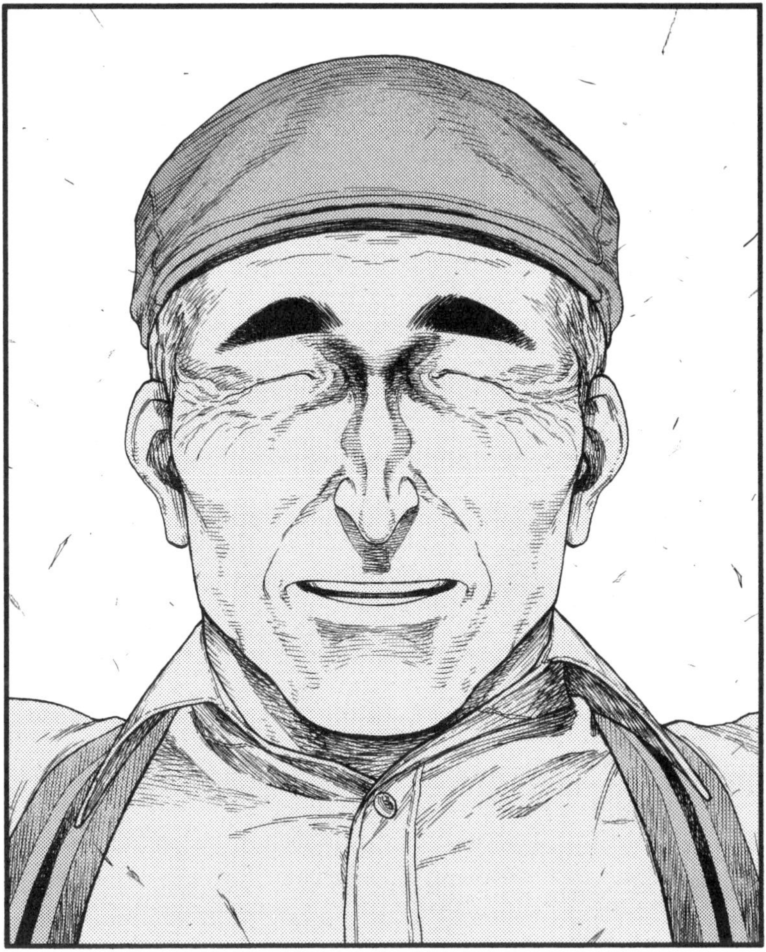

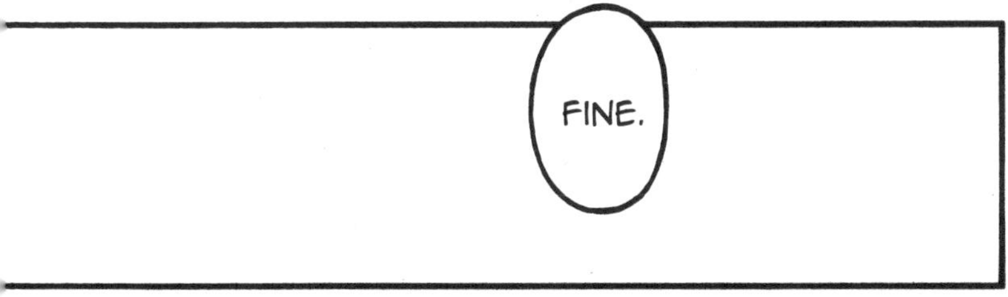
FINE.

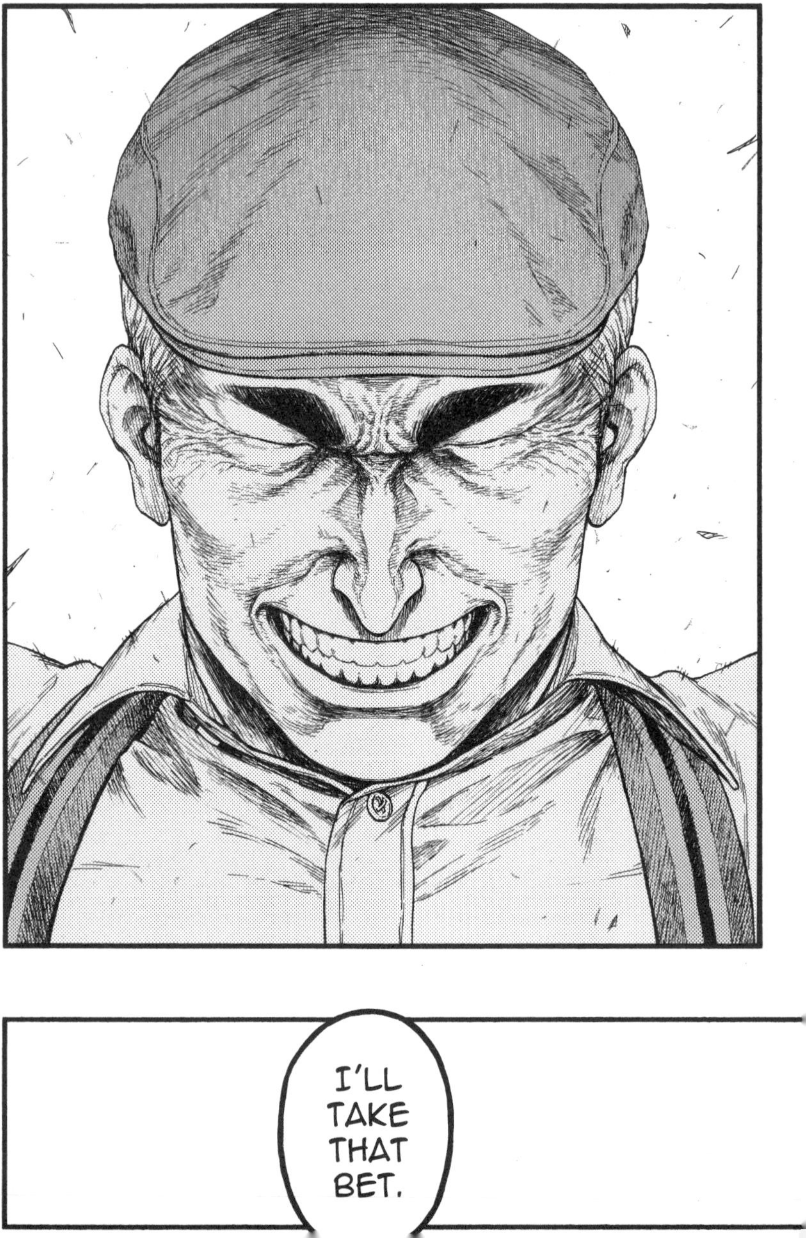
I'LL TAKE THAT BET.

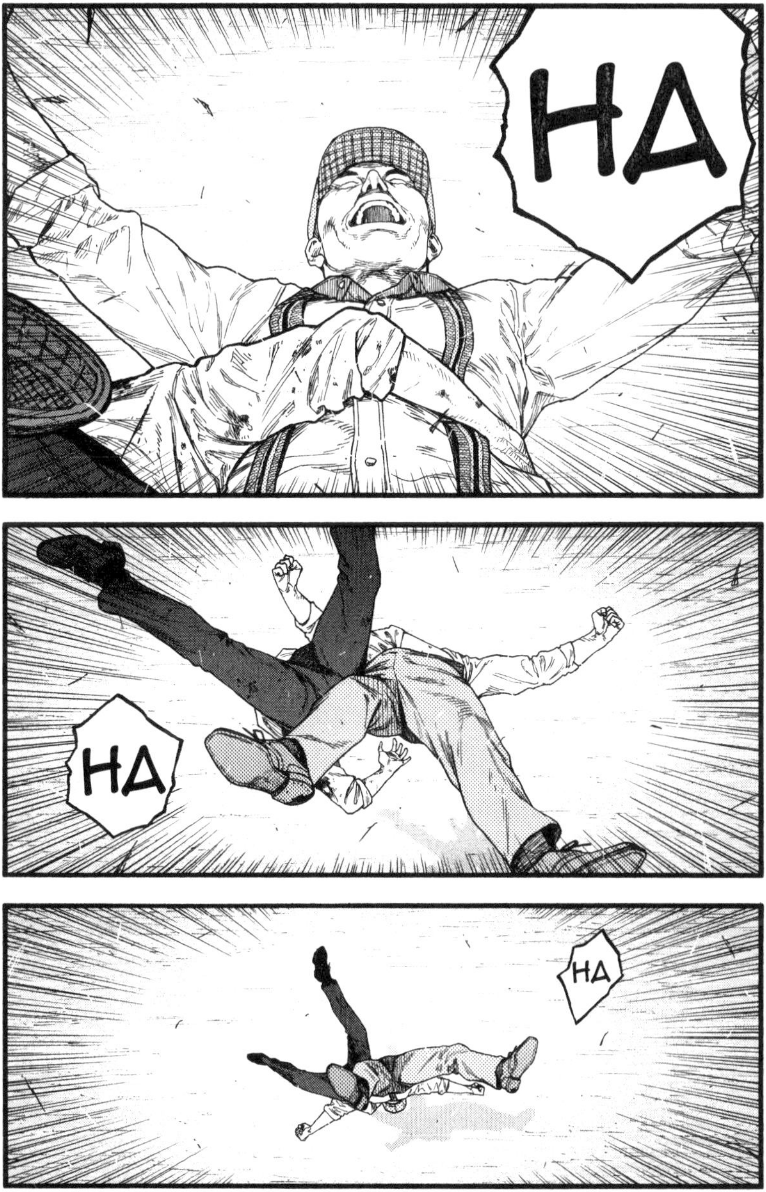
HA
HA
HA

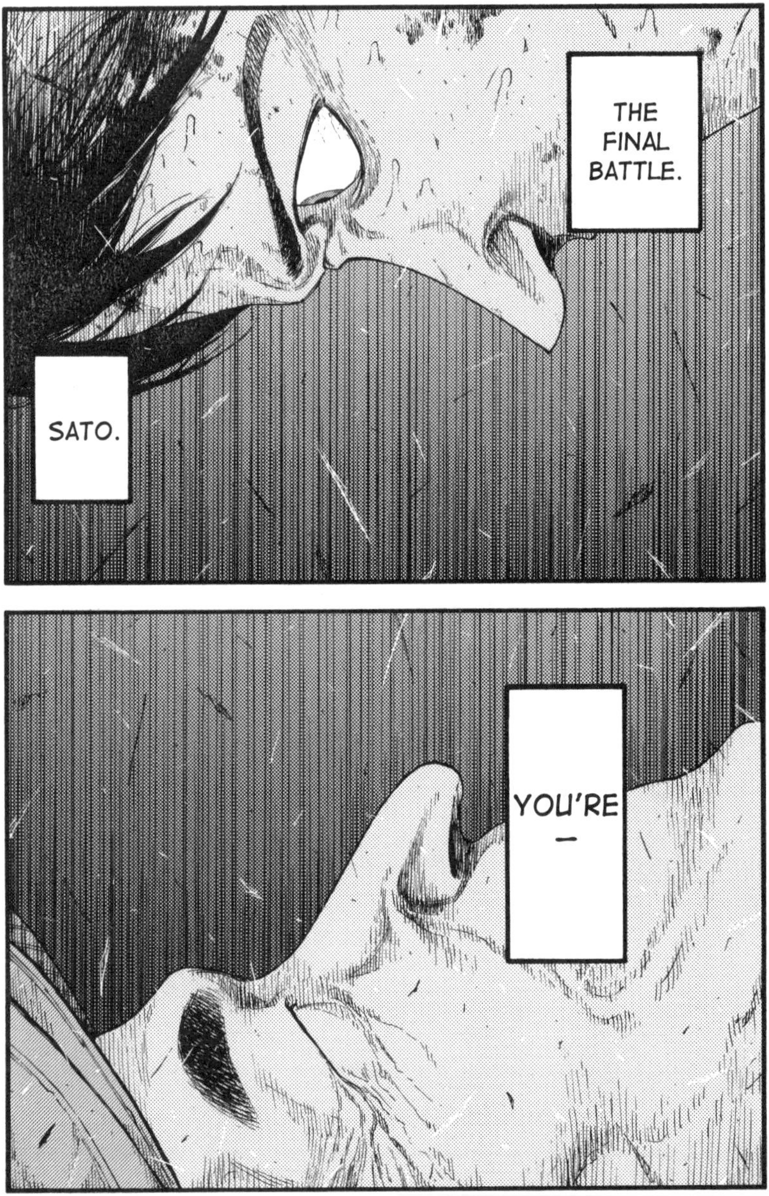
THE FINAL BATTLE.
SATO.
YOU'RE —

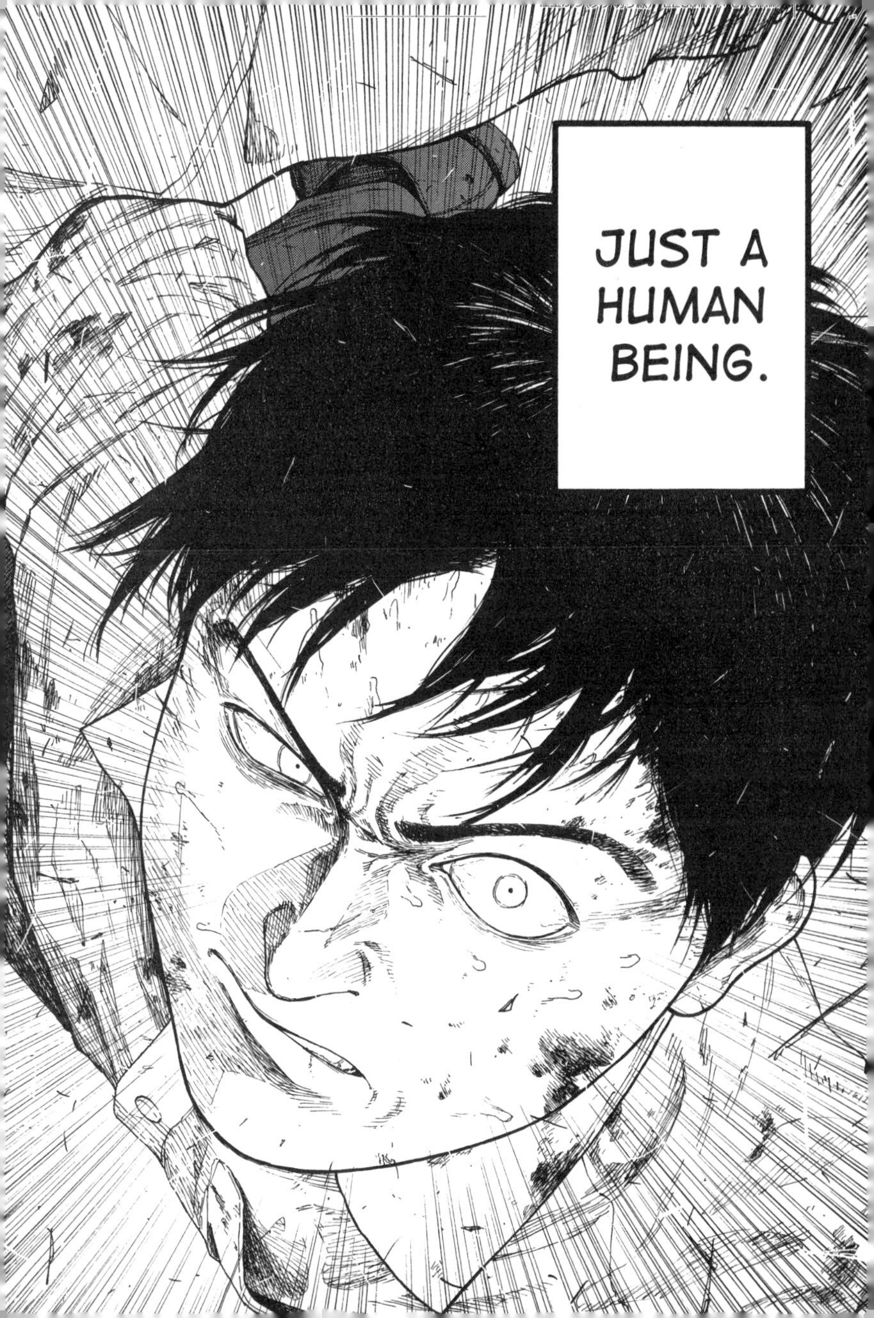
JUST A HUMAN BEING.

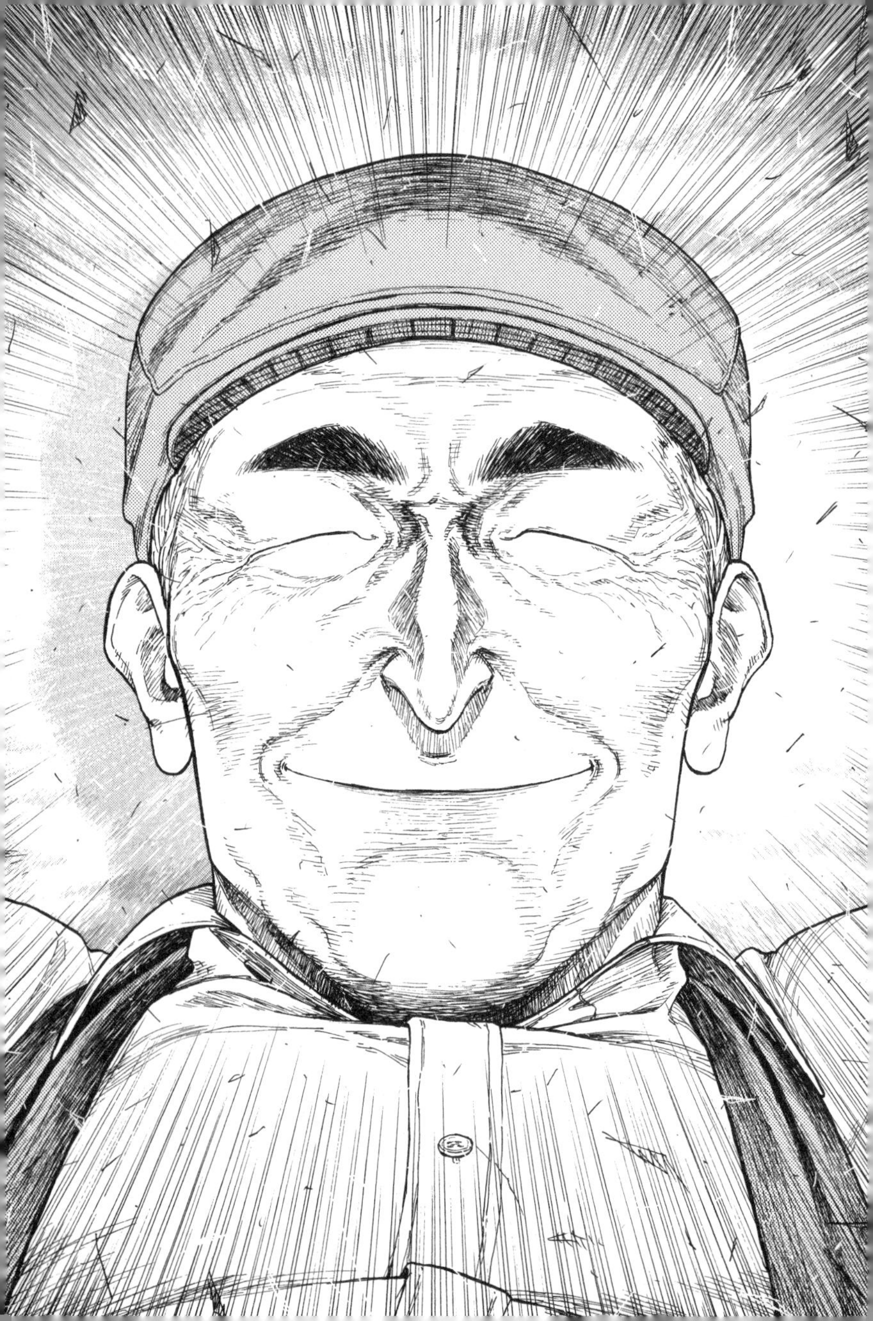

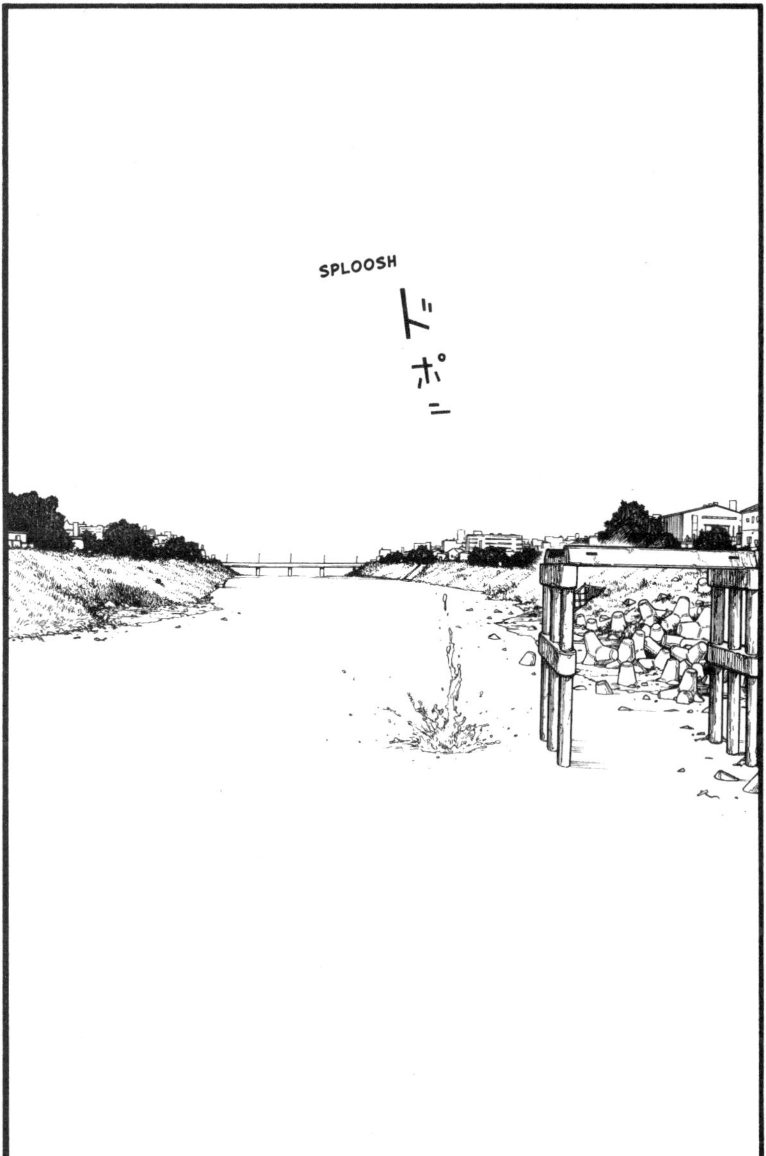
SPLOOSH
ドポン

File:81 End

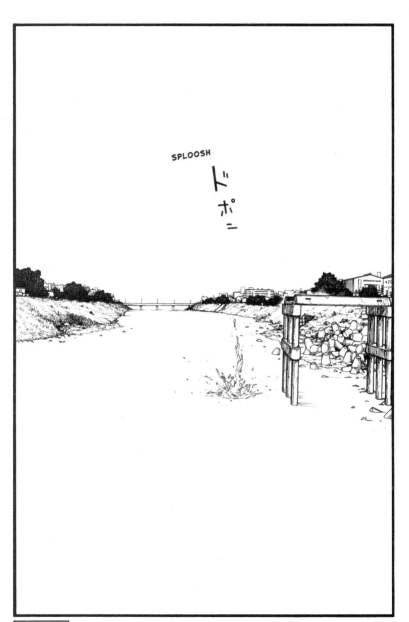

File: 82

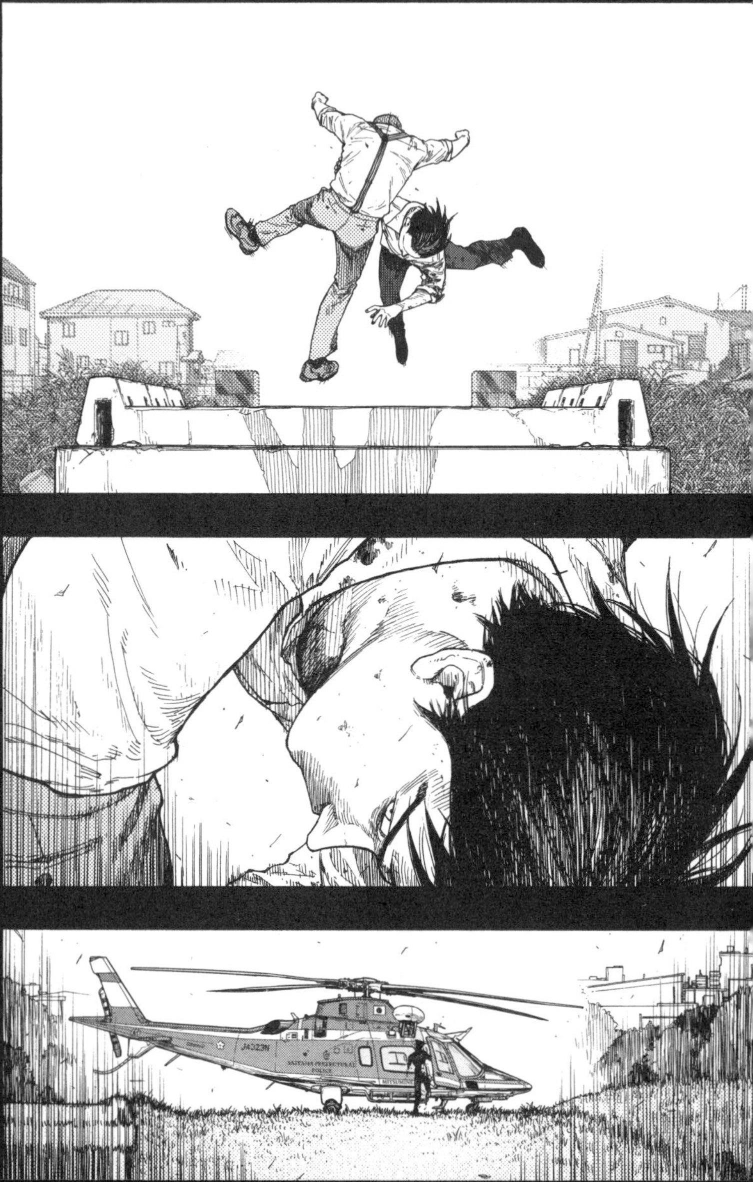
JA323N
MITSUMINE

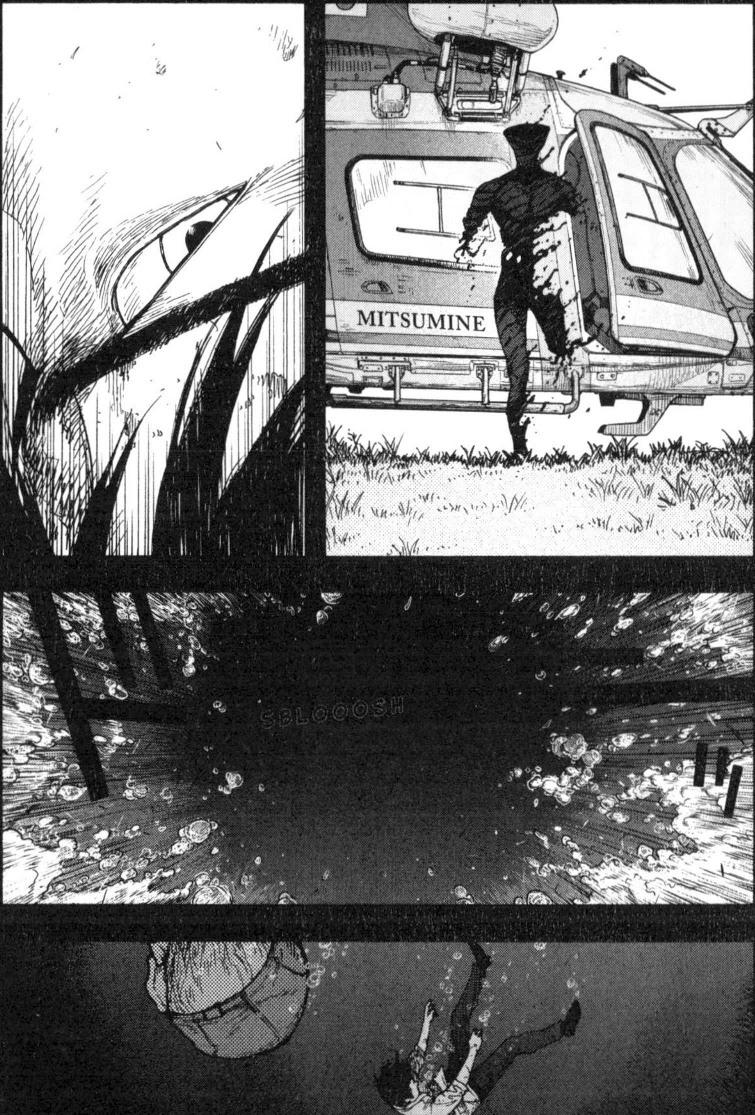
MITSUMINE
SBLOOOSH

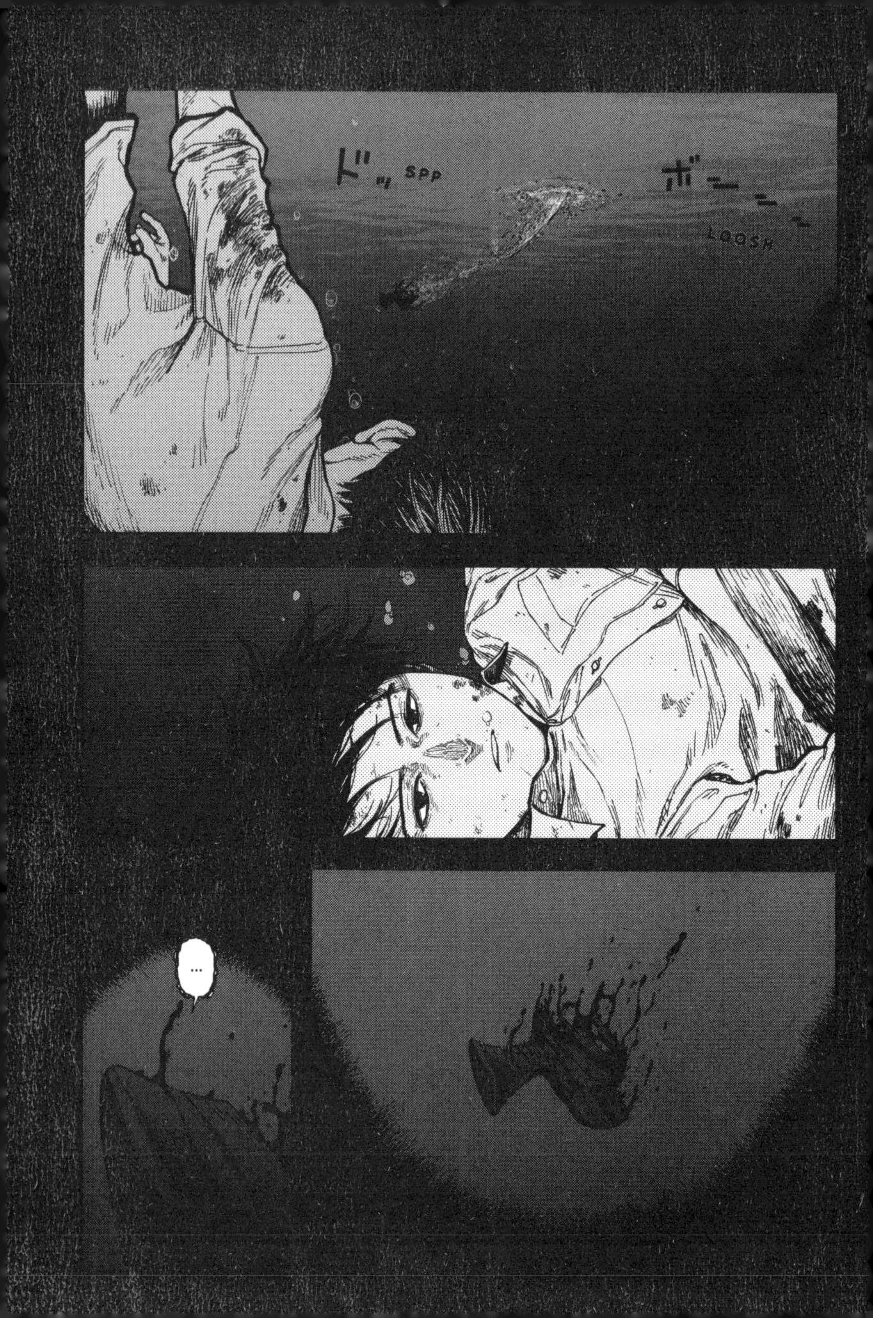
LOOSH
SPP
...

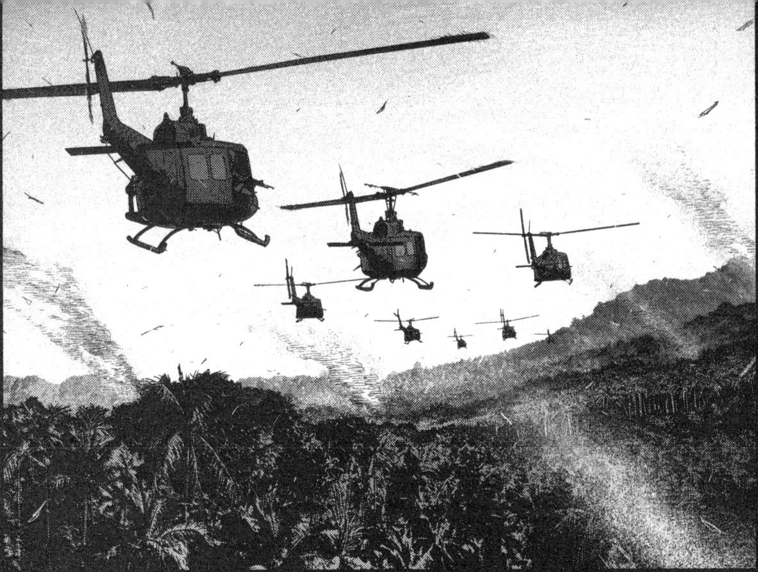
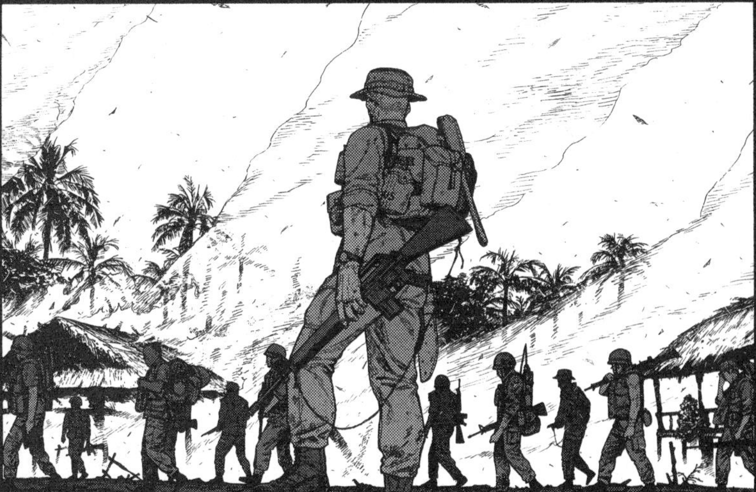

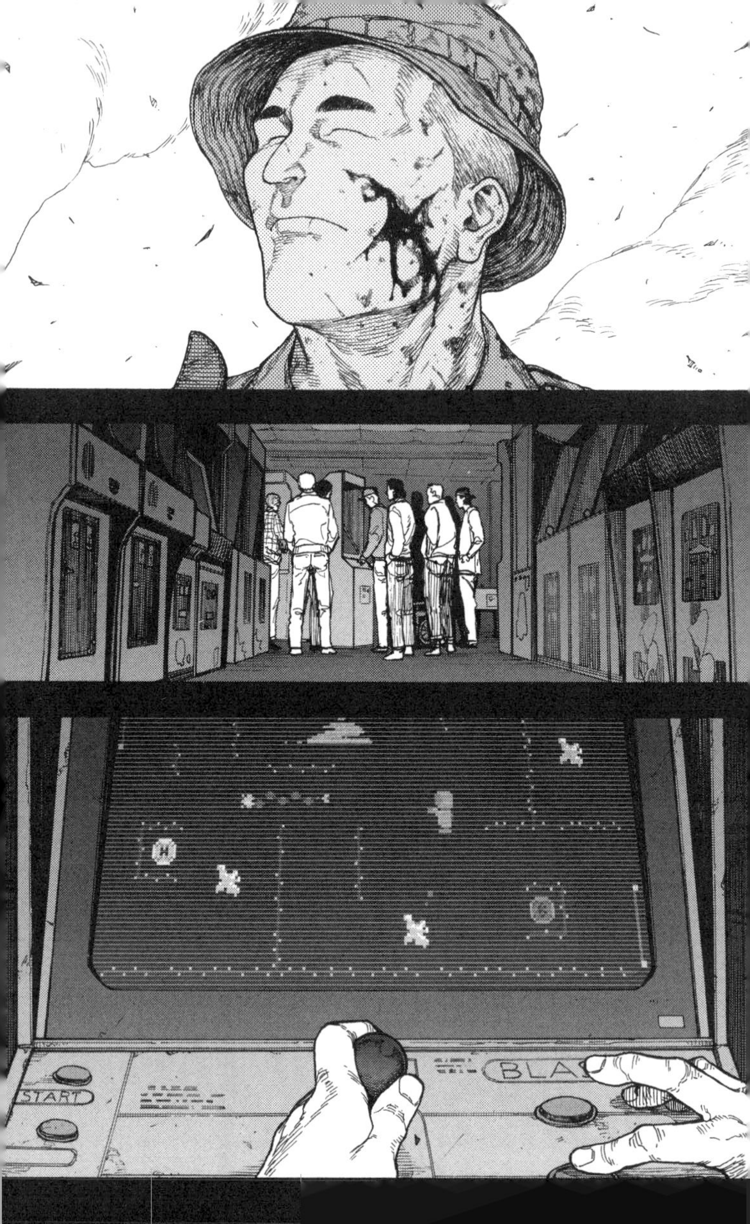

BLAS
START

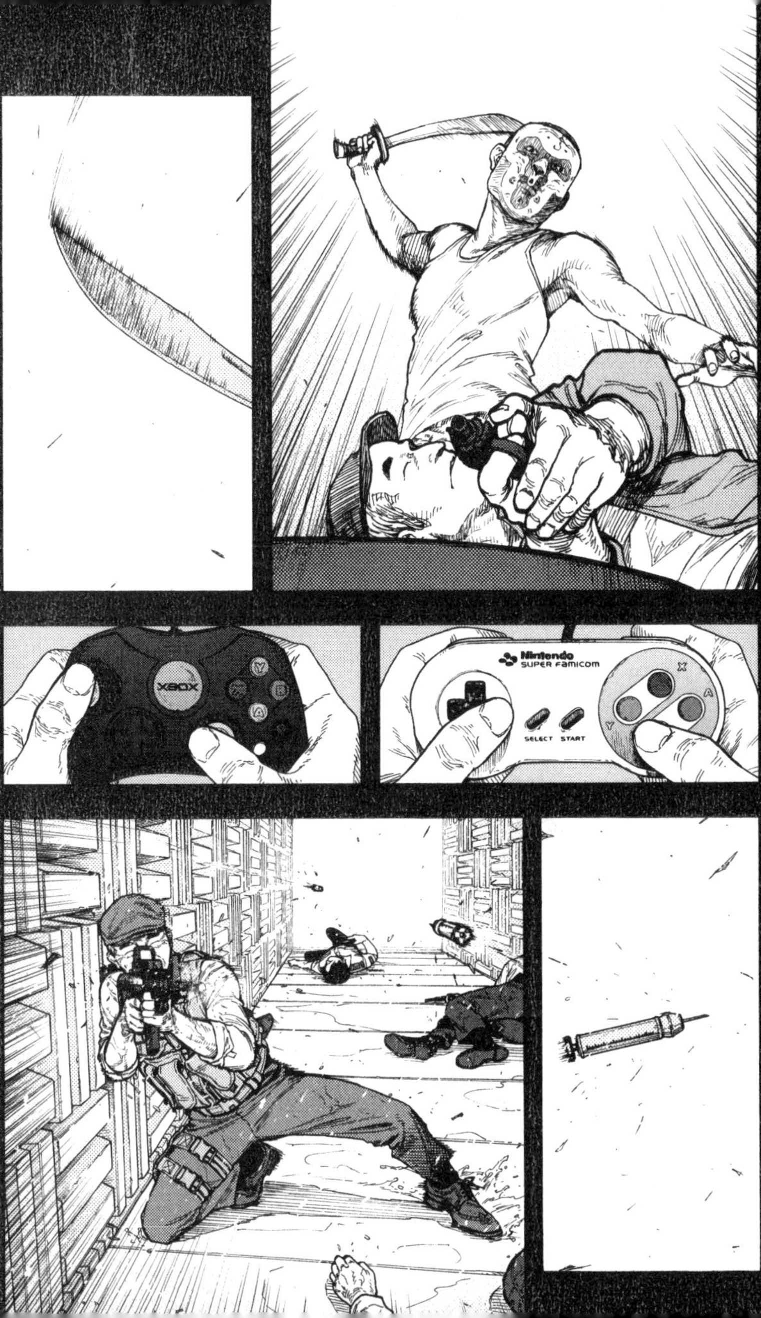
Nintendo
SUPER FAMICOM
SELECT
START
XBOX

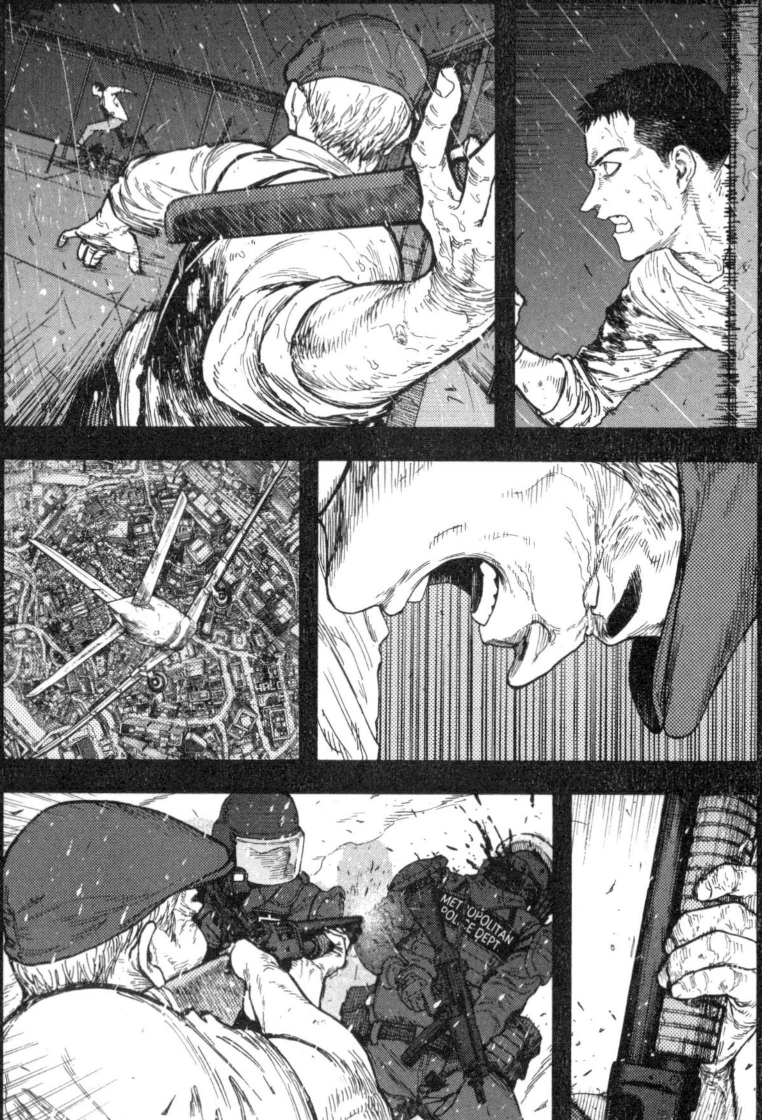
MET OPOLITAN
POL CE DEPT.

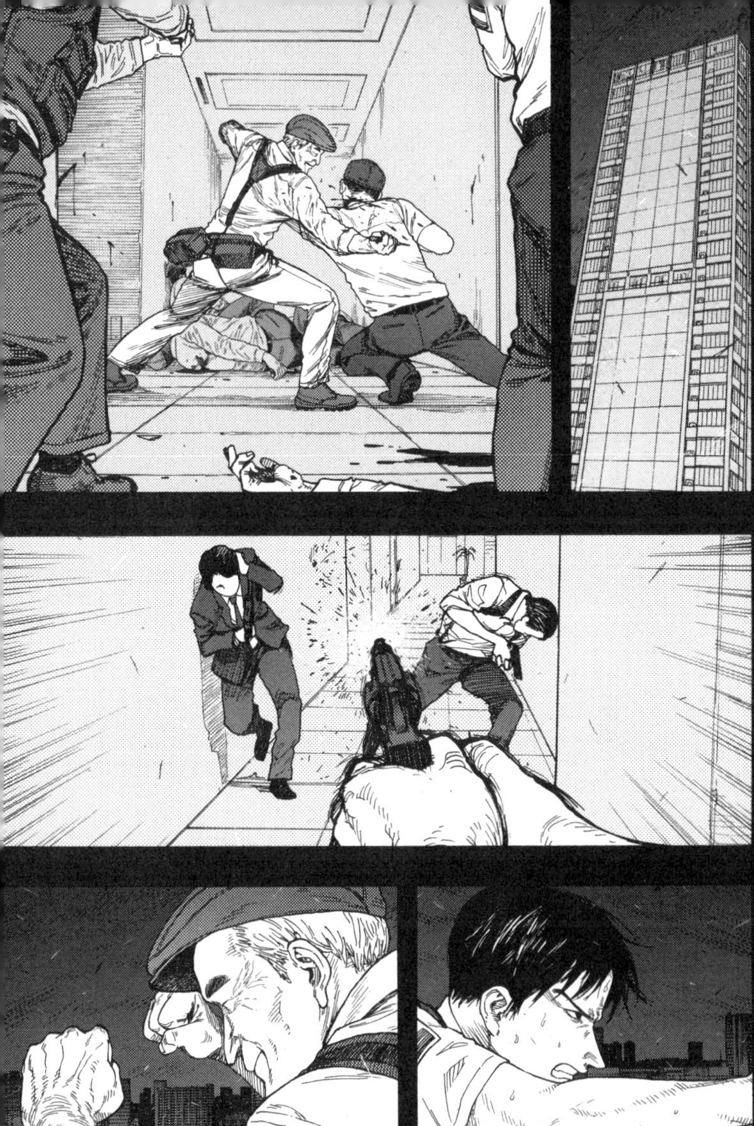

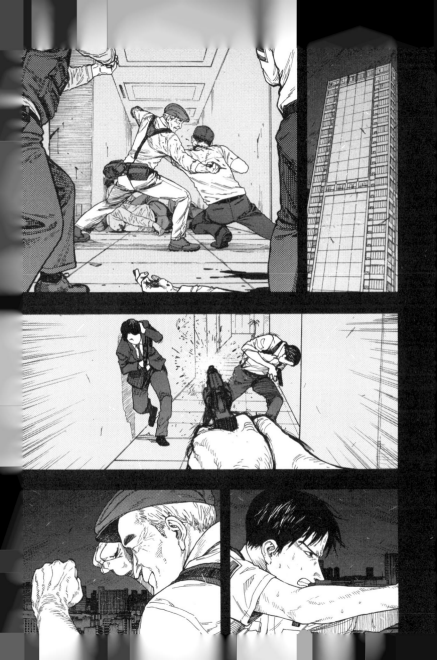

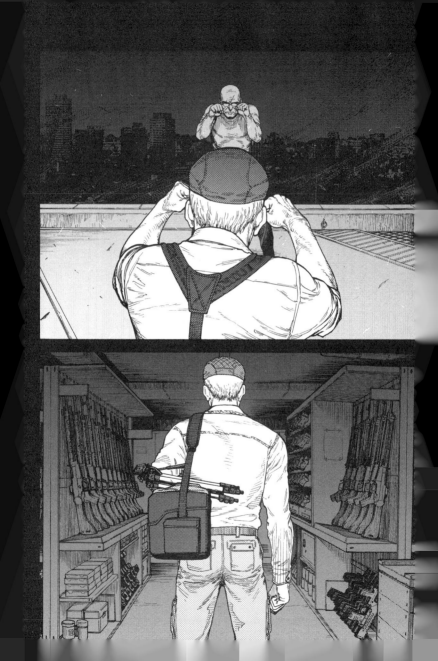

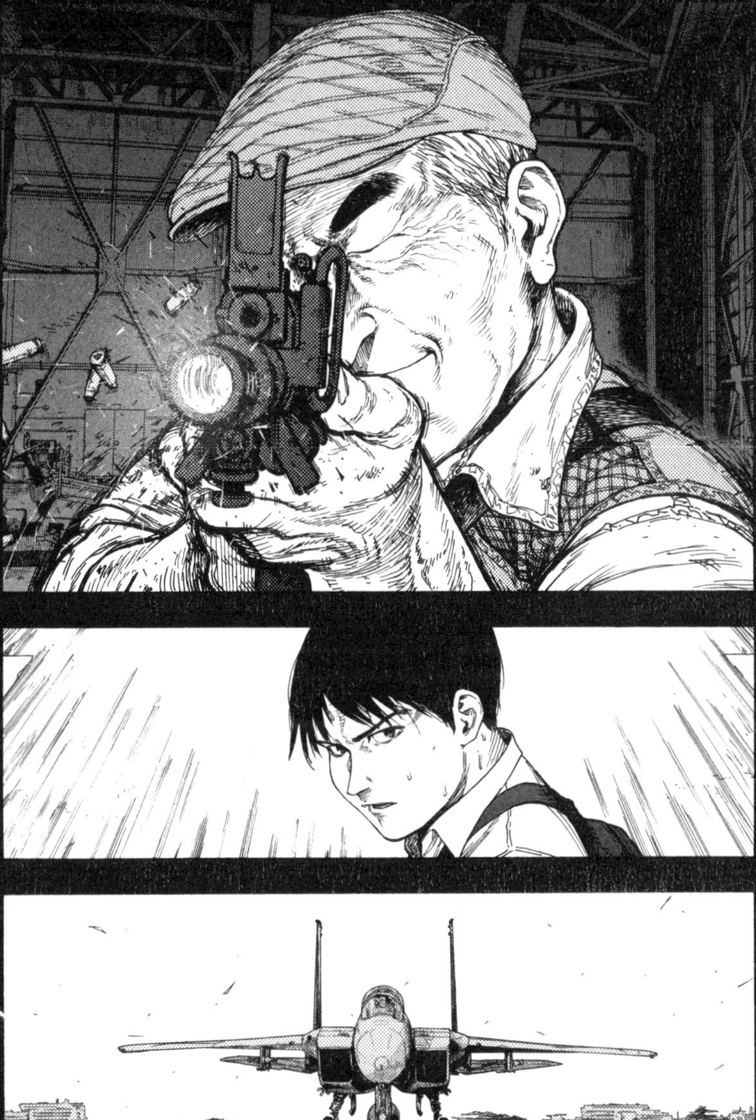

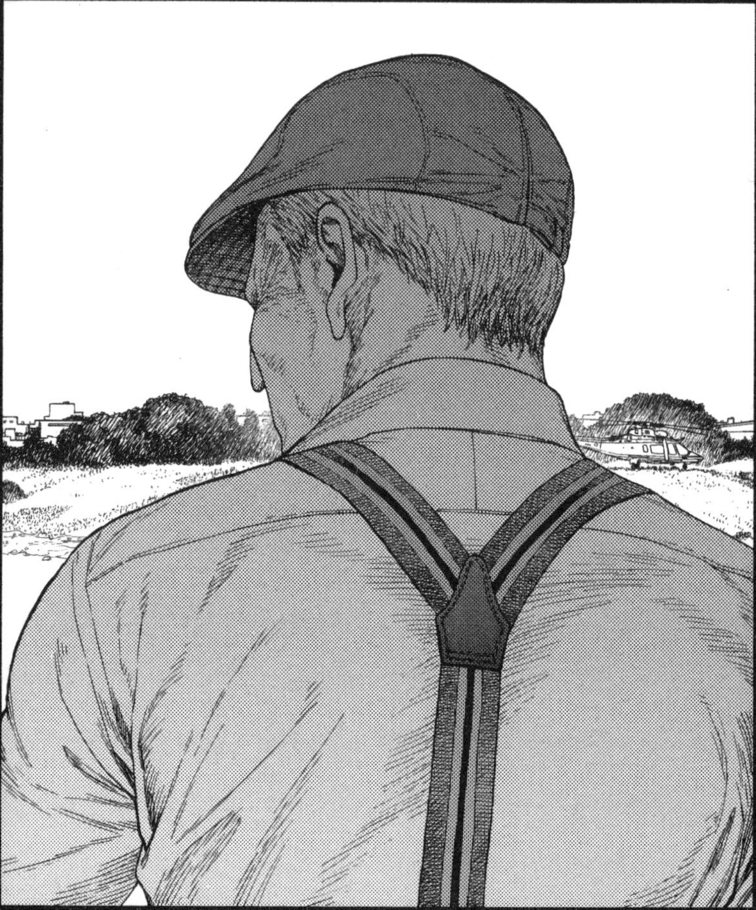
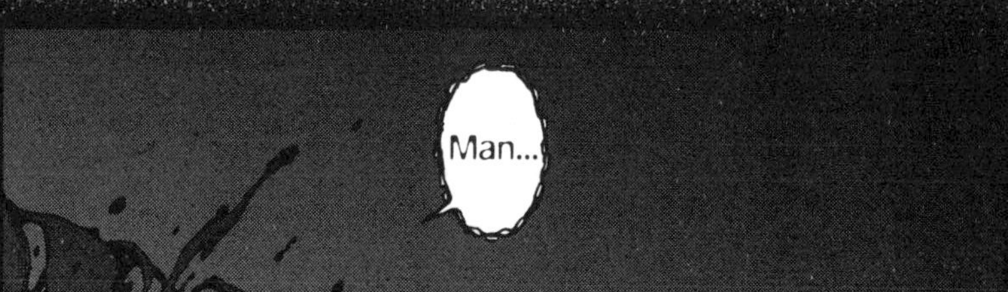
Man...

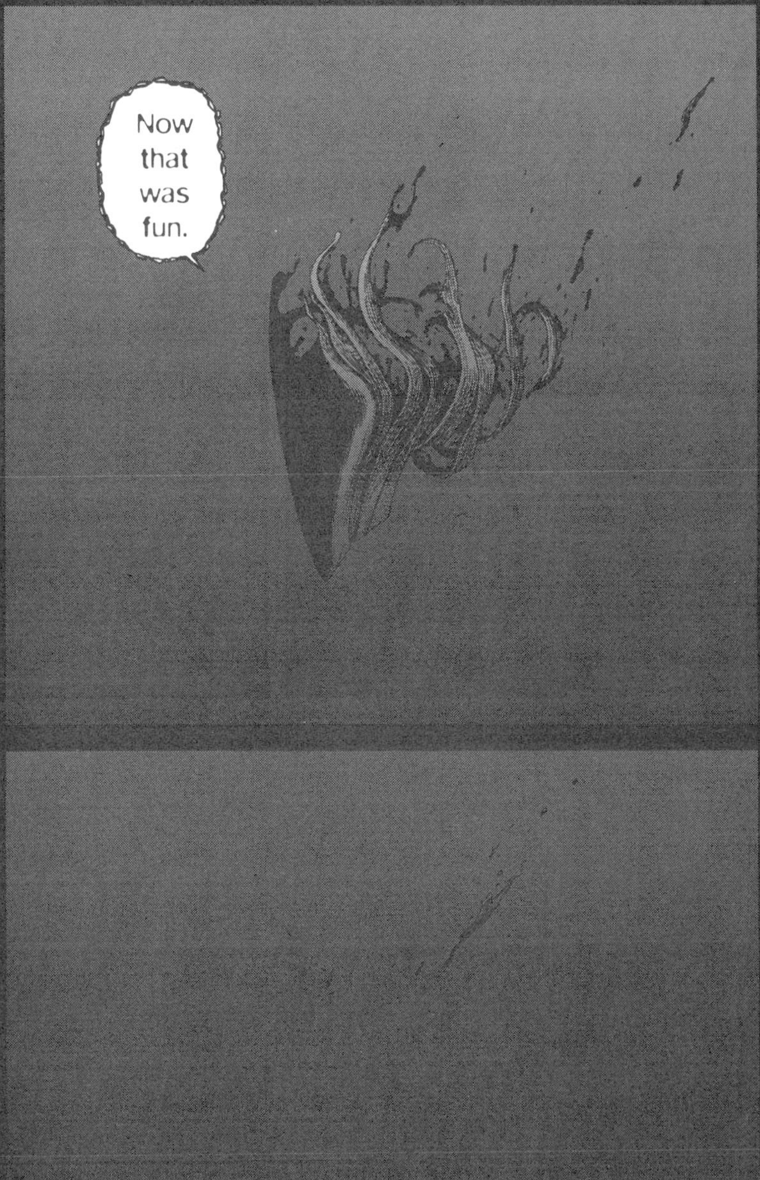
Now that was fun.

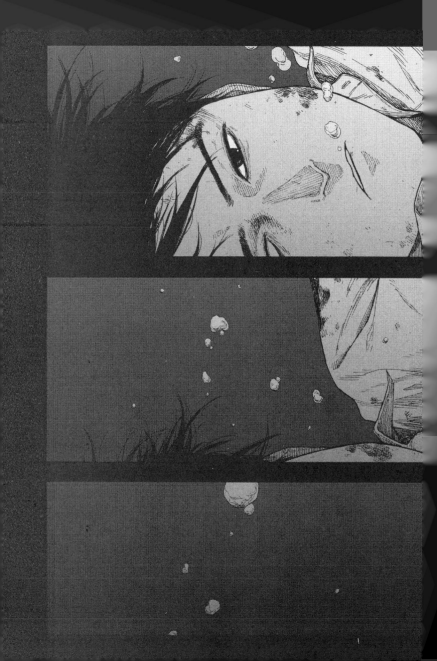

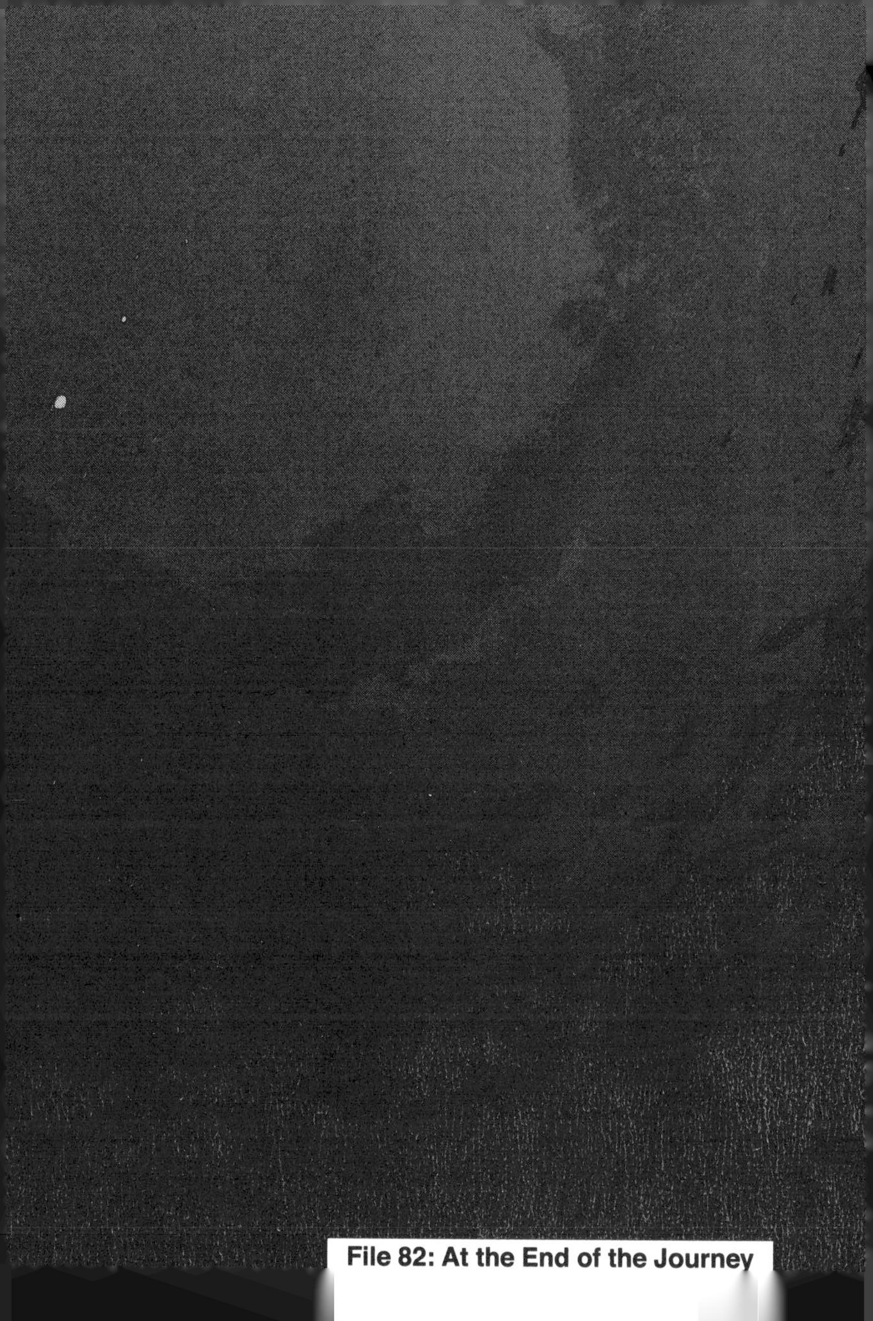

File 82: At the End of the Journey

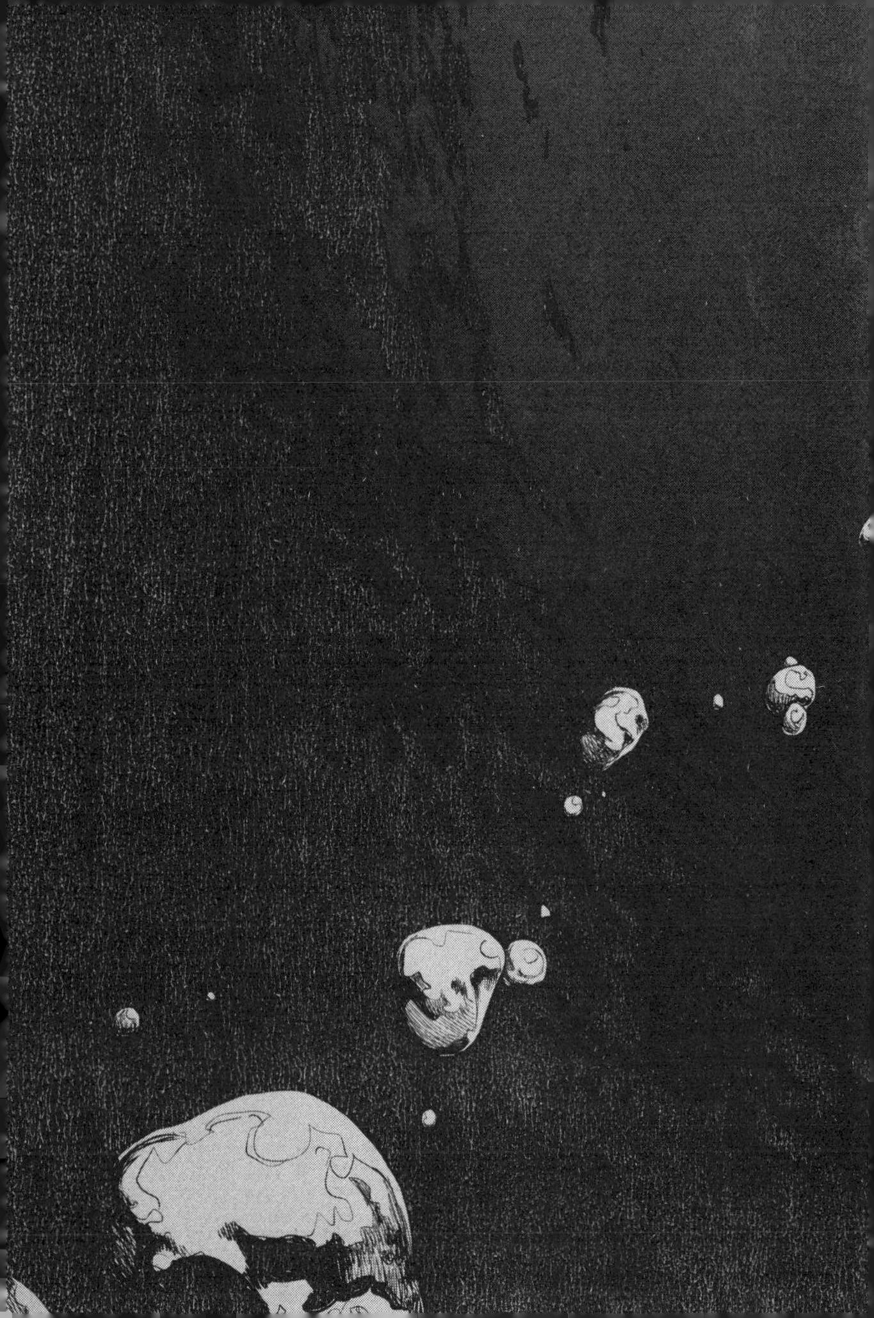

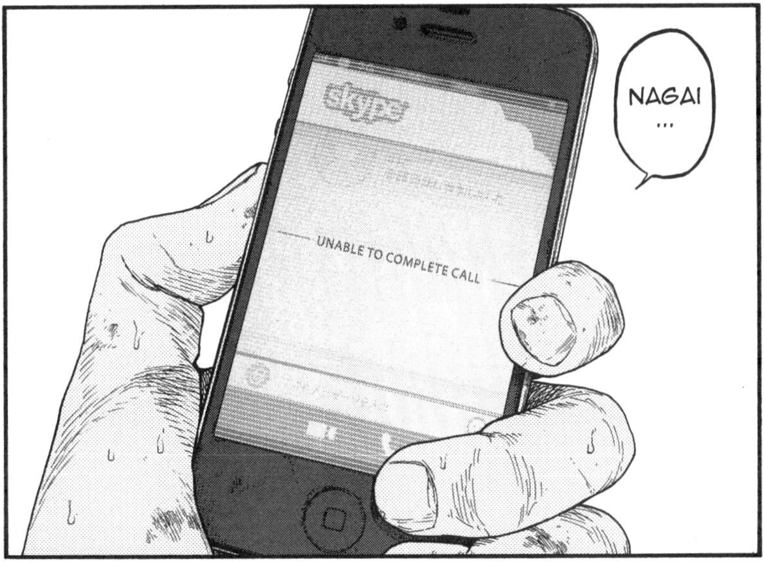
NAGAI
...
skype
UNABLE TO COMPLETE CALL

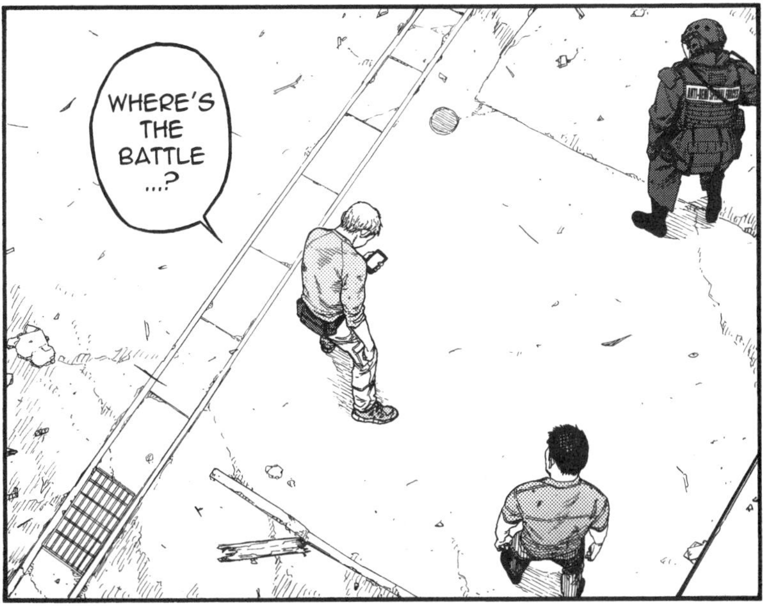
WHERE'S THE BATTLE ...?

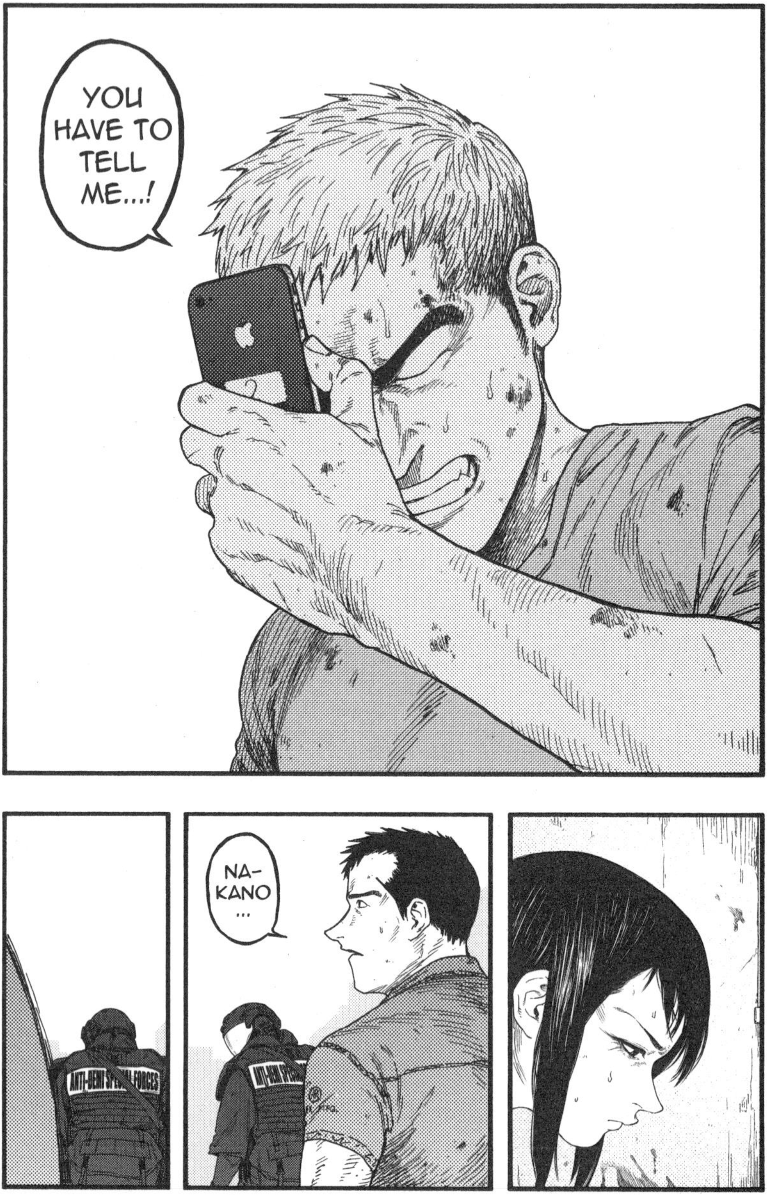
YOU HAVE TO TELL ME...!
NA-KANO ...

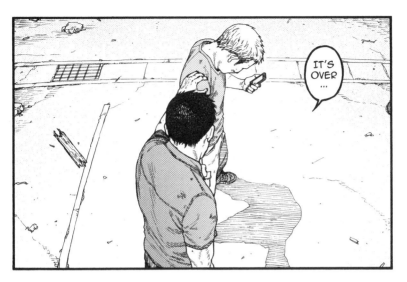

IT'S
OVER
...

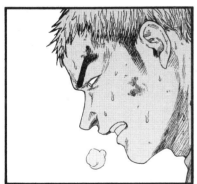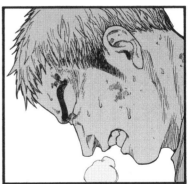

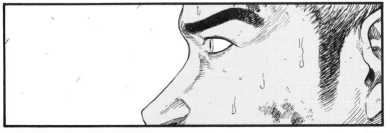

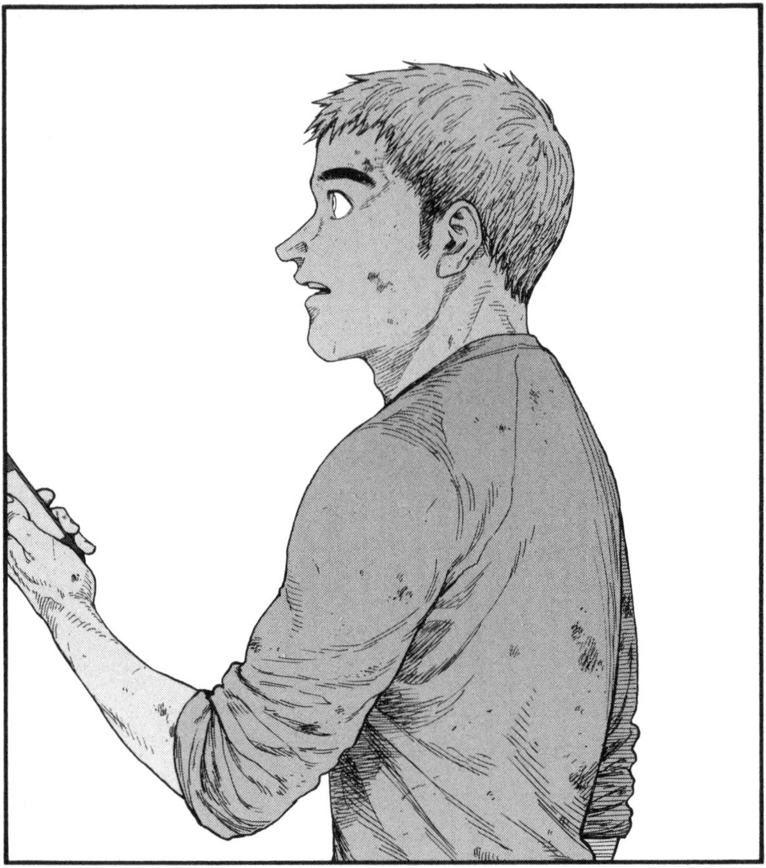

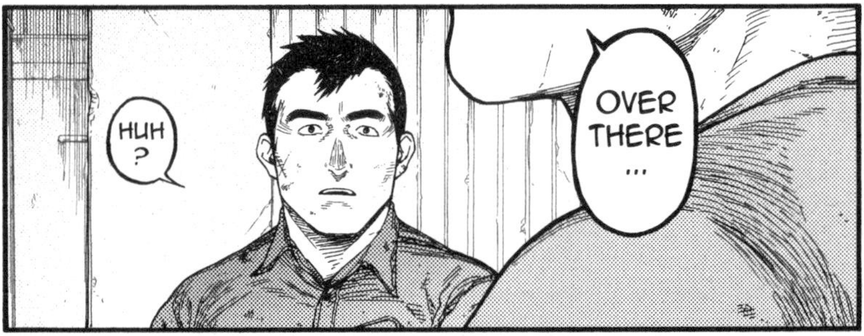
OVER THERE ...
HUH?

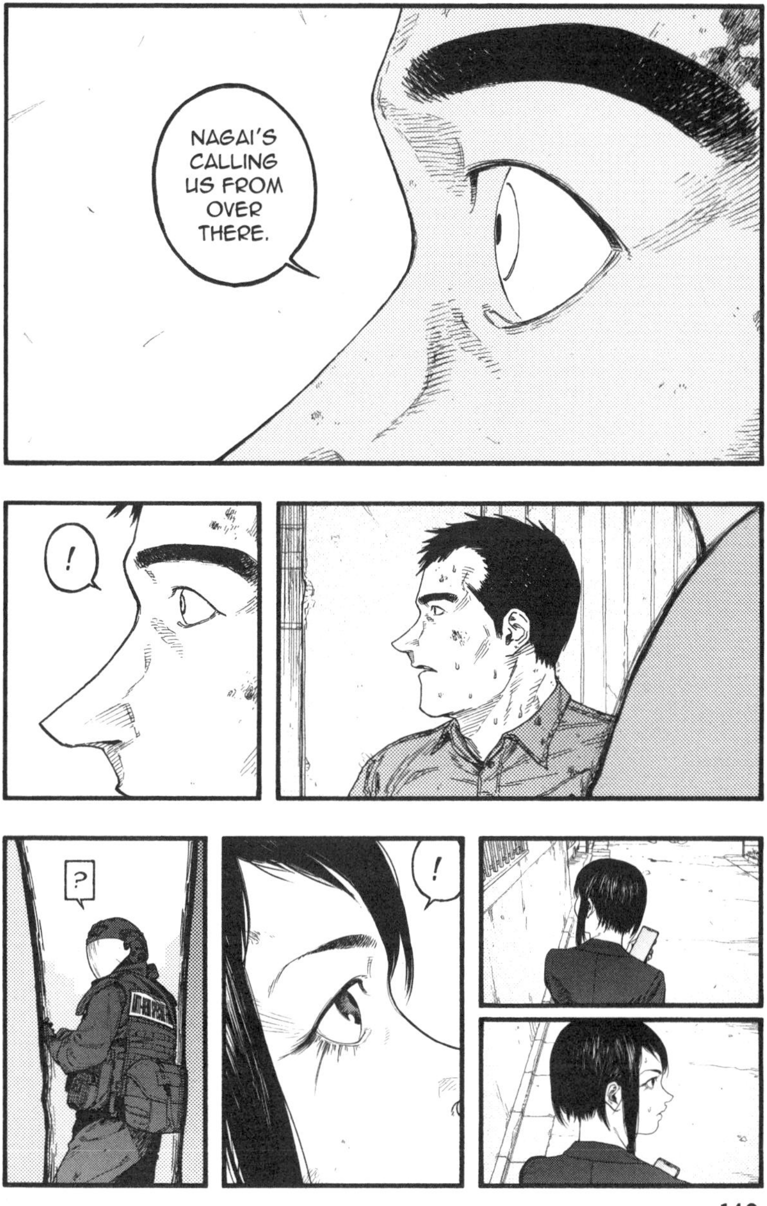
NAGAI'S CALLING US FROM OVER THERE.
!
!
?

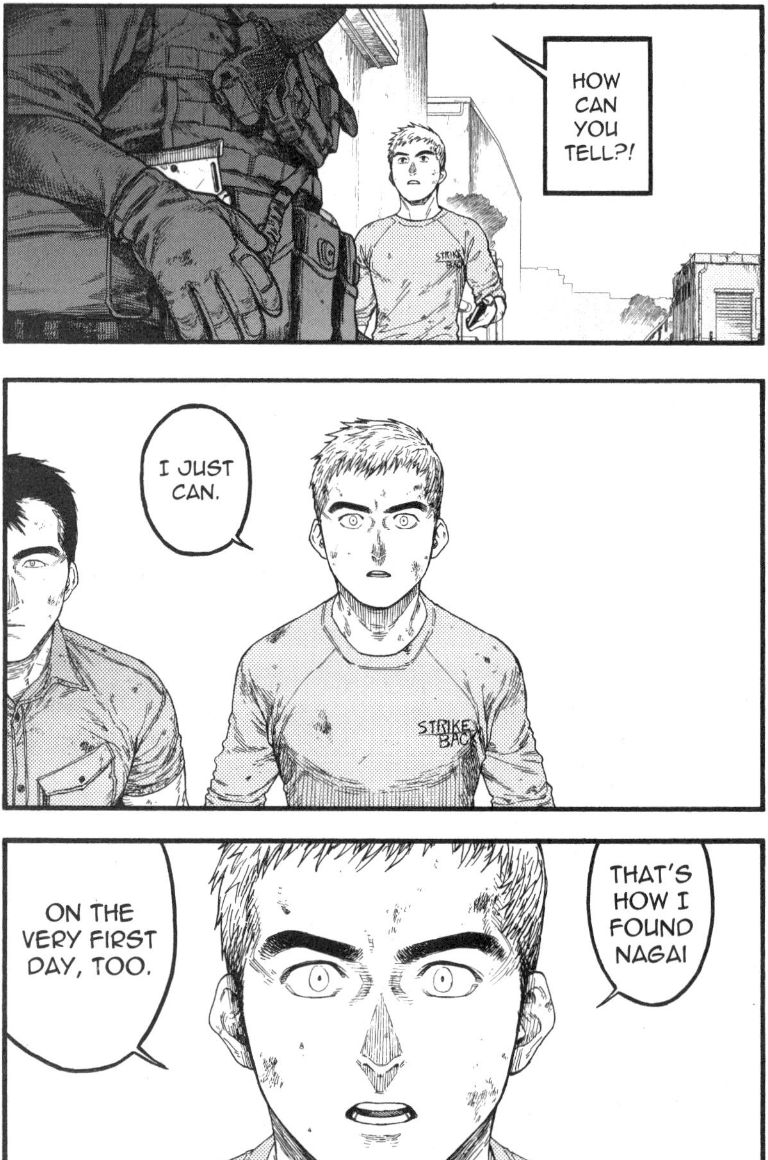
HOW CAN YOU TELL?!
STRIKE BACK
I JUST CAN.
STRIKE BACK
THAT'S HOW I FOUND NAGAI
ON THE VERY FIRST DAY, TOO.

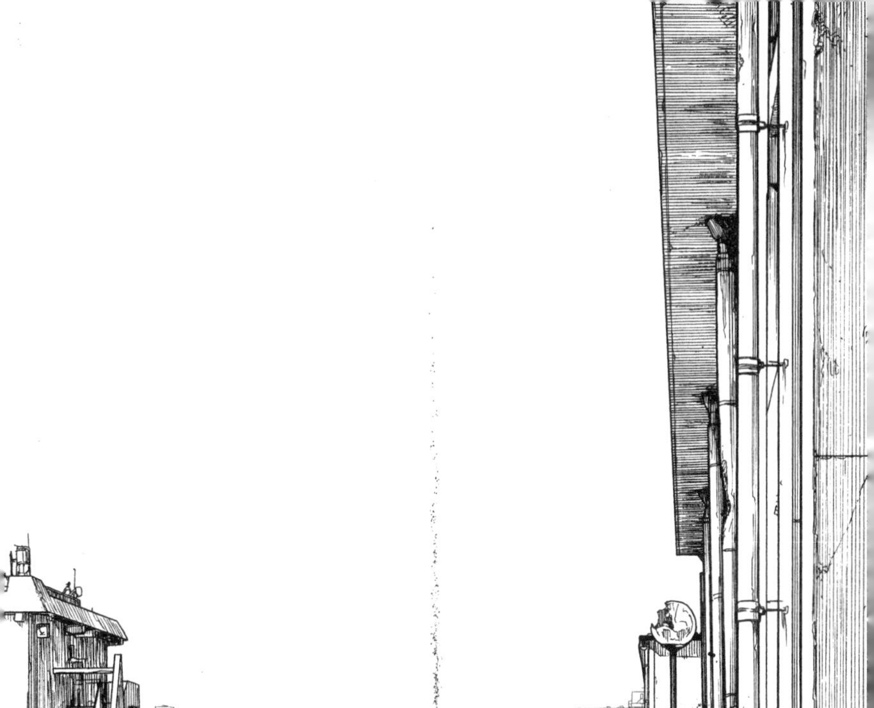

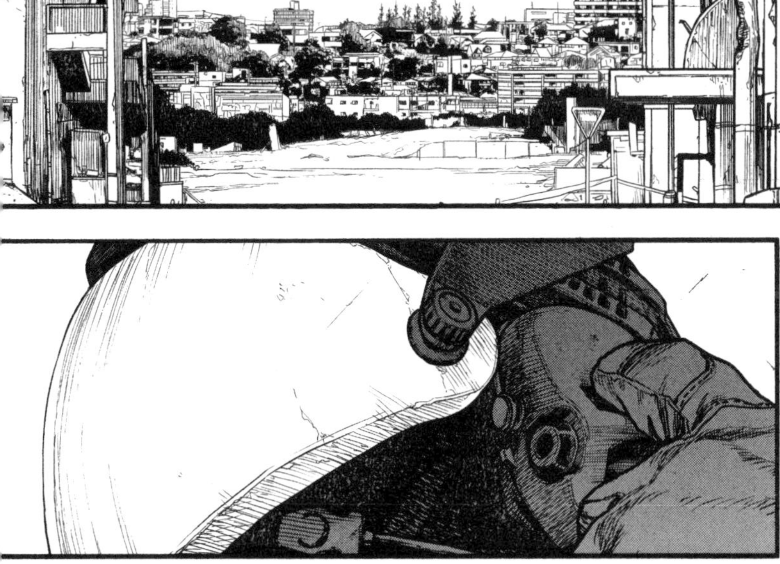

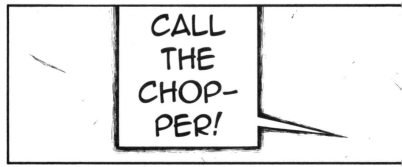

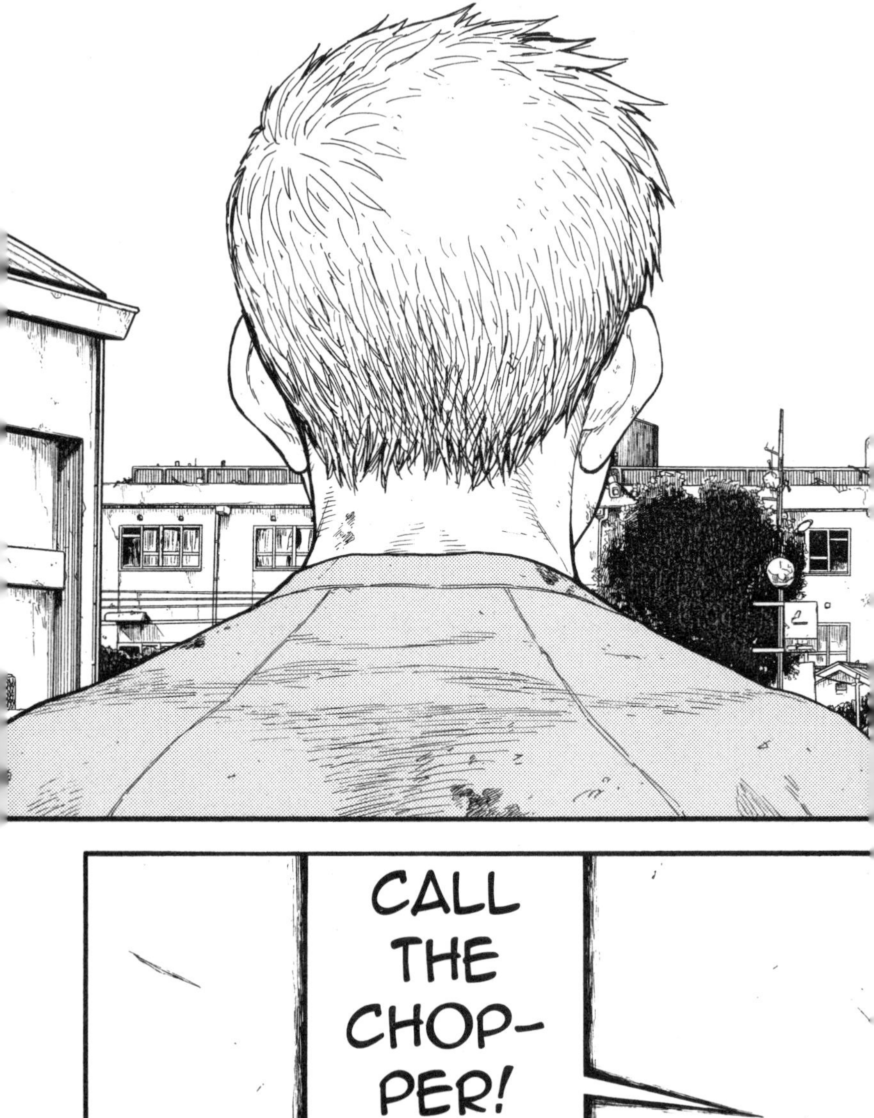
CALL THE CHOP-PER!

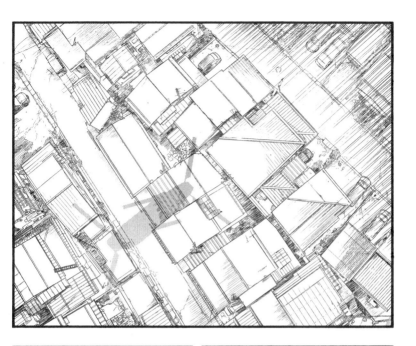

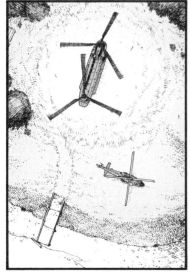

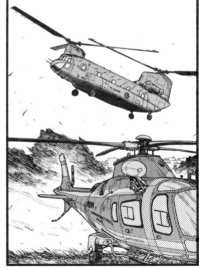

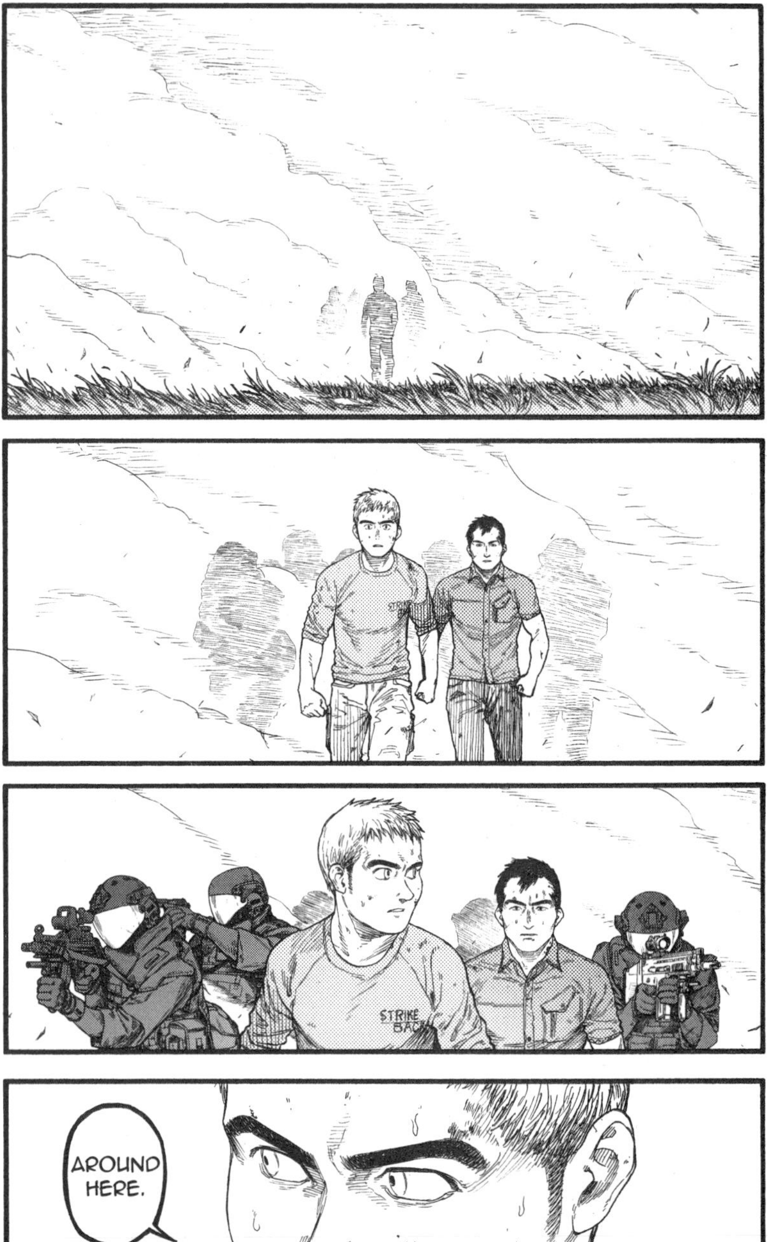
STRIKE BACK
AROUND HERE.

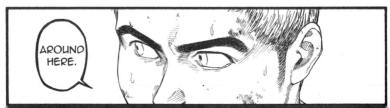

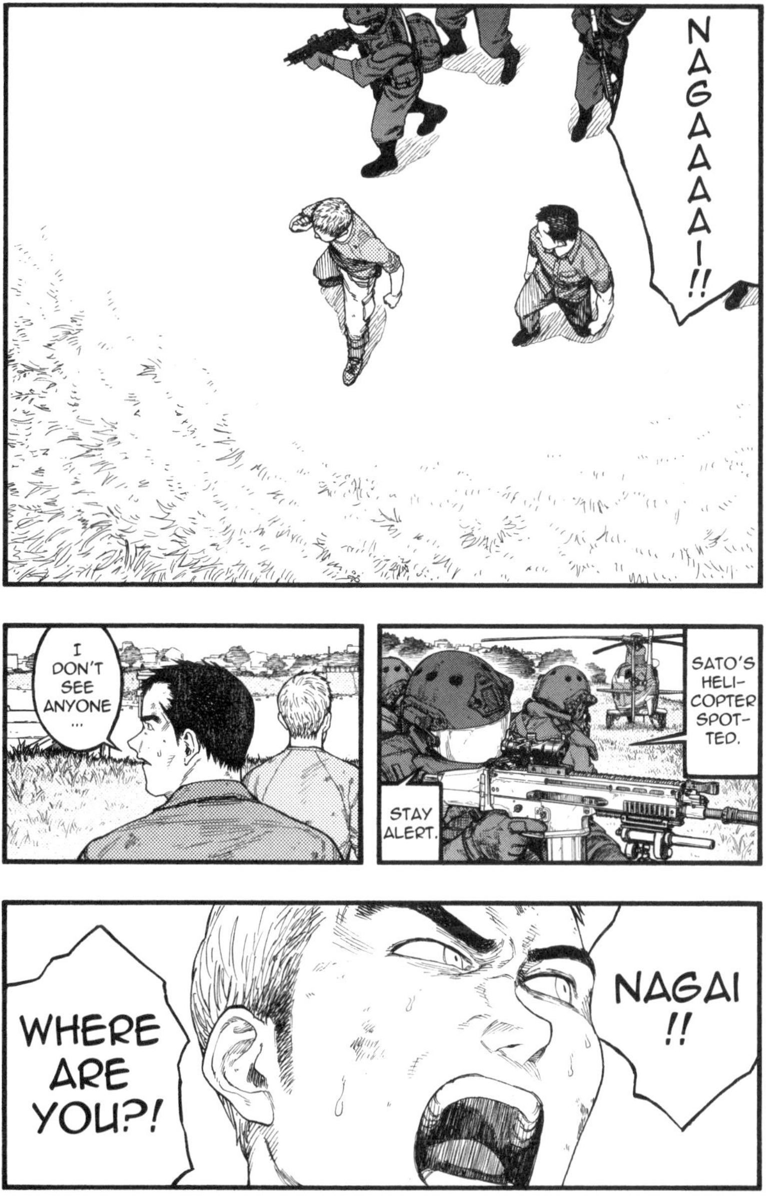
NAGAAAAAI!!
SATO'S HELI-COPTER SPOT-TED.
STAY ALERT.
I DON'T SEE ANYONE...
NAGAI!!
WHERE ARE YOU?!

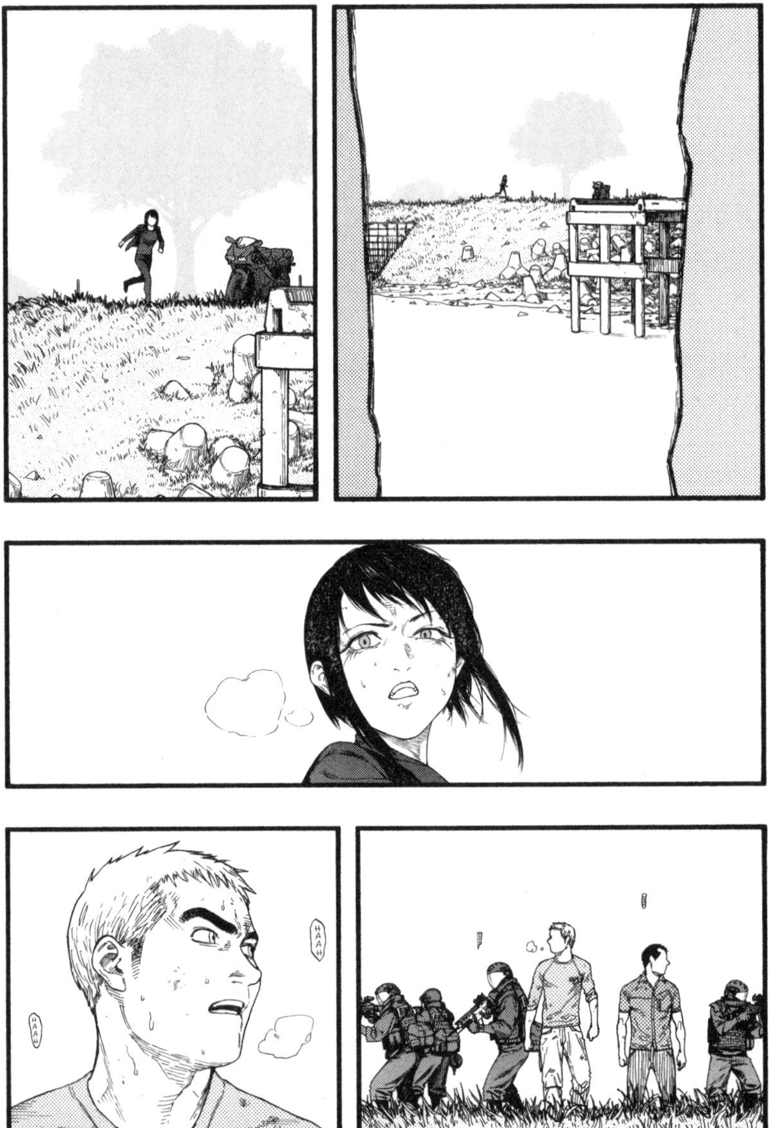
!
!
HAAH
HAAH

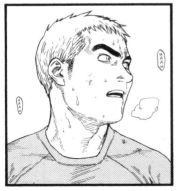

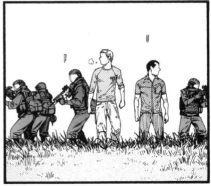

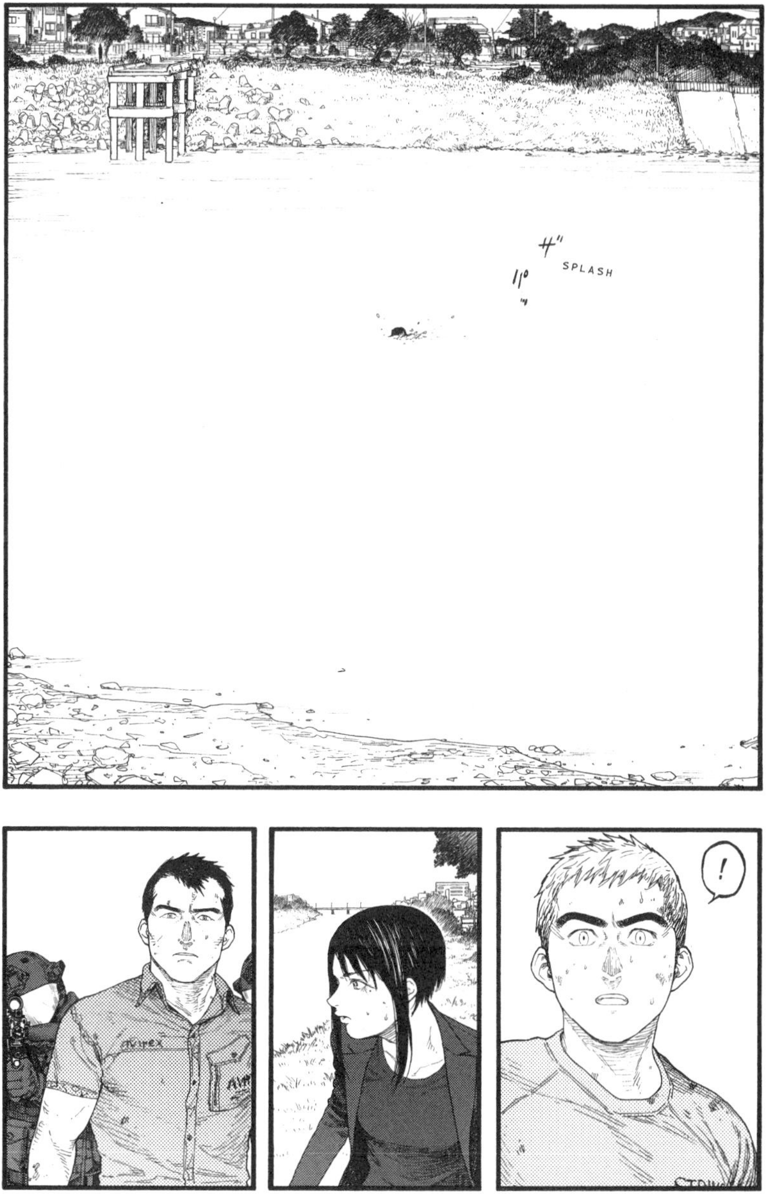
SPLASH
!

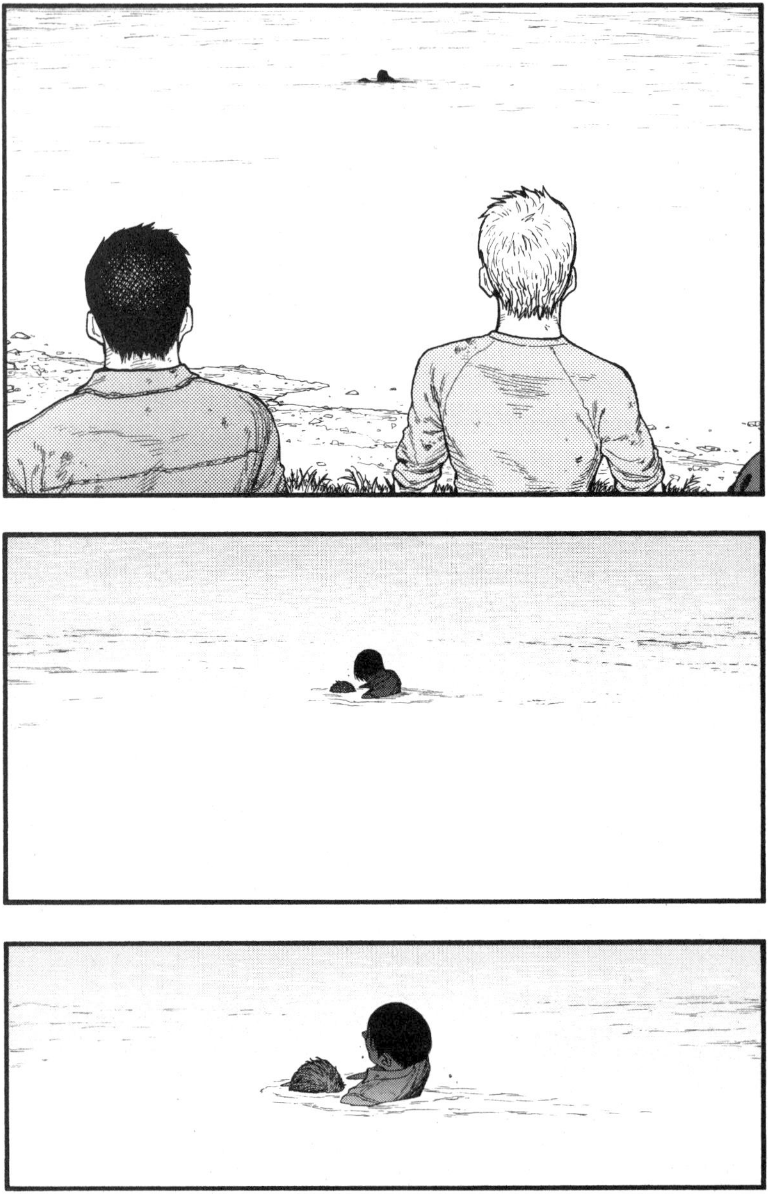

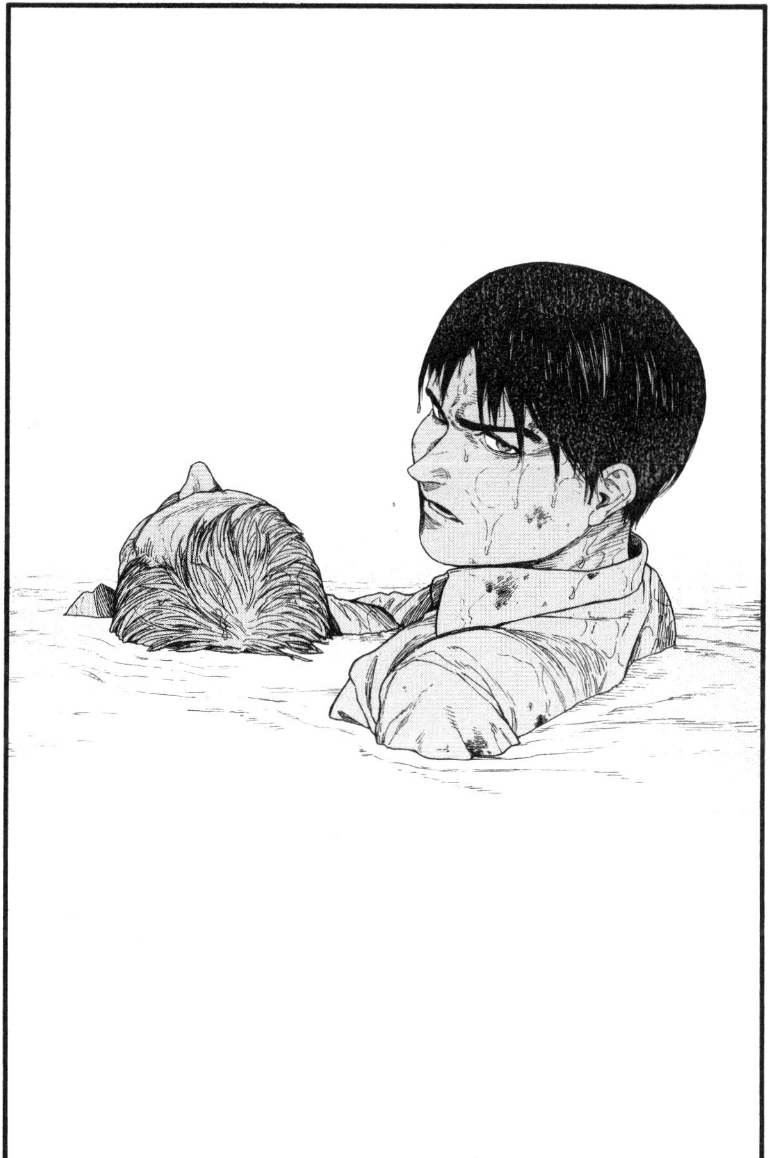

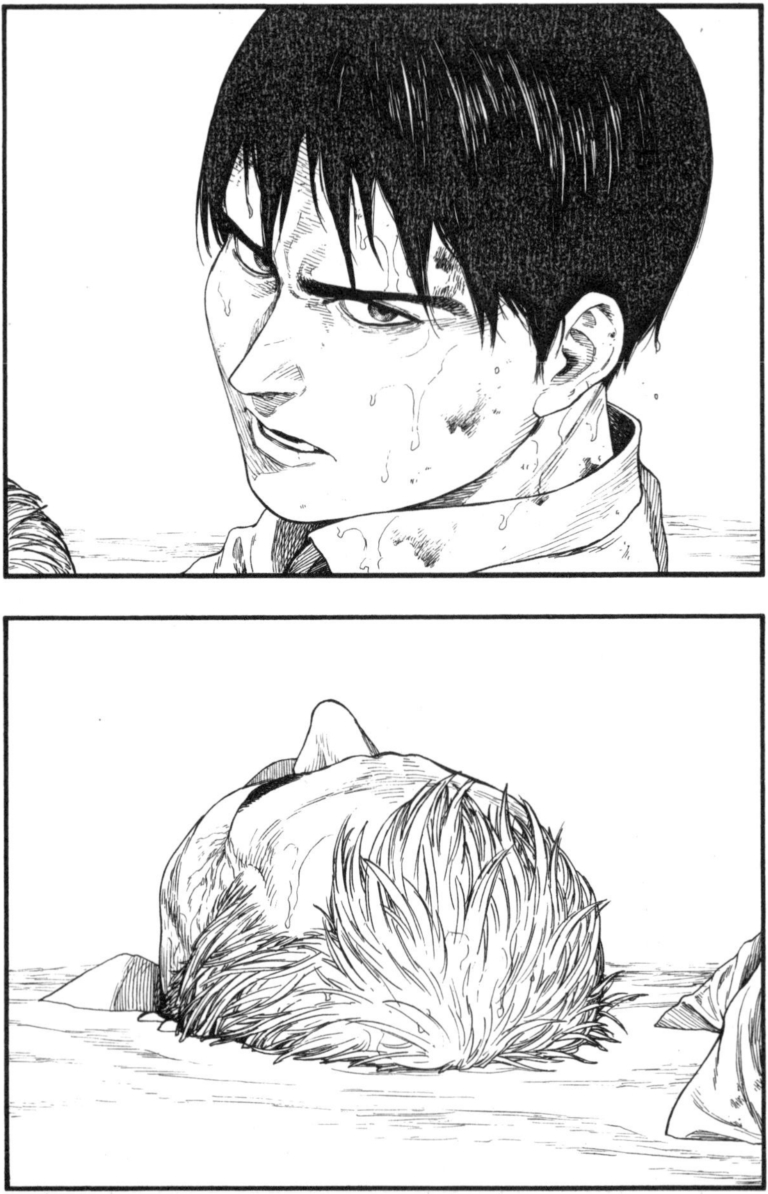

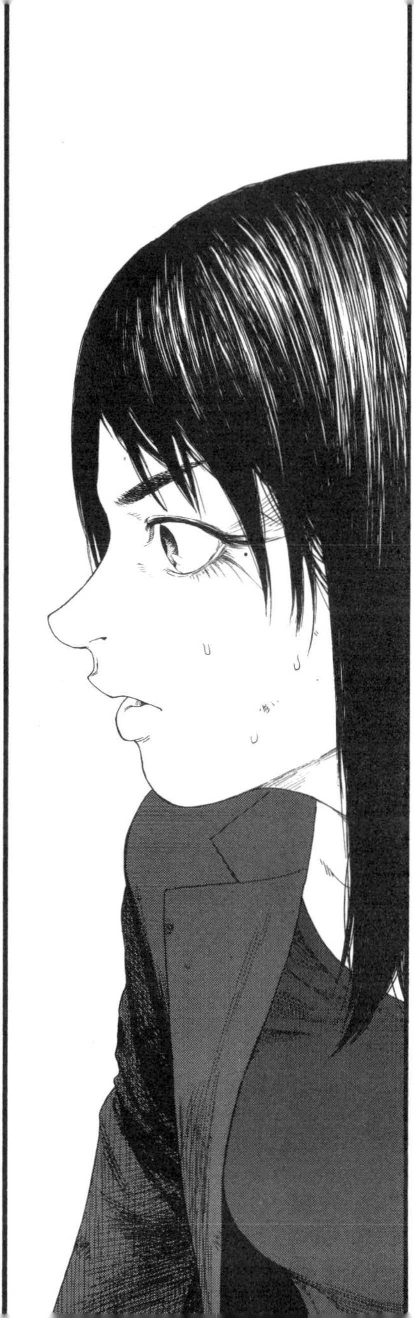

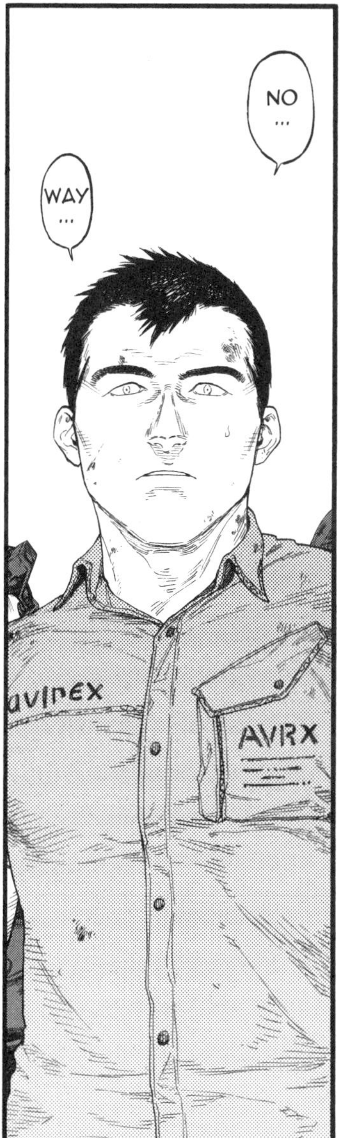
NO
...
WAY
...
avirex
AVRX

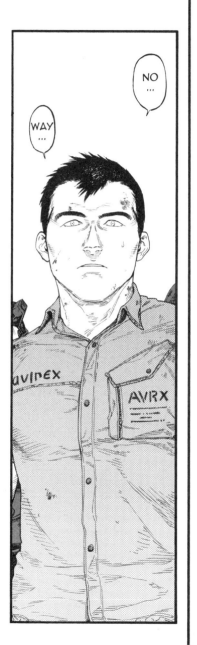

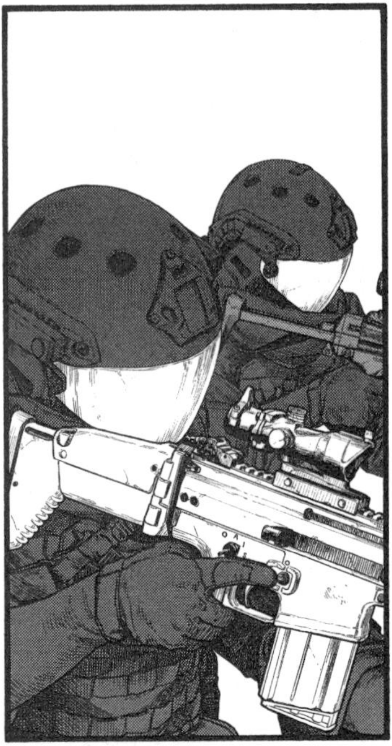

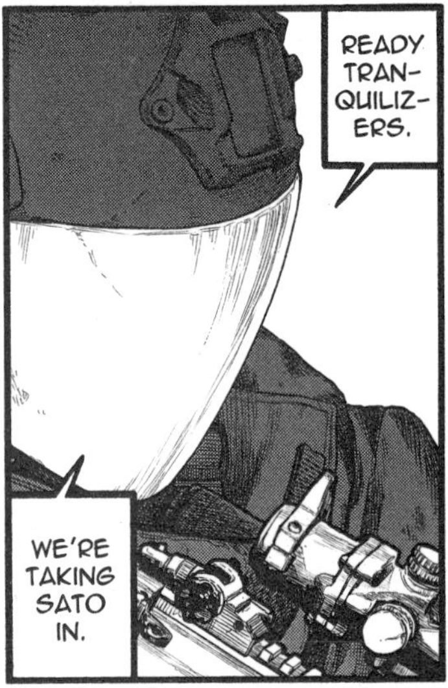
READY TRAN-QUILIZ-ERS.
WE'RE TAKING SATO IN.

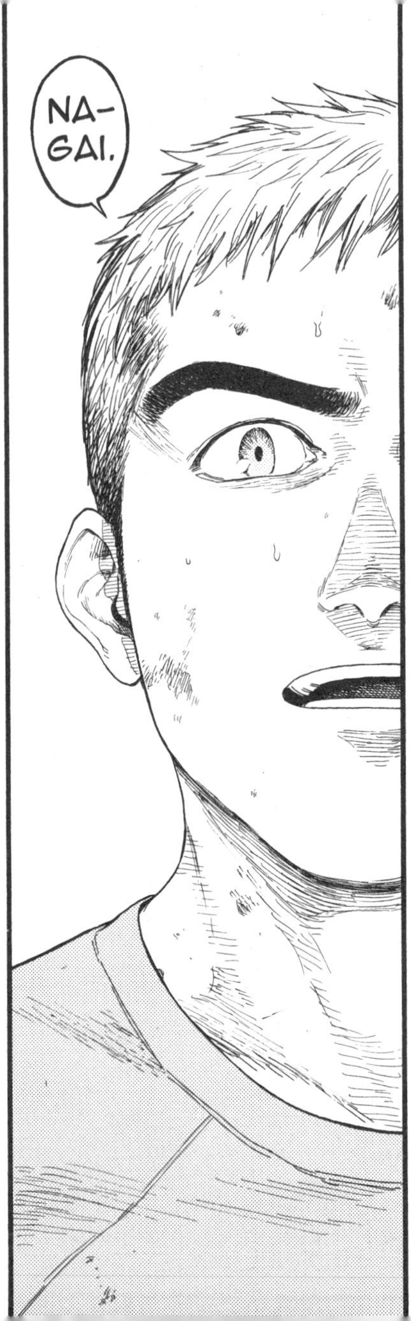
NA-GAI.

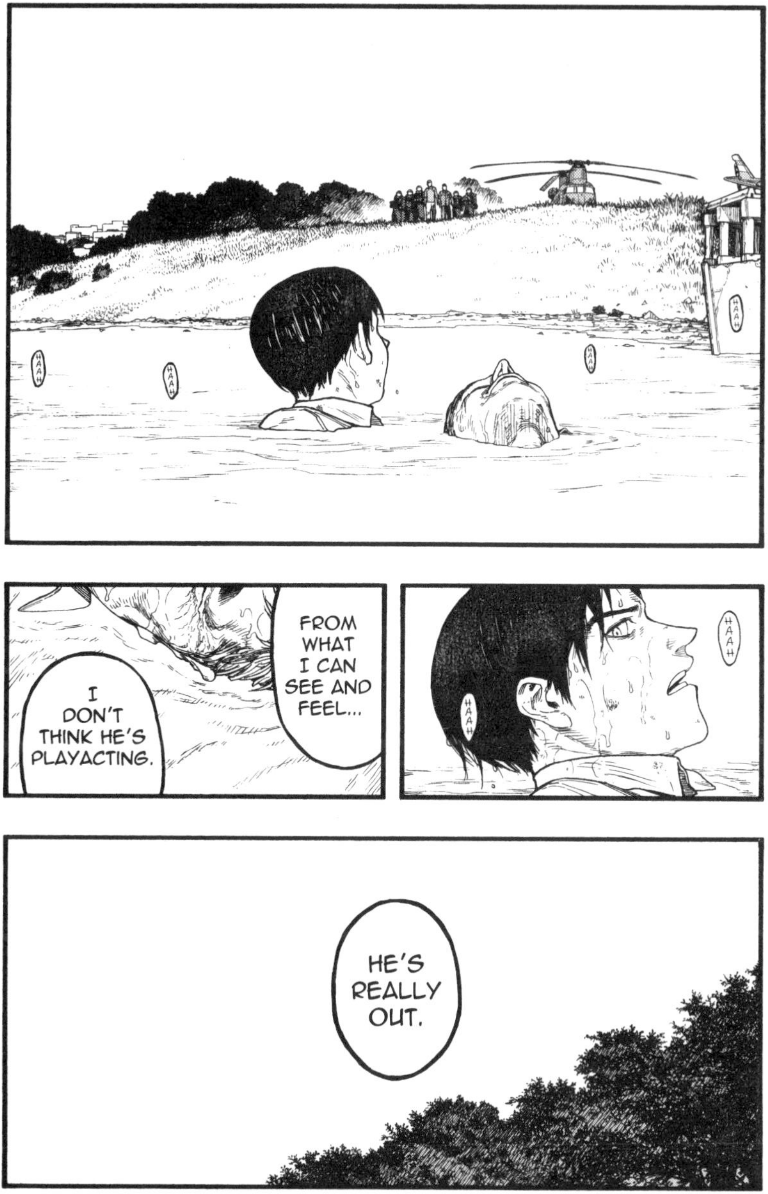
HAAH
HAAH
HAAH
HAAH
HAAH
HAAH
FROM WHAT I CAN SEE AND FEEL...
I DON'T THINK HE'S PLAYACTING.
HE'S REALLY OUT.

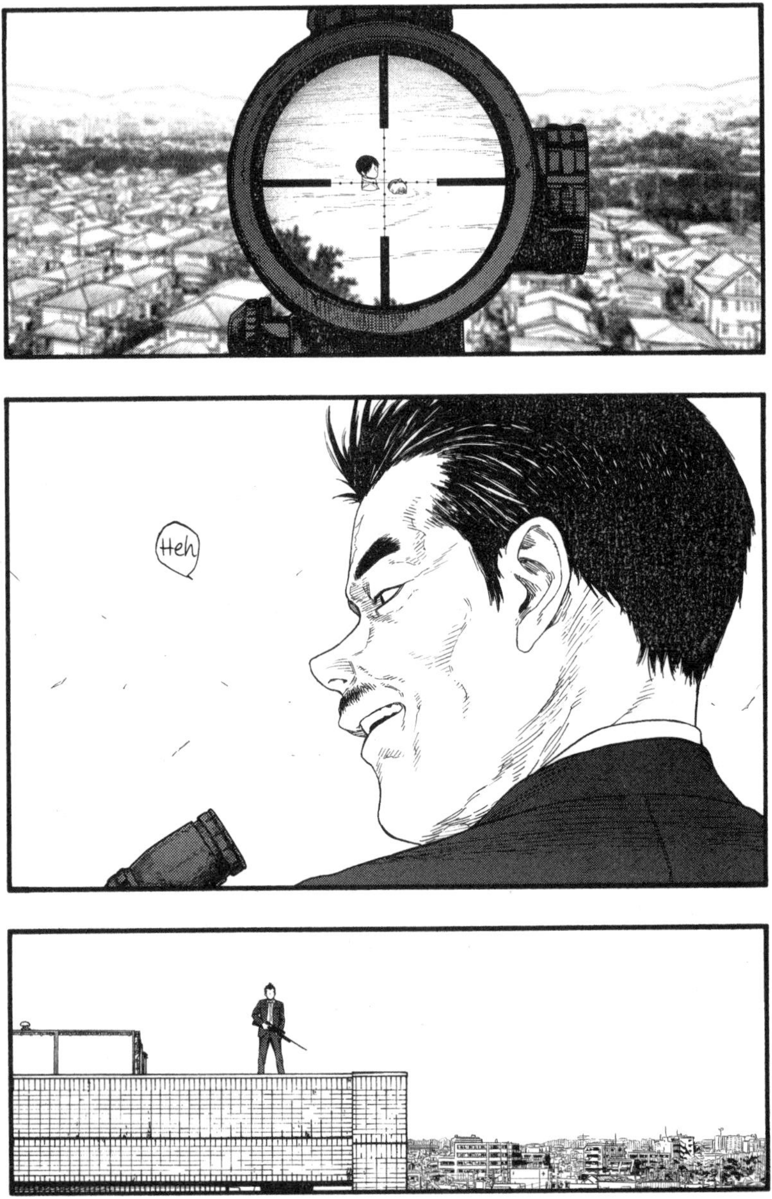
Heh

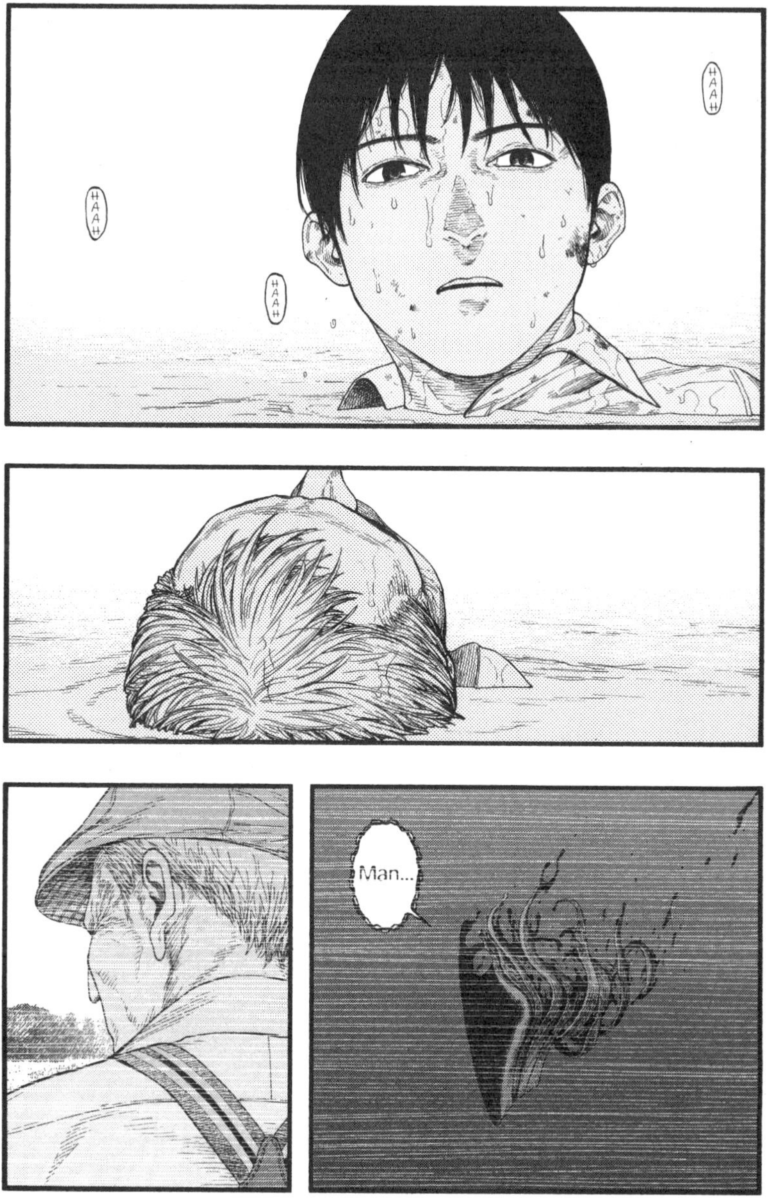
HAAH
HAAH
HAAH
Man...

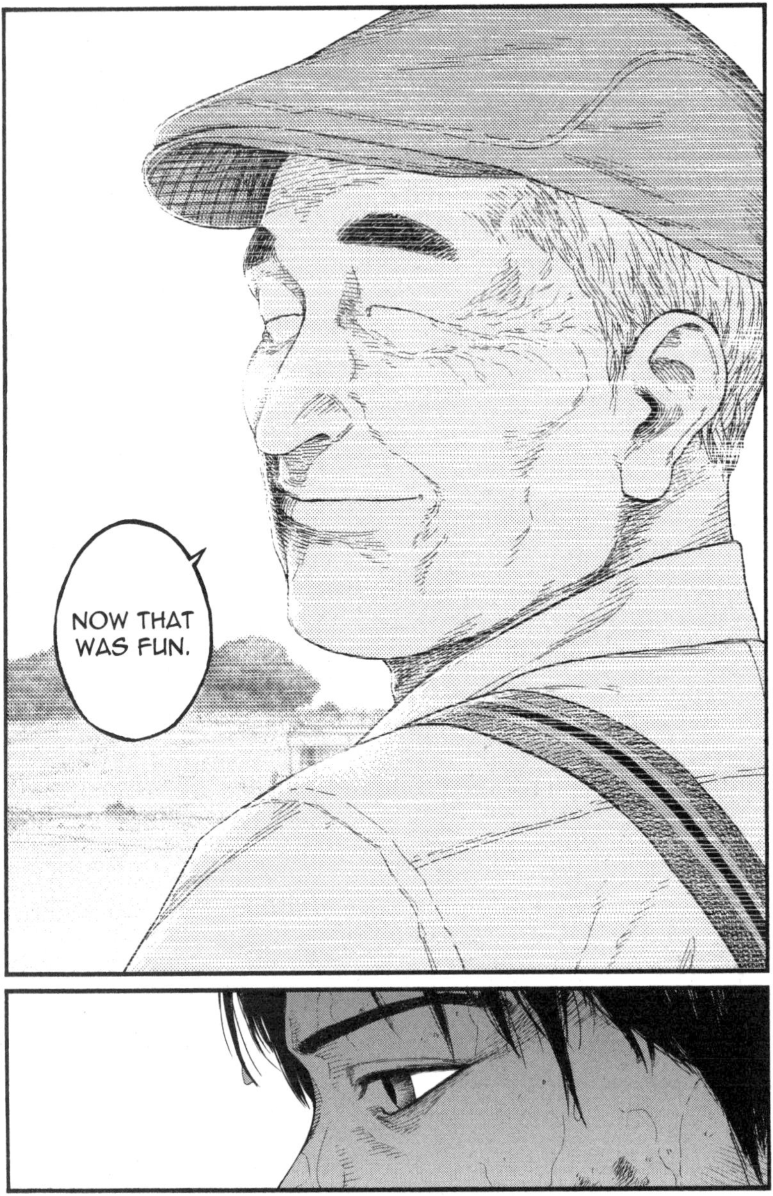
NOW THAT WAS FUN.

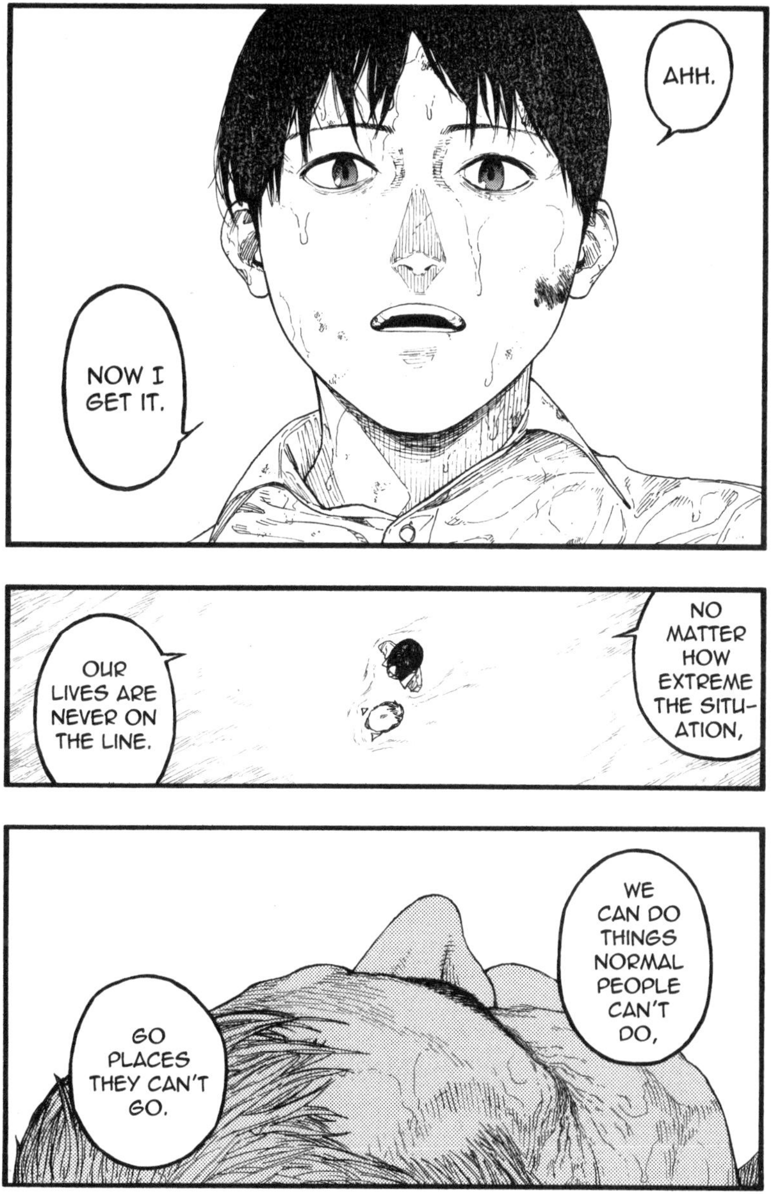
AHH.
NOW I GET IT.
NO MATTER HOW EXTREME THE SITU-ATION,
OUR LIVES ARE NEVER ON THE LINE.
WE CAN DO THINGS NORMAL PEOPLE CAN'T DO,
GO PLACES THEY CAN'T GO.

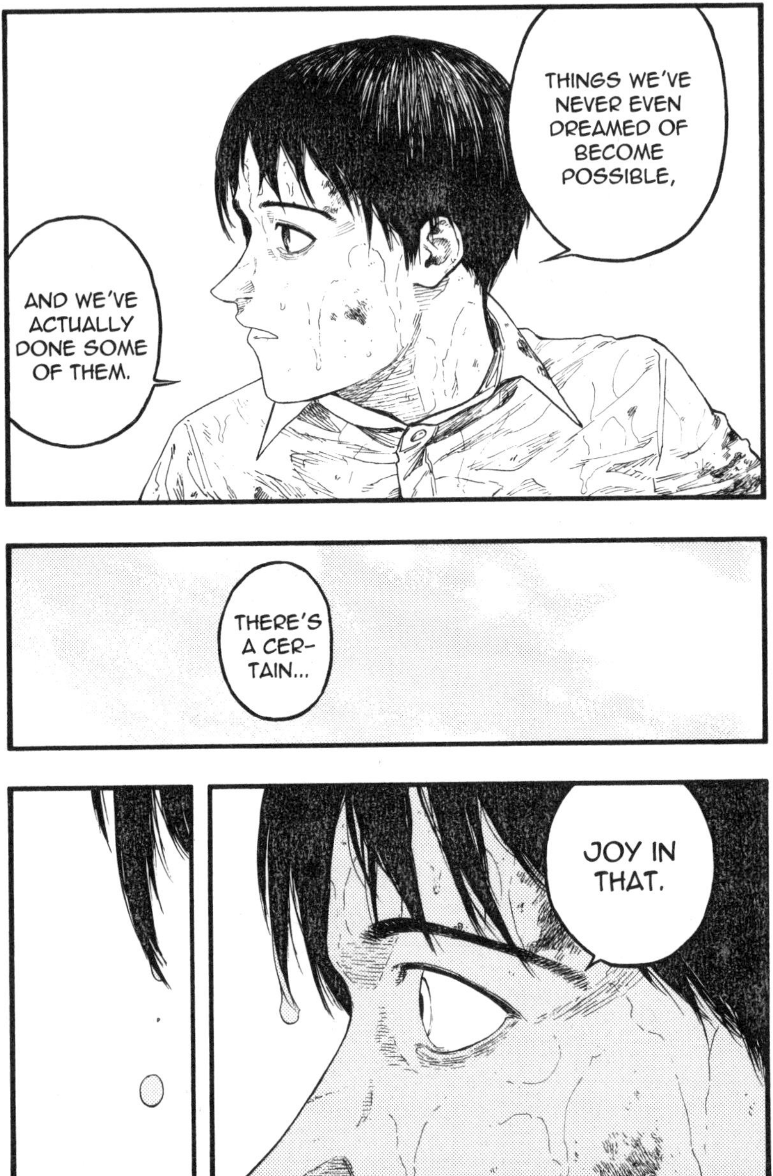
THINGS WE'VE NEVER EVEN DREAMED OF BECOME POSSIBLE,
AND WE'VE ACTUALLY DONE SOME OF THEM.
THERE'S A CER-TAIN...
JOY IN THAT.

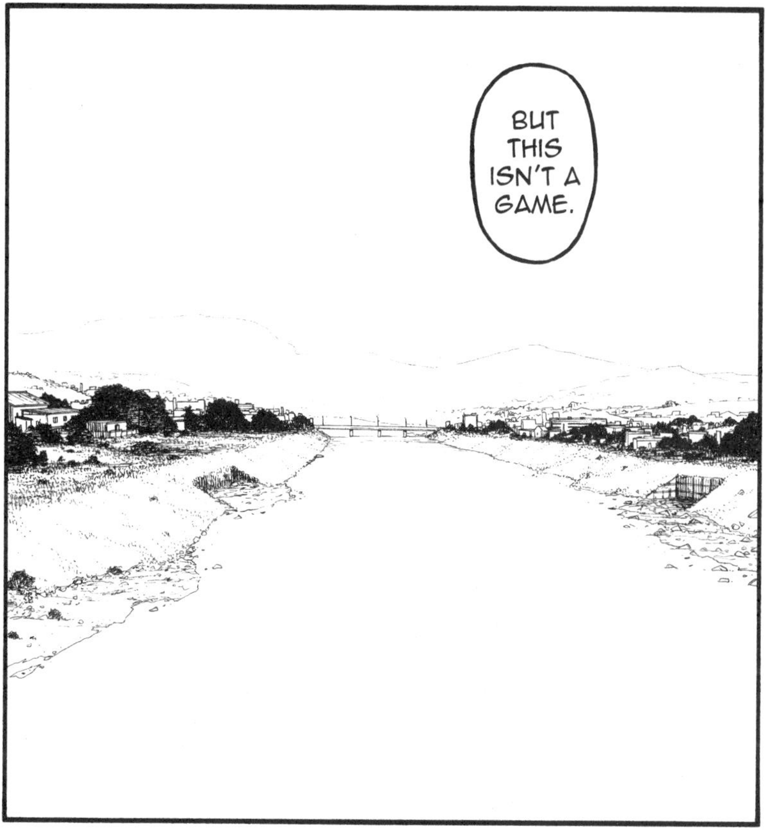
BUT THIS ISN'T A GAME.

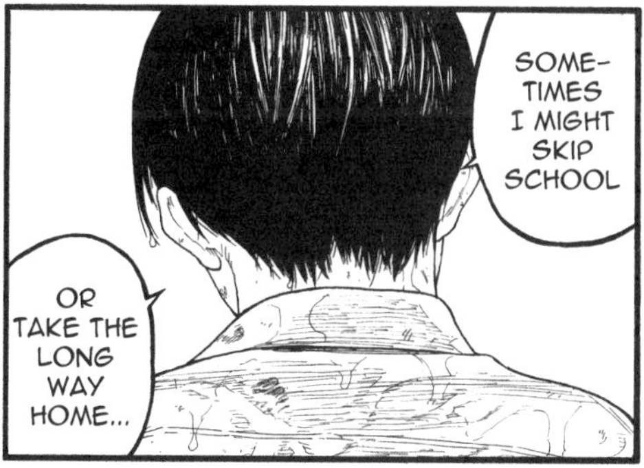
SOME-TIMES I MIGHT SKIP SCHOOL
OR TAKE THE LONG WAY HOME...

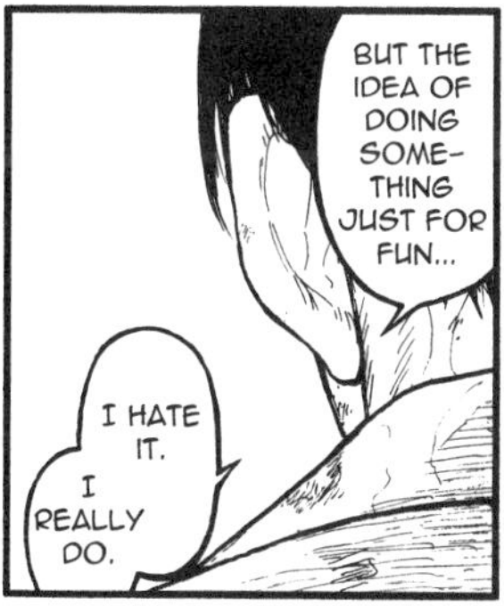
BUT THE IDEA OF DOING SOME-THING JUST FOR FUN...
I HATE IT. I REALLY DO.

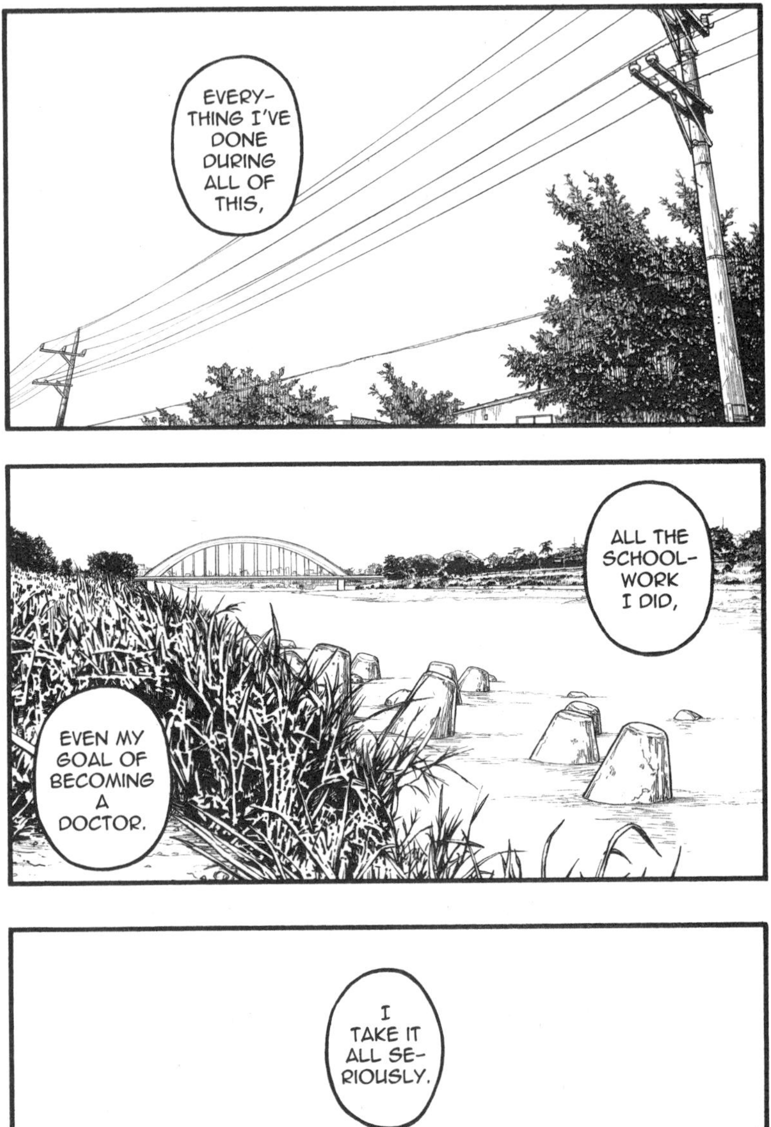
EVERY-THING I'VE DONE DURING ALL OF THIS,
ALL THE SCHOOL-WORK I DID,
EVEN MY GOAL OF BECOMING A DOCTOR.
I TAKE IT ALL SE-RIOUSLY.

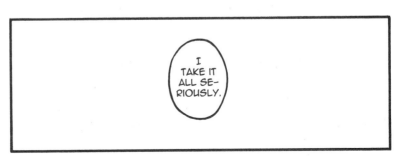

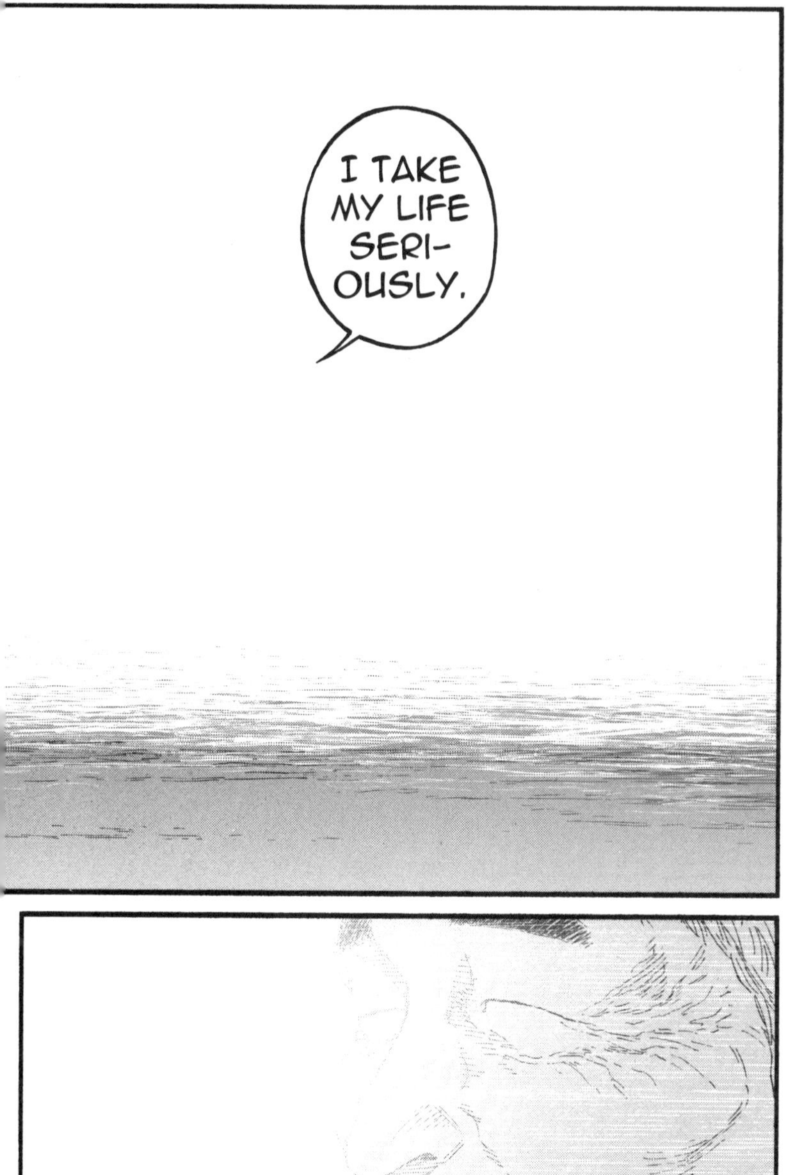
I TAKE MY LIFE SERI-OUSLY.

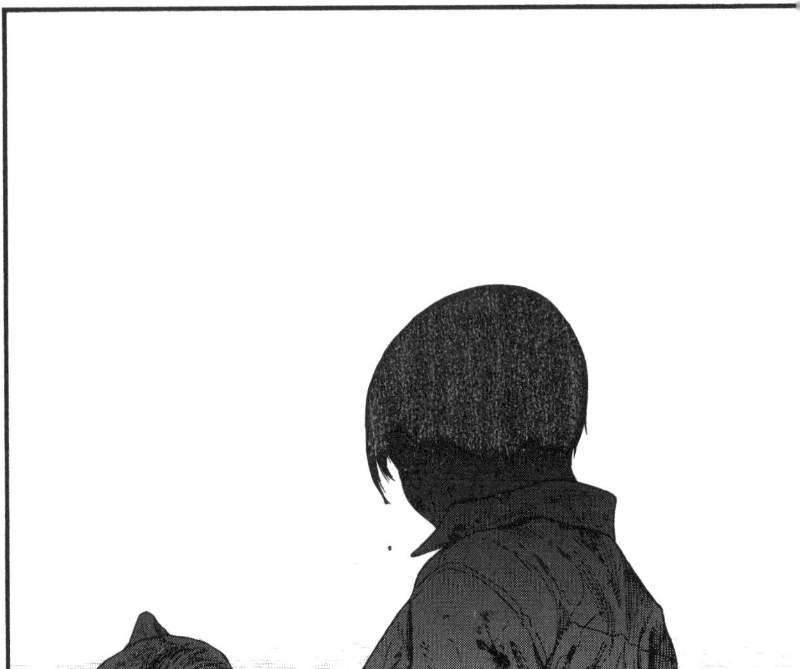
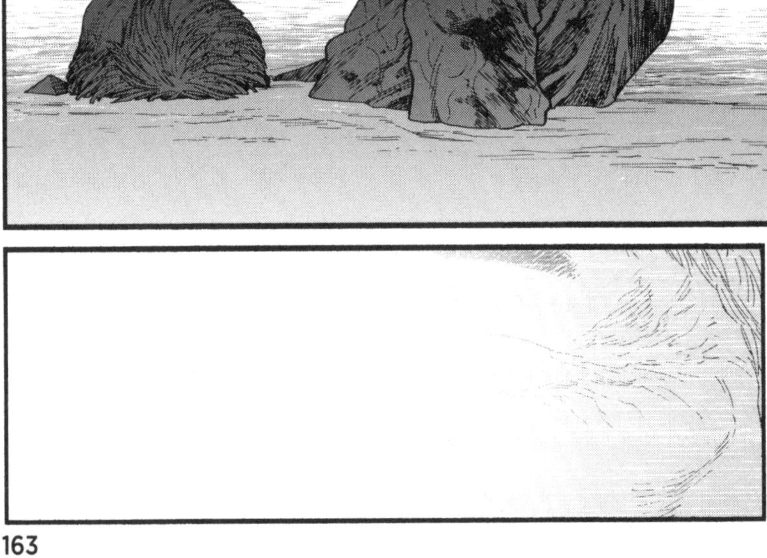

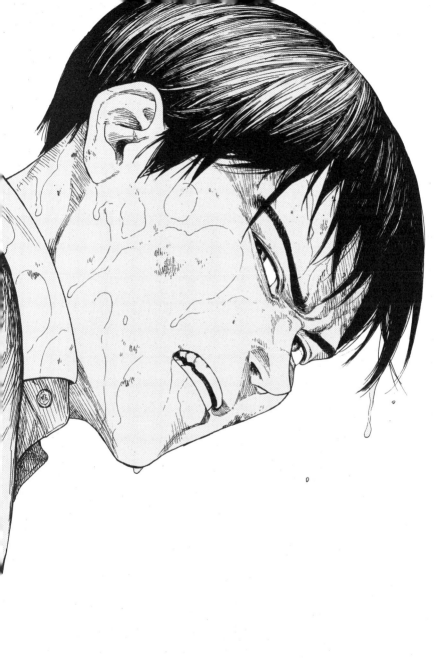

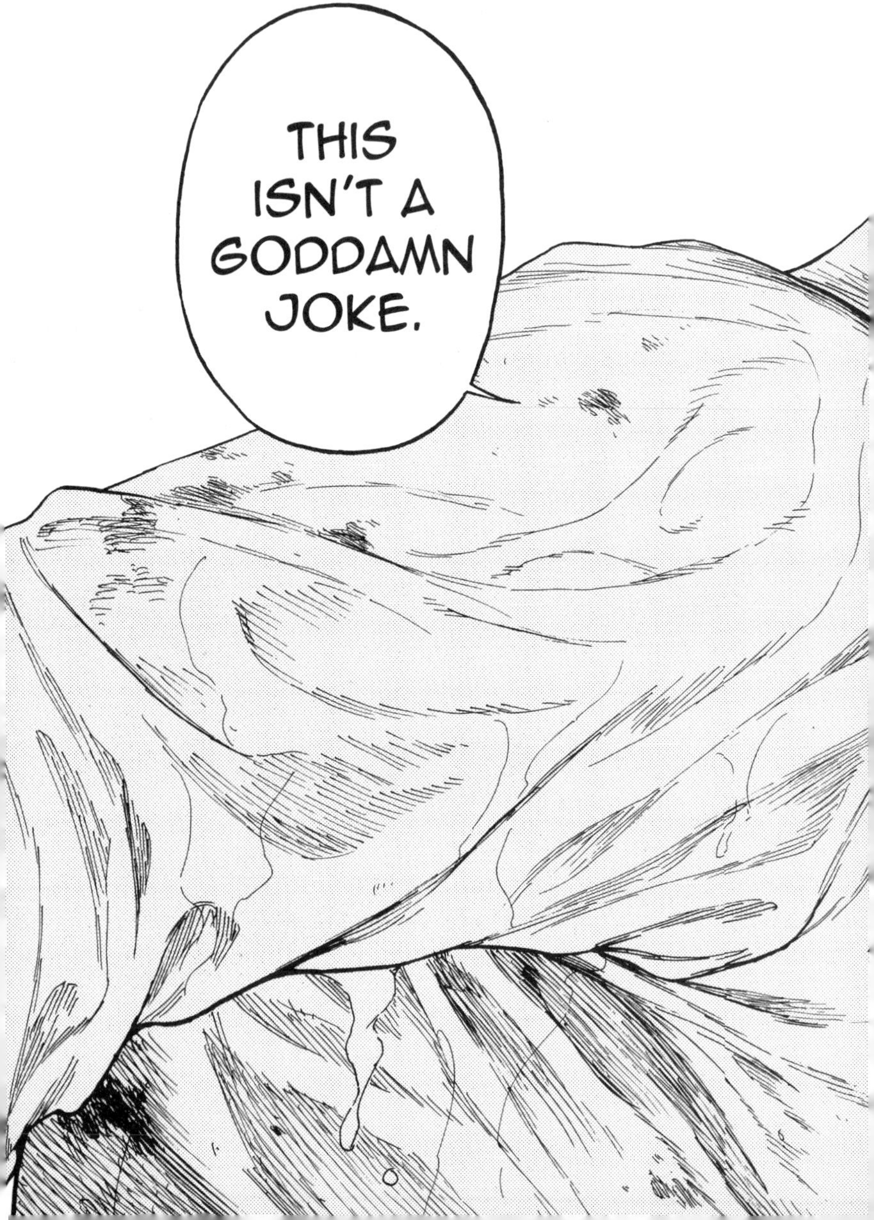
THIS ISN'T A GODDAMN JOKE.

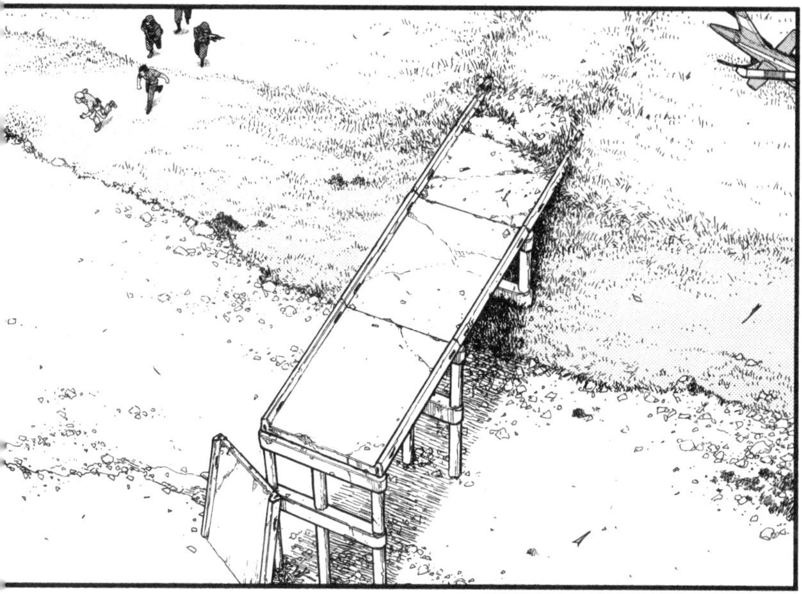
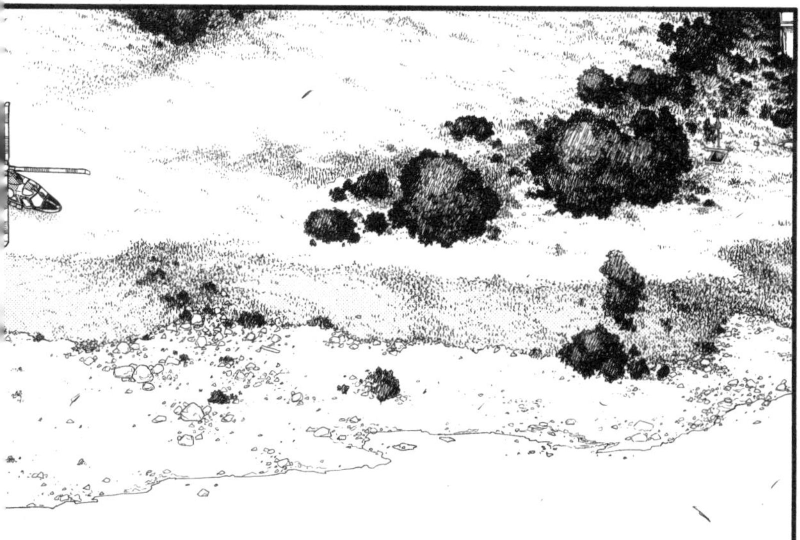

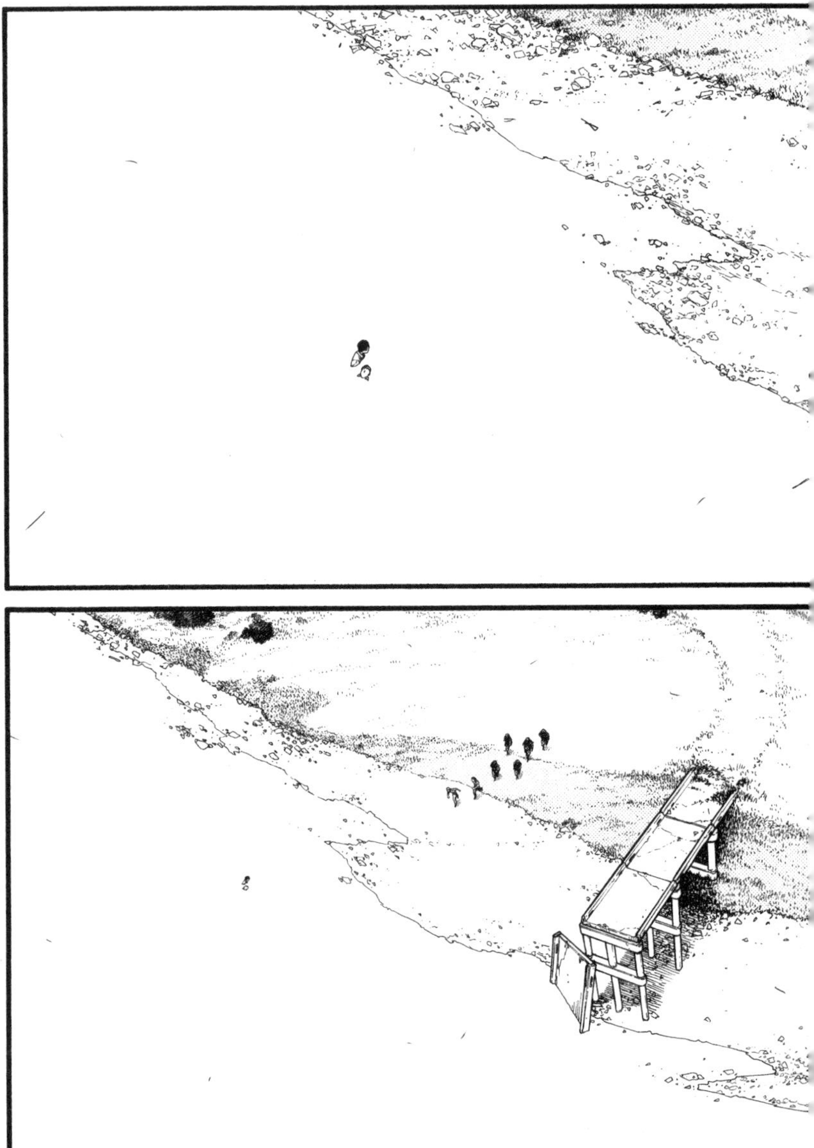

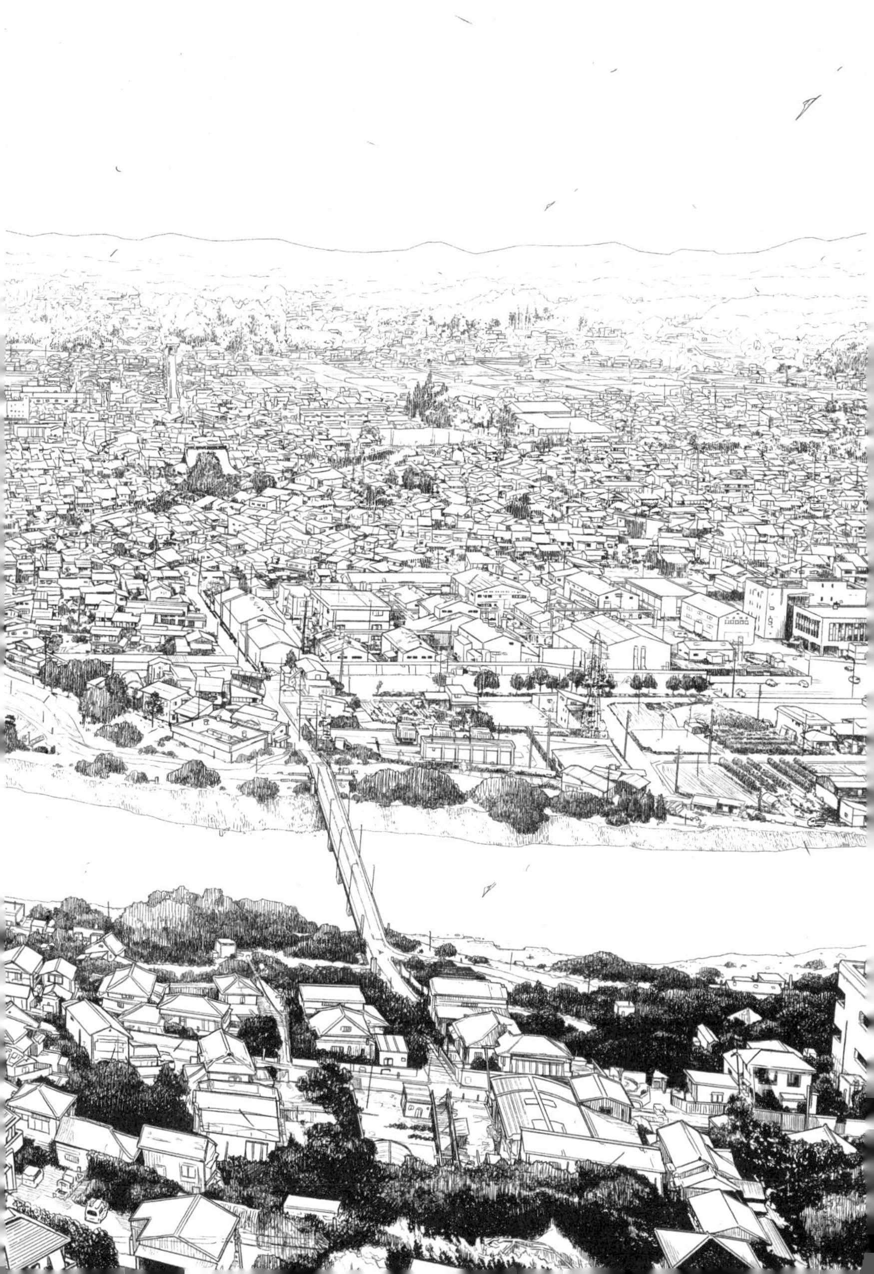

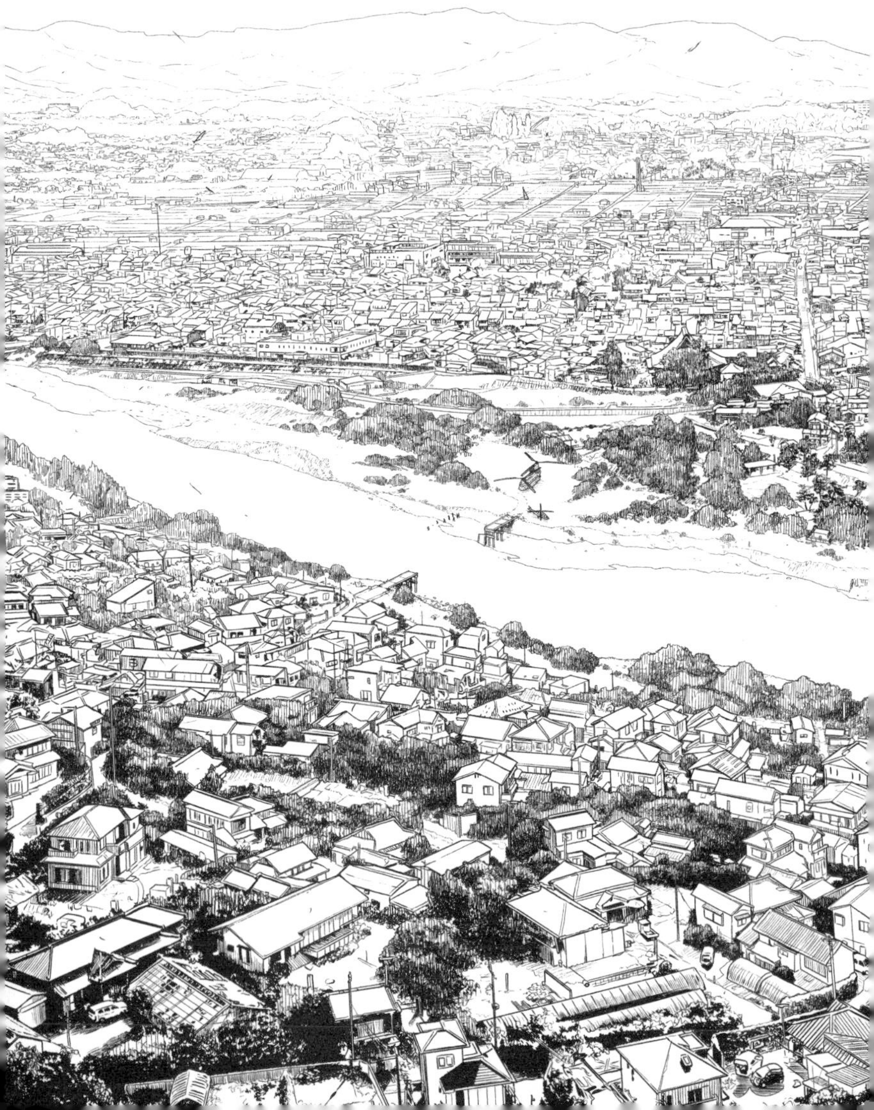

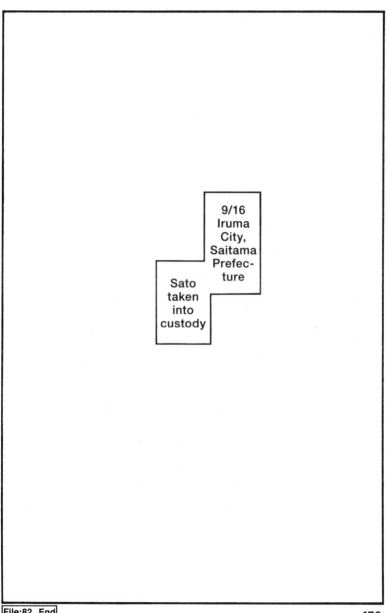

9/16
Iruma
City,
Saitama
Prefec-
ture

Sato
taken
into
custody

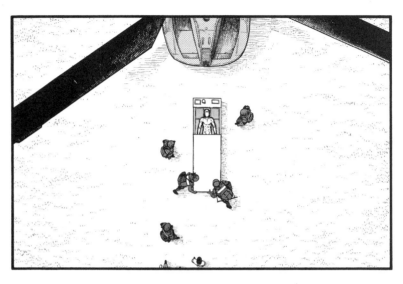

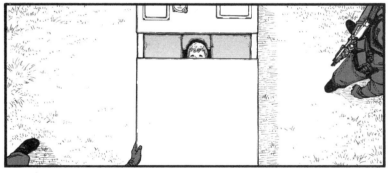

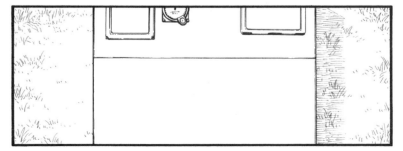

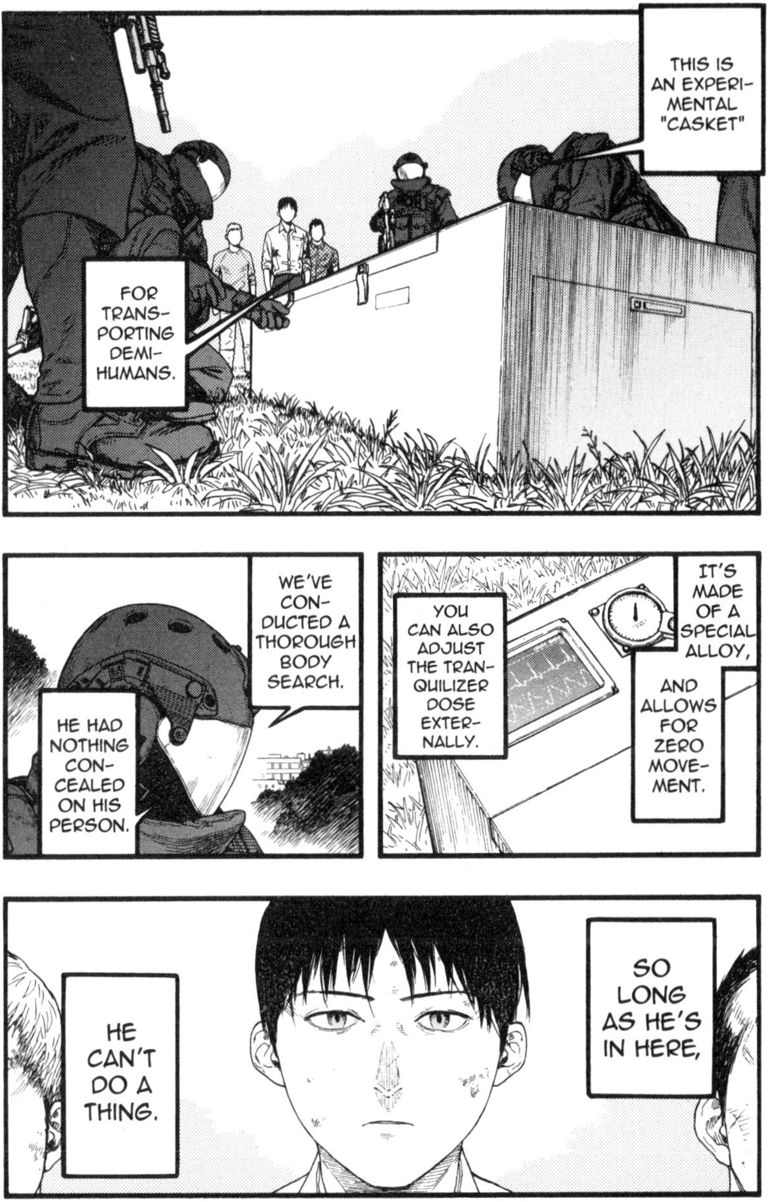
THIS IS AN EXPERIMENTAL "CASKET"
FOR TRANSPORTING DEMIHUMANS.
IT'S MADE OF A SPECIAL ALLOY,
AND ALLOWS FOR ZERO MOVEMENT.
YOU CAN ALSO ADJUST THE TRANQUILIZER DOSE EXTERNALLY.
WE'VE CONDUCTED A THOROUGH BODY SEARCH.
HE HAD NOTHING CONCEALED ON HIS PERSON.
SO LONG AS HE'S IN HERE,
HE CAN'T DO A THING.

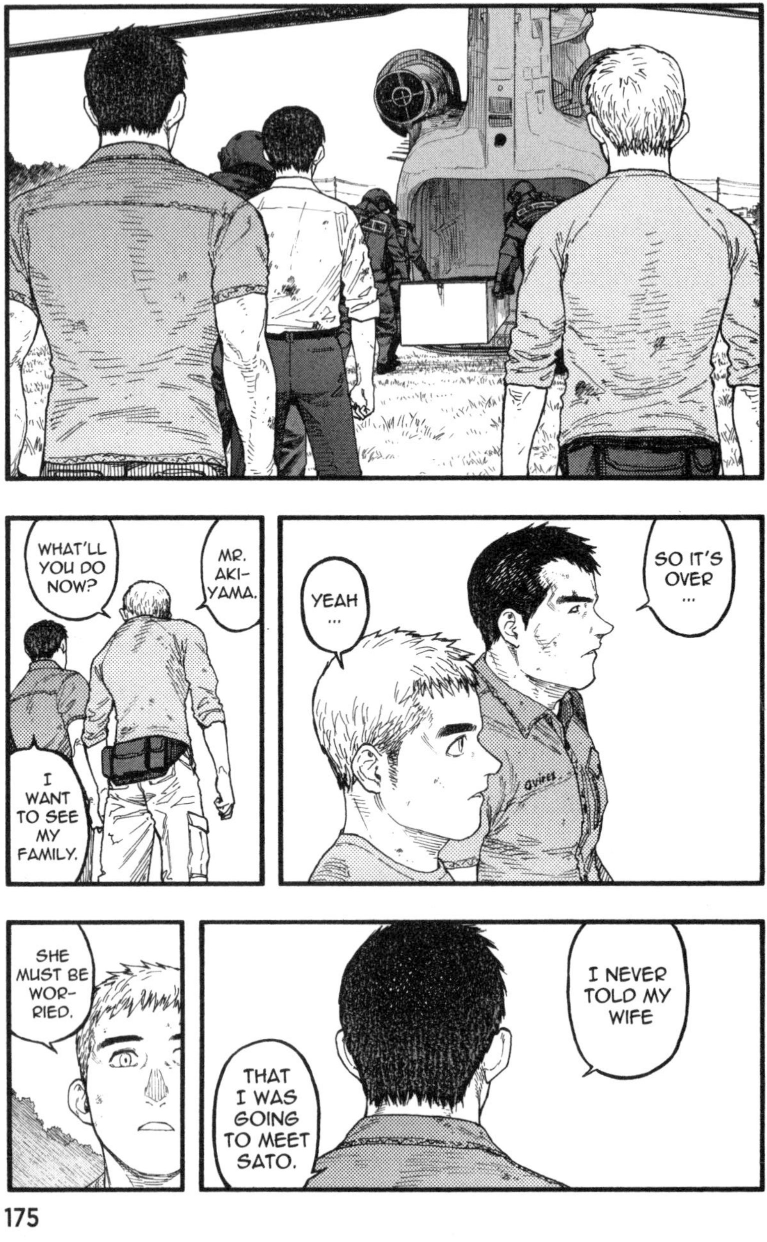
SO IT'S OVER ...
YEAH ...
MR. AKI-YAMA.
WHAT'LL YOU DO NOW?
I WANT TO SEE MY FAMILY.
I NEVER TOLD MY WIFE
THAT I WAS GOING TO MEET SATO.
SHE MUST BE WOR-RIED.

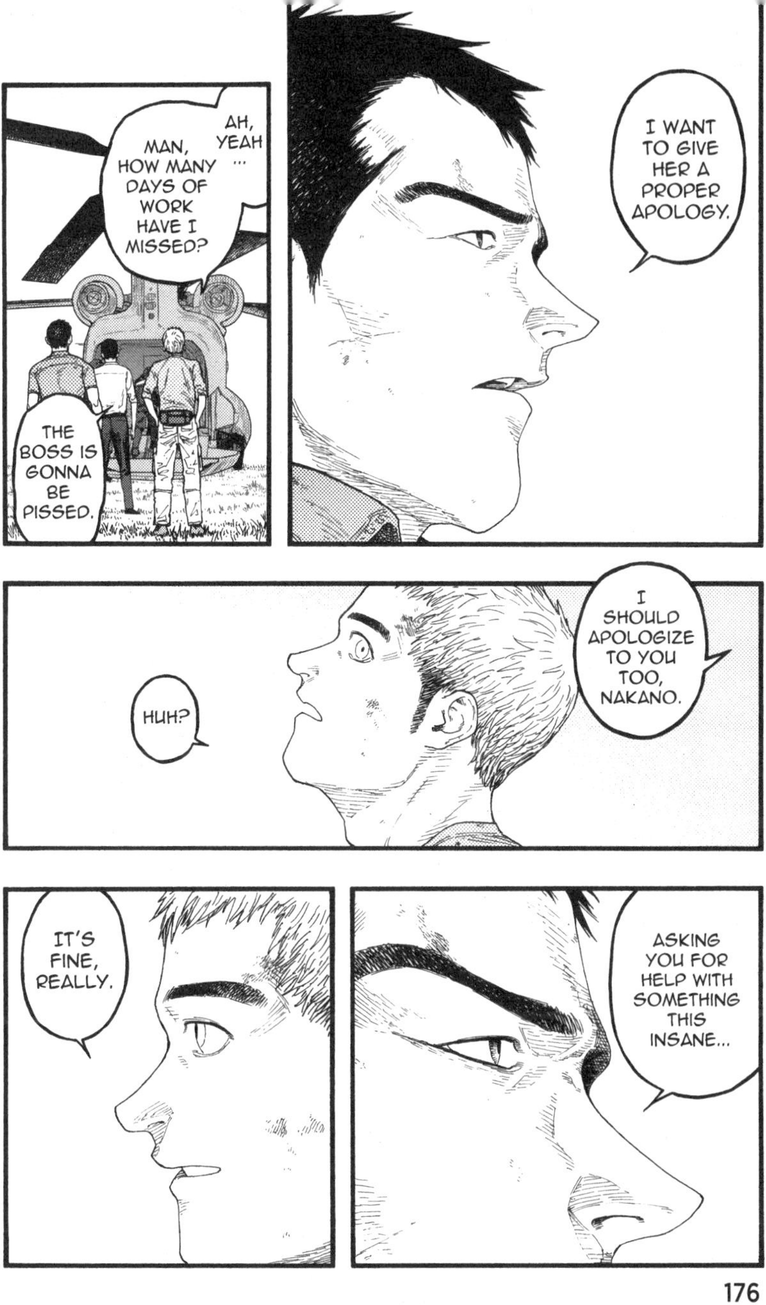
I WANT TO GIVE HER A PROPER APOLOGY.
AH, YEAH ...
MAN, HOW MANY DAYS OF WORK HAVE I MISSED?
THE BOSS IS GONNA BE PISSED.
I SHOULD APOLOGIZE TO YOU TOO, NAKANO.
HUH?
ASKING YOU FOR HELP WITH SOMETHING THIS INSANE...
IT'S FINE, REALLY.

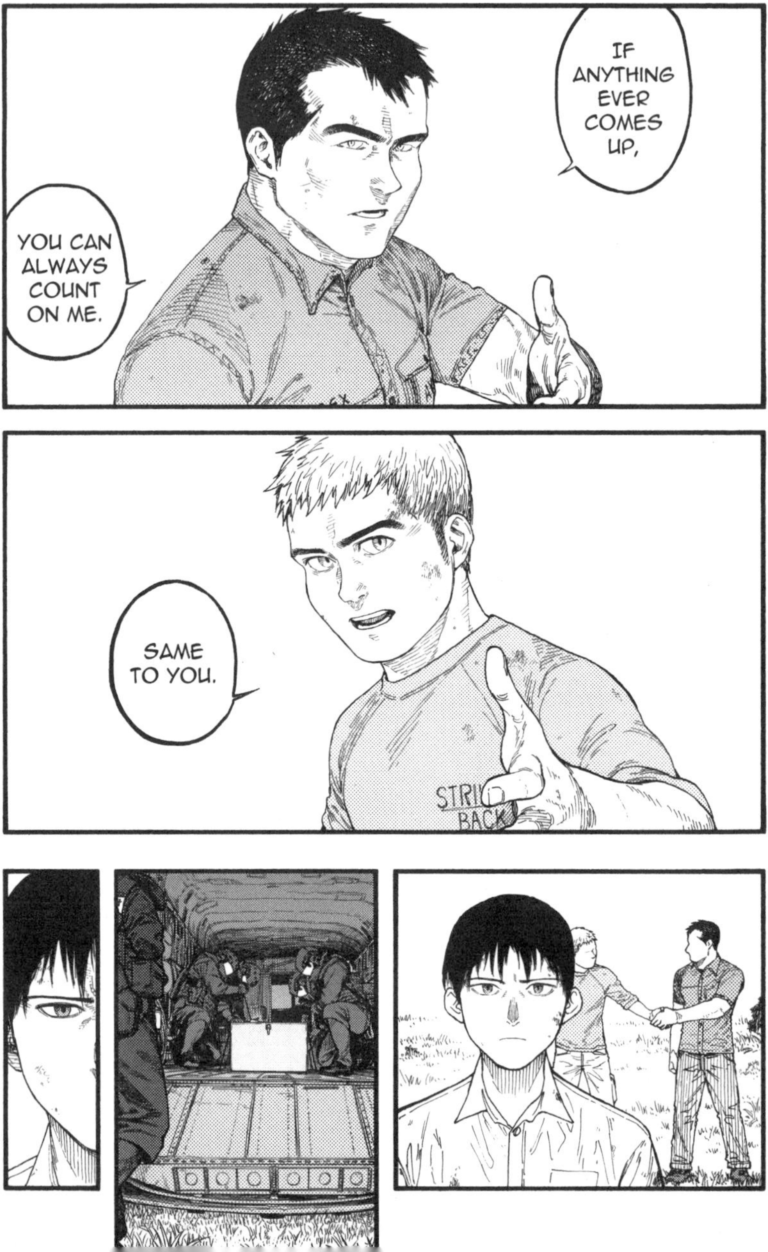
IF ANYTHING EVER COMES UP,
YOU CAN ALWAYS COUNT ON ME.
SAME TO YOU.

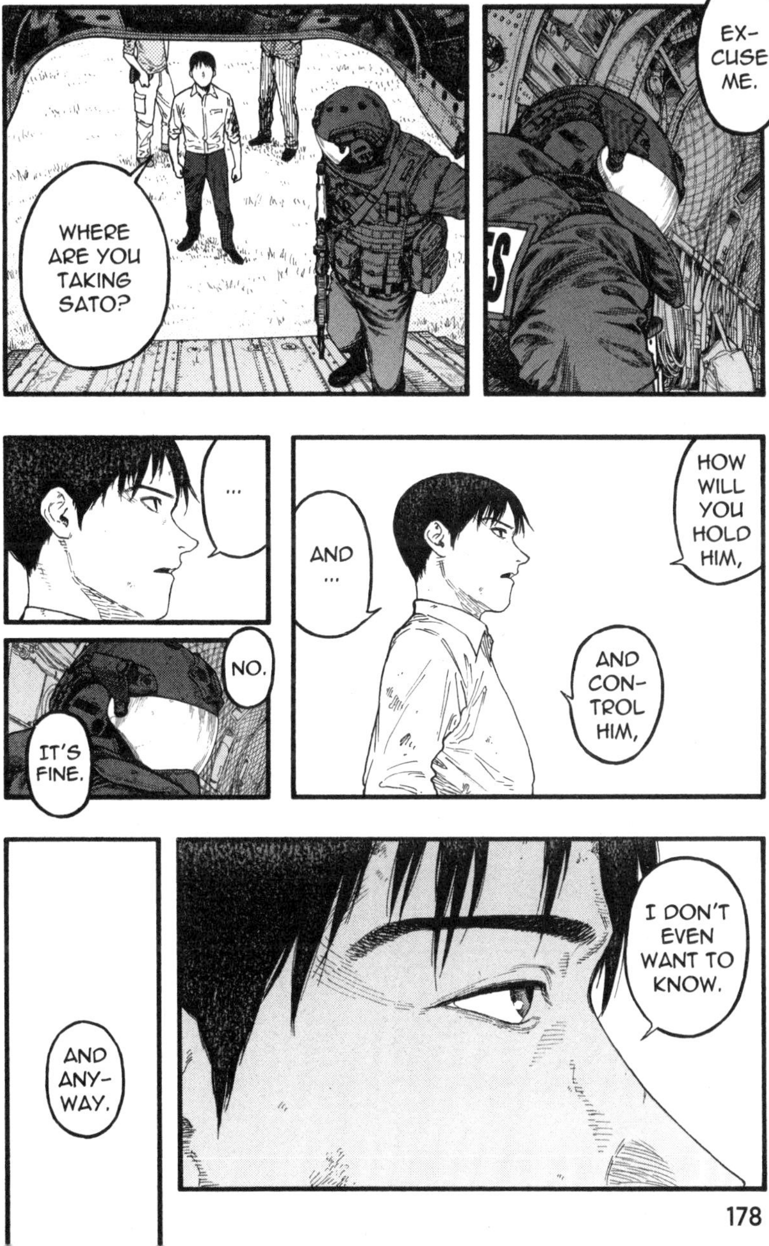
EX-CUSE ME.
WHERE ARE YOU TAKING SATO?
HOW WILL YOU HOLD HIM,
AND CON-TROL HIM,
AND ...
...
NO.
IT'S FINE.
I DON'T EVEN WANT TO KNOW.
AND ANY-WAY.

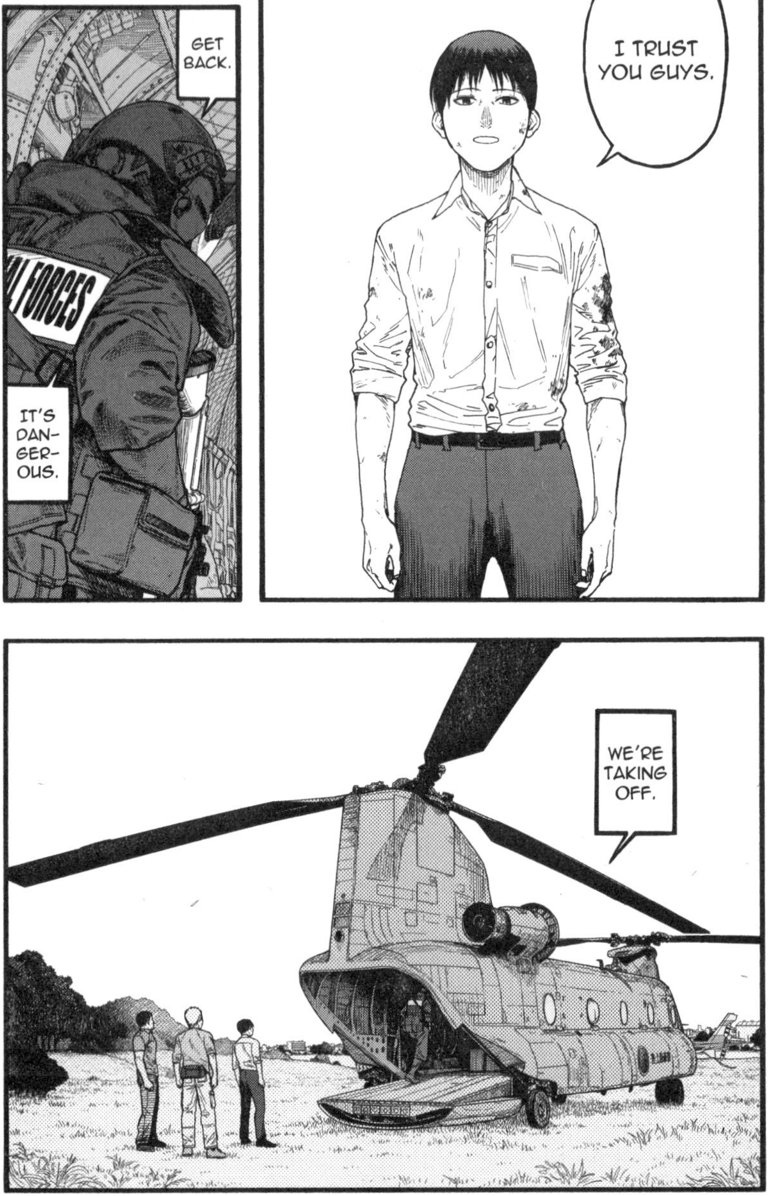
I TRUST YOU GUYS.
GET BACK.
IT'S DAN-GER-OUS.
WE'RE TAKING OFF.

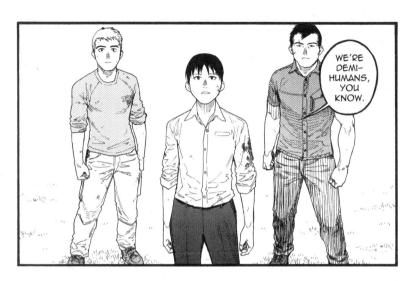

WE'RE DEMI-HUMANS, YOU KNOW.

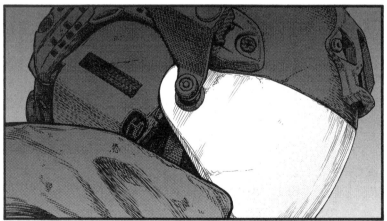

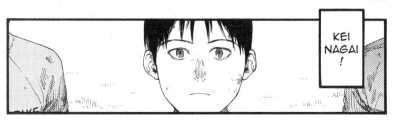

KEI NAGAI!

180

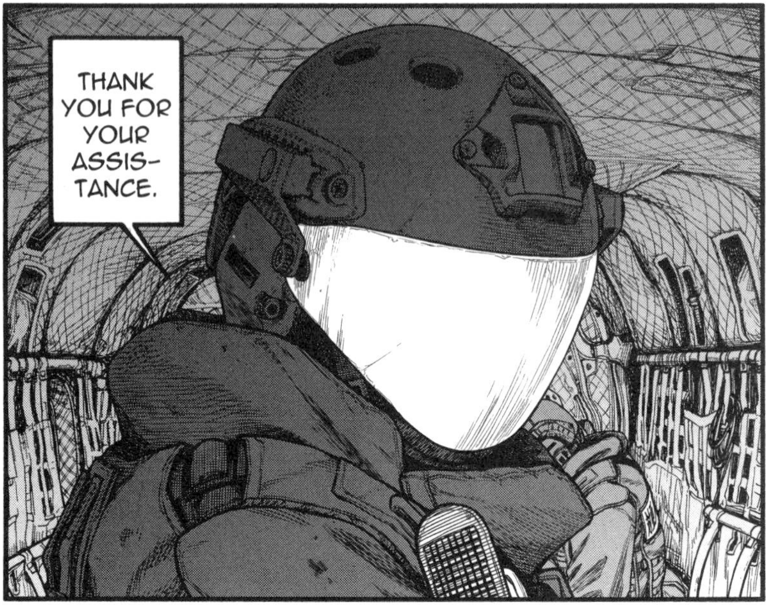
THANK YOU FOR YOUR ASSIS-TANCE.

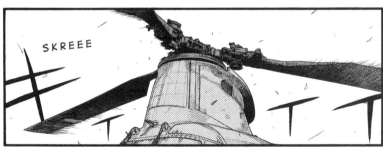

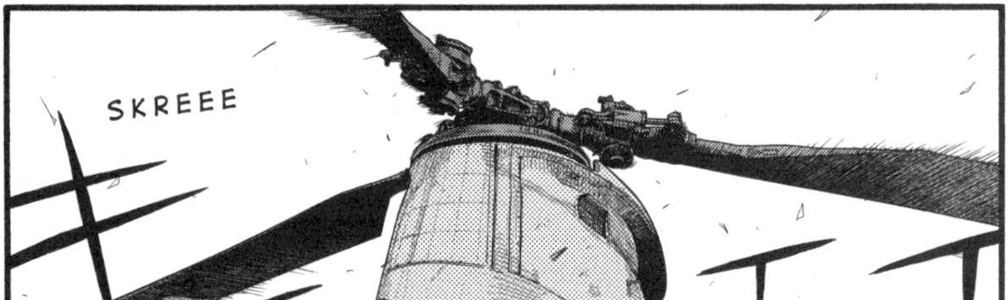
SKREEE

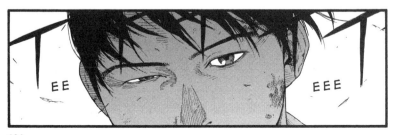

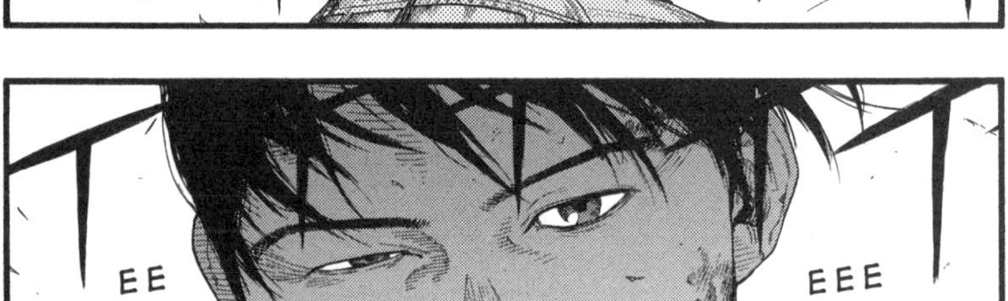
EE
EEE

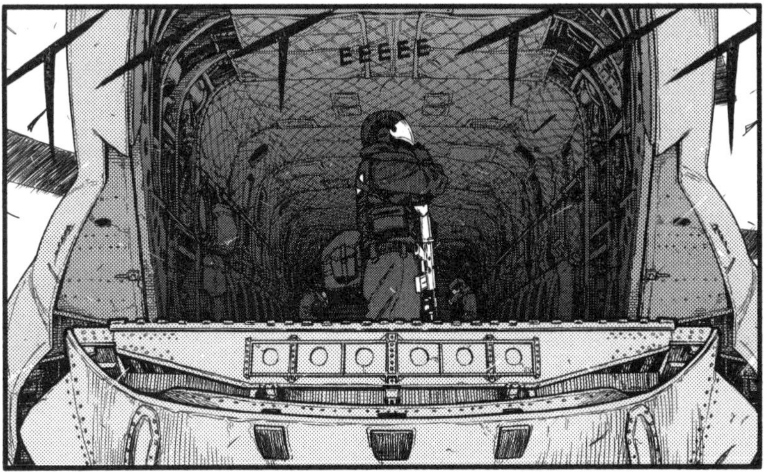
EEEEE
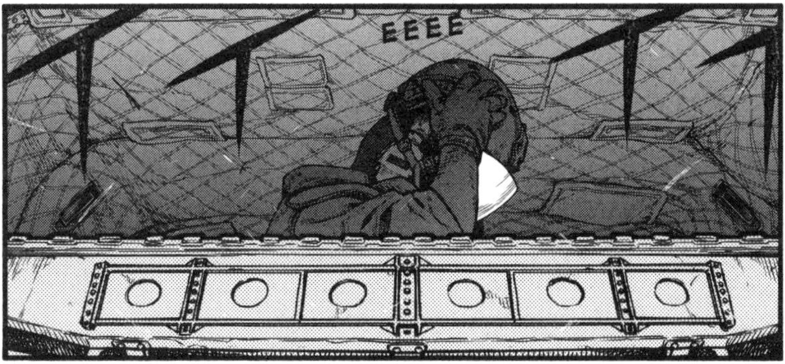
EEEE
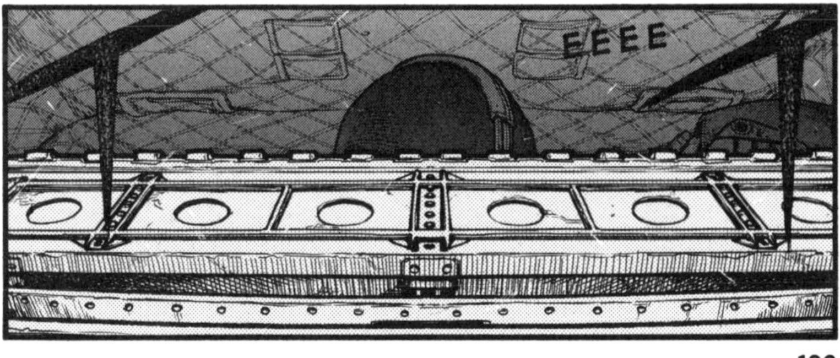
EEEE

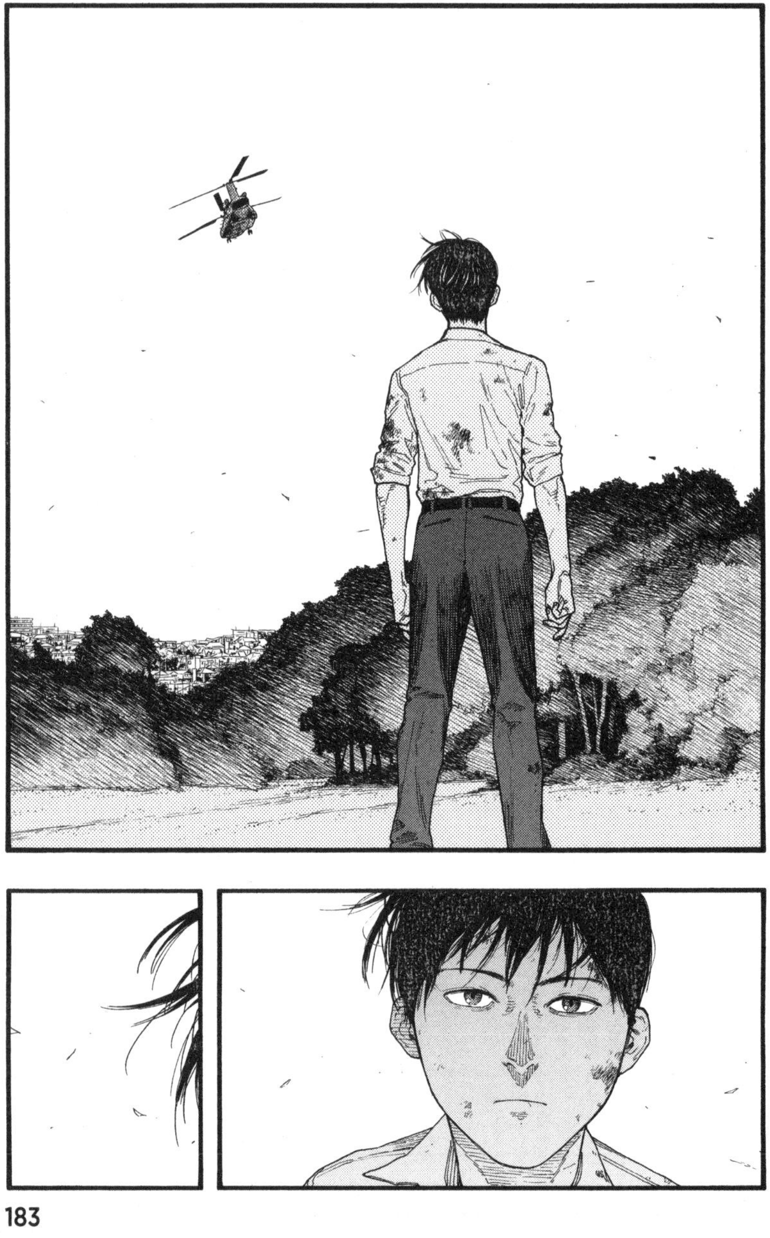

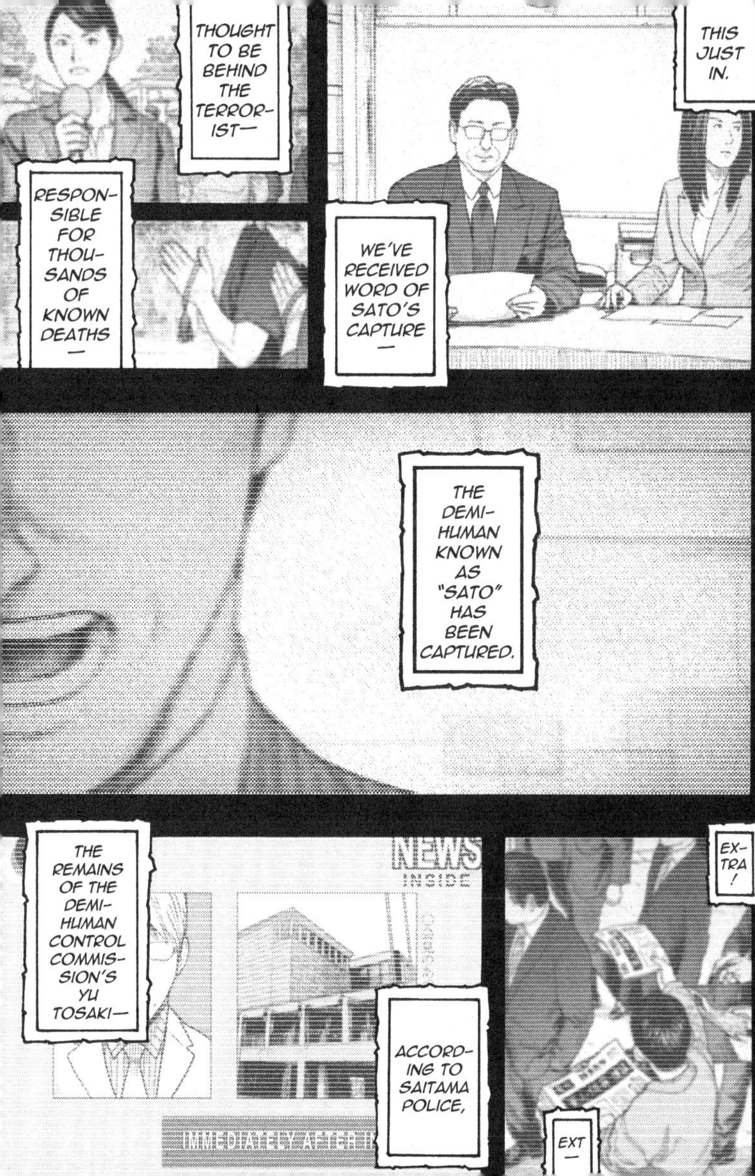
THIS JUST IN.
WE'VE RECEIVED WORD OF SATO'S CAPTURE—
THOUGHT TO BE BEHIND THE TERRORIST—
RESPONSIBLE FOR THOUSANDS OF KNOWN DEATHS—
THE DEMI-HUMAN KNOWN AS "SATO" HAS BEEN CAPTURED.
EXTRA!
EXT—
NEWS INSIDE
THE REMAINS OF THE DEMI-HUMAN CONTROL COMMISSION'S YU TOSAKI—
ACCORDING TO SAITAMA POLICE,
IMMEDIATELY AFTER

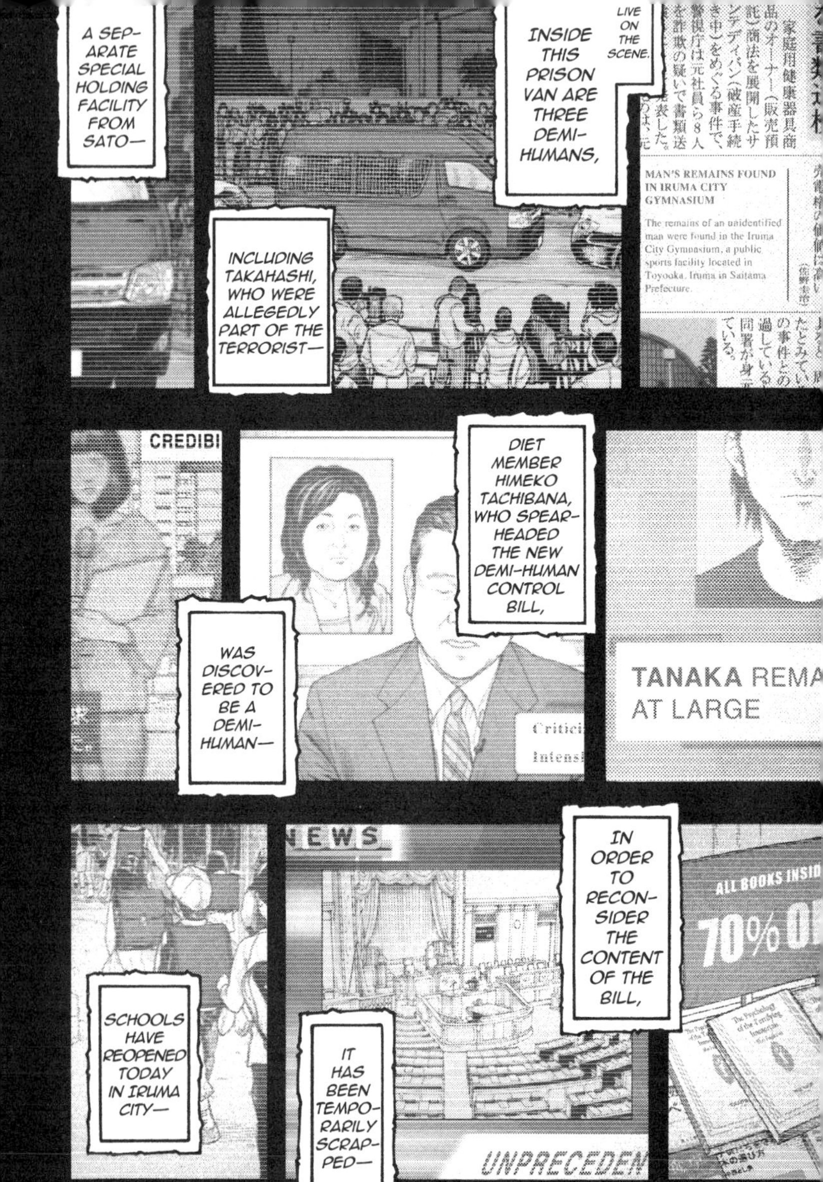
家庭用健康器具商品のオーナー（販売預託）商法を展開したサンデディバン（破産手続き中）をめぐる事件で、警視庁は元社員ら8人を詐欺の疑いで書類送
MAN'S REMAINS FOUND IN IRUMA CITY GYMNASIUM
The remains of an unidentified man were found in the Iruma City Gymnasium, a public sports facility located in Toyooka, Iruma in Saitama Prefecture.
LIVE ON THE SCENE.
INSIDE THIS PRISON VAN ARE THREE DEMI-HUMANS,
INCLUDING TAKAHASHI, WHO WERE ALLEGEDLY PART OF THE TERRORIST—
A SEP-ARATE SPECIAL HOLDING FACILITY FROM SATO—
TANAKA REMA
AT LARGE
DIET MEMBER HIMEKO TACHIBANA, WHO SPEAR-HEADED THE NEW DEMI-HUMAN CONTROL BILL,
WAS DISCOV-ERED TO BE A DEMI-HUMAN—
Critici
Intensi
CREDIBI
ALL BOOKS INSID
IN ORDER TO RECON-SIDER THE CONTENT OF THE BILL,
NEWS
IT HAS BEEN TEMPO-RARILY SCRAP-PED—
UNPRECEDEN
SCHOOLS HAVE REOPENED TODAY IN IRUMA CITY—

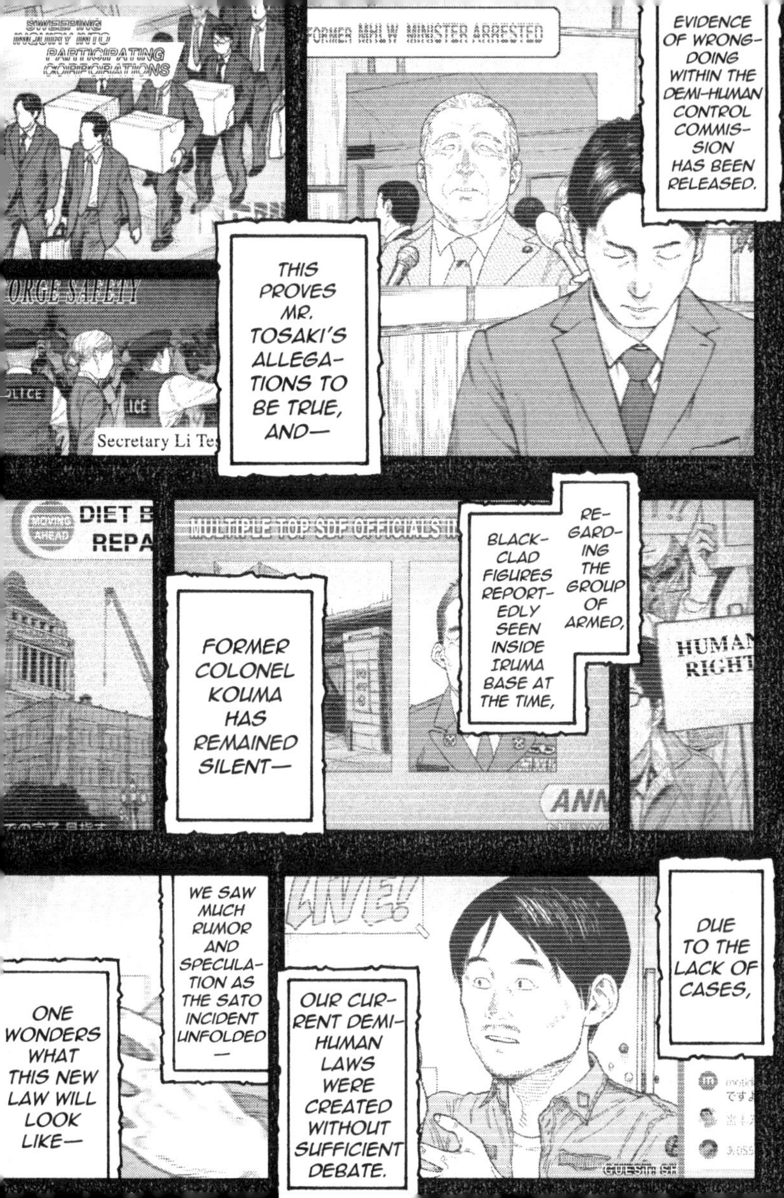
FORMER MHLW MINISTER ARRESTED
EVIDENCE OF WRONG-DOING WITHIN THE DEMI-HUMAN CONTROL COMMISSION HAS BEEN RELEASED.
THIS PROVES MR. TOSAKI'S ALLEGATIONS TO BE TRUE, AND—
SWEEPING INQUIRY INTO PARTICIPATING CORPORATIONS
REGARDING THE GROUP OF ARMED,
BLACK-CLAD FIGURES REPORTEDLY SEEN INSIDE IRUMA BASE AT THE TIME,
FORMER COLONEL KOUMA HAS REMAINED SILENT—
MOVING AHEAD
DUE TO THE LACK OF CASES,
OUR CURRENT DEMI-HUMAN LAWS WERE CREATED WITHOUT SUFFICIENT DEBATE.
WE SAW MUCH RUMOR AND SPECULATION AS THE SATO INCIDENT UNFOLDED—
ONE WONDERS WHAT THIS NEW LAW WILL LOOK LIKE—

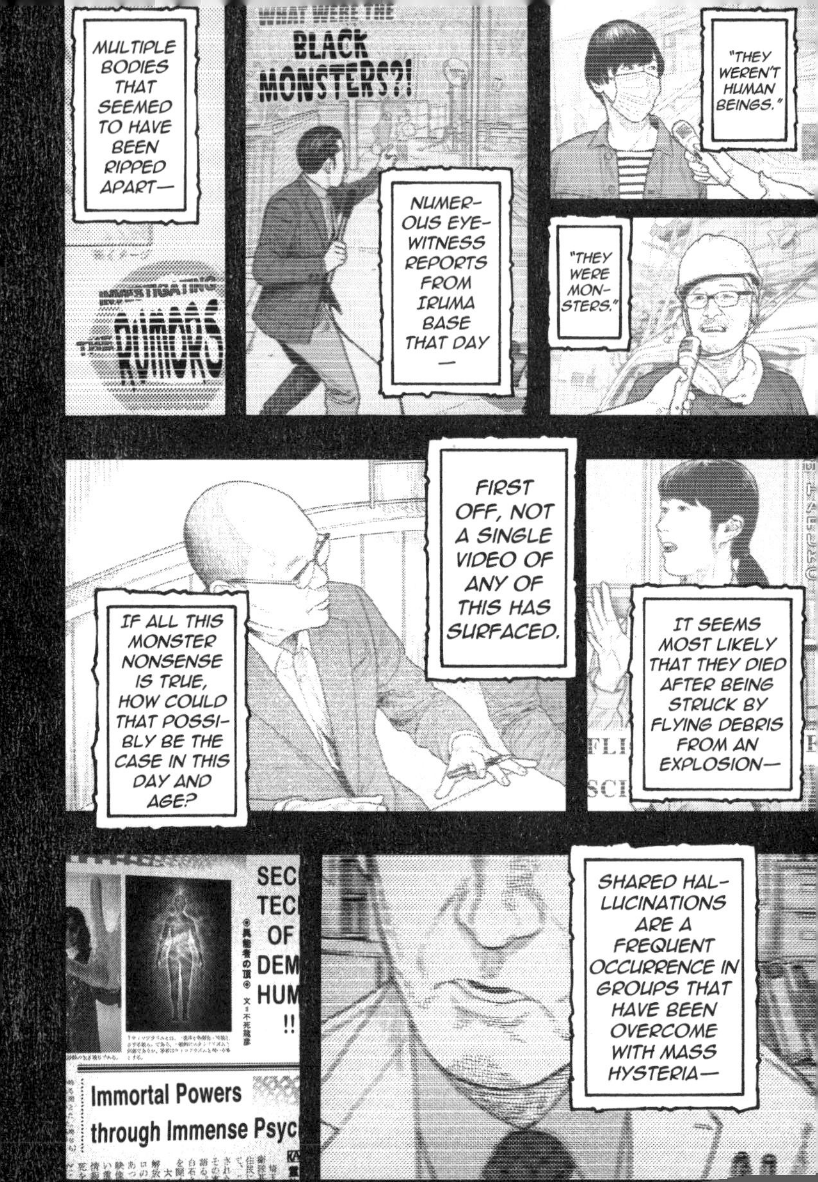
"THEY WEREN'T HUMAN BEINGS."
"THEY WERE MONSTERS."
WHAT WERE THE BLACK MONSTERS?!
NUMEROUS EYEWITNESS REPORTS FROM IRUMA BASE THAT DAY—
MULTIPLE BODIES THAT SEEMED TO HAVE BEEN RIPPED APART—
INVESTIGATING THE RUMORS
IT SEEMS MOST LIKELY THAT THEY DIED AFTER BEING STRUCK BY FLYING DEBRIS FROM AN EXPLOSION—
FIRST OFF, NOT A SINGLE VIDEO OF ANY OF THIS HAS SURFACED.
IF ALL THIS MONSTER NONSENSE IS TRUE, HOW COULD THAT POSSIBLY BE THE CASE IN THIS DAY AND AGE?
SHARED HALLUCINATIONS ARE A FREQUENT OCCURRENCE IN GROUPS THAT HAVE BEEN OVERCOME WITH MASS HYSTERIA—
Immortal Powers
through Immense Psyc

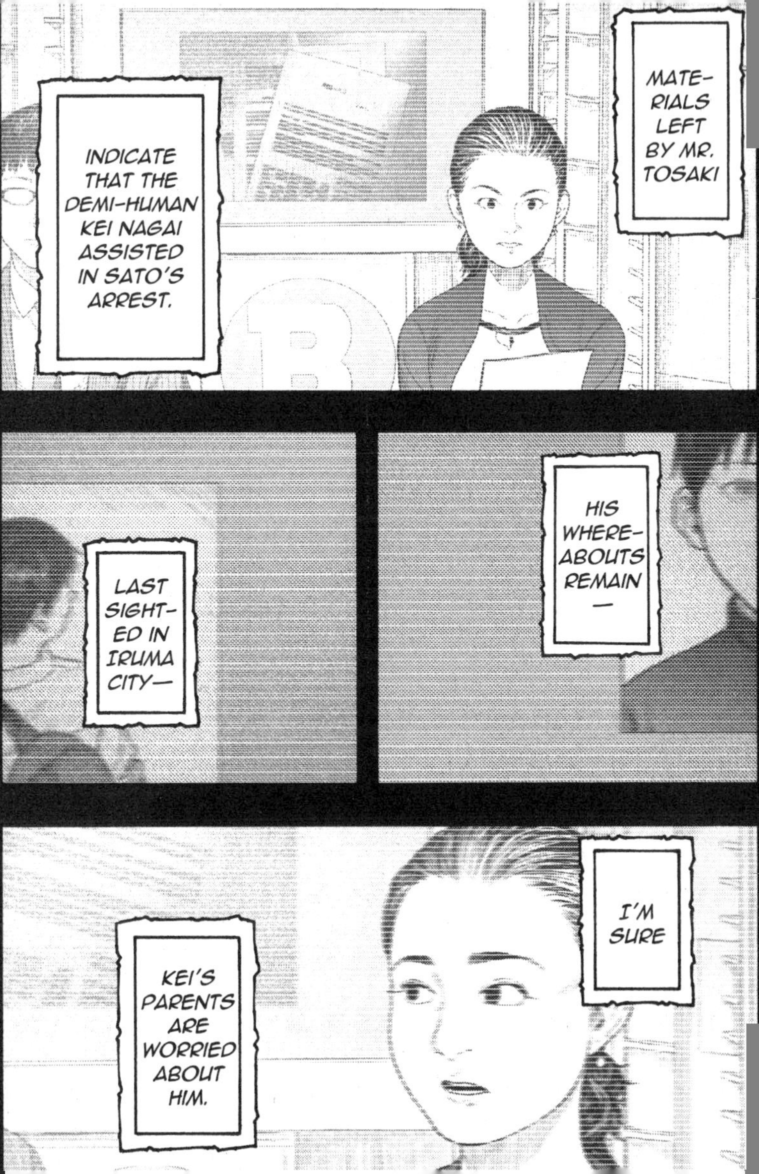
MATERIALS LEFT BY MR. TOSAKI
INDICATE THAT THE DEMI-HUMAN KEI NAGAI ASSISTED IN SATO'S ARREST.
HIS WHEREABOUTS REMAIN—
LAST SIGHTED IN IRUMA CITY—
I'M SURE
KEI'S PARENTS ARE WORRIED ABOUT HIM.

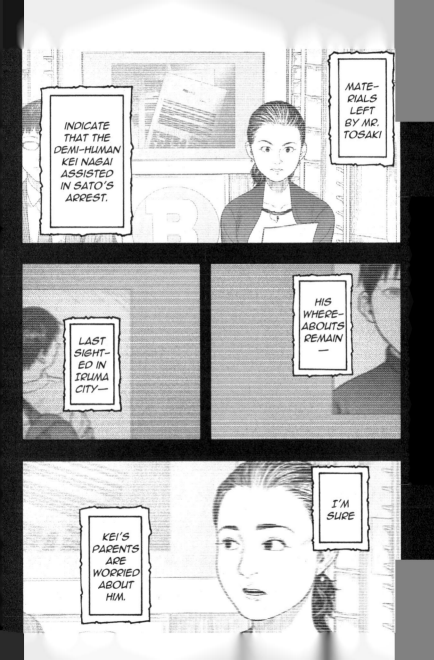

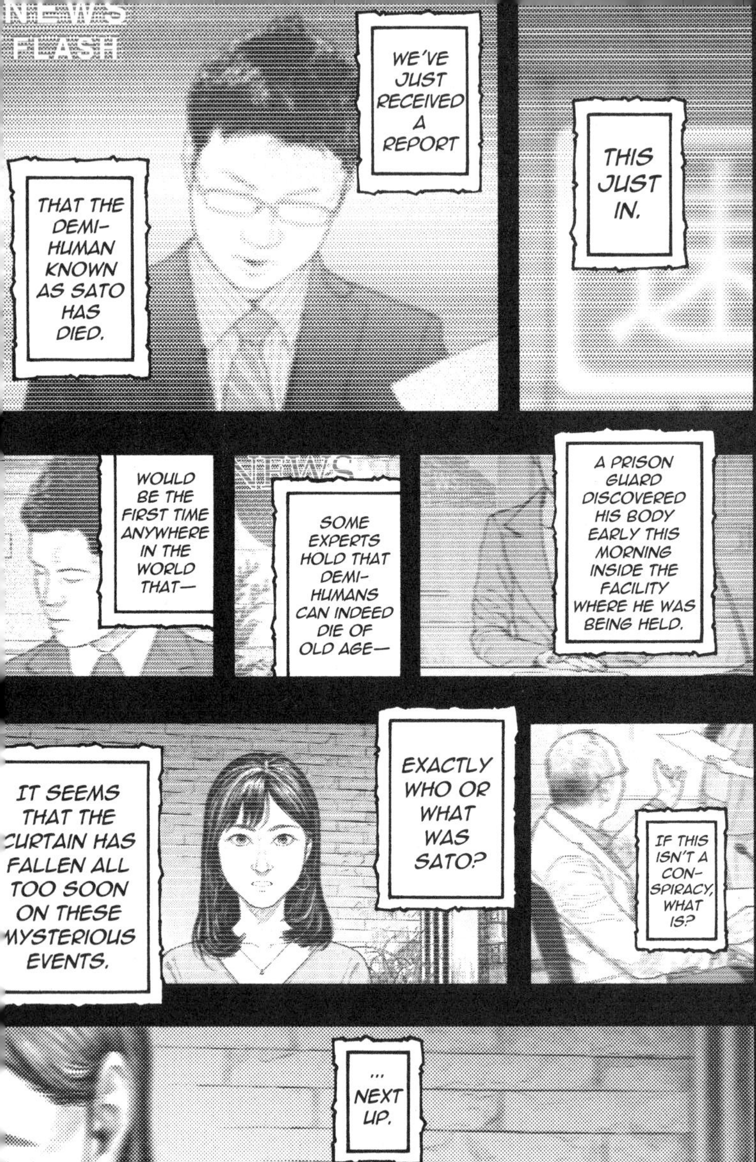
THIS JUST IN.
NEWS FLASH
WE'VE JUST RECEIVED A REPORT
THAT THE DEMI-HUMAN KNOWN AS SATO HAS DIED.
A PRISON GUARD DISCOVERED HIS BODY EARLY THIS MORNING INSIDE THE FACILITY WHERE HE WAS BEING HELD.
SOME EXPERTS HOLD THAT DEMI-HUMANS CAN INDEED DIE OF OLD AGE—
WOULD BE THE FIRST TIME ANYWHERE IN THE WORLD THAT—
IF THIS ISN'T A CON-SPIRACY, WHAT IS?
EXACTLY WHO OR WHAT WAS SATO?
IT SEEMS THAT THE CURTAIN HAS FALLEN ALL TOO SOON ON THESE MYSTERIOUS EVENTS.
... NEXT UP.

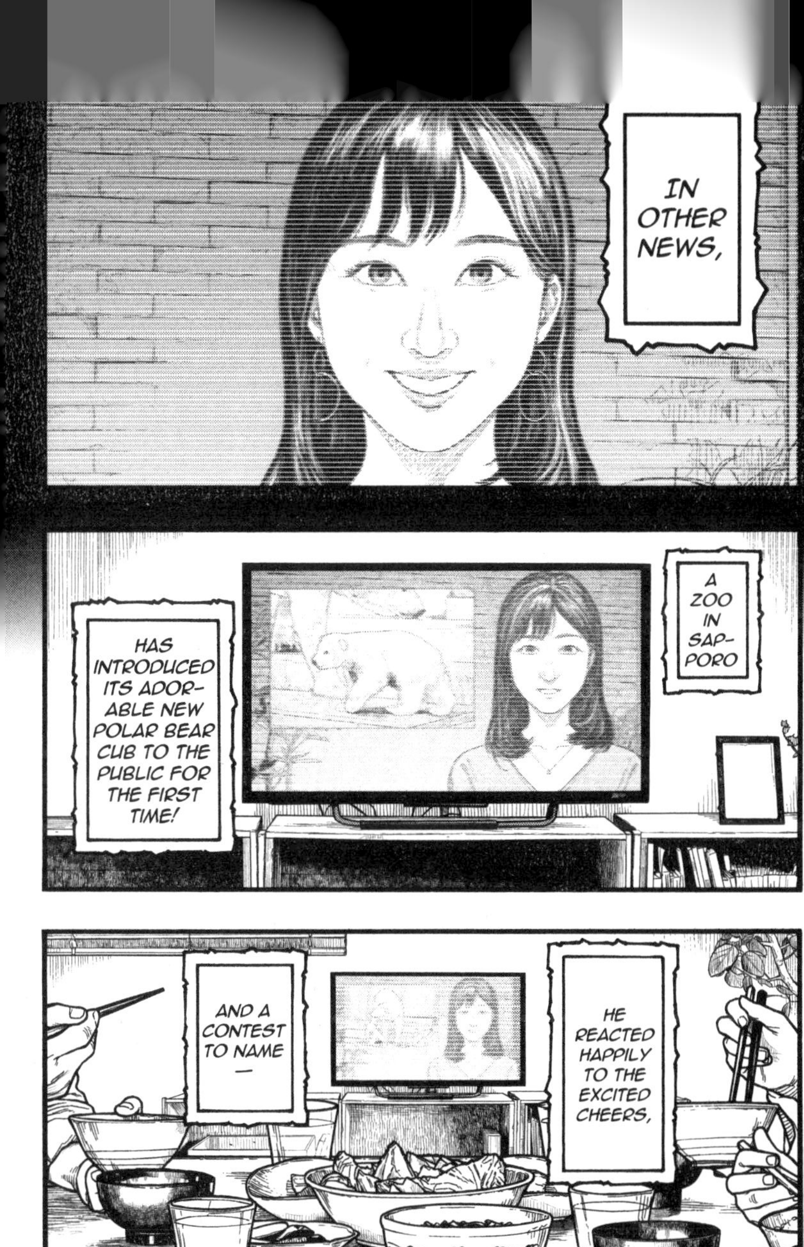
IN OTHER NEWS,
A ZOO IN SAPPORO
HAS INTRODUCED ITS ADORABLE NEW POLAR BEAR CUB TO THE PUBLIC FOR THE FIRST TIME!
HE REACTED HAPPILY TO THE EXCITED CHEERS,
AND A CONTEST TO NAME —

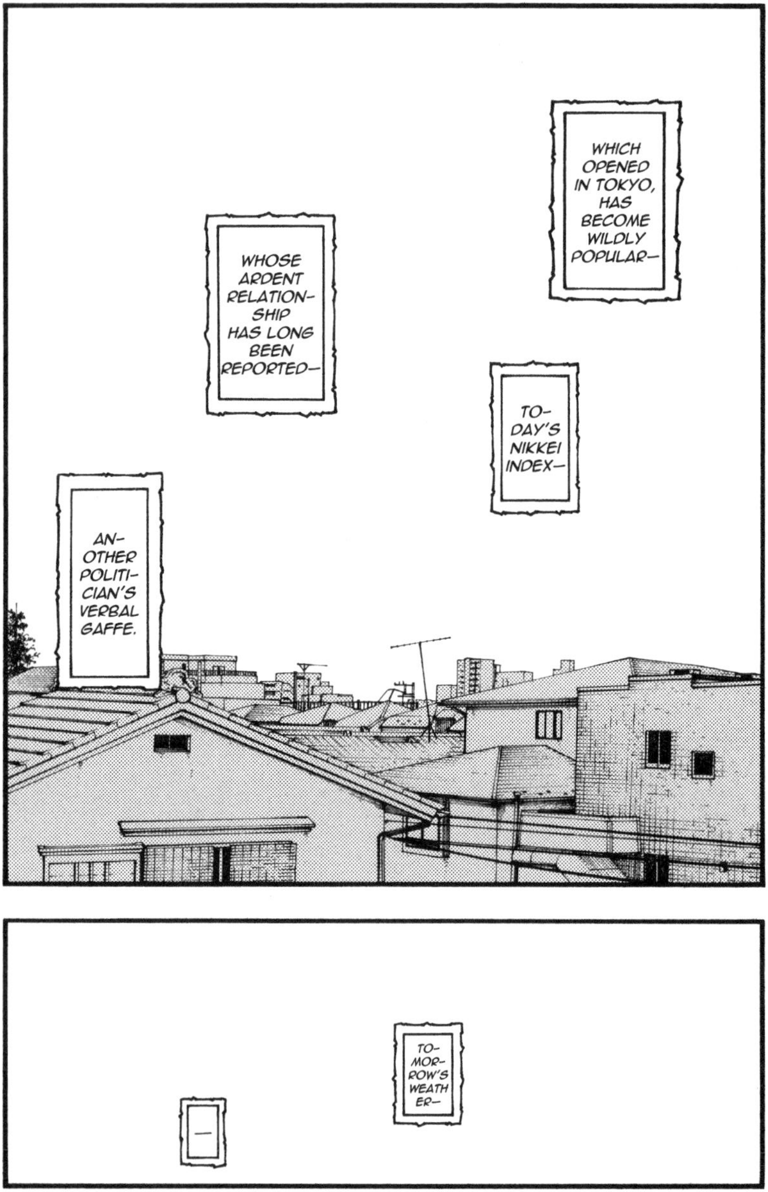
WHICH OPENED IN TOKYO, HAS BECOME WILDLY POPULAR—
WHOSE ARDENT RELATION-SHIP HAS LONG BEEN REPORTED—
TO-DAY'S NIKKEI INDEX—
AN-OTHER POLITI-CIAN'S VERBAL GAFFE.
TO-MOR-ROW'S WEATH ER—
—

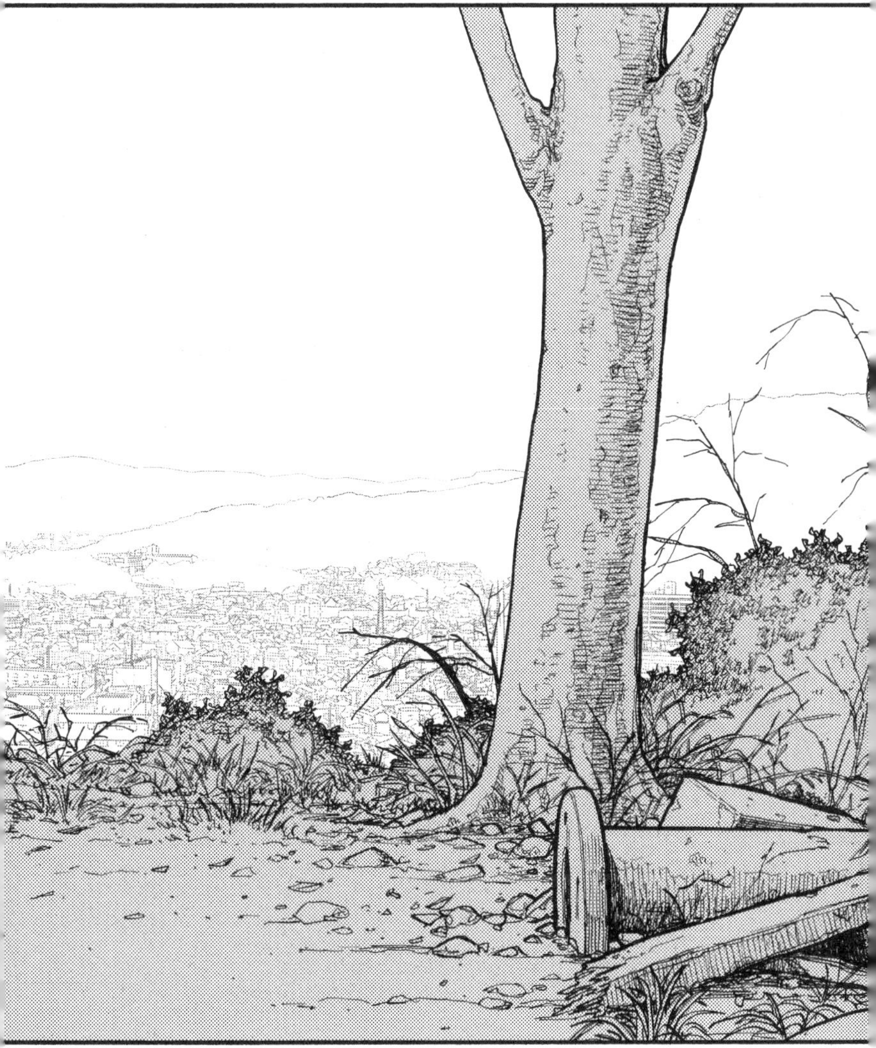

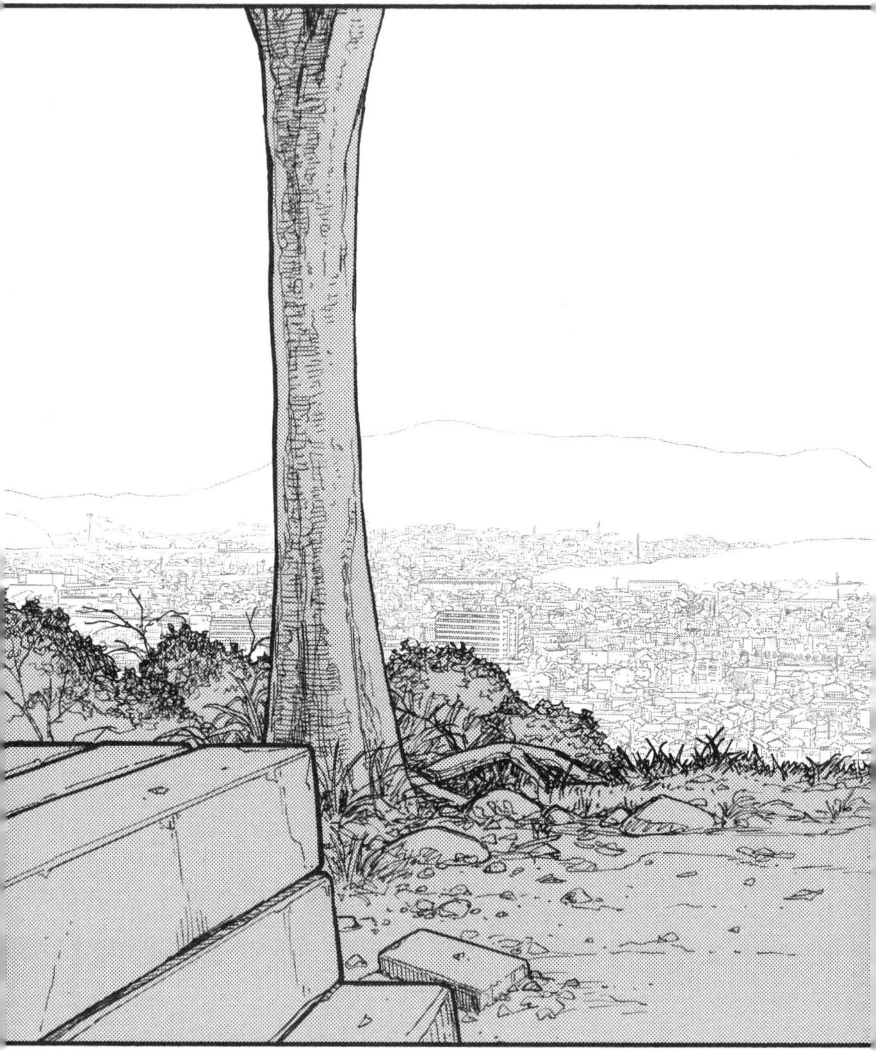

Final File: As Long as It Lasts

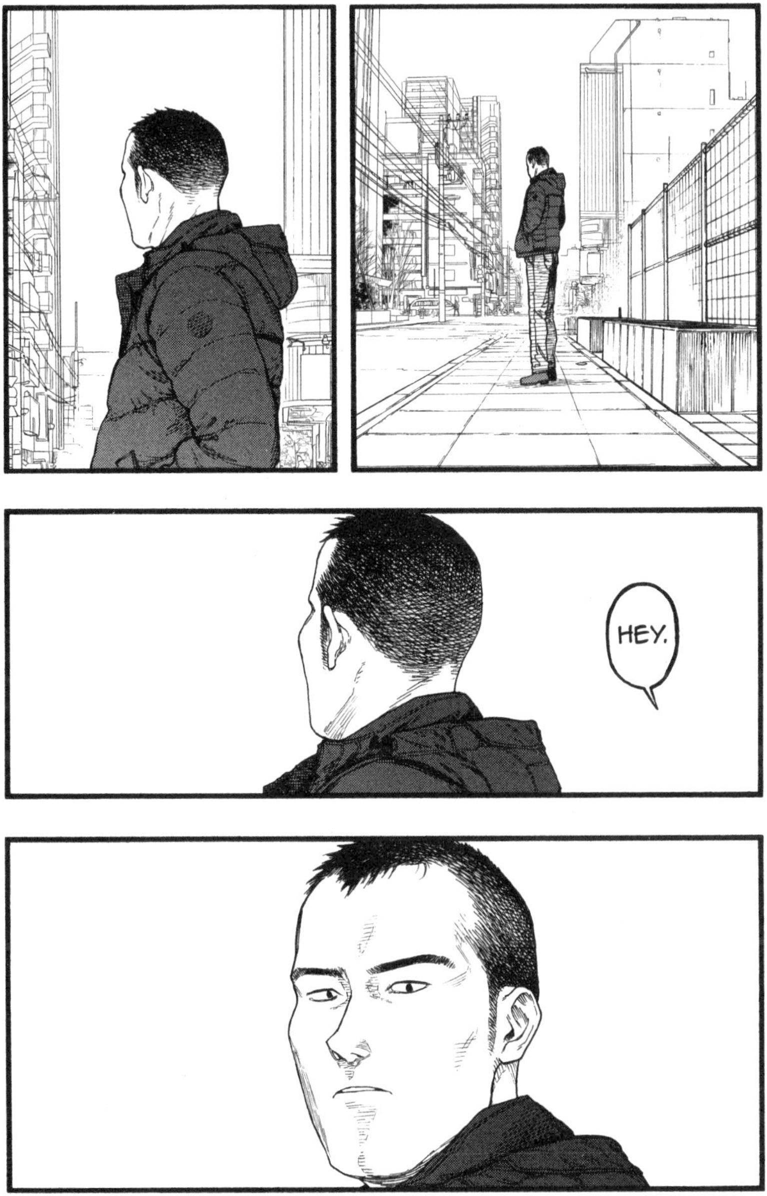
HEY.

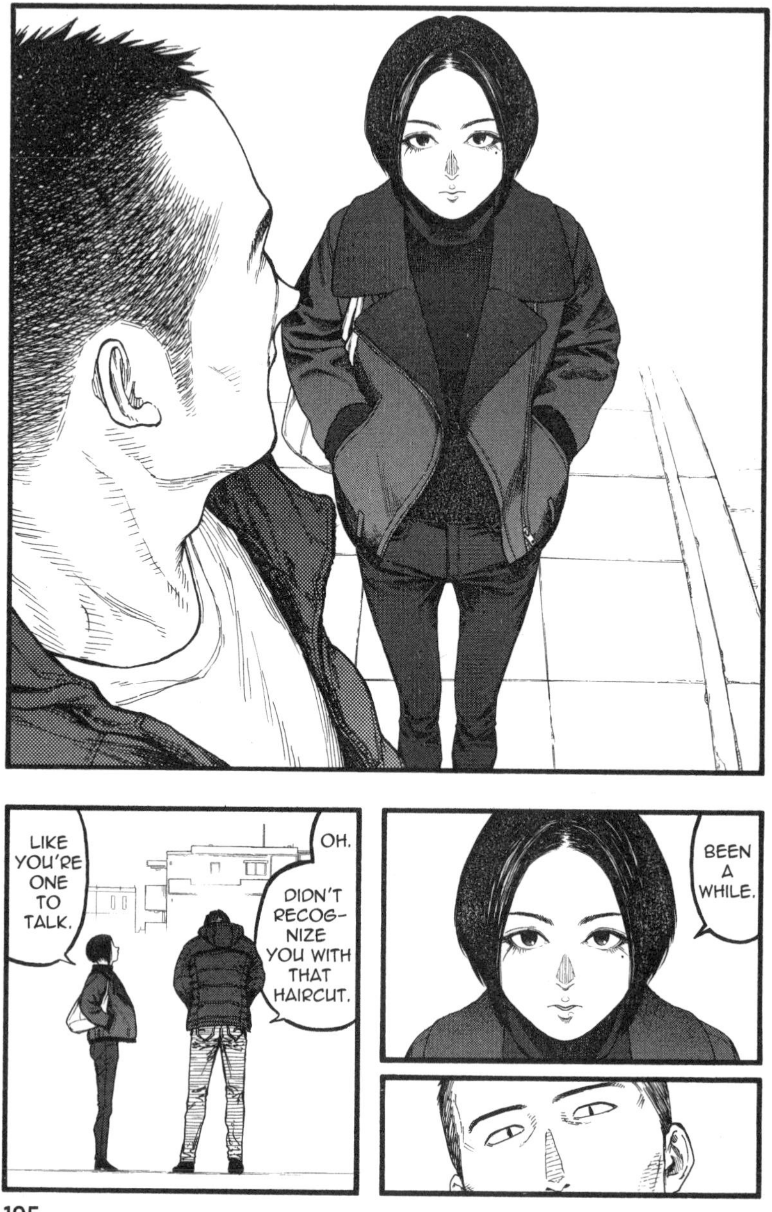
BEEN A WHILE.
OH.
DIDN'T RECOG-NIZE YOU WITH THAT HAIRCUT.
LIKE YOU'RE ONE TO TALK.

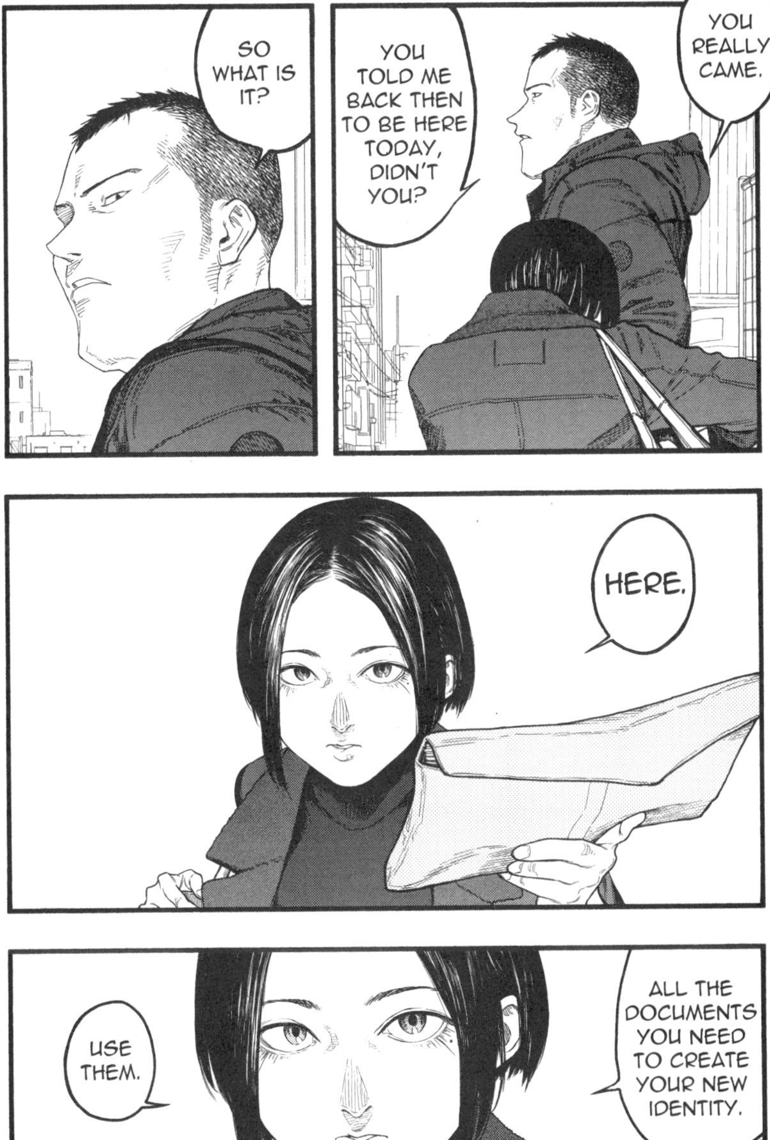
YOU REALLY CAME.
YOU TOLD ME BACK THEN TO BE HERE TODAY, DIDN'T YOU?
SO WHAT IS IT?
HERE.
ALL THE DOCUMENTS YOU NEED TO CREATE YOUR NEW IDENTITY.
USE THEM.

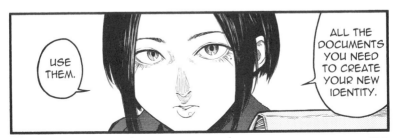

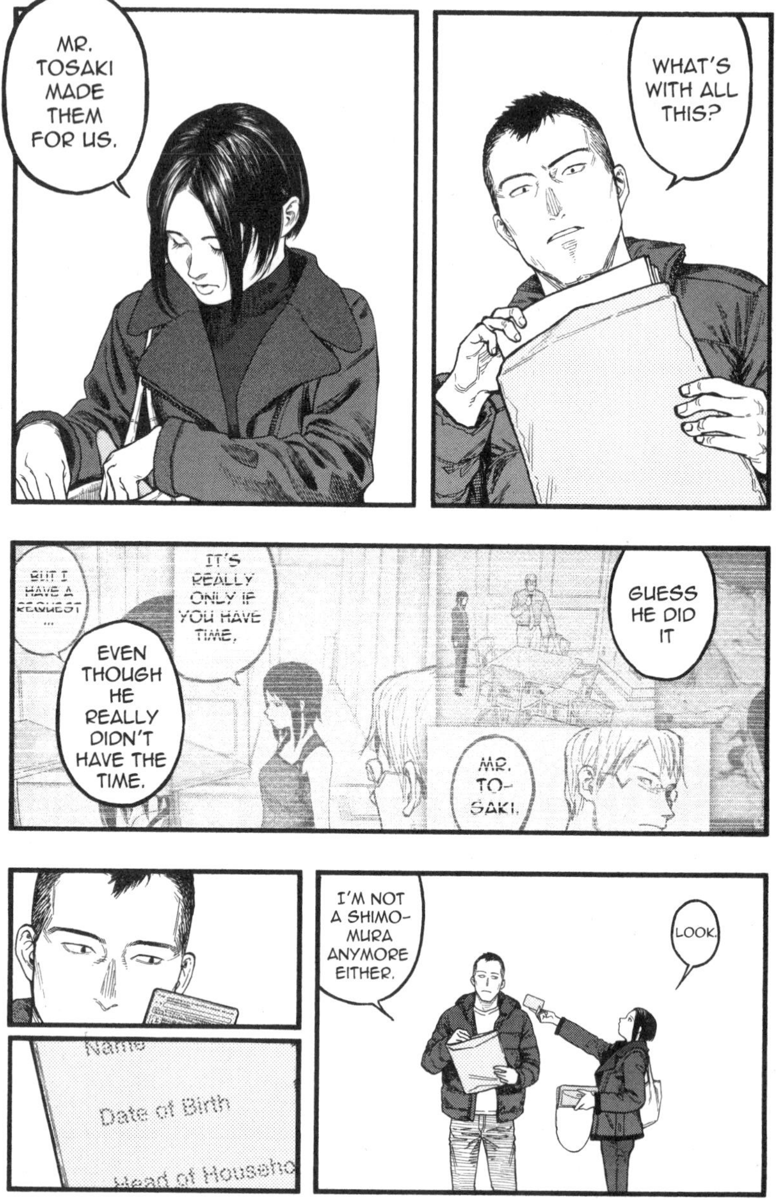
WHAT'S WITH ALL THIS?
MR. TOSAKI MADE THEM FOR US.
GUESS HE DID IT
MR. TO-SAKI.
IT'S REALLY ONLY IF YOU HAVE TIME.
BUT I HAVE A REQUEST ...
EVEN THOUGH HE REALLY DIDN'T HAVE THE TIME.
LOOK.
I'M NOT A SHIMOMURA ANYMORE EITHER.
Name
Date of Birth
Head of Househo

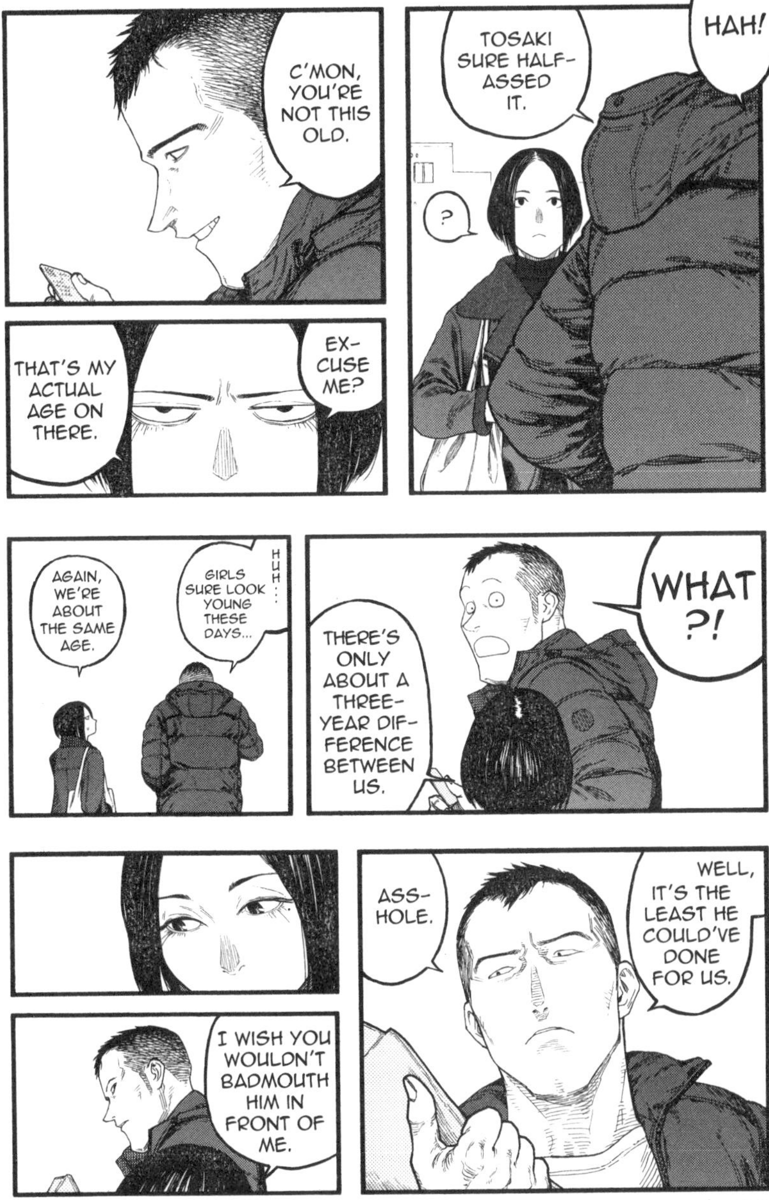
HAH!
TOSAKI SURE HALF-ASSED IT.
?
C'MON, YOU'RE NOT THIS OLD.
EX-CUSE ME?
THAT'S MY ACTUAL AGE ON THERE.
WHAT?!
THERE'S ONLY ABOUT A THREE-YEAR DIF-FERENCE BETWEEN US.
HUH...
GIRLS SURE LOOK YOUNG THESE DAYS...
AGAIN, WE'RE ABOUT THE SAME AGE.
WELL, IT'S THE LEAST HE COULD'VE DONE FOR US.
ASS-HOLE.
I WISH YOU WOULDN'T BADMOUTH HIM IN FRONT OF ME.

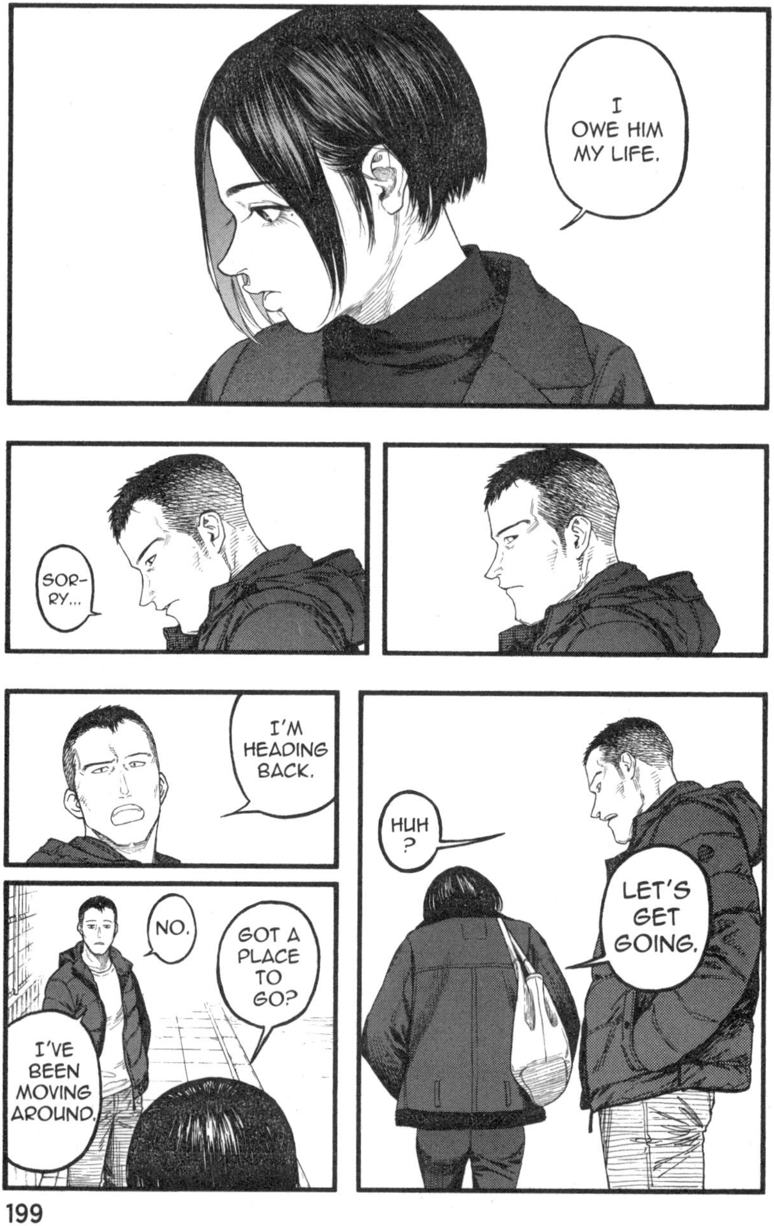
I OWE HIM MY LIFE.
SORRY...
HUH?
LET'S GET GOING.
I'M HEADING BACK.
GOT A PLACE TO GO?
NO.
I'VE BEEN MOVING AROUND.

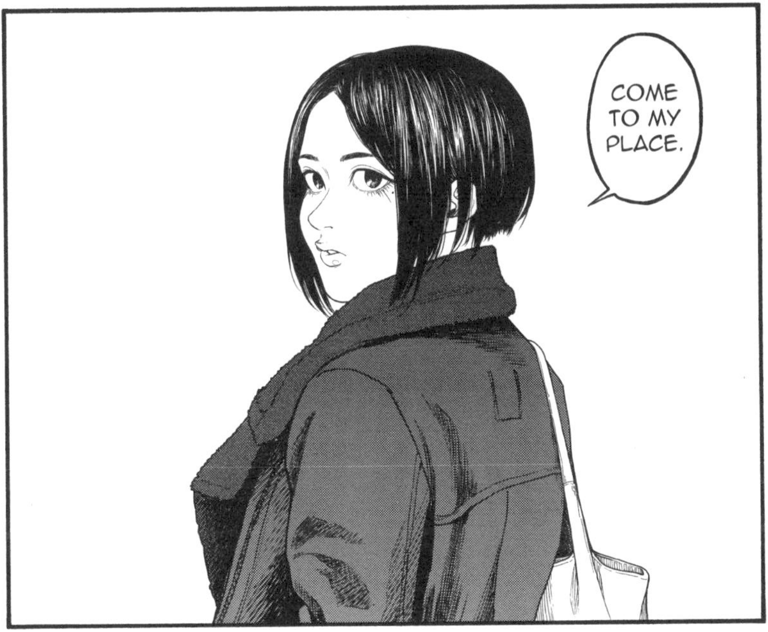
COME TO MY PLACE.

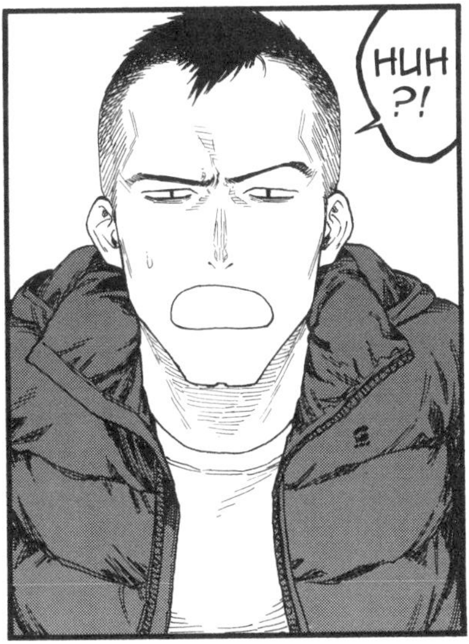
HUH ?!

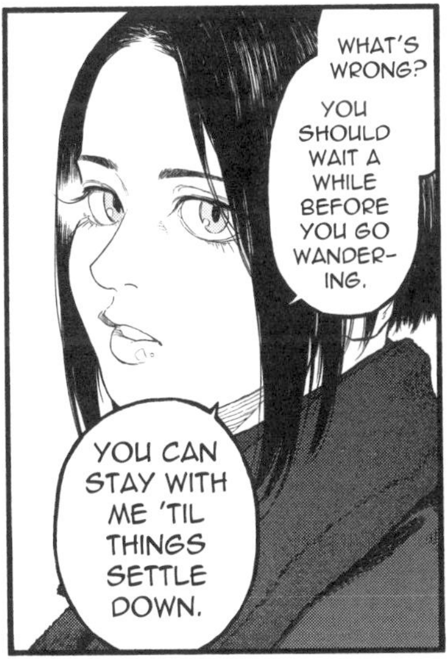
WHAT'S WRONG?
YOU SHOULD WAIT A WHILE BEFORE YOU GO WANDER-ING.
YOU CAN STAY WITH ME 'TIL THINGS SETTLE DOWN.

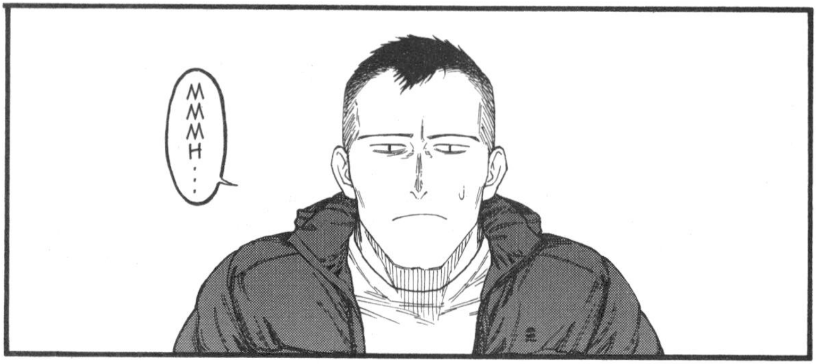
MMMH...

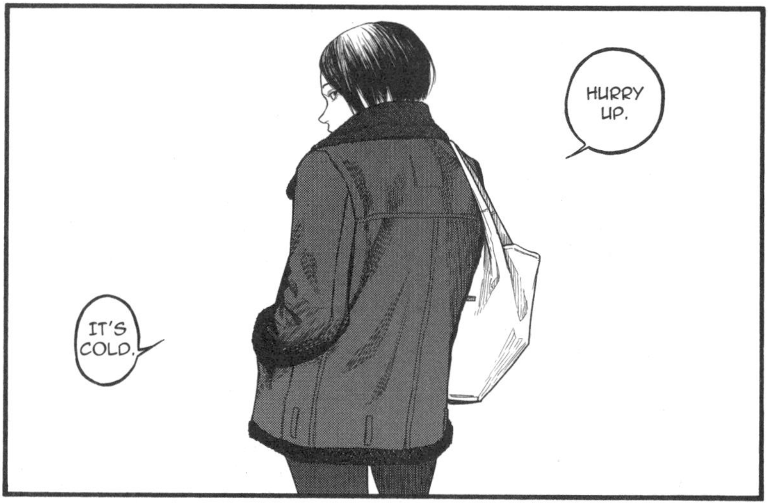
HURRY UP.
IT'S COLD.

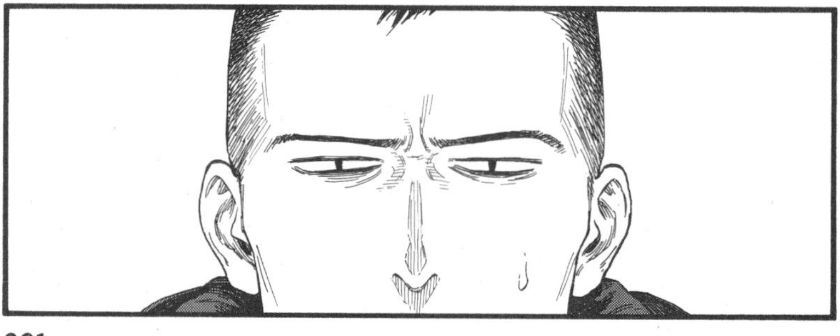

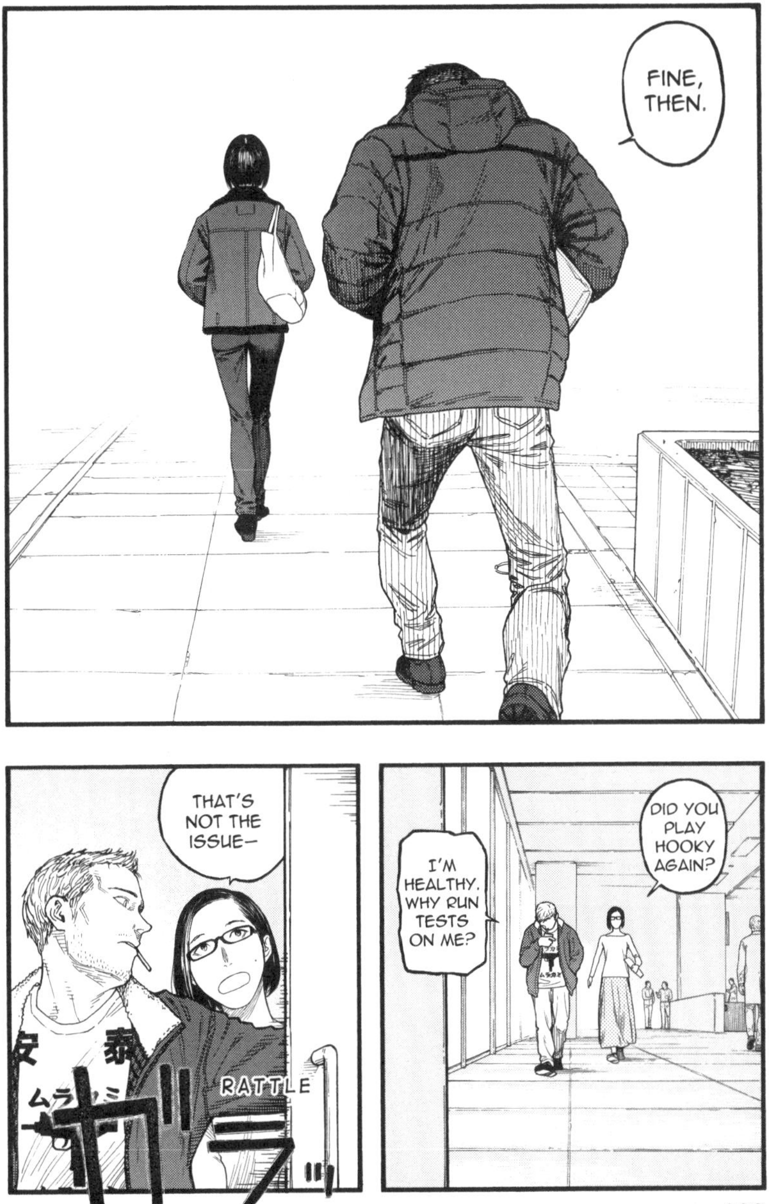
FINE, THEN.
DID YOU PLAY HOOKY AGAIN?
I'M HEALTHY. WHY RUN TESTS ON ME?
THAT'S NOT THE ISSUE—
RATTLE

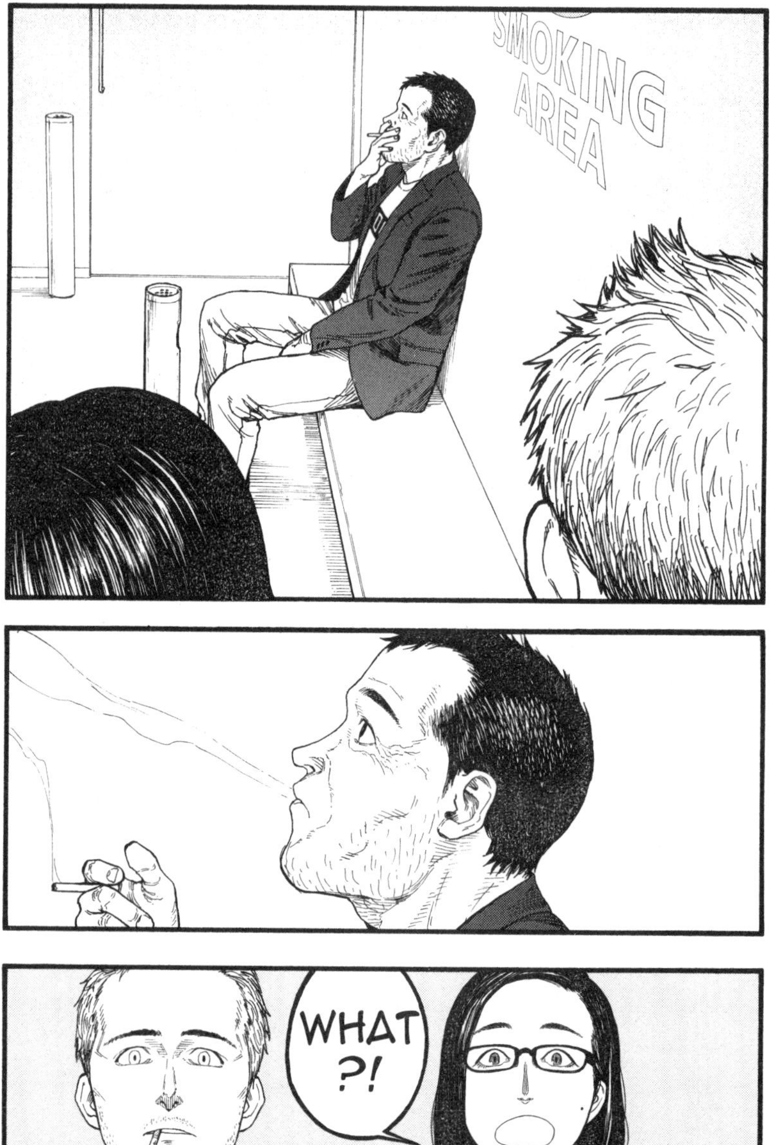
SMOKING AREA
WHAT ?!

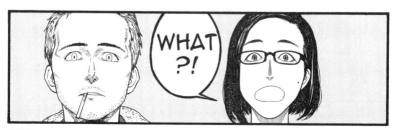

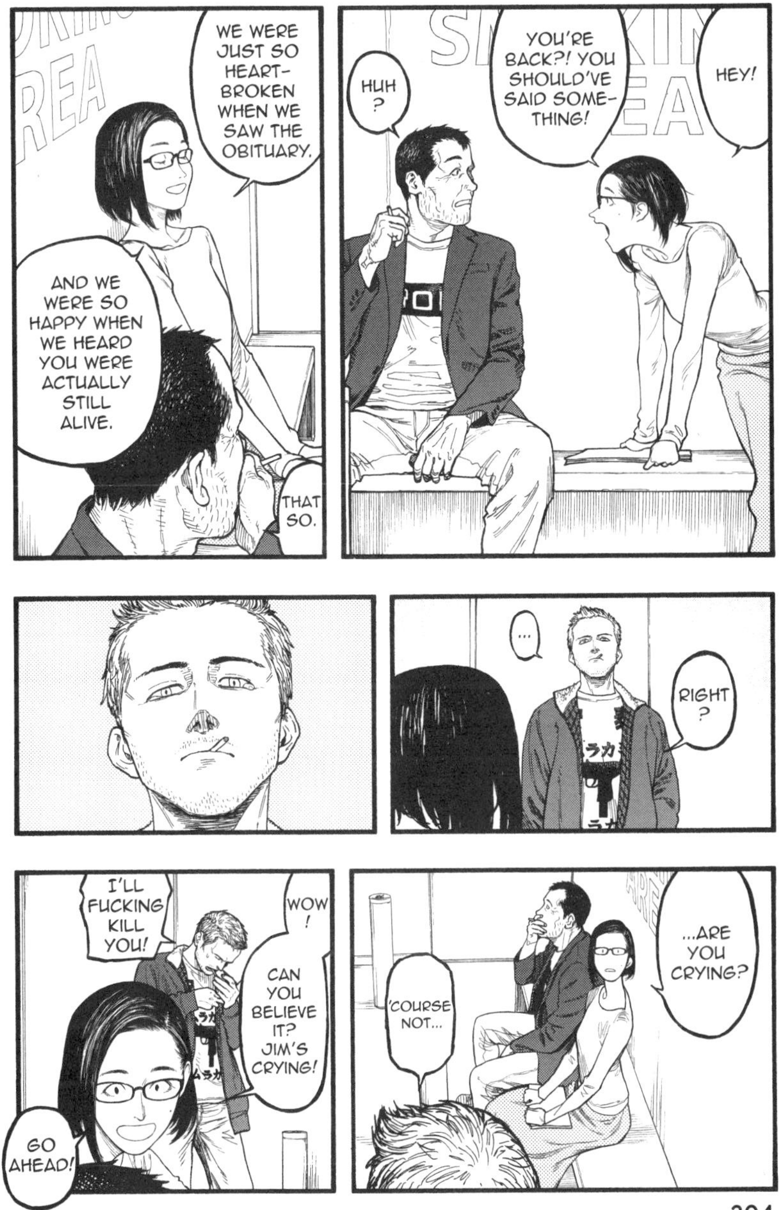
HEY!
YOU'RE BACK?! YOU SHOULD'VE SAID SOME-THING!
HUH?
WE WERE JUST SO HEART-BROKEN WHEN WE SAW THE OBITUARY.
AND WE WERE SO HAPPY WHEN WE HEARD YOU WERE ACTUALLY STILL ALIVE.
THAT SO.
RIGHT?
...
...ARE YOU CRYING?
'COURSE NOT...
WOW!
CAN YOU BELIEVE IT? JIM'S CRYING!
I'LL FUCKING KILL YOU!
GO AHEAD!

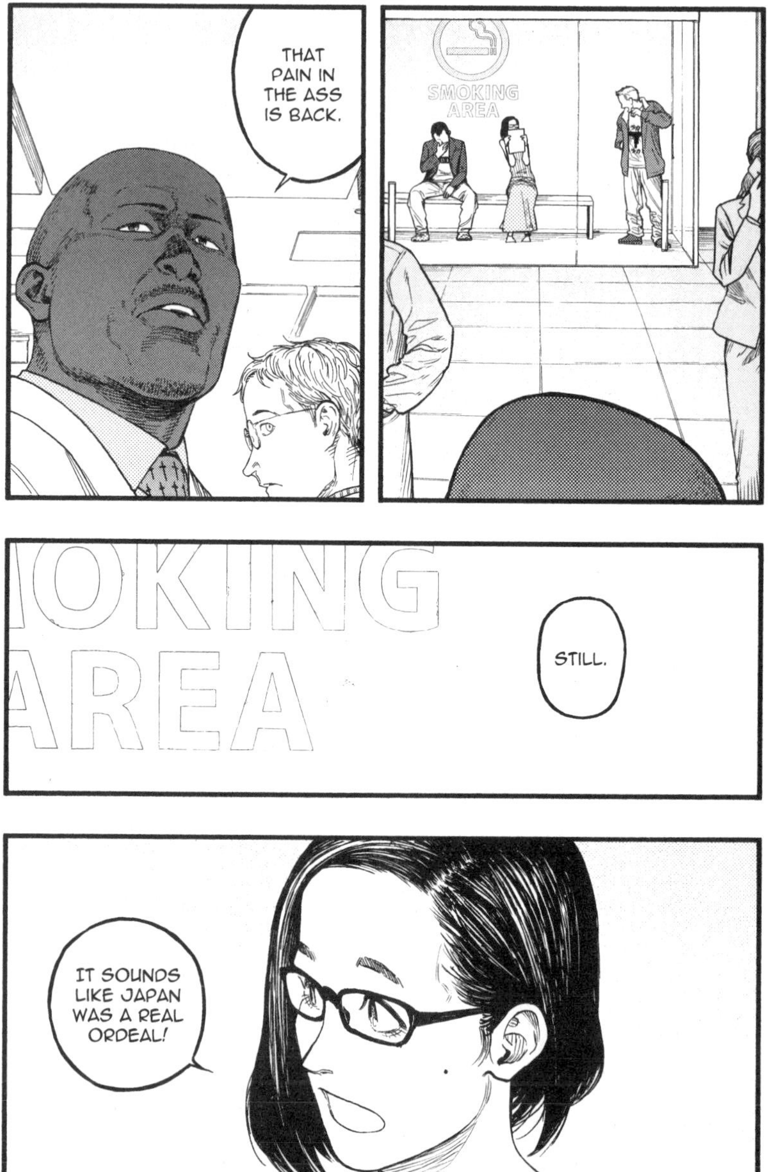
SMOKING AREA
THAT PAIN IN THE ASS IS BACK.
STILL.
IT SOUNDS LIKE JAPAN WAS A REAL ORDEAL!

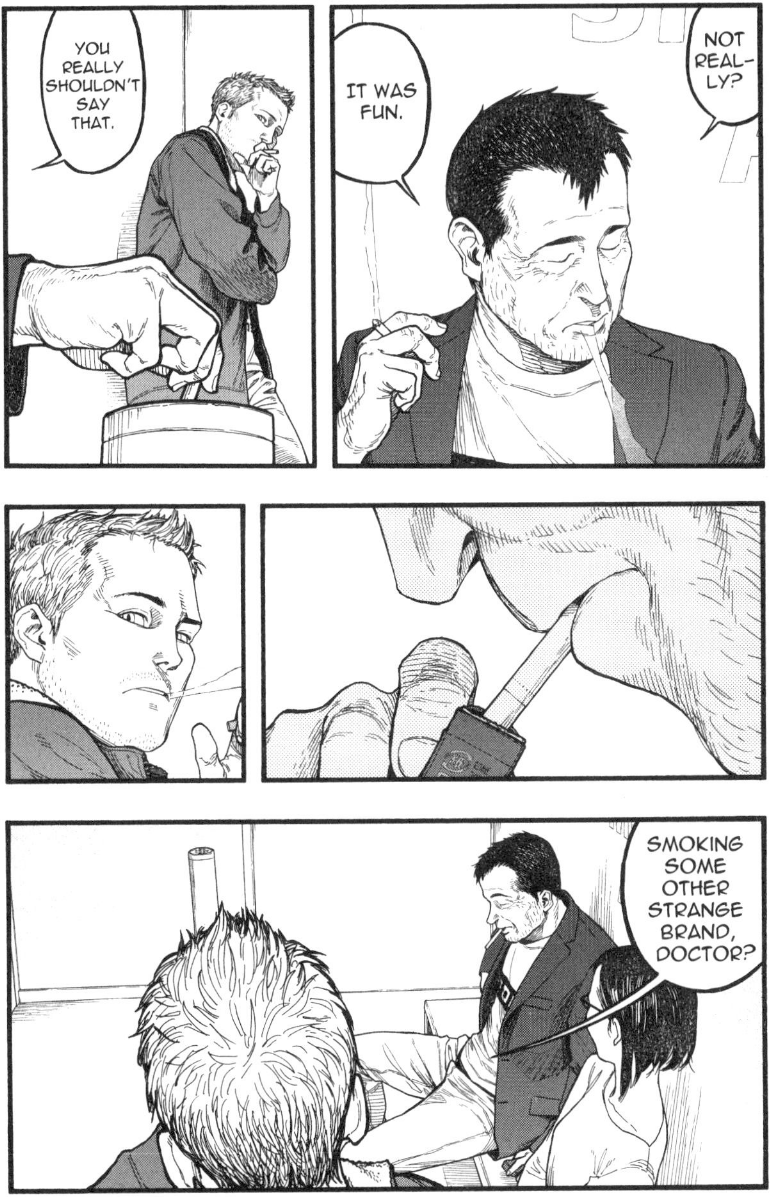
NOT REALLY?
IT WAS FUN.
YOU REALLY SHOULDN'T SAY THAT.
SMOKING SOME OTHER STRANGE BRAND, DOCTOR?

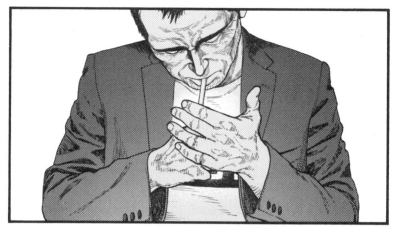

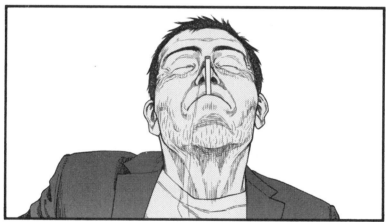

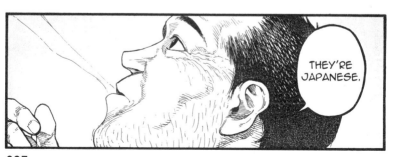

THEY'RE JAPANESE.

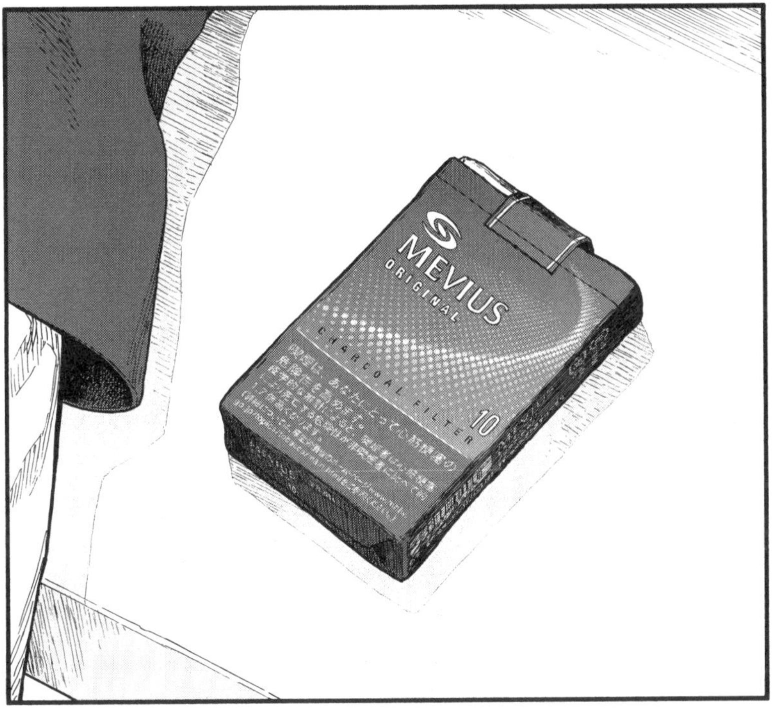
MEVIUS
ORIGINAL
CHARCOAL FILTER
10

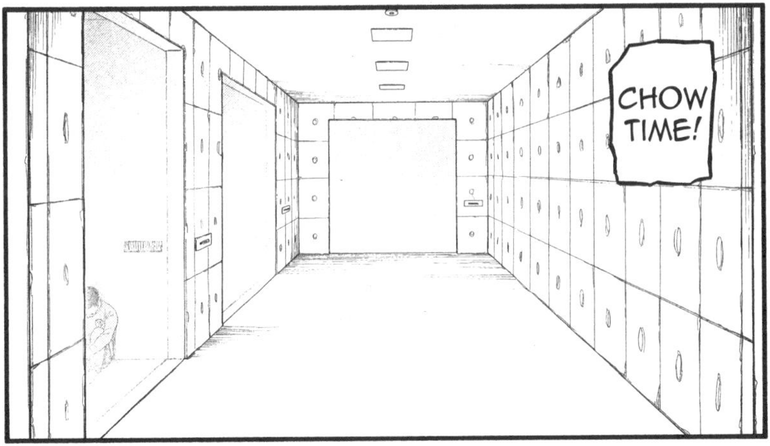
CHOW TIME!

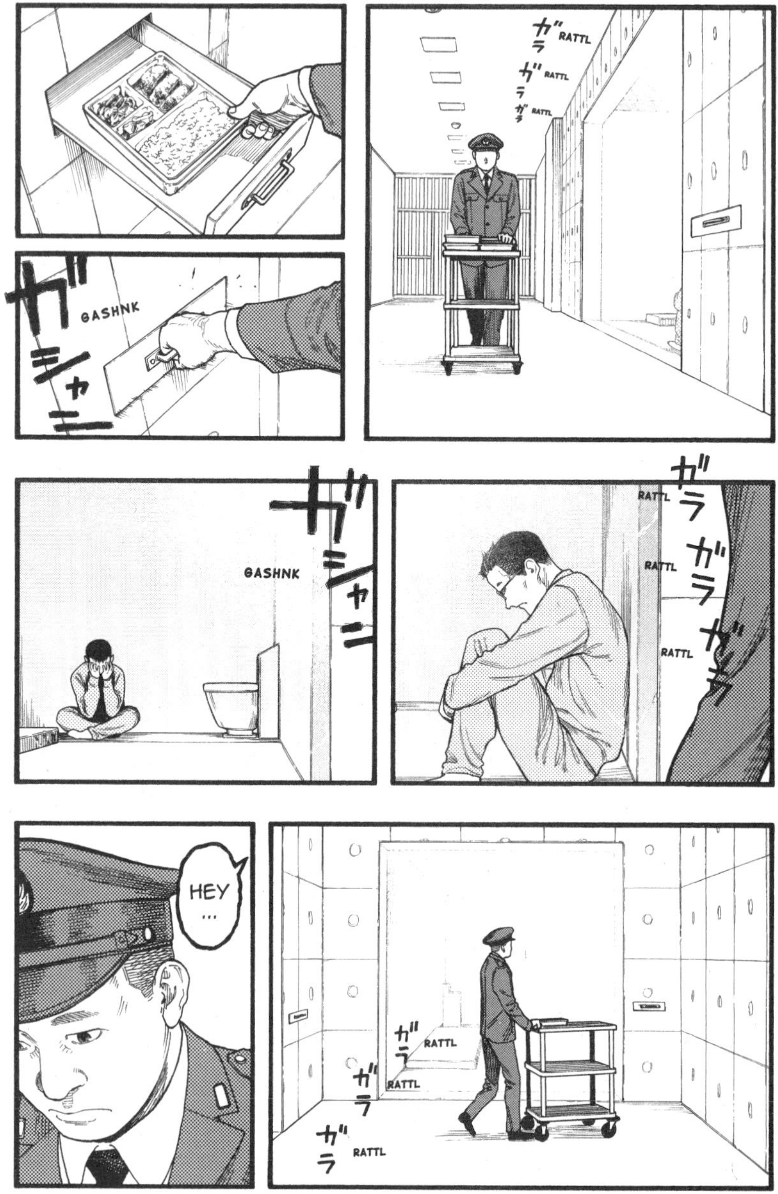

ガラ RATTL
ガラ RATTL
ガラ RATTL
ガシャン GASHNK
ガラ RATTL
ガラ RATTL
RATTL
ガシャン GASHNK
ガラ RATTL
ガラ RATTL
ガラ RATTL
HEY …

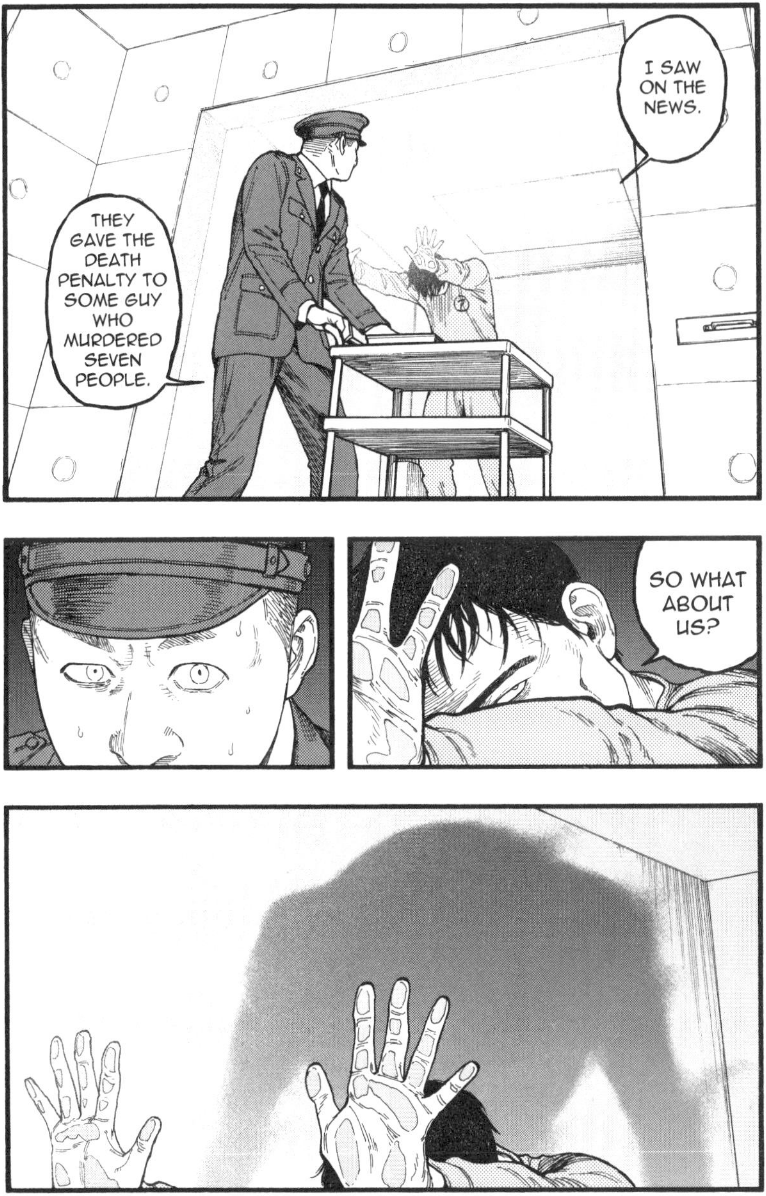
I SAW ON THE NEWS.
THEY GAVE THE DEATH PENALTY TO SOME GUY WHO MURDERED SEVEN PEOPLE.
SO WHAT ABOUT US?

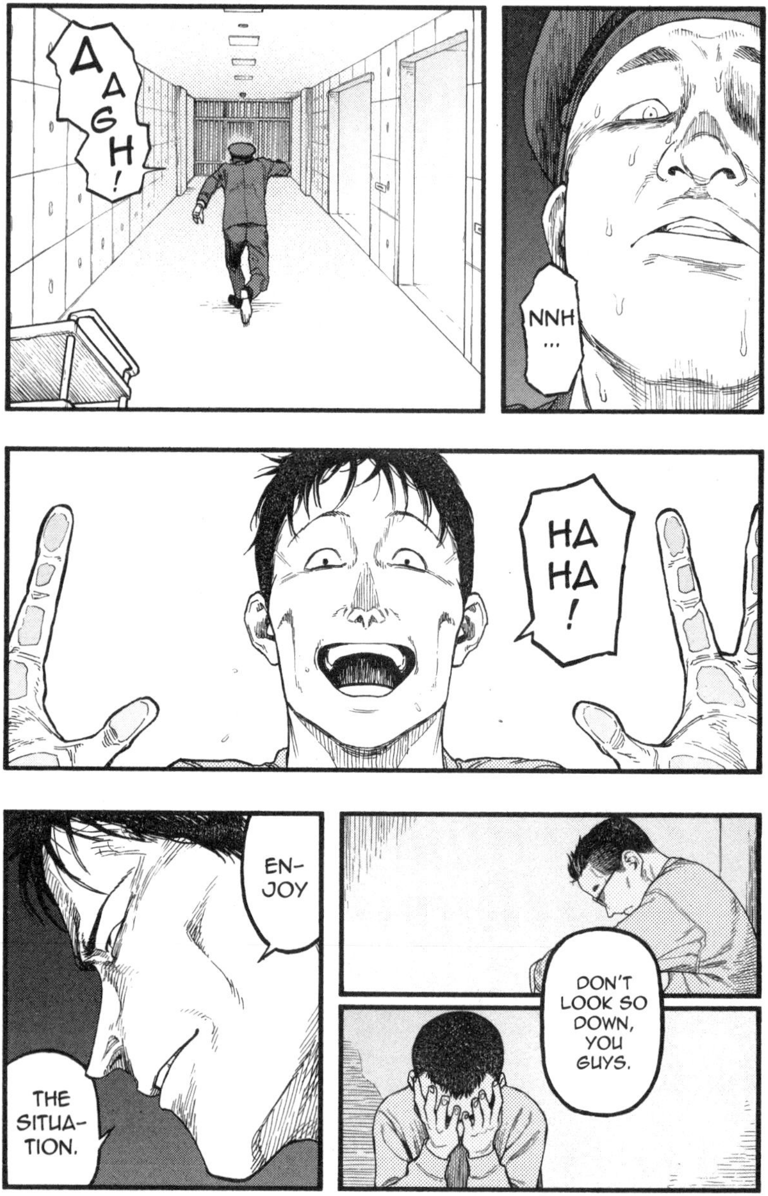
NNH ...
AAGH!
HA HA!
DON'T LOOK SO DOWN, YOU GUYS.
EN-JOY
THE SITUA-TION.

HA
HA
HA
HA
SO. SOUNDS LIKE THEY'RE RELEASING US, HUH?

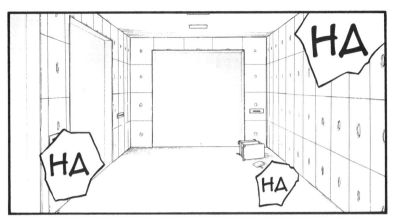

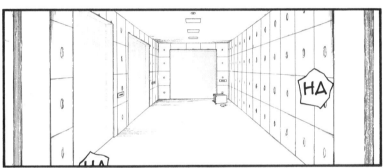

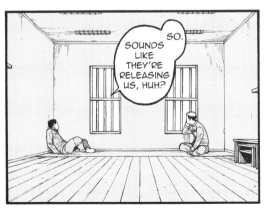

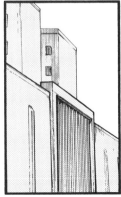

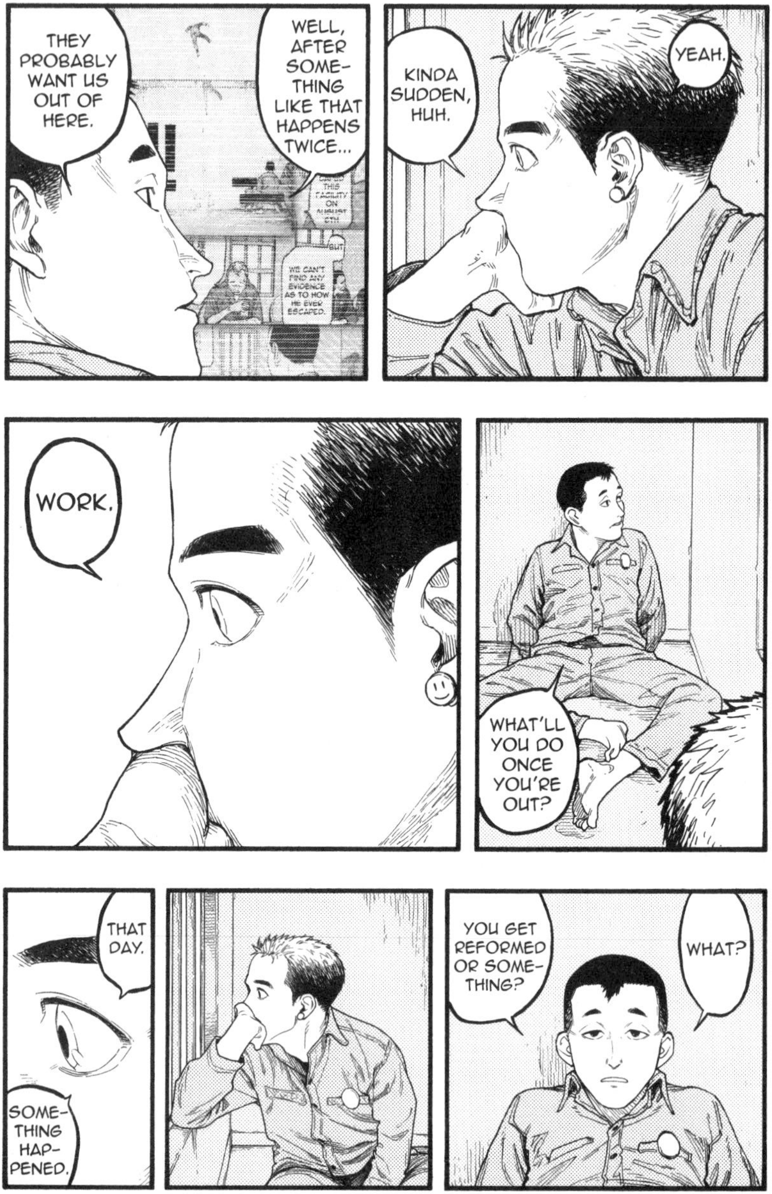
YEAH.
KINDA SUDDEN, HUH.
WELL, AFTER SOME-THING LIKE THAT HAPPENS TWICE...
BUT
WE CAN'T FIND ANY EVIDENCE AS TO HOW HE EVER ESCAPED.
THEY PROBABLY WANT US OUT OF HERE.
WHAT'LL YOU DO ONCE YOU'RE OUT?
WORK.
WHAT?
YOU GET REFORMED OR SOME-THING?
THAT DAY.
SOME-THING HAP-PENED.

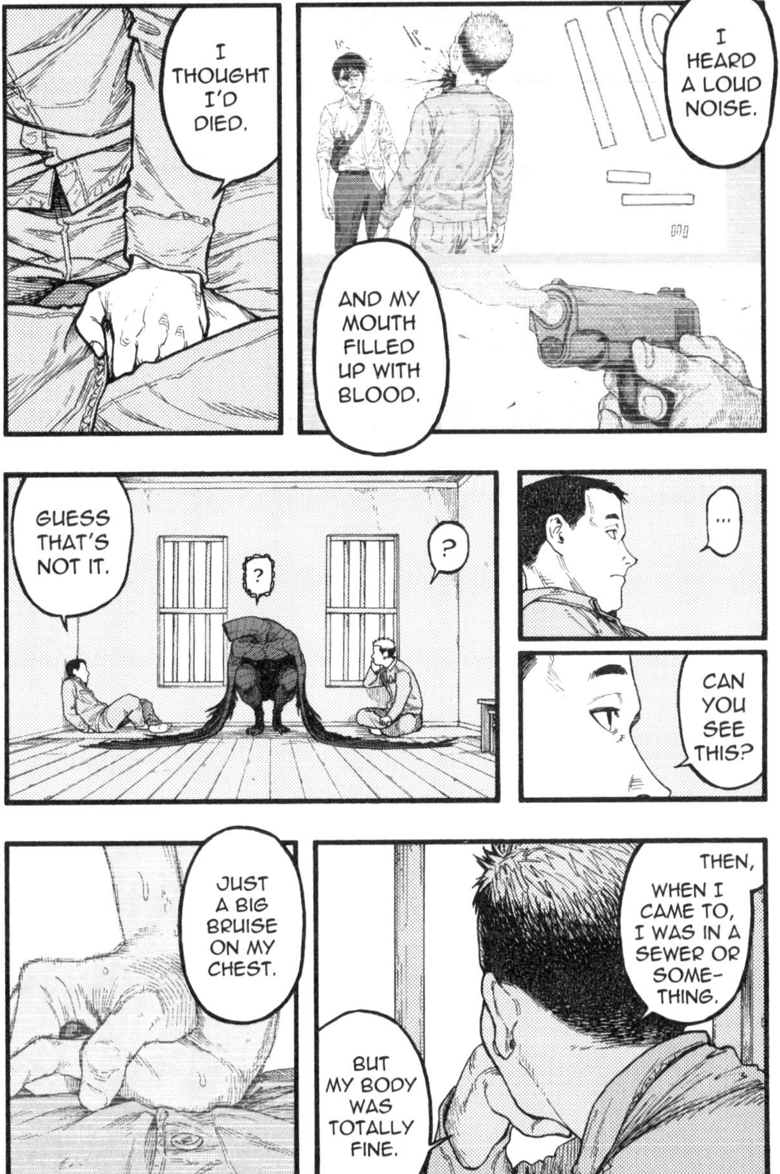
I HEARD A LOUD NOISE.
AND MY MOUTH FILLED UP WITH BLOOD.
I THOUGHT I'D DIED.
...
CAN YOU SEE THIS?
?
?
GUESS THAT'S NOT IT.
THEN, WHEN I CAME TO, I WAS IN A SEWER OR SOME-THING.
BUT MY BODY WAS TOTALLY FINE.
JUST A BIG BRUISE ON MY CHEST.

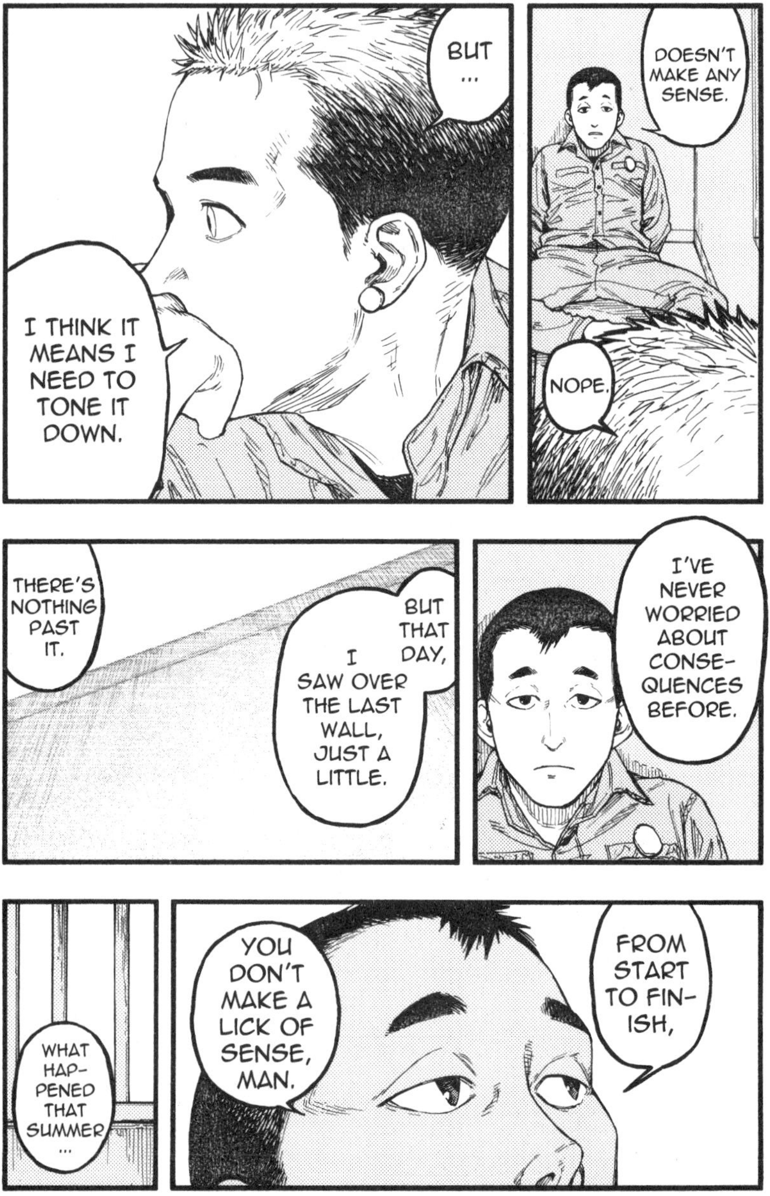
DOESN'T MAKE ANY SENSE.
NOPE.
BUT ...
I THINK IT MEANS I NEED TO TONE IT DOWN.
I'VE NEVER WORRIED ABOUT CONSE-QUENCES BEFORE.
BUT THAT DAY,
I SAW OVER THE LAST WALL, JUST A LITTLE.
THERE'S NOTHING PAST IT.
FROM START TO FIN-ISH,
YOU DON'T MAKE A LICK OF SENSE, MAN.
WHAT HAP-PENED THAT SUMMER ...

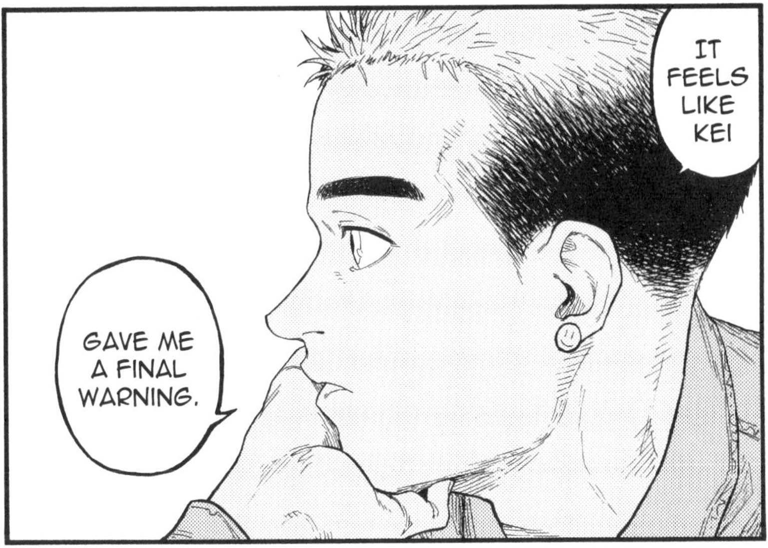
IT FEELS LIKE KEI
GAVE ME A FINAL WARNING.

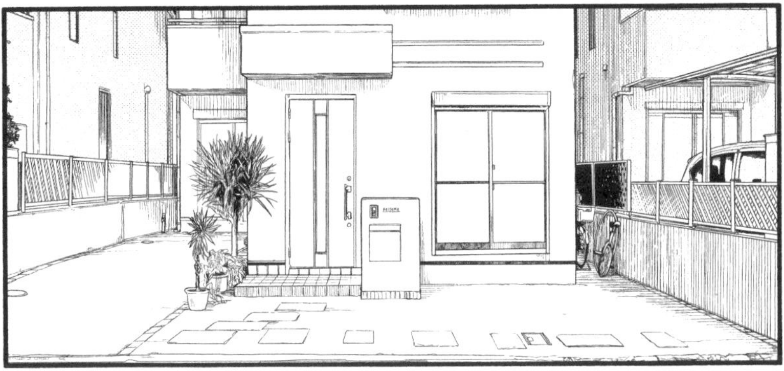

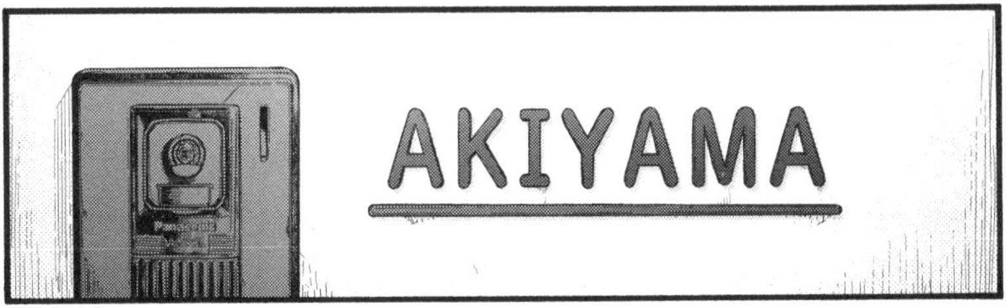
AKIYAMA

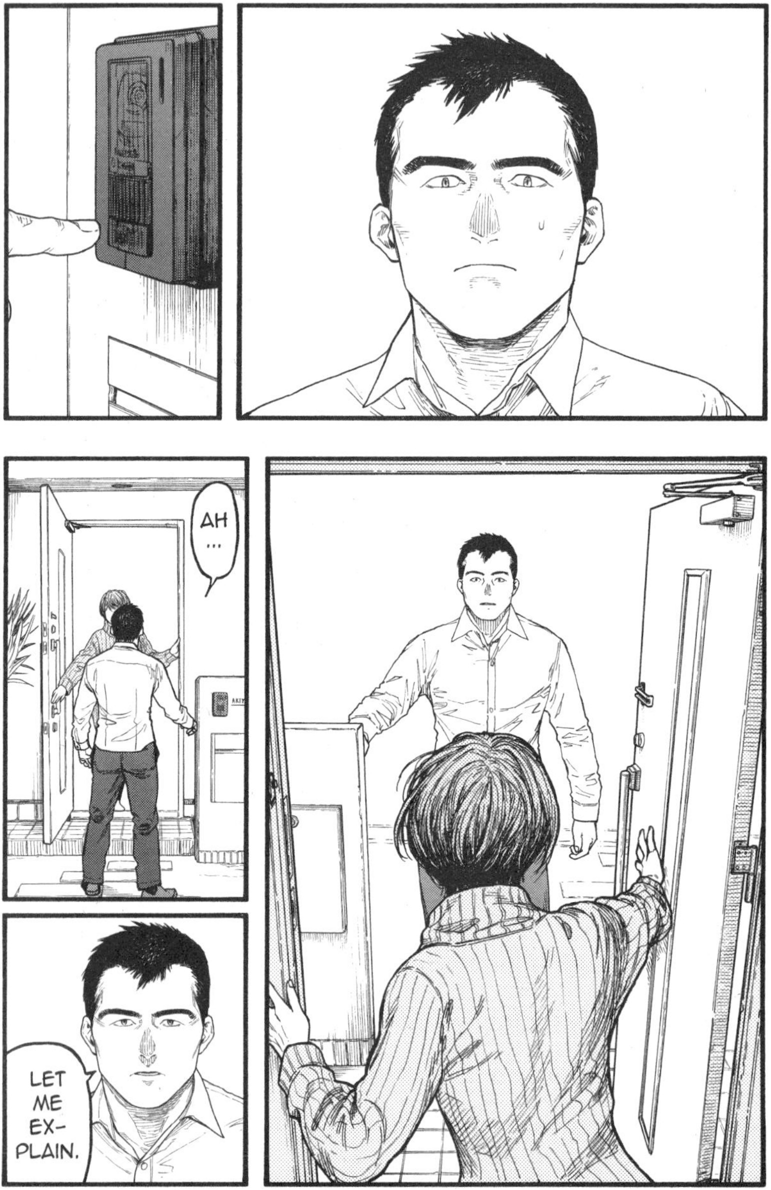
AH ...
LET ME EX- PLAIN.

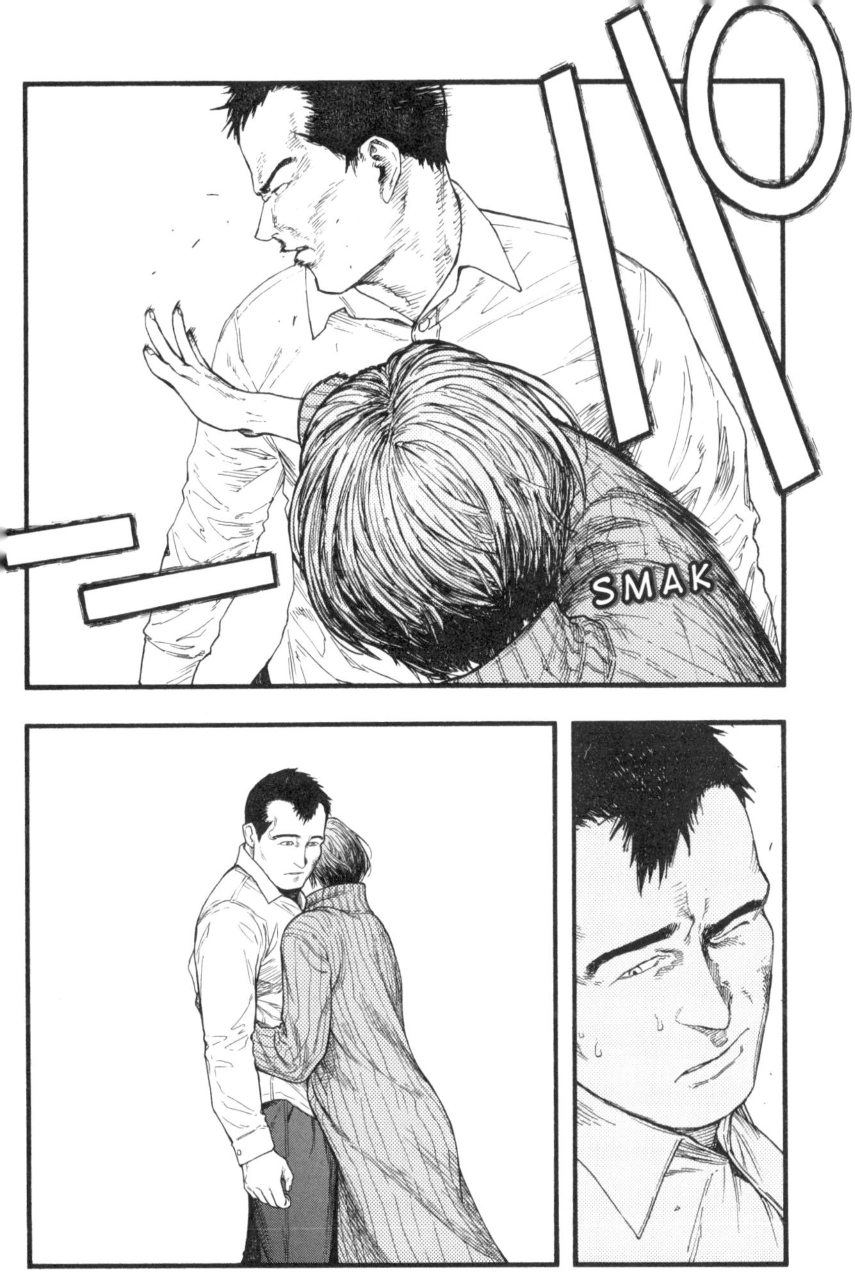
SMAK

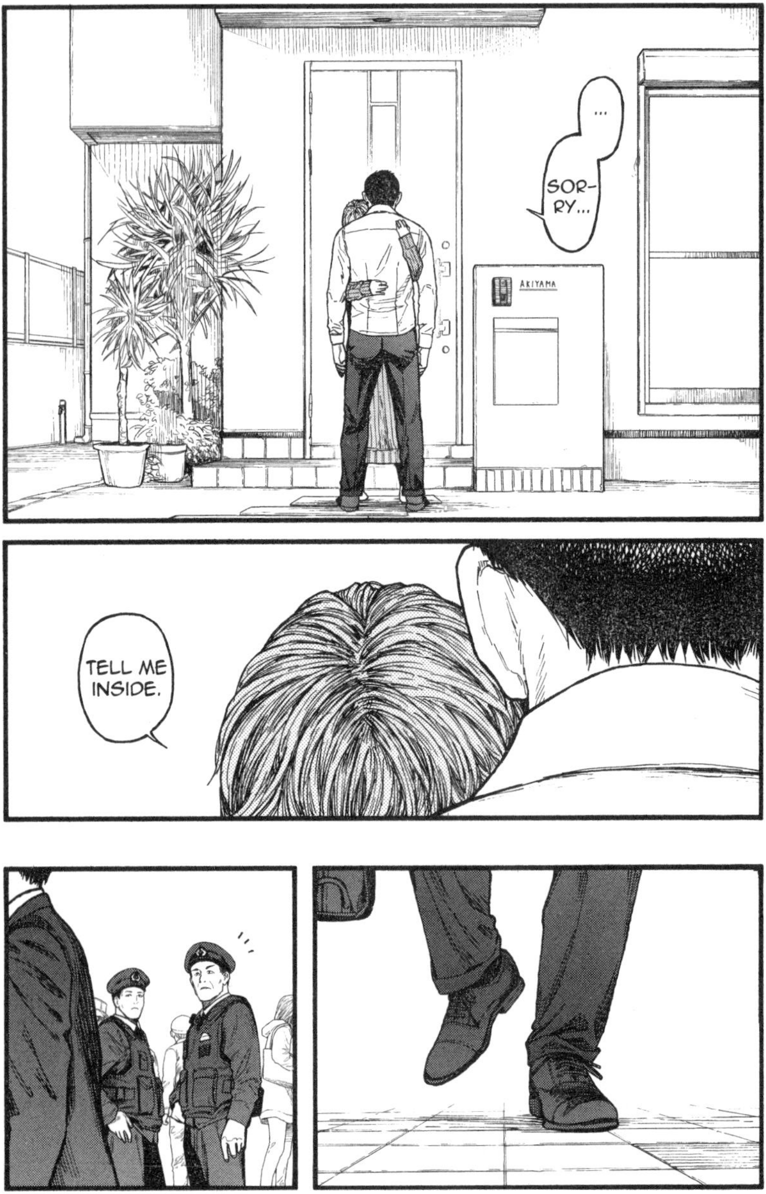
...
SOR-
RY...
TELL ME INSIDE.

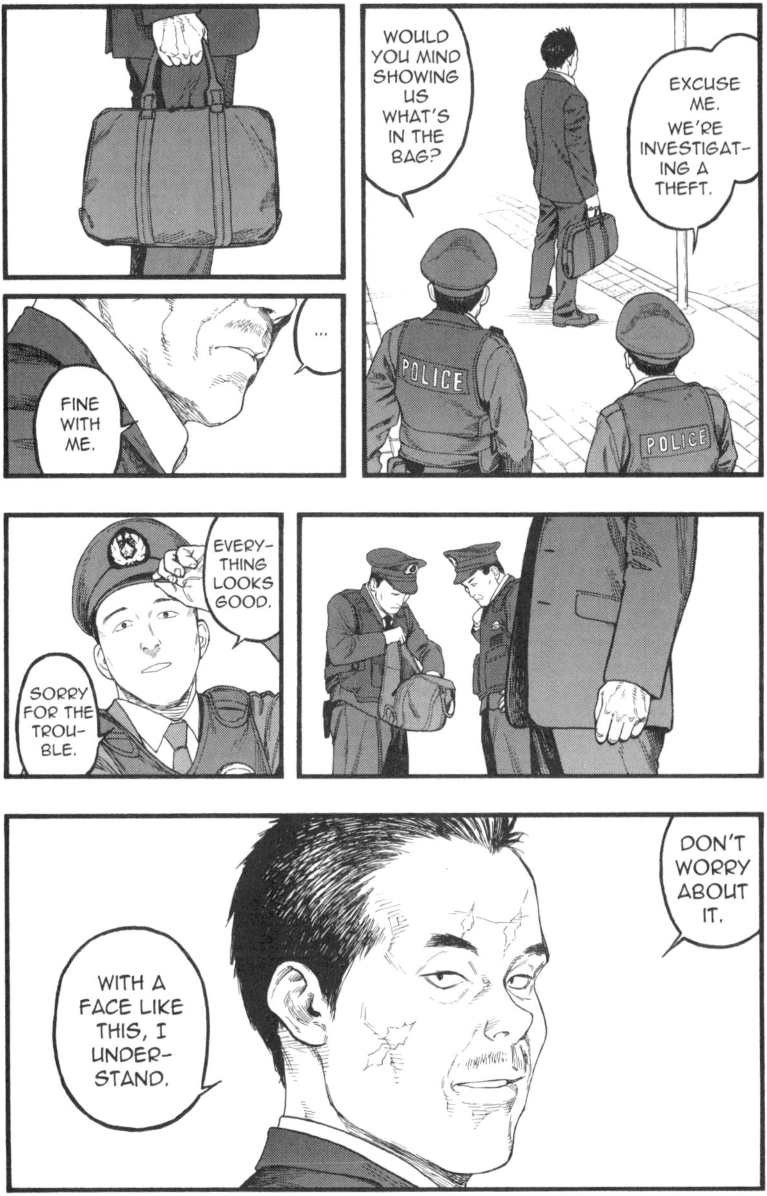
EXCUSE ME. WE'RE INVESTIGATING A THEFT.
WOULD YOU MIND SHOWING US WHAT'S IN THE BAG?
...
FINE WITH ME.
EVERYTHING LOOKS GOOD.
SORRY FOR THE TROUBLE.
DON'T WORRY ABOUT IT.
WITH A FACE LIKE THIS, I UNDERSTAND.

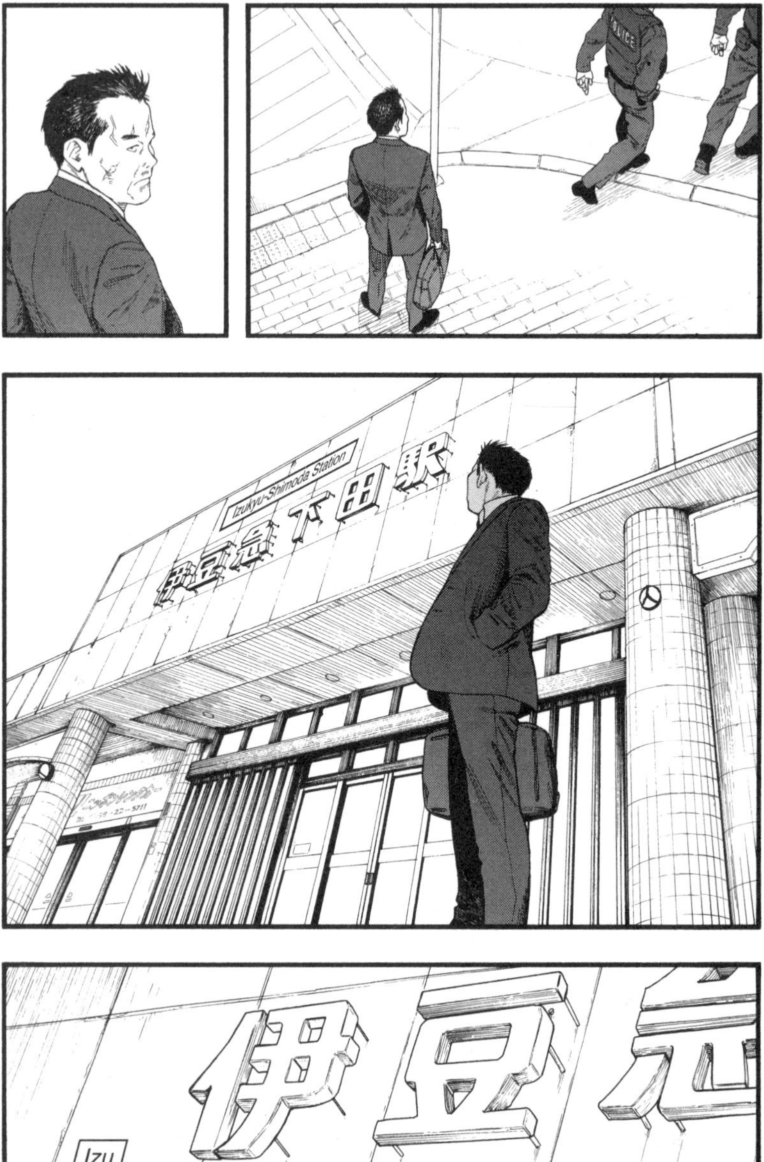
Izukyu-Shimoda Station
伊豆急下田駅
伊豆
Izu

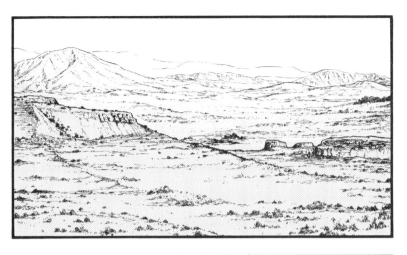

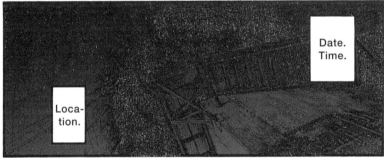

Date.
Time.

Loca-
tion.

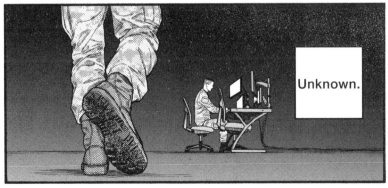

Unknown.

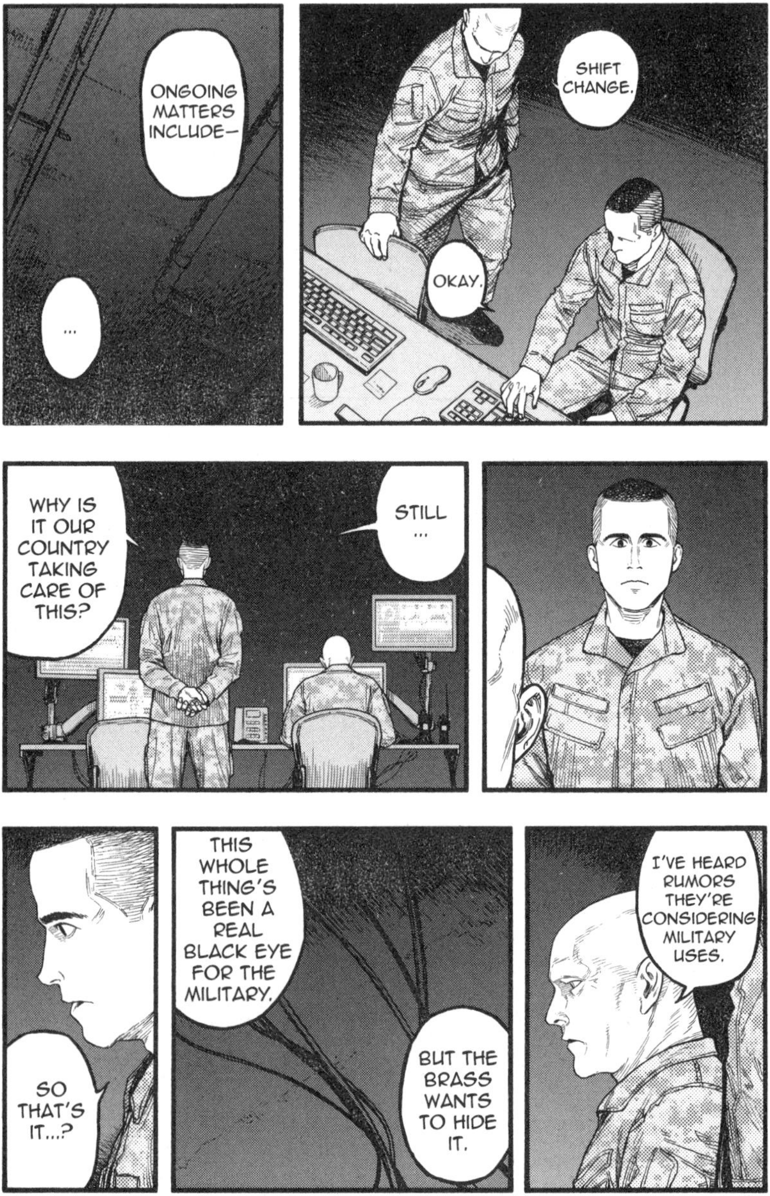
SHIFT CHANGE.
OKAY.
ONGOING MATTERS INCLUDE—
...
STILL ...
WHY IS IT OUR COUNTRY TAKING CARE OF THIS?
I'VE HEARD RUMORS THEY'RE CONSIDERING MILITARY USES.
THIS WHOLE THING'S BEEN A REAL BLACK EYE FOR THE MILITARY.
BUT THE BRASS WANTS TO HIDE IT.
SO THAT'S IT...?

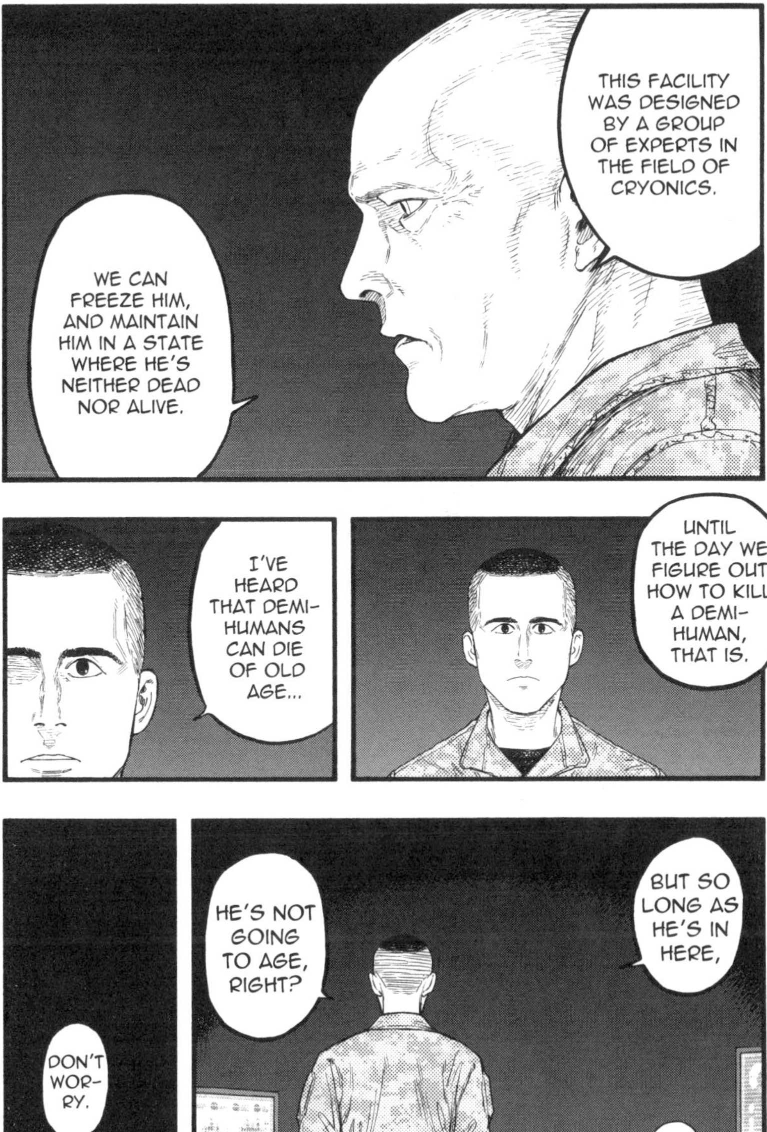
THIS FACILITY WAS DESIGNED BY A GROUP OF EXPERTS IN THE FIELD OF CRYONICS.
WE CAN FREEZE HIM, AND MAINTAIN HIM IN A STATE WHERE HE'S NEITHER DEAD NOR ALIVE.
UNTIL THE DAY WE FIGURE OUT HOW TO KILL A DEMI-HUMAN, THAT IS.
I'VE HEARD THAT DEMI-HUMANS CAN DIE OF OLD AGE...
BUT SO LONG AS HE'S IN HERE,
HE'S NOT GOING TO AGE, RIGHT?
DON'T WOR-RY.

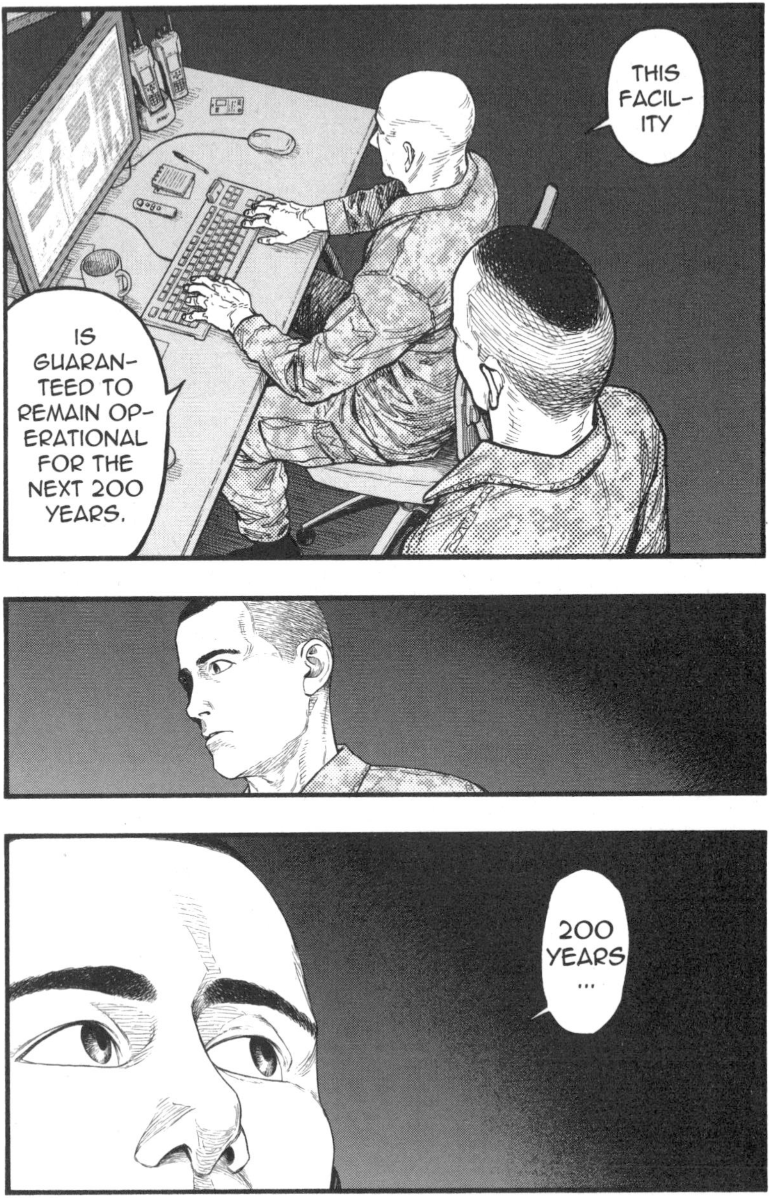
THIS FACIL- ITY
IS GUARAN- TEED TO REMAIN OP- ERATIONAL FOR THE NEXT 200 YEARS.
200 YEARS ...

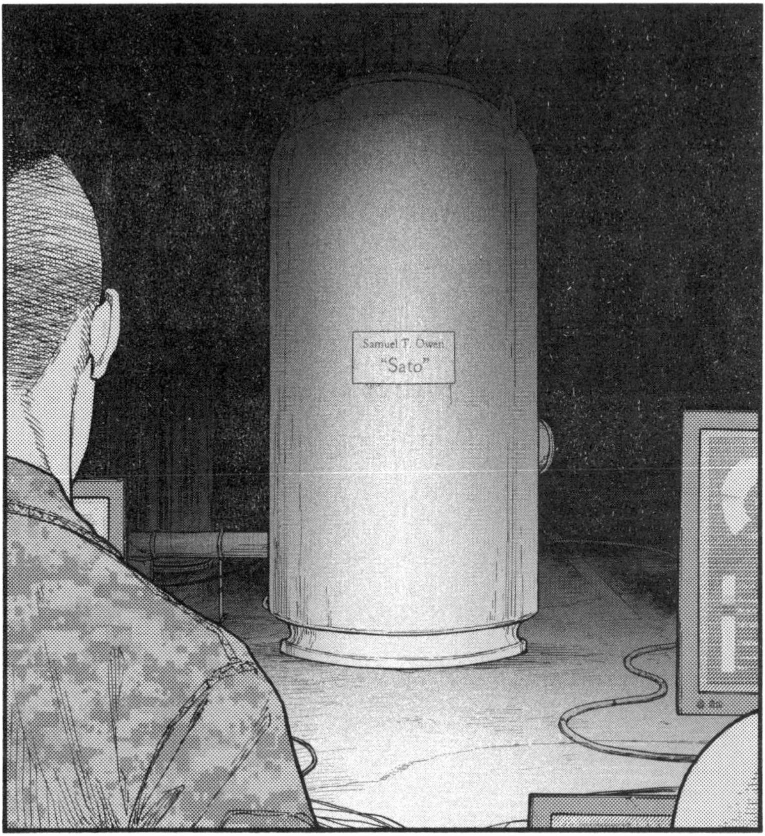
Samuel T. Owen
“Sato”

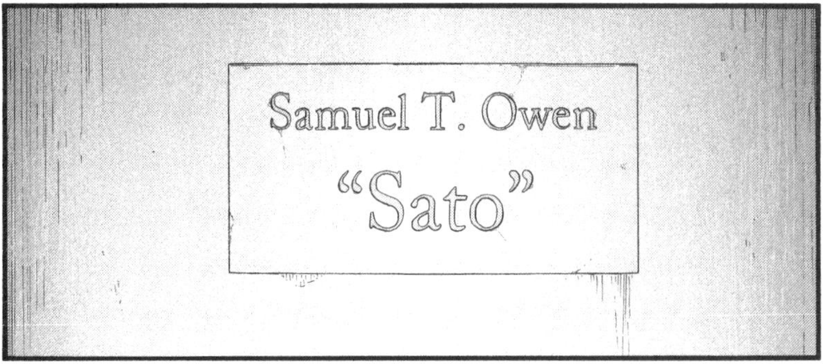
Samuel T. Owen
“Sato”

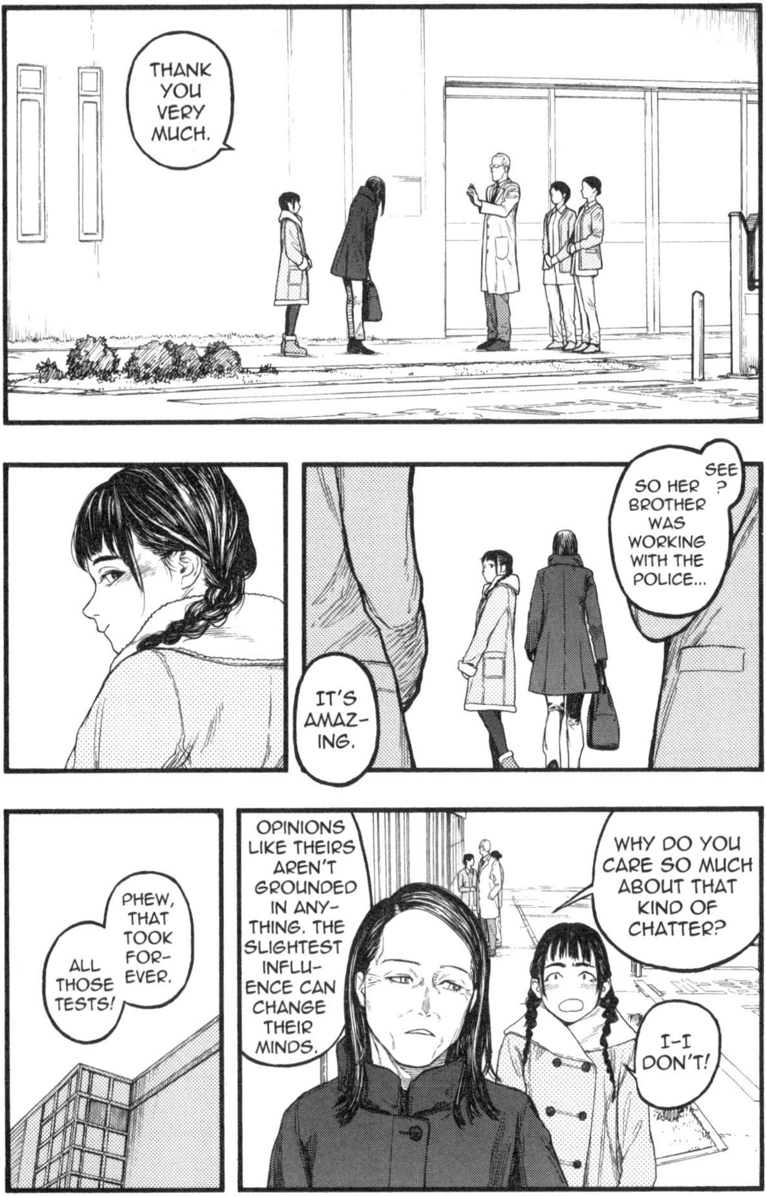
THANK YOU VERY MUCH.
SEE?
SO HER BROTHER WAS WORKING WITH THE POLICE...
IT'S AMAZ-ING.
WHY DO YOU CARE SO MUCH ABOUT THAT KIND OF CHATTER?
OPINIONS LIKE THEIRS AREN'T GROUNDED IN ANY-THING. THE SLIGHTEST INFLU-ENCE CAN CHANGE THEIR MINDS.
I-I DON'T!
PHEW, THAT TOOK FOR-EVER.
ALL THOSE TESTS!

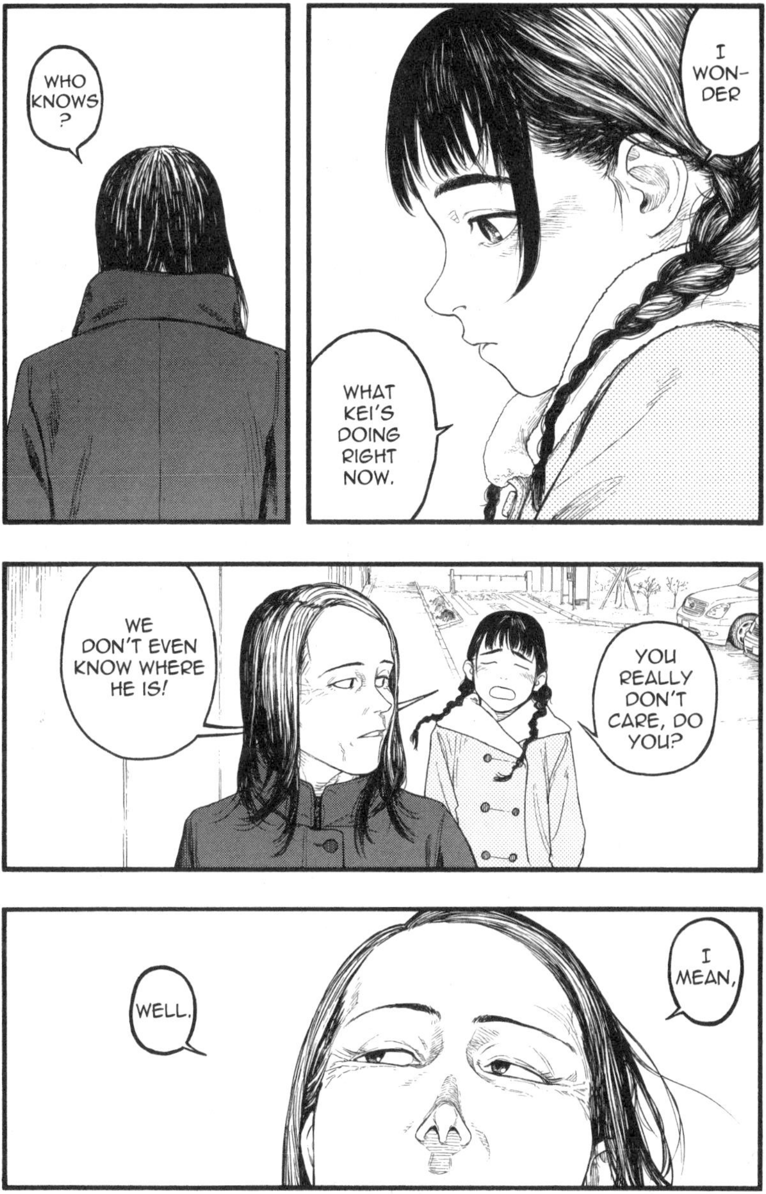
I WON-DER
WHAT KEI'S DOING RIGHT NOW.
WHO KNOWS?
YOU REALLY DON'T CARE, DO YOU?
WE DON'T EVEN KNOW WHERE HE IS!
I MEAN,
WELL.

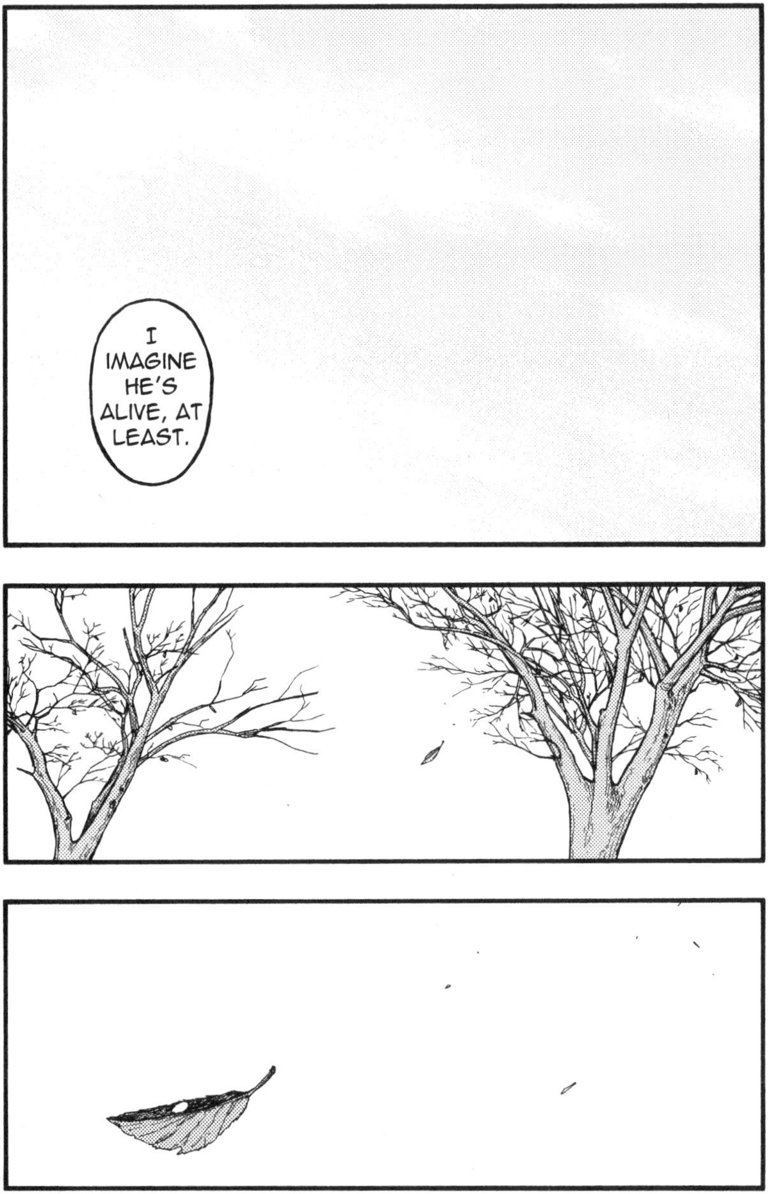
I IMAGINE HE'S ALIVE, AT LEAST.

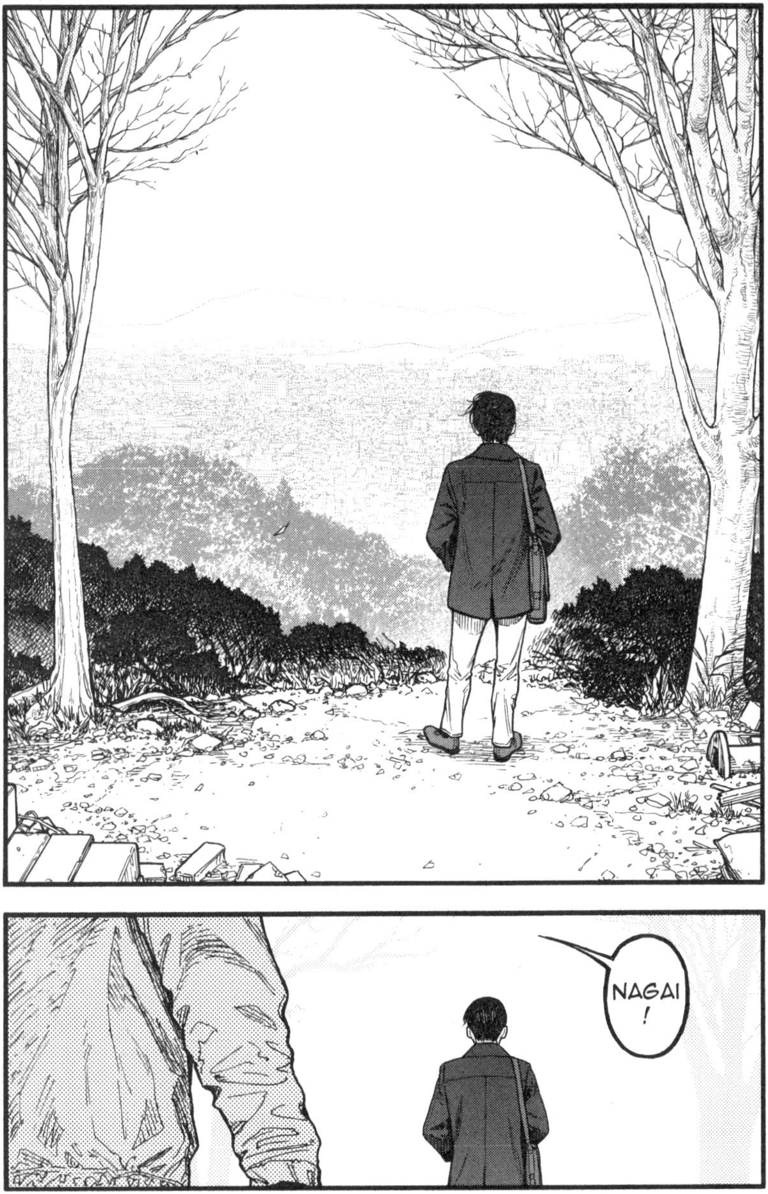
NAGAI !

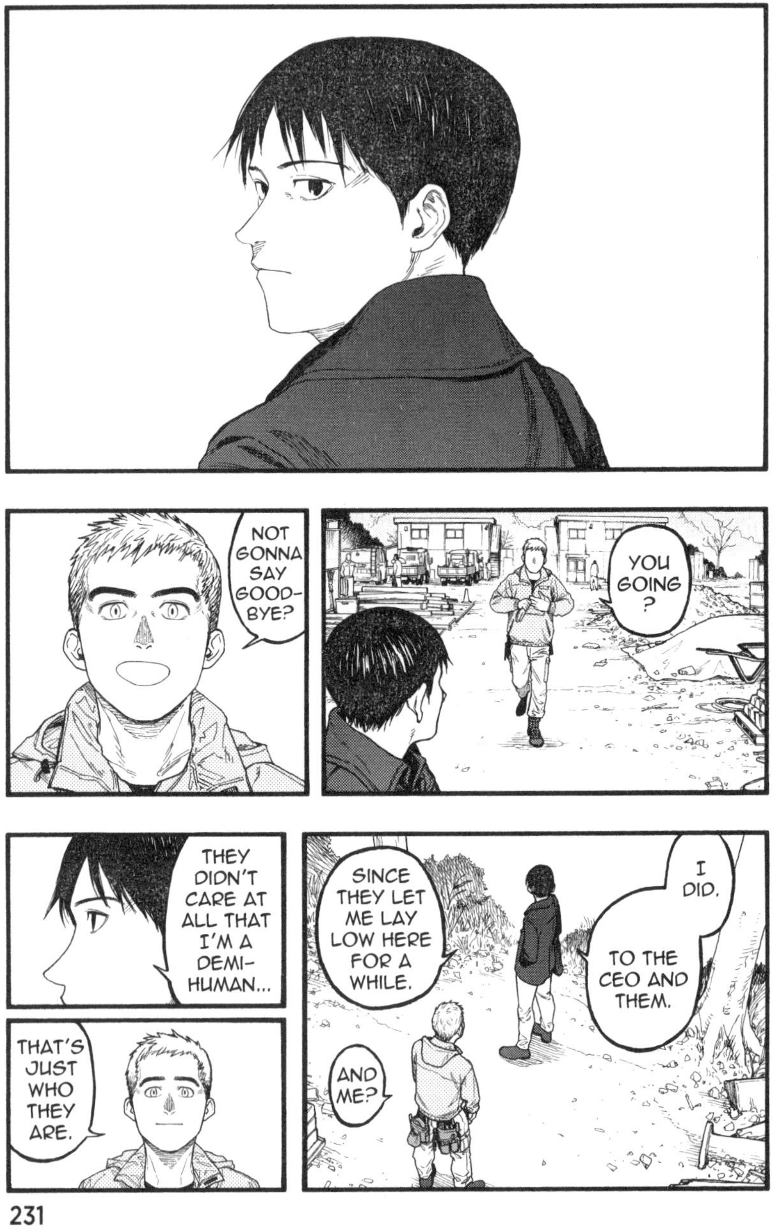
YOU GOING?
NOT GONNA SAY GOODBYE?
I DID.
TO THE CEO AND THEM.
SINCE THEY LET ME LAY LOW HERE FOR A WHILE.
AND ME?
THEY DIDN'T CARE AT ALL THAT I'M A DEMI-HUMAN...
THAT'S JUST WHO THEY ARE.

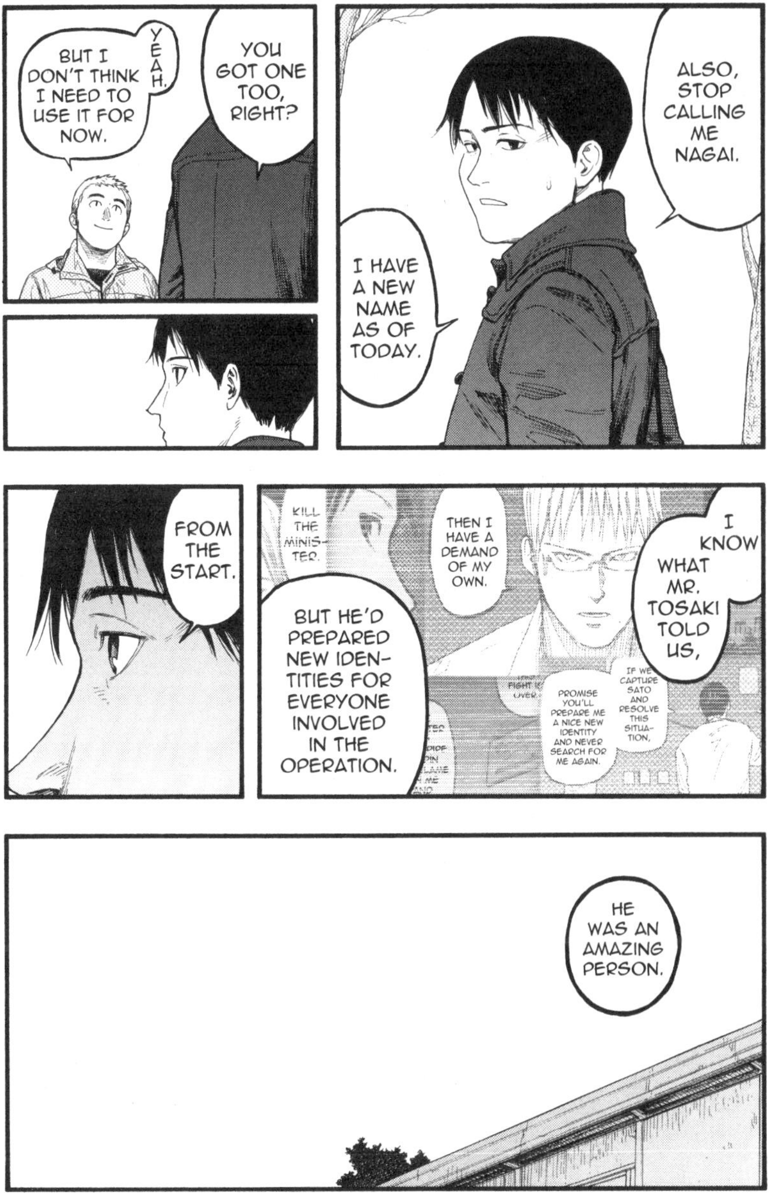
ALSO, STOP CALLING ME NAGAI.
I HAVE A NEW NAME AS OF TODAY.
YOU GOT ONE TOO, RIGHT?
YEAH.
BUT I DON'T THINK I NEED TO USE IT FOR NOW.
I KNOW WHAT MR. TOSAKI TOLD US,
THEN I HAVE A DEMAND OF MY OWN.
KILL THE MINISTER.
IF WE CAPTURE SATO AND RESOLVE THIS SITUATION,
PROMISE YOU'LL PREPARE ME A NICE NEW IDENTITY AND NEVER SEARCH FOR ME AGAIN.
BUT HE'D PREPARED NEW IDENTITIES FOR EVERYONE INVOLVED IN THE OPERATION.
FROM THE START.
HE WAS AN AMAZING PERSON.

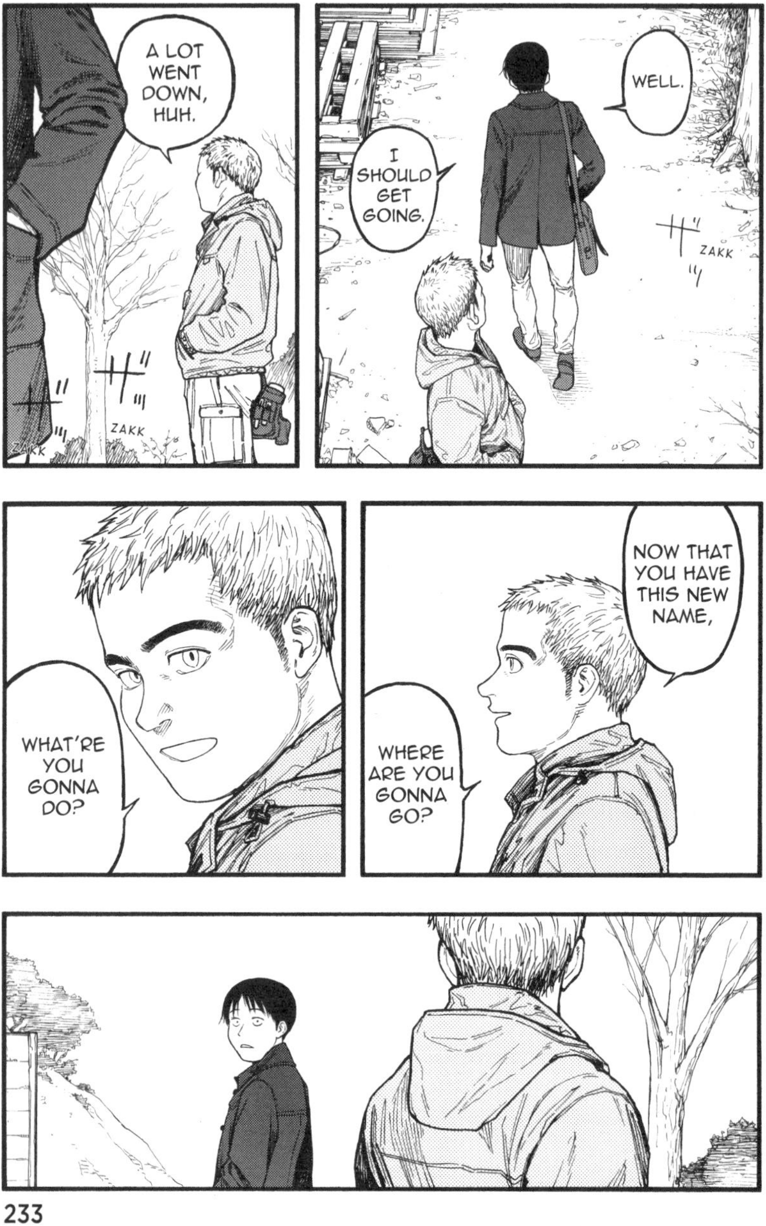
WELL.
I SHOULD GET GOING.
ZAKK
A LOT WENT DOWN, HUH.
ZAKK
ZAKK
NOW THAT YOU HAVE THIS NEW NAME,
WHERE ARE YOU GONNA GO?
WHAT'RE YOU GONNA DO?

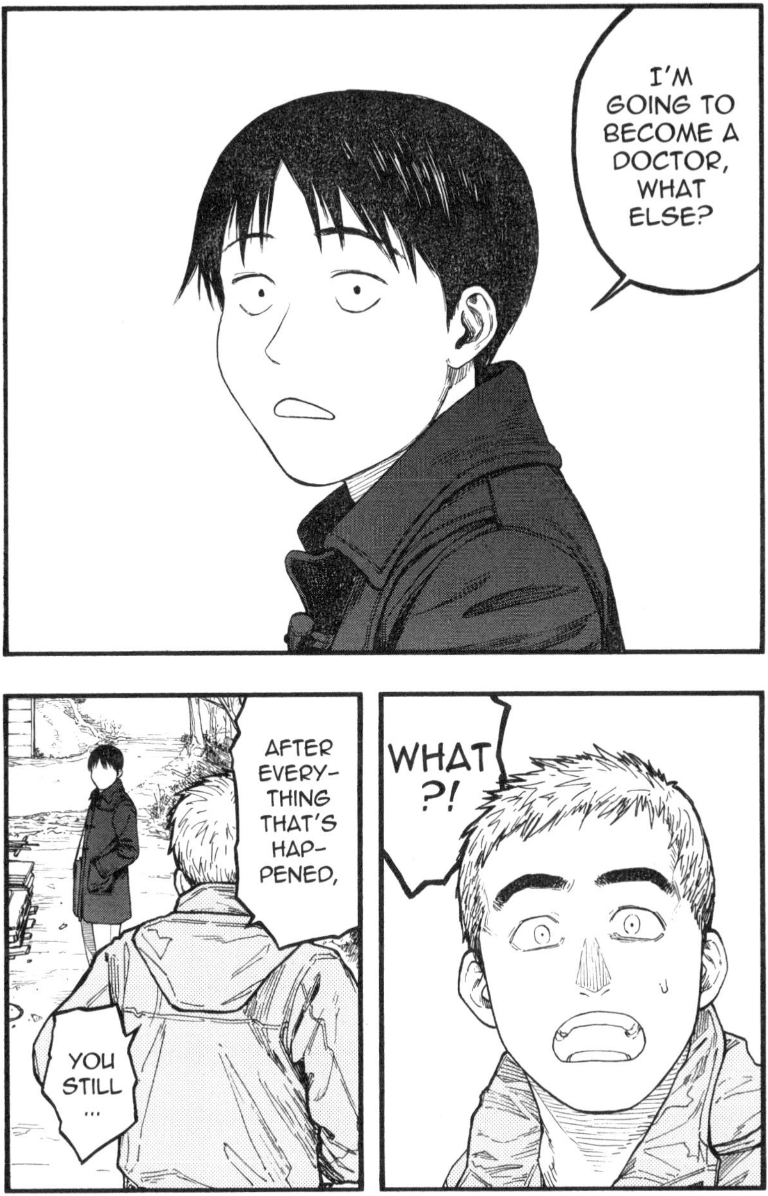
I'M GOING TO BECOME A DOCTOR, WHAT ELSE?
WHAT?!
AFTER EVERY-THING THAT'S HAP-PENED,
YOU STILL ...

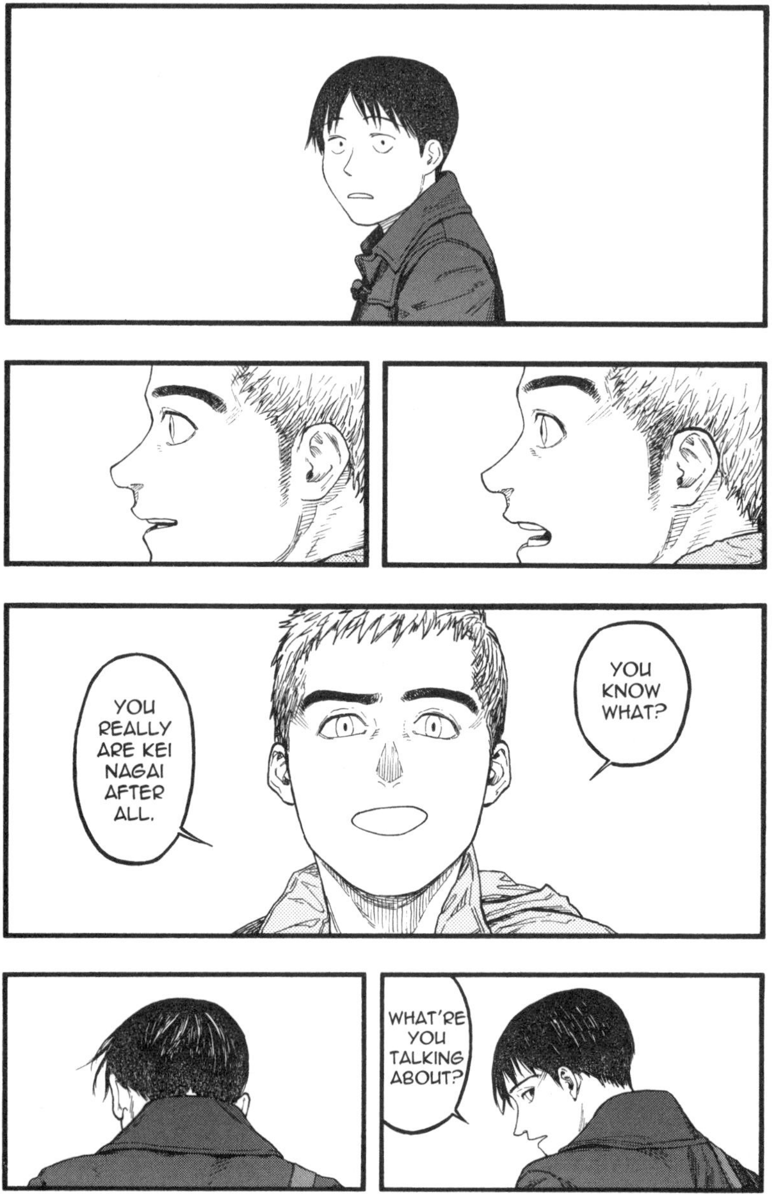
YOU KNOW WHAT?
YOU REALLY ARE KEI NAGAI AFTER ALL.
WHAT'RE YOU TALKING ABOUT?

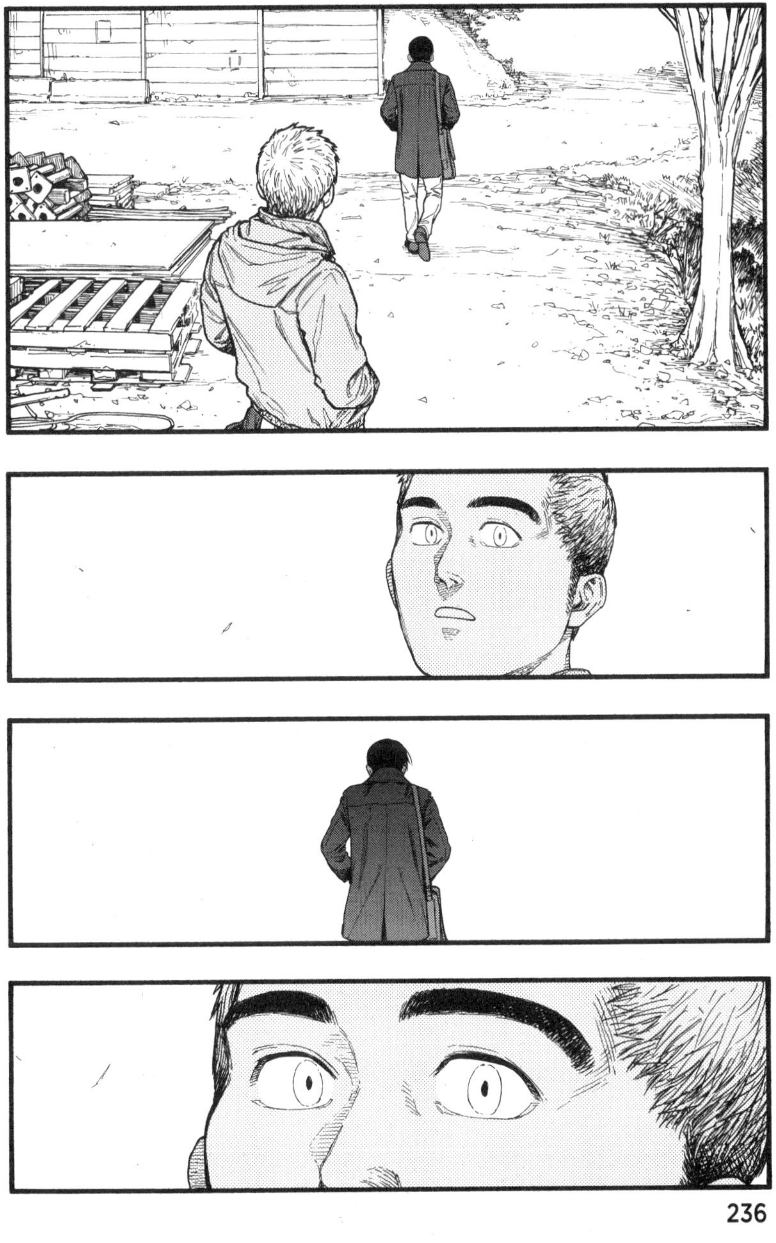

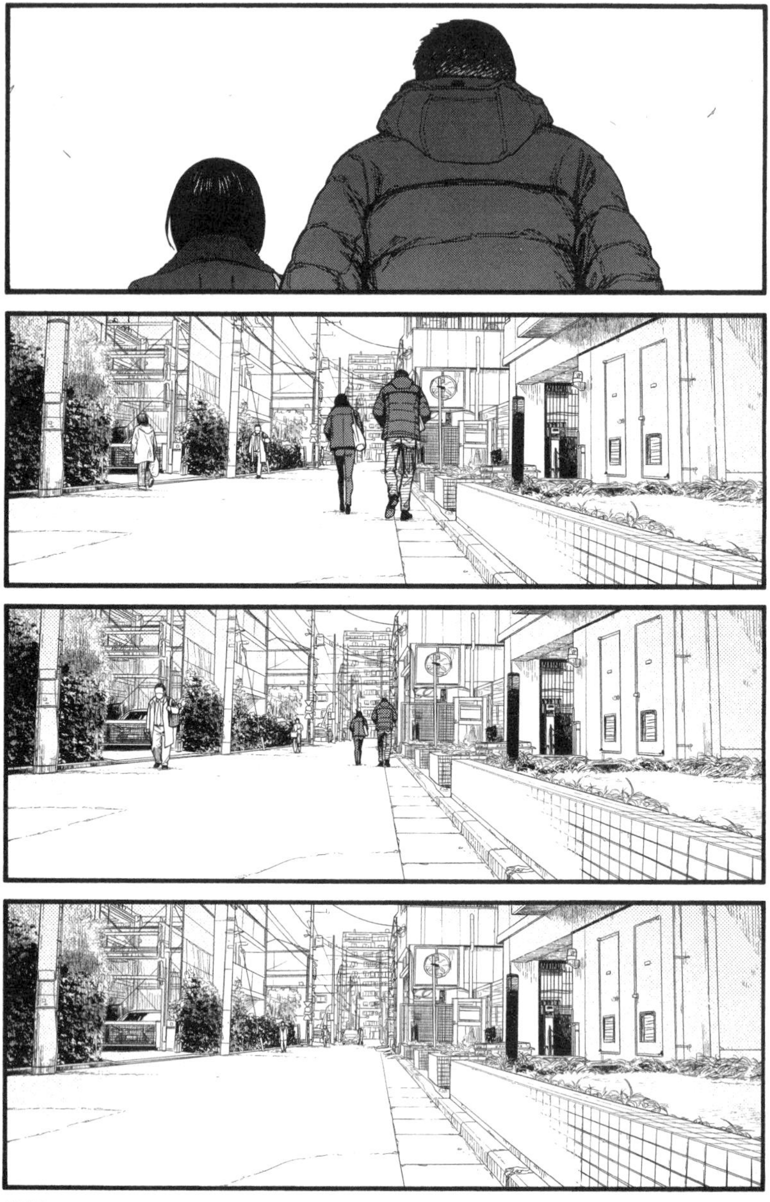

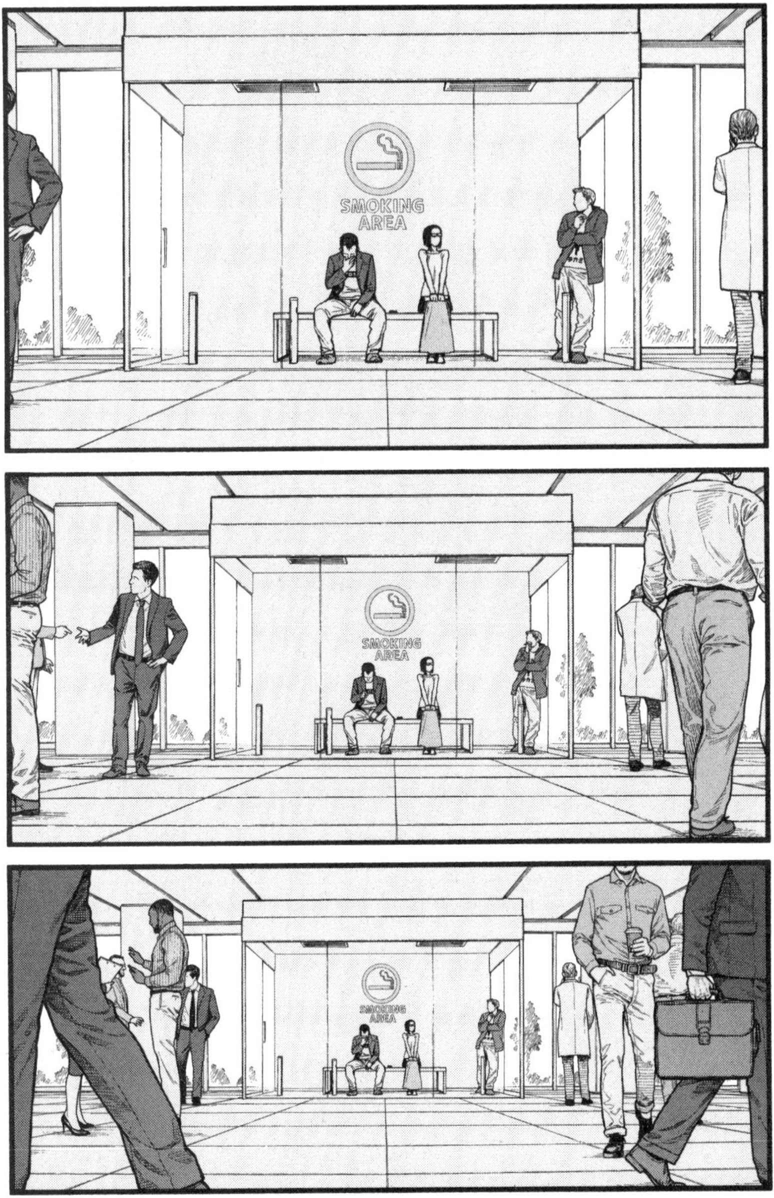
SMOKING AREA
SMOKING AREA
SMOKING AREA

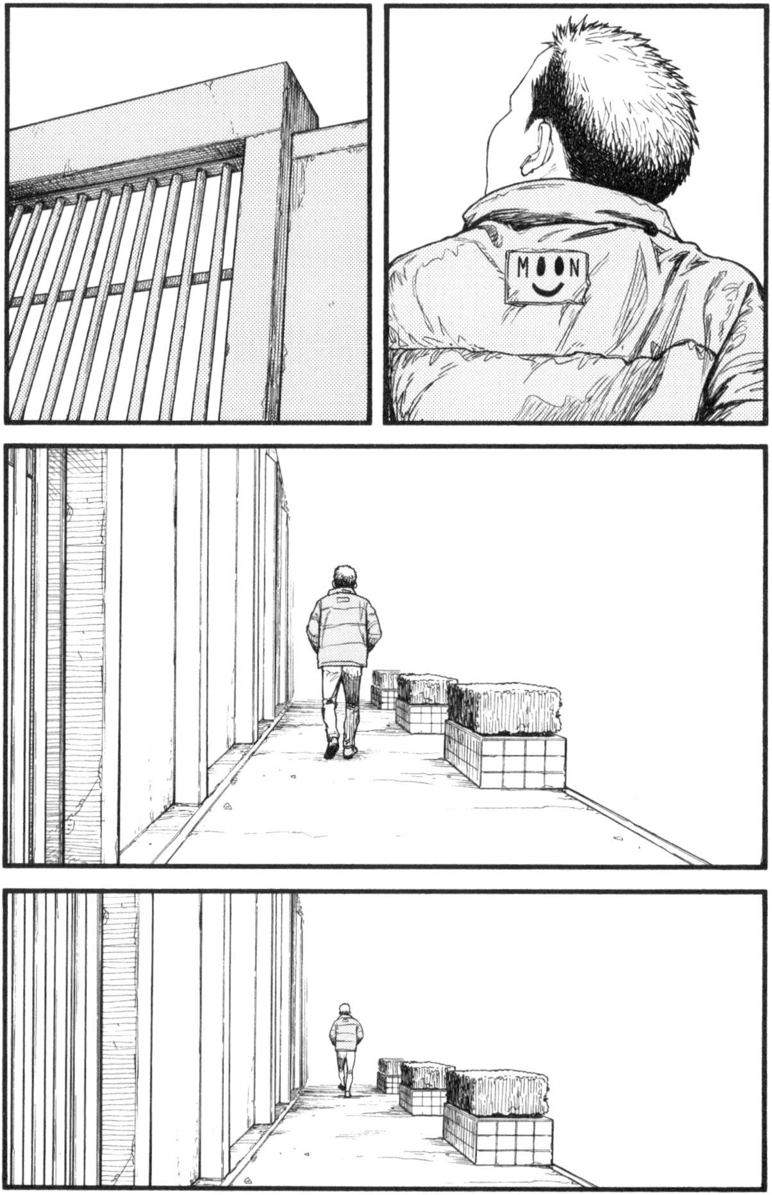
MOON

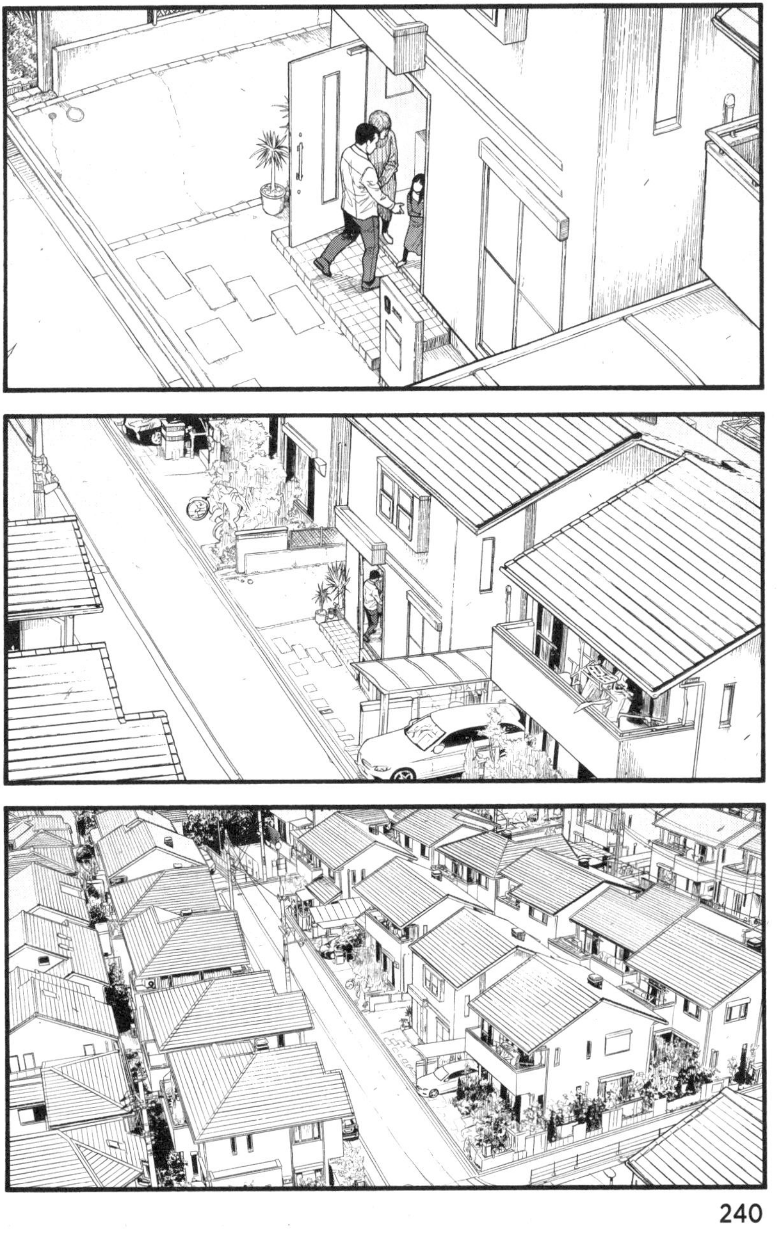

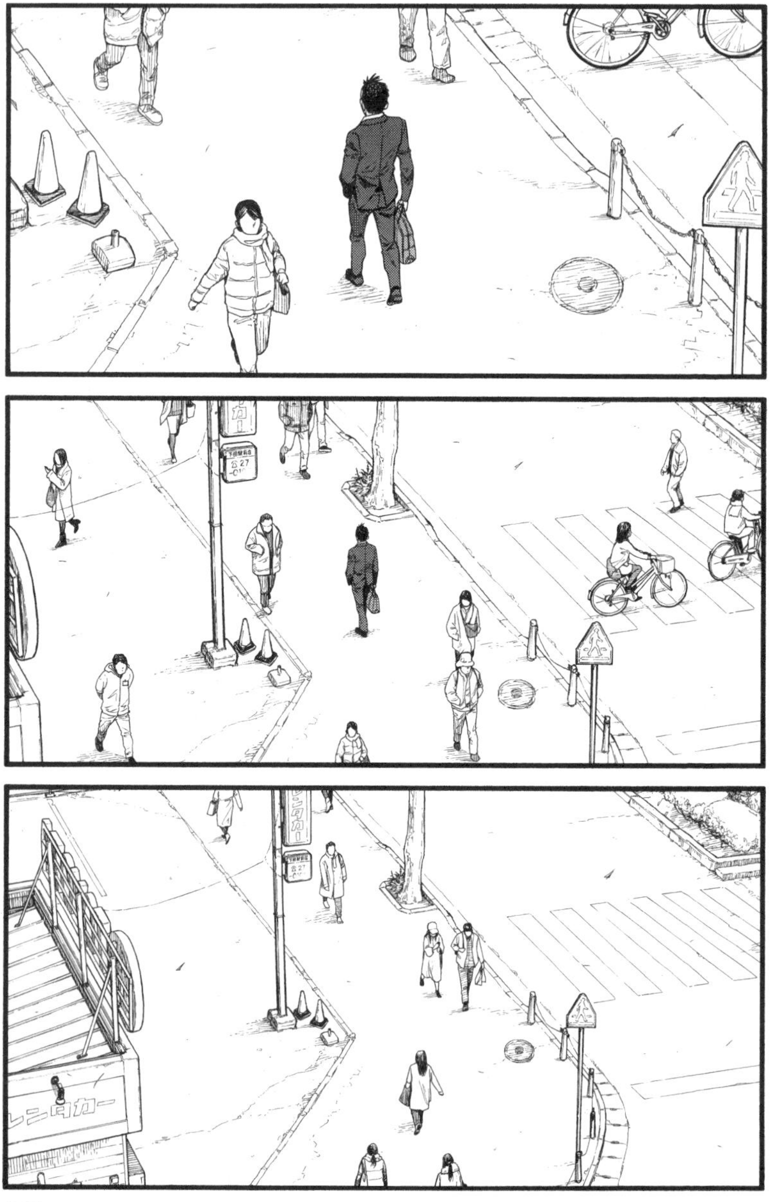
レンタカー

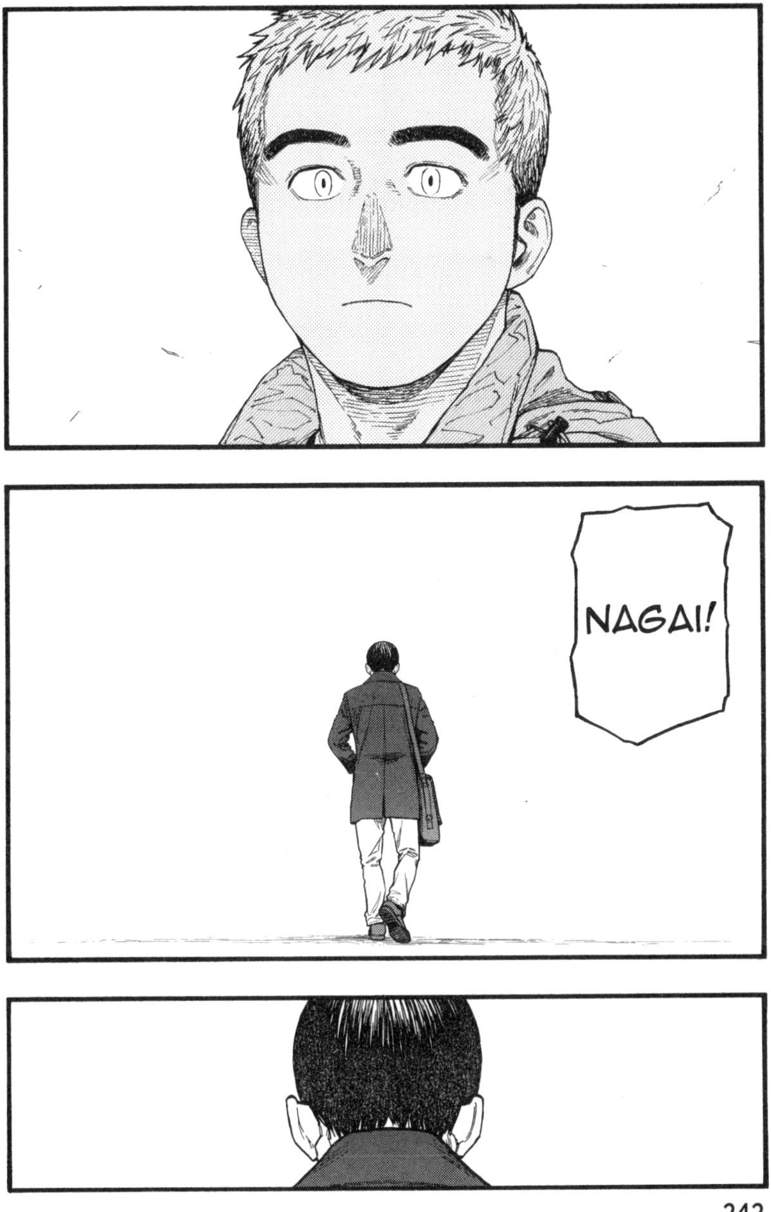
NAGAI!

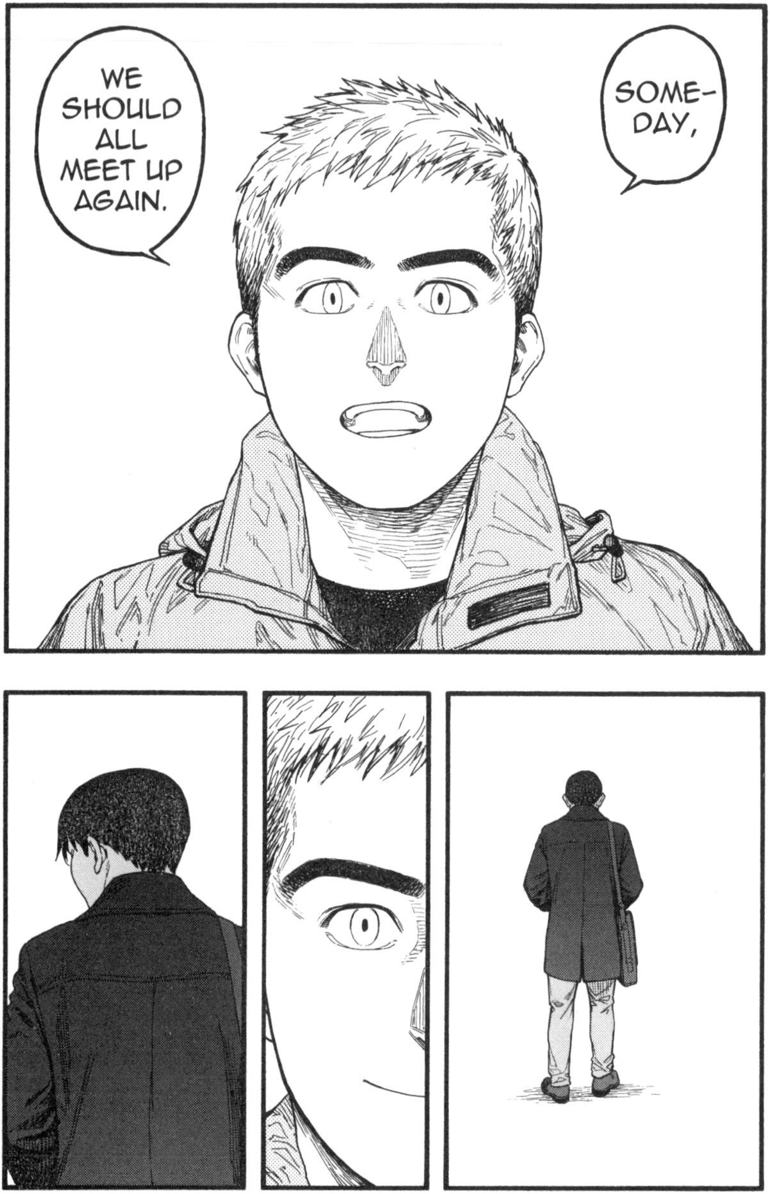
SOME-DAY,
WE SHOULD ALL MEET UP AGAIN.

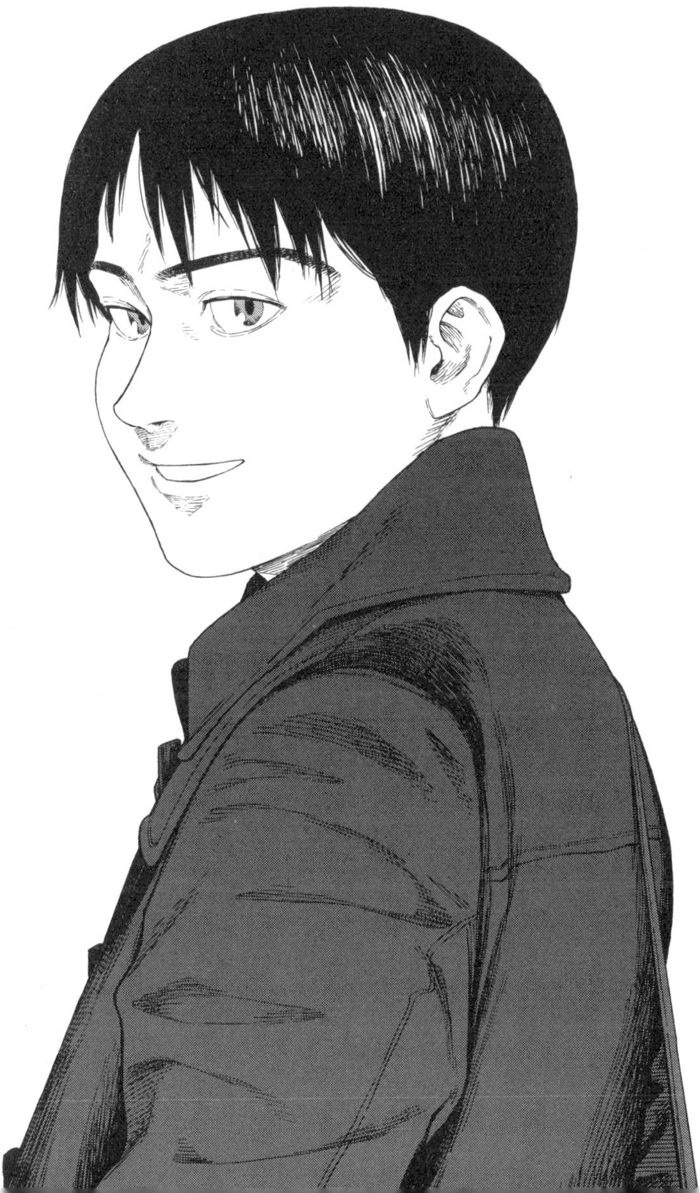

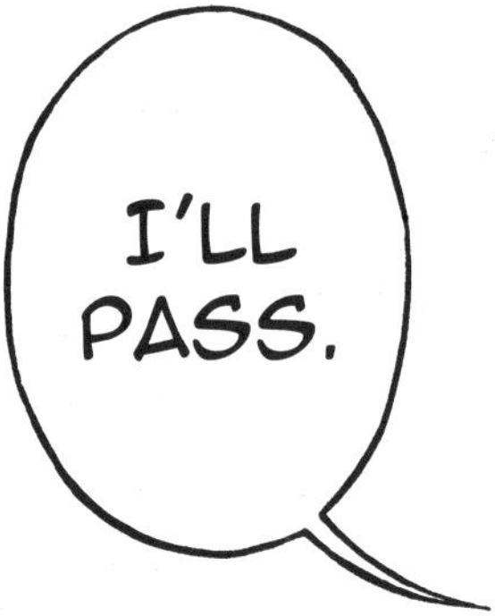
I'LL PASS.

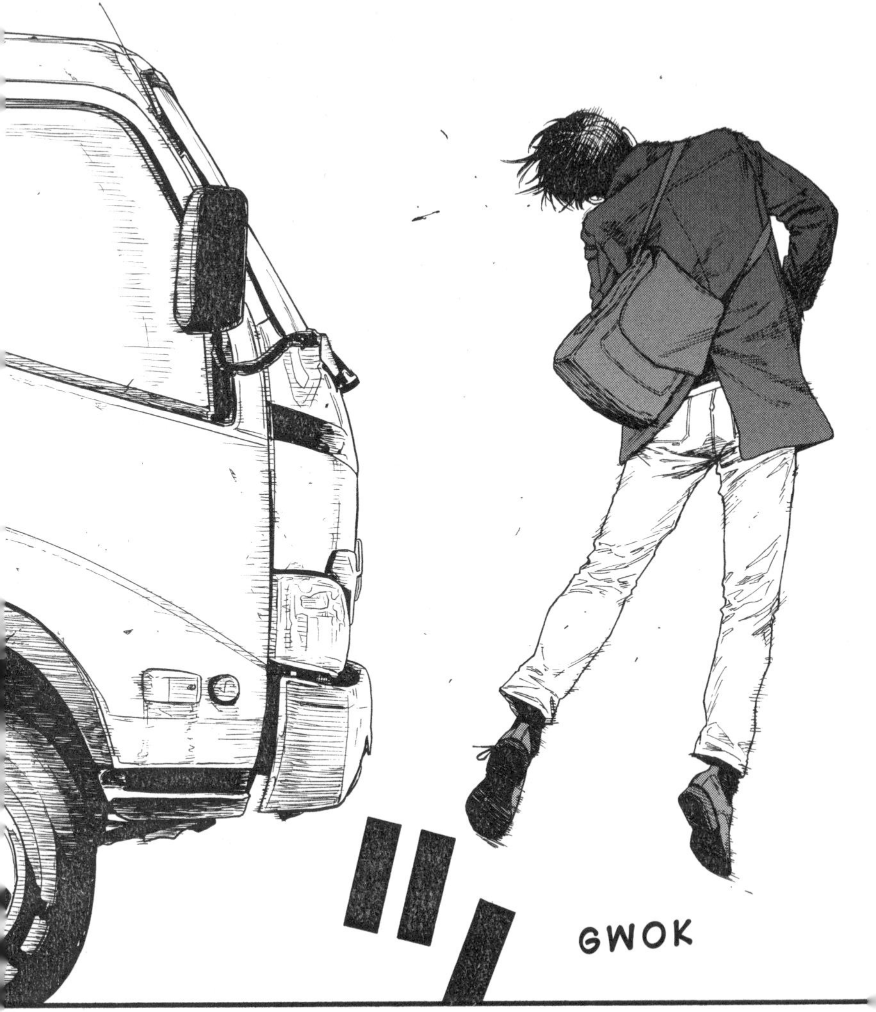
GWOK
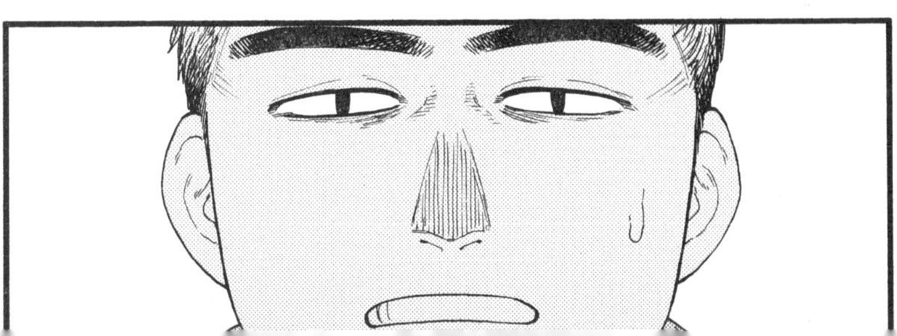

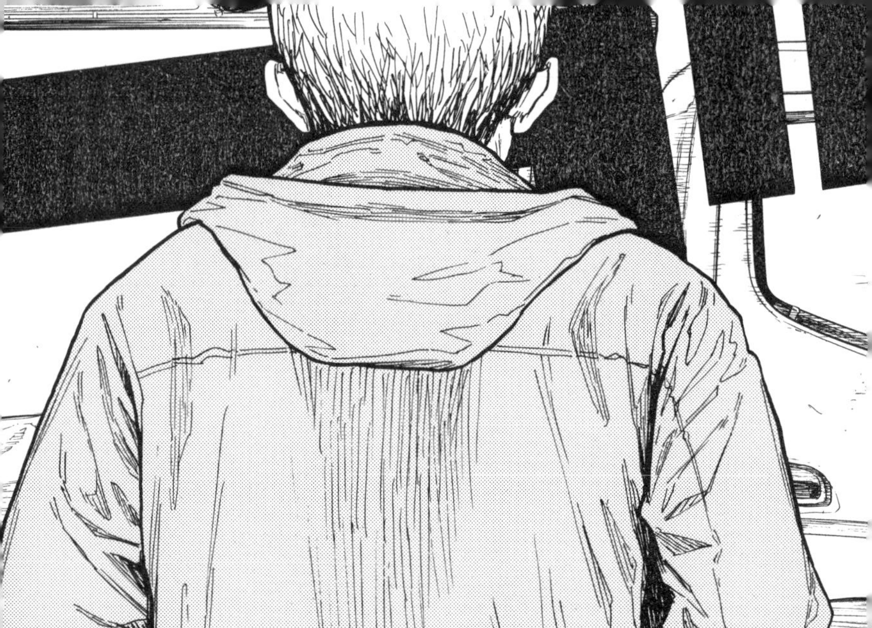

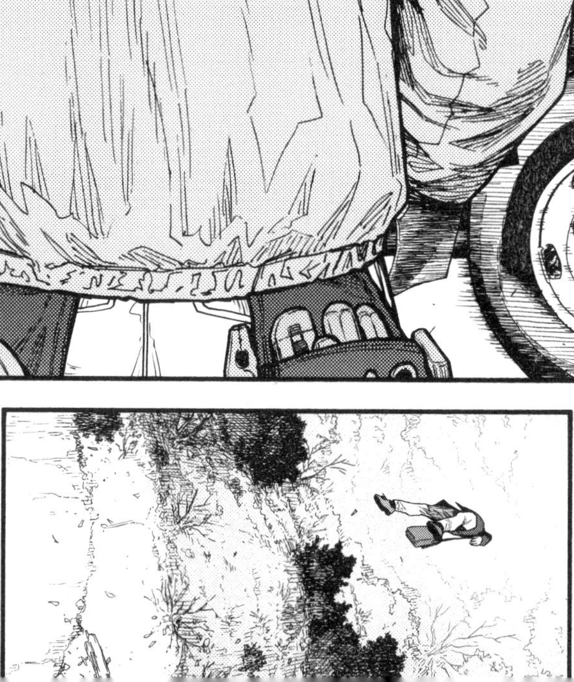

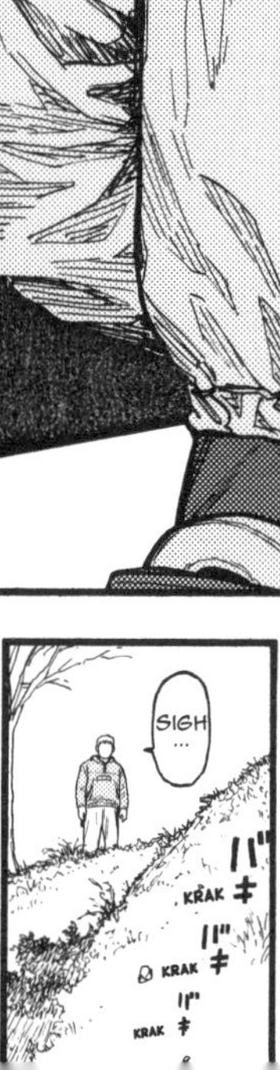
SIGH ...
バキ
KRAK
バキ
KRAK
バキ
KRAK

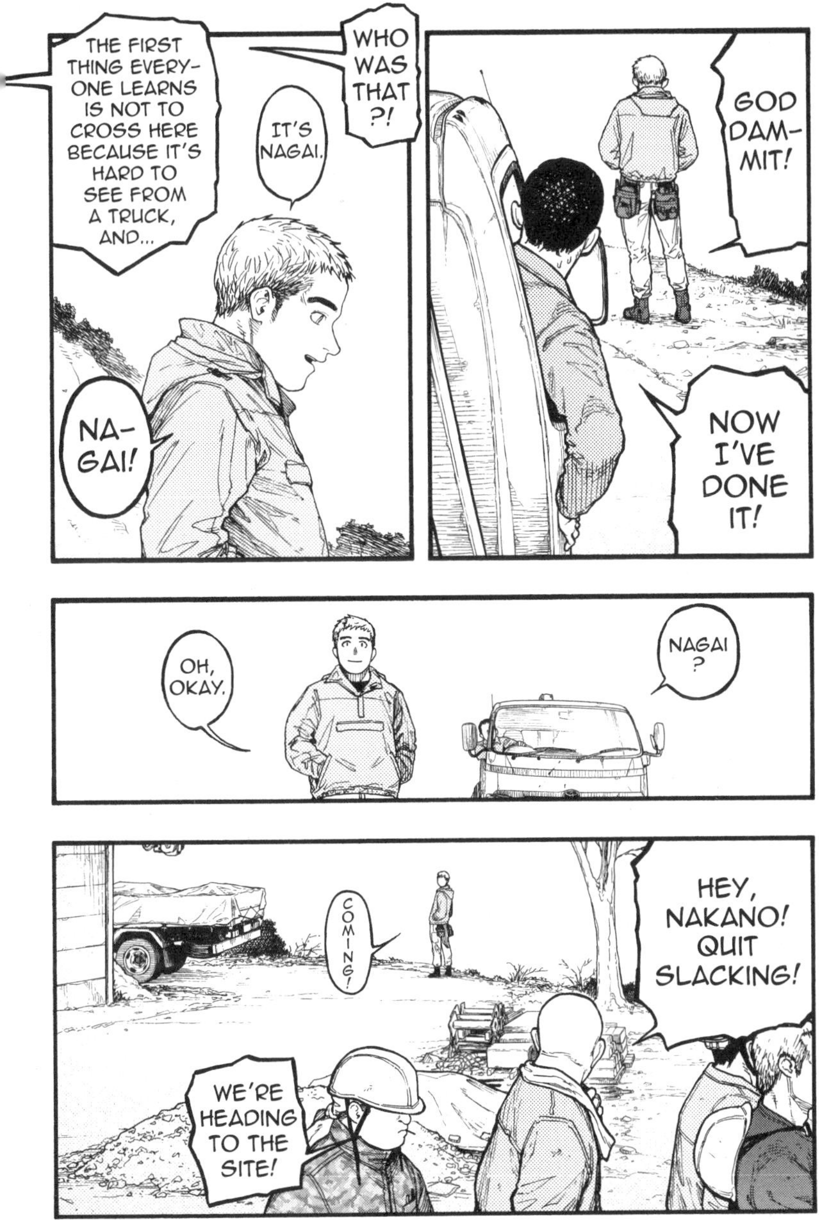
GOD DAMMIT!
NOW I'VE DONE IT!
WHO WAS THAT?!
IT'S NAGAI.
THE FIRST THING EVERYONE LEARNS IS NOT TO CROSS HERE BECAUSE IT'S HARD TO SEE FROM A TRUCK, AND...
NA-GAI!
NAGAI?
OH, OKAY.
HEY, NAKANO! QUIT SLACKING!
COMING!
WE'RE HEADING TO THE SITE!

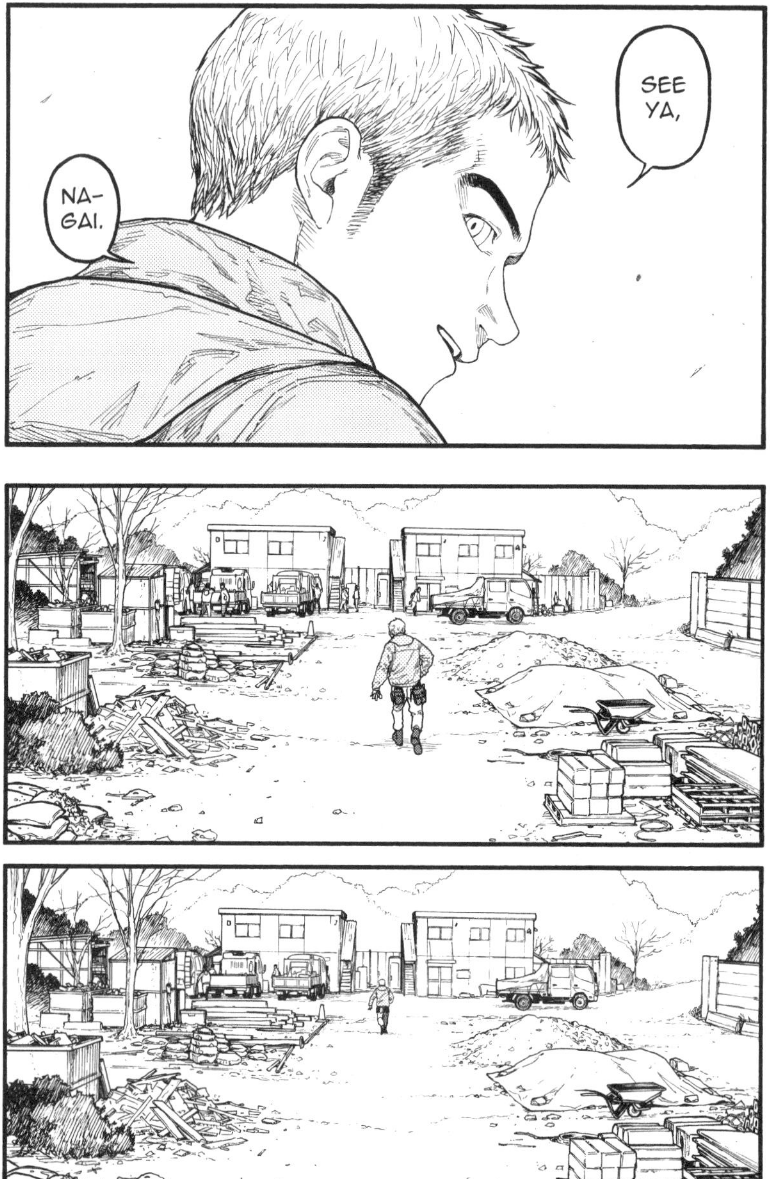
SEE YA,
NA-GAI.

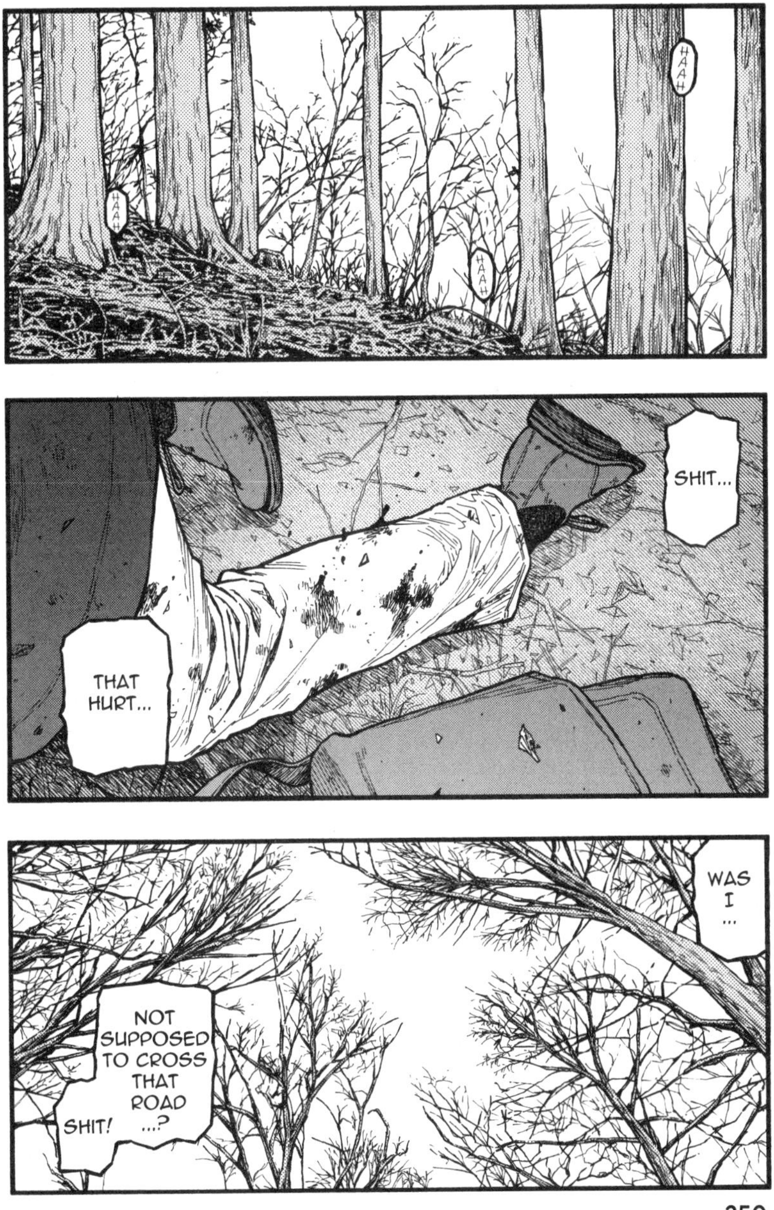
HAAH
HAAH
HAAH
SHIT...
THAT HURT...
WAS I ...
NOT SUPPOSED TO CROSS THAT ROAD ...?
SHIT!

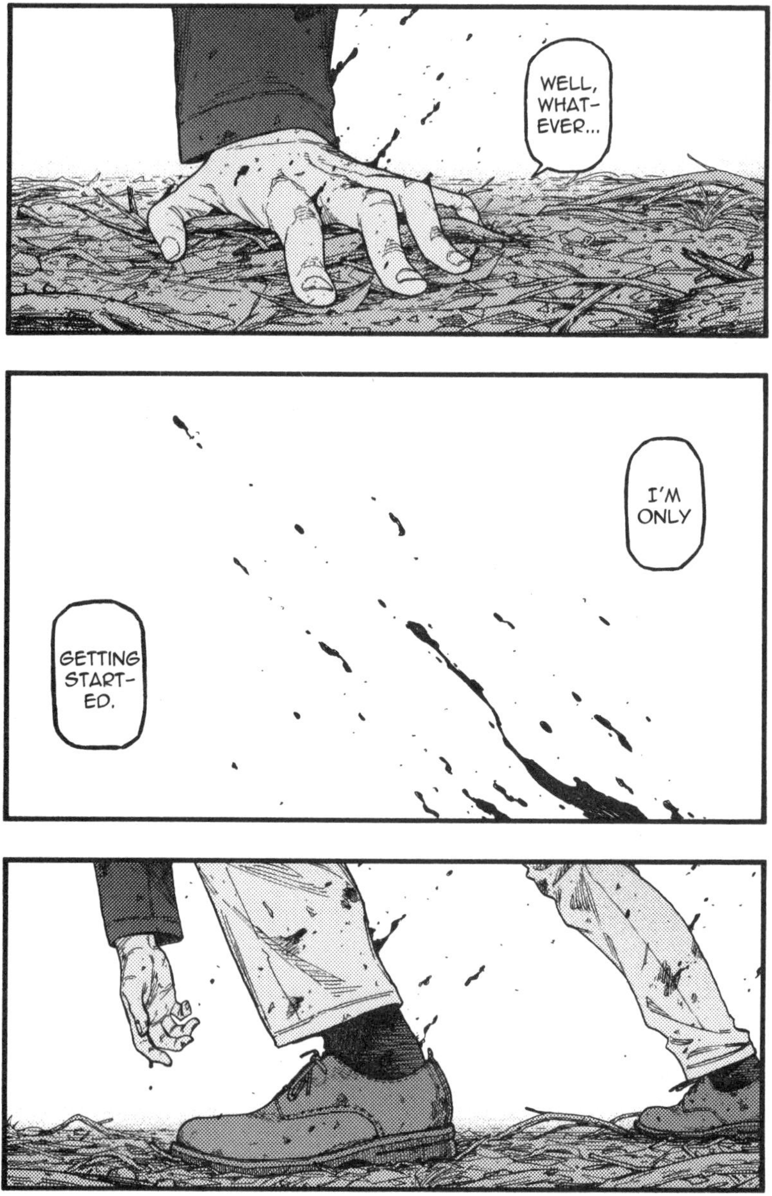
WELL, WHAT-EVER...
I'M ONLY
GETTING START-ED.

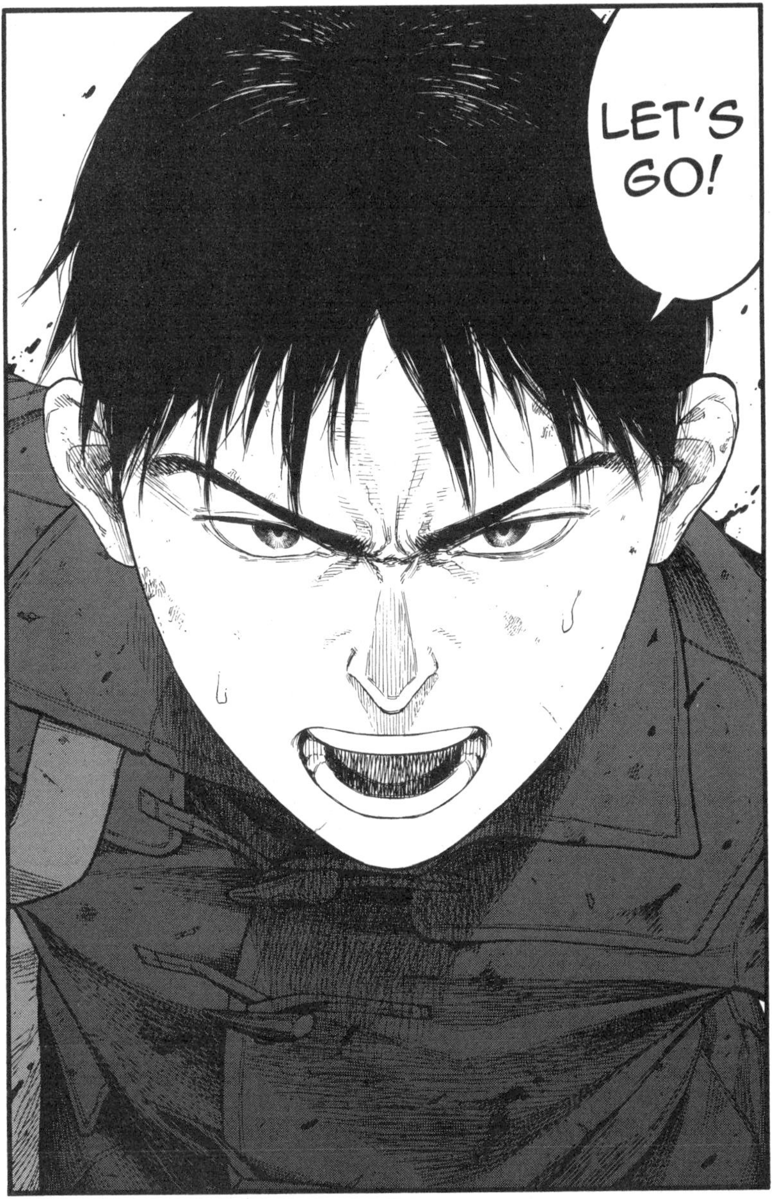
LET'S GO!

AJIN

DEMI-HUMAN

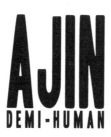

END

KURAI

almost all tone range masking]

Line drawings

Volume 17: throughout: Anti-Demi logo: 90%]

[File 79: p. 32, panel 2: background: 90%] [File 79: p. 33, panels 3, 4, 5: background: 90%] [File 79: p. 36, panel 1: shoe: 99%] [File 79: p. 37, panel 1: panel contents: 80%]

[File 80: p. 41, panels 1, 2, 3: motorcycle and helicopter: 95%] [File 80: p.41, panel 1: background: 93%] [File 80: p.42, panel 3: cars: 93%] [File 80: p. 43, panels 2, 6: cars: 90%] [File 80: p. 43, panel 5: panel contents: 91%] [File 80: p. 44, panel 2: background: 65%] [File 80: p. 45, panel 6: person and cell phone: 90%] [File 80: p. 46, panel 1: car: 90%] [File 80: p. 47, panel 2: hand and cell phone: 72%] [File 80: p. 49, panels 2, 3: hand and cell phone: 73%] [File 80: p. 50, panel 4: background: 95%] [File 80: p. 53, panel 3: background: 70%] [File 80: p. 55, panel 2: gun and hand: 60%] [File 80: p. 59, panels 1, 2: helicopter: 80%] [File 80: p. 60, panels 1, 3, 5: helicopter and motorcycle: 63%] [File 80: p. 61, panel 1: helicopter: 90%] [File 80: p. 62, panels 2, 4: feet, hand, and cellphone: 75%] [File 80: p. 63, panel 1: hand and cell phone: 80%] [File 80: p. 64, panel 3: hand and cell phone: 80%] [File 80: p. 65, panels 1, 2: car: 83%]]

[File 81: throughout: helicopter and motorcycle: 80%] [File 81: p. 71, panel 1: feet: 40%] [File 81: p. 74, panel 1: background: 70%] [File 81: p. 77, panel 2: panel contents: 95%] [File 81: p. 84, panel 3: panel contents: 90%] [File 81: p. 85, panel 2: foot: 40%] [File 81: p. 90, panel 3: foot: 42%] [File 81: p. 98, panel 2: panel contents: 61%] [File 81: p. 99, panel 1: telephone pole and wires: 90%] [File 81: p. 101, panel 2: foot: 42%] [File 81: p. 109, panel 2: body: 87%]

[File 82: throughout: Mitsumine, Chinook, and motorcycle: 69%] [File 82: p. 124, panel 1: helicopters: 80%] [File 82: p.124, panel 2: Sato's gun, houses, and trees: 65%] [File 82: p. 126, panels 3, 4: controllers and hands: 80%] [File 82: p. 127, panel 5: panel contents: 25%] [File 82: p. 127, panel 6: guns: 40%] [File 82: p.128, panel 1: building: 90%] [File 82: p.130, panel 1: background: 84%] [File 82: p. 130, panel 3: fighter: 90%] [File 82: p. 136, panel 1: hand and cell phone: 66%] [File 82: p. 142-143, panel 1: background: 70%] [File 82: p. 144, panel 1: background: 65%] [File 82: p. 145, panel 3: MP5 and SCAR: 95%] [File 82: p. 146, panel 2: SCAR: 90%] [File 82: p. 153, panels 1, 2: SCAR: 90%] [File 82: p. 155, panels 1, 2: scope: 84%] [File 82: p. 155, panel 3: background: 59%] [File 82: p. 161, panel 1: panel contents: 80%] [File 82: p. 161, panel 2: panel contents: 37%] [File 82: p. 168-169, panel 1: landscape: 70%]

[Final File: throughout: smoking area logo: 90%] [Final File: throughout: computer keys: 99%] [Final File: p. 173, panel 1: helicopter: 95%] [Final File: p. 175, panel 1: helicopter: 88%] [Final File: p. 176, panel 2: helicopter: 95%] [Final File: p. 178, panel 2: helicopter: 98%] [Final File: p. 179, panel 3: helicopter: 70%] [Final File: p. 181, panel 2: helicopter: 92%] [Final File: p. 183, panel 1: helicopter: 100%] [Final File: p. 184, panel 1: panel contents: 60%] [Final File: p. 184, panels 5, 6: men in suits and photograph of building: 90%] [Final File: p. 185, panels, 2,3: cars: 90%] [Final File: p. 185, panel 5: announcer: 95%] [Final File: p. 185, panel 9: panel contents: 96%] [Final File: p. 186, panels 3, 4, 6: everything other than Lee and the police: 90%] [Final File: p. 186, panel 5: photograph of building: 99%] [Final File: p. 187, panels 1, 2, 5, 6: panel contents: 93%] [Final File: p. 187, panel 3: background: 99%] [Final File: p. 188, panels 1, 4: background: 90%] [Final File: p. 189, panels 5, 6: panel contents: 90%] [Final File: p. 189, panels 7, 8: background: 92] [Final File: p. 190, panels 1, 2, 3: everything other than the announcer: 93%] [Final File: p. 192-193, panel 1: distant background: 88%] [Final File: p. 194, panels 1, 2: background: 77%] [Final File: p. 196, panels 1, 2: background: 80%] [Final File: p. 197, panel 6: writing: 100%] [Final File: p. 208, panel 1: cigarette pack: 80%] [Final File: p. 216, panels 2, 3: panel contents: 45%] [Final File: p. 217, panel 2: intercom: 94%] [Final File: p. 222, panel 2: panel contents: 98%] [Final File: p. 222, panel 3: shoe sole: 99%] [Final File: p. 226, panels 1, 2: background: 75%] [Final File: p. 230, panel 1: distant background: 97%] [Final File: p. 237, panels 2, 3, 4: background other than people: 97%] [Final File: p.240, panels 2, 3: background: 92%] [Final File: p. 246-247, panel 1: truck: 75%] [Final File: p. 248, panels 1, 3: truck: 77%]

Line drawings

[File 79: p. 12, panels 3, 4: background: 100%] [File 79: p. 32, panel 2: folding chairs: 100%]

[File 80: p. 45, panels 1, 3: background: 90%] [File 80: p. 47, panels 2, 4: news images: 68%] [File 80: p. 48, panel 1: announcer and background of photograph: 90%] [File 80: p. 61, panels 3, 4: background: 70%]

[File 81: p. 70, panels 3, 4: panel contents: 85%]

[File 82: p. 124, panel 1: jungle: 70%] [File 82: p. 128, panels 4, 5: background 90%] [File 82: p. 129, panels 1, 2: buildings and Type 64 pistols: 92%] [File 82: p. 154, panel 4: foliage: 84%] [File 82: p. 155, panel 3: background: 39%] [File 82: p. 161: panel 2: panel contents: 37%]

[Final File: p. 184, panel 2: announcer: 93%] [Final File: p. 185, panel 6: announcer: 99%] [Final File: p. 185, panel 8: photograph of Diet chamber: 100%] [Final File: p. 186, panel 1: announcer: 97%] [Final File: p. 189, panel 3: panel contents: 85%] [Final File: p. 191, panel 1: background: 100%] [Final File: p. 209, panel 2: bento box: 85%] [Final File: p. 221, panel 3: background 90%] [Final File: p. 250, panels 1, 3: panel contents: 86%]]

DRAWINGS VIA LINE EXTRACTION (IN PREVIOUS VOLUMES THIS WAS LISTED AS "LT CONVERSION FUNCTION," BUT THIS IS PERHAPS MORE ACCURATE)

AFTERWORD

AJIN had something of a slapdash beginning.

"It starts as an escape story, and then it's going to gradually move towards combat. I expect it'll be the kind of manga that isn't thought out too far in advance, so we'll just figure out the most exciting ways for it to develop from scene to scene"—that's how this series began. I remember the editor telling me this in early 2011, when I had been selected to do the art. (I had heard there would be "black ghosts, phantoms the demi-humans could see," but I was startled when they started engaging in physical combat.)

I suspect that people who follow me on social media already know this, but the first five chapters of AJIN were written by someone else. I was originally just in charge of the art, but from the sixth chapter on, I started handling the story as well.

So, the rest of this is an apology.

As I said, it hadn't been decided where the comic would go, which meant that when I took over, everything—the rest of the story, the setting, the ways foreshadowing would pay off, the characters' pasts and futures—was going to be invented by someone with a completely different authorial voice and vision. And what would that bring…? Well, having just read the final volume, you know the answer.

The point is that it's become a manga with a different sensibility than it had at the beginning.

Which means it's betrayed the expectations of everyone who, after reading Volume 1, thought to themselves, "So the story's going to go on like this, then…?" And all I can do is offer an apology. I'm truly sorry. (Starting with Volume 2, I tried to move the art gradually closer to my own style, but I sure got a lot of comments from readers that "the art had suddenly changed.")

The thing is, this is what I do. I love American action movies of the late '80s-early '00s from the bottom of my heart. This is the only kind of manga I can draw.

Lastly, it wasn't the publisher or the editors or even me myself who supported the serialization of AJIN; it was all the readers who paid to read it. I'm not trying to toss off some maudlin message here, I'm talking about the structure of society.

So thank you for sticking with AJIN over the course of these past nine years. I'm truly grateful to each and every one of you for reading.

Gamon Sakurai   March 2021

Ajin: Demi-Human, volume 17

Editor: Daniel Joseph
Translation: Ko Ransom
Production: Risa Cho
Hiroko Mizuno

First published in Japan in 2021 by Kodansha, Ltd., Tokyo
Publication for this English edition arranged through Kodansha, Ltd., Tokyo

Published by Vertical, an imprint of Kodansha USA Publishing, LLC

Originally published in Japanese as *Ajin 17* by Kodansha, Ltd.
Ajin first serialized in *good! Afternoon*, Kodansha, Ltd., 2012-2021

This is a work of fiction.

ISBN: 978-1-64729-045-0

Manufactured in the United States of America

First Edition

Kodansha USA Publishing, LLC
451 Park Avenue South
7th Floor
New York, NY 10016
www.kodansha.us

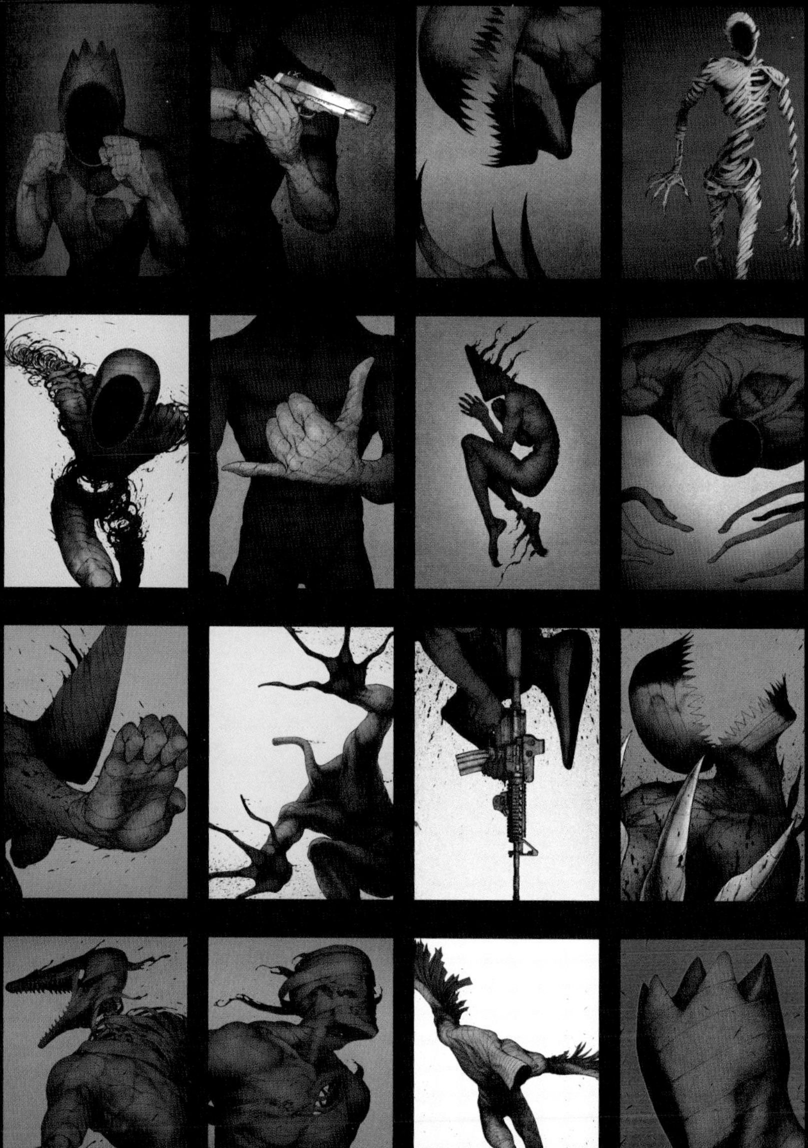

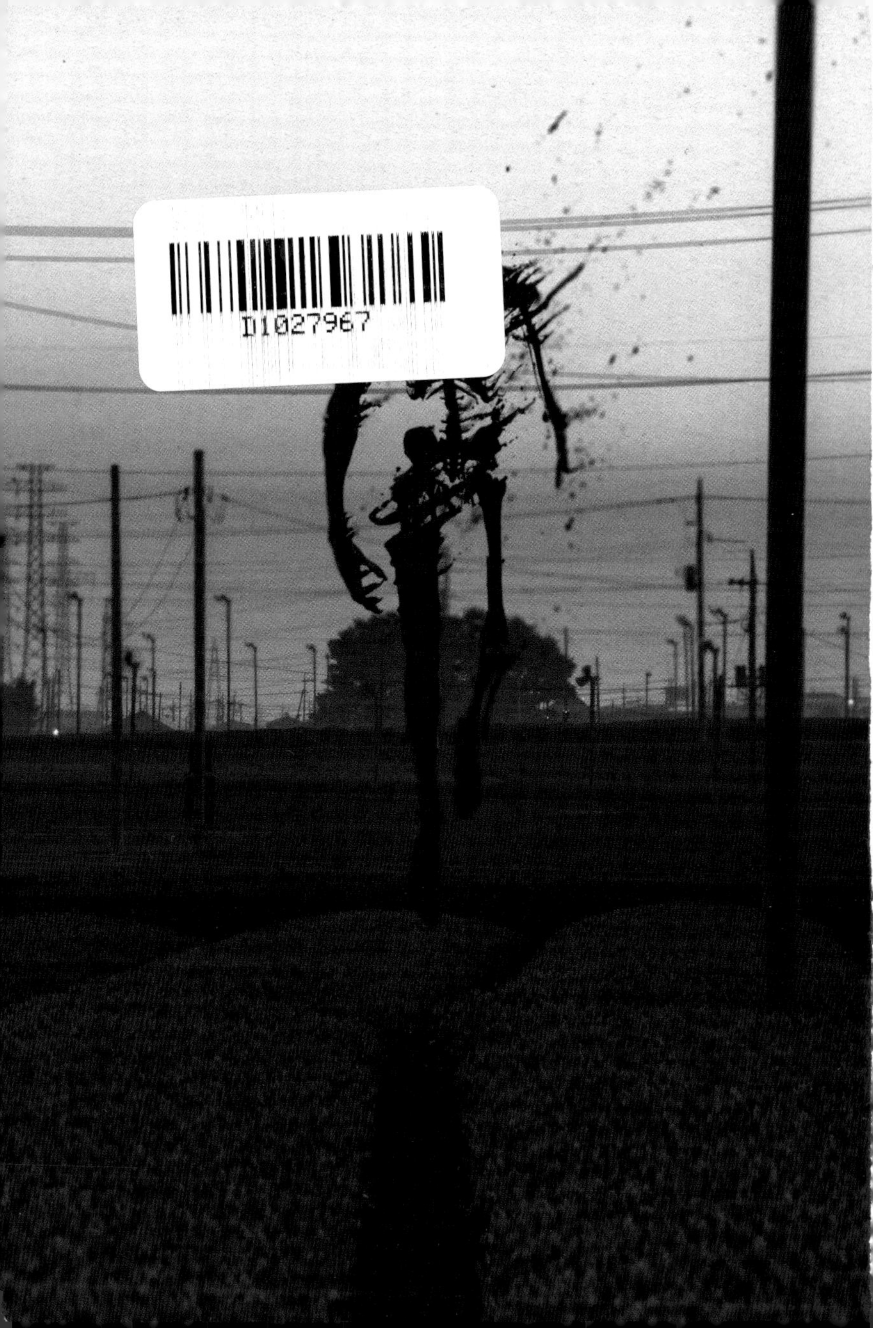